Living with DEBT

How to Limit the Risks of Sovereign Finance

Economic and Social Progress in Latin America

2007 REPORT

Eduardo Borensztein
Eduardo Levy Yeyati
Ugo Panizza
Coordinators

GW00481909

INTER-AMERICAN DEVELOPMENT BANK

DAVID ROCKEFELLER CENTER FOR LATIN AMERICAN STUDIES
HARVARD UNIVERSITY

LIVING WITH DEBT
How to Limit the Risks of Sovereign Finance

©2006 Inter-American Development Bank
        1300 New York Avenue, NW
        Washington, DC 20577

Co-published by
        David Rockefeller Center
        for Latin American Studies
        Harvard University
        1730 Cambridge Street
        Cambridge, MA 02138

Distributed by
        Harvard University Press
        Cambridge, Massachusetts
        London, England

To order this book, contact
IDB Bookstore
Tel: 202-623-1753
Fax: 202-623-1709
E-mail: idb-books@iadb.org
www.iadb.org/pub

ISBN: 1-59782-033-4
ISSN: 0095-2850

Production Editor	Michael Harrup
Editorial Assistant	Cathy Conkling-Shaker
Graphic Designers	Leilany Garron
	Dolores Subiza

CONTENTS

PREFACE

THE 2007 REPORT ON ECONOMIC AND SOCIAL PROGRESS IN LATIN AMERICA analyzes the nature and evolution of sovereign debt in Latin America and discusses the policies that can be followed by countries and international financial institutions (IFIs) to reduce the vulnerabilities associated with it. Although this is not a time of debt crises or financial emergencies, the report is timely because policies implemented in tranquil times can help prevent future problems. There is currently a receptive attitude in international markets to new financial instruments, such as obligations denominated in domestic currencies, which opens up opportunities for improving the profile and risk characteristics of Latin American public debt. This report seeks to contribute, as well, to the debate regarding the current international financial architecture, and to discuss ideas and initiatives aimed at improving the management of key risks such as those associated with rollovers, currency denomination, commodity price volatility, and economic shocks.

Governments can use debt for valuable purposes, including financing of investment in infrastructure and expenditures in human capital, and responding to cyclical downturns and to exceptional events such as natural disasters or financial crashes. Excessive public debt, however, can have serious consequences: it can create a burden on future generations, it may crowd out private investment, and, perhaps most importantly, it may increase the propensity for financial crises. The report concludes that governments can leverage the benefits of public debt, while minimizing vulnerability to crises, by improving debt management, developing domestic bond markets, and applying prudent fiscal policies backed by transparent rules.

The IFIs, for their part, have an important role to play in reforming the international financial architecture with a view to limiting the risks of sovereign finance. They can contribute to reducing global vulnerabilities by focusing on the creation of fast-disbursing liquidity facilities to soften the impact of sudden stops and prevent contagion. They can help to overcome the inefficiency of self-insurance strategies by promoting and supporting reserve-pooling agreements. The IFIs can also promote, through various means, the development of markets for contingent and local currency financial instruments, for instance, by including these features in their own bonds placed in the markets and passing these features through their loans to countries in the region.

This is a broad agenda, and it is unlikely that every aspect of it will gain international consensus. But the lessons of recent years indicate that the risks of inaction are higher than the risks of adopting a reform initiative that seems too ambitious. If some of the proposals end up being unnecessary, they will not be applied in practice, but if they are needed and they are not available, the consequences could be serious.

This report contains a review of existing and new data, a survey of standard literature and conventional views on past debt crises, and a window into the new analysis and ideas that are a result of the research work that is ongoing at the Inter-American Development Bank and elsewhere. As such, it can serve as a tool for dialogue, a reference for researchers, a guide for policymakers, and a source of ideas for the design of systemic reforms.

Luis Alberto Moreno
President
Inter-American Development Bank

ACKNOWLEDGMENTS

ECONOMIC AND SOCIAL PROGRESS IN LATIN AMERICA is the flagship publication of the Inter-American Development Bank. This issue was produced by the Research Department and was coordinated by Eduardo Borensztein, Eduardo Levy Yeyati, and Ugo Panizza under the supervision of Guillermo Calvo and Eduardo Lora. Carlos Andrés Gómez-Peña, who was project assistant, and Rita Funaro and John Dunn Smith, who edited a preliminary version of the report, completed the coordinating team.

Although all chapters were reviewed and approved by all three coordinators, the principal responsibility for each chapter was as follows:

Chapter 1: Eduardo Borensztein, Eduardo Levy Yeyati, and Ugo Panizza
Chapter 2: Ugo Panizza
Chapter 3: Ugo Panizza
Chapter 4: Eduardo Borensztein
Chapter 5: Eduardo Borensztein
Chapter 6: Eduardo Fernández-Arias and Andrew Powell
Chapter 7: Eduardo Borensztein, Barry Eichengreen, and Ugo Panizza
Chapter 8: Ugo Panizza
Chapter 9: Ugo Panizza
Chapter 10: Eduardo Lora and Ugo Panizza
Chapter 11: Alejandro Izquierdo and Igor Zuccardi
Chapter 12: Eduardo Levy Yeyati
Chapter 13: Eduardo Borensztein, Eduardo Levy Yeyati, and Ugo Panizza
Chapter 14: Eduardo Borensztein, Barry Eichengreen, Eduardo Levy Yeyati, and Ugo Panizza
Appendix: María Laura Devoto and Ugo Panizza

The chapters were in part based on background research papers written specifically for this report by Laura Alfaro (Chapter 13), Matteo Bobba (Chapter 6), Patrick Bolton (Chapter 7), Eduardo Borensztein (Chapters 5, 7, 12, 13, and 14), Camila Campos (Chapter 3), Daniel Cohen (Chapter 13), Kevin Cowan (Chapters 2, 5, and 7), Gerardo della Paolera (Chapter 4), Barry Eichengreen (Chapter 7), Marcela Eslava (Chapter 9), Eduardo Fernández-Arias (Chapter 6), Xavier Freixas (Chapter 7), Eloy García (Chapter 14), Martín González Rozada (Chapter 5), Alejandro Izquierdo (Chapter 11), Dany Jaimovich (Chapters 2 and 3), Fabio Kanczuk (Chapter 13), Miguel Kiguel (Chapter 8), Eduardo Levy Yeyati (Chapters 2, 5, 11, 12, 13, and 14), Eduardo Lora (Chapter 10), Mauricio Olivera (Chapter 10), Ugo Panizza (Chapters 2, 3, 7,

12, 13, and 14), Andrew Powell (Chapter 6), Roberto Rigobón (Chapter 14), Jean-Charles Rochet (Chapter 9), Federico Sturzenegger (Chapters 2 and 11), Alan Taylor (Chapter 4), Patricio Valenzuela (Chapters 5 and 9), and Igor Zuccardi (Chapter 11). Chapter 7 also drew on the papers of the IDB Latin American and Caribbean Research Network project on the development of the Latin American bond market.

Overall research assistance was provided by Mariano Álvarez, Matteo Bobba, Laura Clavijo, Fabio Dorso, María Fernández, Dany Jaimovich, Gonzalo Llosa, Juan Francisco Martínez, Patricio Valenzuela, Mónica Yáñez, and Igor Zuccardi.

The long list of individuals who participated in the production of this report by attending various seminars at the Inter-American Development Bank, Universidad Torcuato Di Tella, and DFID on the outline and preliminary results of the report and providing comments on background papers and the preliminary chapters includes Miguel Braun, Ricardo Caballero, Eduardo Cavallo, Marcos Chamon, Bill Cline, Tito Cordella, Enrique Cosio Pascal, Enrica Detragiache, Eugenio Díaz-Bonilla, Koldo Echebarría, Germán Fermo, Roque Fernández, Franco Fornasari, Javier Game, Márcio Garcia, Pablo Guidotti, John Hauge, Ricardo Hausmann, Fidel Jaramillo, Graciela Kaminsky, Ricardo Leal, Joaquim Levy, Lorenza Martínez, Ricardo Martner, Pietro Masci, Paolo Mauro, Enrique Mendoza, Gian Maria Milesi-Ferretti, Marcus Miller, Juan Pablo Nicolini, Juan Ricardo Ortega, Sergio Pernice, Fernando Quevedo, Luca Ricci, Liliana Rojas-Suárez, João Sayad, Sergio Schmukler, Nemat Shafik, Jorge Streb, Rogério Studart, Ernesto Talvi, Vito Tanzi, Toni Venables, Alejandro Werner, John Williamson, and Jeromin Zettelmeyer.

The IDB's Office of External Relations, under the direction of Alfredo Barnechea, was responsible for the editorial production of the report.

EXECUTIVE SUMMARY

THIS REPORT FOCUSES ON TOTAL GOVERNMENT DEBT in Latin America and the Caribbean, comprising both international and domestic debt. The difference between the two types of debt has narrowed considerably in recent years, as the holders of bonds issued in domestic markets may be international investors and domestic investors may hold bonds issued in international markets.[1] Moreover, instruments such as credit derivatives can be used to shift risk among different investors almost instantaneously, and there is no practical way to trace results of the increasingly large volume of such derivatives. Using total government debt, which is a more comprehensive measure, turns out to be important because focusing exclusively on external debt has led some observers to conclude—erroneously—that government debt is decreasing in Latin America. The complete story is that the ongoing decline in external debt ratios in the countries of the region is often compensated for by an increase in domestic debt. All things considered, the average level of public debt in the region is now similar to that prevailing in the early 1990s.

Examination of the sources of debt growth yields a striking finding: recorded budget deficits play only a secondary role in explaining debt growth in developing countries. Most debt volatility, especially sudden explosions in debt levels, is the result of balance sheet effects due to exchange rate adjustments, the resolution of contingent liabilities, and extrabudgetary items. For example, in the Dominican Republic, the debt-to-GDP ratio rose from 25 percent of GDP in 2002 to 55 percent of GDP by the end of 2003 owing to a costly banking crisis. Debt-to-GDP ratios in Argentina and Uruguay more than doubled in 2002 as a result of currency depreciations in those two countries. This underscores the conclusion that the structure of debt and contingent liabilities often involves more risks than the level of debt itself and that countries need to improve debt management to limit their debt vulnerability.

The international private market has been a prime source of financing for Latin America for over 200 years. Although the international sovereign debt market is liquid and deep, emerging market premiums have been extremely volatile at times, with a tendency to experience large spikes and subsequent reversals, and external factors have often been

---

[1] Information on total debt is not readily available. Databases such as those included in the IMF's *International Financial Statistics* and the World Bank's *Global Development Finance* contain scant information on domestic debt level and composition. This report introduces a new database for 24 Latin American and Caribbean countries, which the IDB will update and publish regularly.

important determinants of emerging market spreads.[2] In recent months, however, global conditions have been quite favorable to emerging market borrowers, and spreads have reached record low levels. The report concludes that there are reasons to be optimistic about these trends, but caution is still in order. The favorable market has resulted in part from a strengthening of fiscal policies and the improvement in current account balances, which has reduced dependence on external savings. But it has also resulted, in part, from abundant liquidity in financial markets, from an expansive phase of the world economy and commodity prices, and from expectations of currency appreciation and domestic interest rate cuts, which cannot continue forever.

Lending by multilateral financial institutions and official bilateral sources is also a traditionally important source of finance and continues to represent a fairly stable share in international borrowing, both for low-income economies with no market access and for the emerging market economies in the region.[3] Despite charges sometimes leveled against multilateral lending, the report finds no evidence of procyclicality in lending by the multilateral banks, but it does find evidence of a catalytic role of multilateral lending, as increases in such lending tend to be followed by subsequent increases in private lending.

Domestic debt markets, although still less developed than their international counterparts, are gaining importance and can play a key role in reducing vulnerabilities. While Latin America does not have comparatively large bond markets, the size of these markets is commensurate with that of overall financial markets in the region. That is, although Latin American bond markets are not large as a proportion of GDP, they are not small as a proportion of bank credit when compared to those in other emerging regions. Government bonds, in contrast, are very sizable in relation to private corporate bonds. A large government bond market may contribute to market development by providing a reference yield curve but may also raise concerns about crowding out private borrowers. Domestic bond markets provide an alternative to keep financial markets running when domestic banks are unable or unwilling to take additional credit risks in their own portfolios, and these markets can promote the use of domestic currency instruments. The growth of institutional investors, such as pension funds, and the appetite shown by international investors will provide the requisite investor base if the legal and institutional framework is supportive of bond market development.

While public borrowing can be applied to worthy projects, it would be naive to ignore political influences that may cause the use of debt to drift away from its legitimate purposes. In particular, decentralized fiscal procedures, widespread fiscal transfers from the central government to states and provinces, and unstable political systems may lead to wasteful borrowing and exacerbate vulnerabilities. One mechanism for ensuring that debt policies are not distorted by political influences is fiscal rules that include limits on the budget deficit, debt, or public spending at various levels of the government, such as those included in the fiscal responsibility laws of several Latin American countries. But fiscal rules can be an ef-

---

[2] These global factors include the behavior of interest rates in large advanced economies, and also sudden stops in capital inflows triggered by events sometimes far removed from Latin American economies, as well as contagion effects that spread a market panic to a whole group of countries in the same asset class.

[3] In fact, the share of official lending in total public debt in the region was higher in 2004 than in the early 1990s, although this was partly reversed in 2005–2006 after Brazil and Argentina repaid their debt to the International Monetary Fund, and will be further undone by Mexico's planned repayment of its debt to the multilateral development banks.

fective mechanism only when the overall institutional framework supports their credibility and enforcement.

It must also be recognized that excessive levels of debt can become a burden on public spending commitments and reduce available resources for poverty-fighting social expenditure. This points to potential benefits of the current debt relief initiatives aimed at helping low-income countries to reach the Millennium Development Goals. Although the empirical studies reviewed in this report do not find strong evidence that past debt relief operations have succeeded in increasing social spending, the fiscal space created by the current, wide-ranging initiatives would provide a broader opportunity for such increases to occur. In fact, there is some preliminary evidence that debt relief brought about under the auspices of the Heavily Indebted Poor Countries initiative has been more effective at increasing social spending than was the case in previous debt relief initiatives.

Debt management and fiscal policies must aim at enhancing sustainability and how it is perceived in markets. The techniques of debt sustainability analysis have undergone radical improvement in recent years, and the new approaches described in this report are part of that trend. These new techniques explicitly consider the fact that variables such as exchange rates, interest rates, and economic growth, for example, are highly volatile in emerging markets and that this high volatility interacts with the debt structure to have a substantial impact on the evolution of debt. From the viewpoint of investors, evaluating debt sustainability implies determining what debt level triggers debt default or restructuring. Finding this level is complicated in the case of sovereign debt because, in contrast to a firm, the point at which a government becomes financially bankrupt is not precisely defined. The theoretical economic literature has traditionally seen the sovereign as calculating the cost implied by a debt default and comparing it to the burden of servicing the country's debt to decide whether or not to keep meeting debt obligations. This type of strategic behavior is not in line with what has been observed in practice. Sovereign defaults most often occur after a country's economy has gone through a serious downturn and other measures have failed. If anything, the empirical evidence suggests that sovereign default does not happen when governments do not need, or do not anticipate the need of, financing from their creditors, but rather in the wake of grave crises.

DEBT POLICIES

In addition to the adoption and implementation of prudent fiscal policies, limiting the risks of sovereign finance should also focus on improving debt management and developing domestic bond markets. Experience has highlighted two key sources of vulnerability: debt denomination (foreign currency debt) and debt maturity (short-term debt). Policies aimed at reducing these vulnerabilities are complicated by the fact that there may be a trade-off along these two dimensions. For example, shifting to domestic currency debt often requires employing short-maturity instruments. Inflation-indexed instruments provide an alternative that can help improve the terms of the trade-off between denomination and maturity, as it may be possible to issue long-term inflation-indexed instruments at moderate cost, because investors are protected from the risk of unexpected inflation. Past experiences in which financial indexation spearheaded widespread indexation of wages, pensions, etc., and created a situation of stubborn inflation and inflexibility of relative prices may make governments wary of such instruments. Still, some countries have been successful in using indexed financial instruments widely without perceptibly worsening inflation persistence.

The high volatility underlying emerging markets' economies and global financial markets creates an argument for introducing into debt contracts contingencies with equity-like features that allow for more efficient sharing of risk. These are instruments that offer lower payoffs during bad times and higher payoffs during good times, which would make them safer for investors and would afford governments the opportunity to manage their fiscal policy stance better over the business cycle. Interest payments could be indexed to commodity prices, the terms of trade, or the rate of growth of GDP. Another option would be to obtain contingent coverage directly from international financial markets through the use of derivative contracts. In practice, however, many futures and option markets lack depth and liquidity and therefore offer only limited scope for insurance. The lack of markets for contingent instruments is more acute in the case of events such as fluctuations in tourism revenue, hurricanes, and other natural disasters. Fortunately, financial market innovation is increasing the scope for using this type of market coverage, as in the case of the recent operation by Mexico securing earthquake insurance for three at-risk geographical areas.

It should be noted, however, that obtaining some form of market insurance, through either derivative contracts or indexed debt, faces a fundamental *domestic* obstacle. By their very nature, these contingent instruments work as an insurance policy for the country as a whole. Because their costs must generally be paid up front, but their payoffs may not occur until years later, the reasons for purchasing the insurance instruments can be easily misunderstood by the public, and they can become a political liability. This may provide little incentive for politicians to enter into large-scale contracts of this type. The international community could contribute to the surmounting of this obstacle by promoting studies and disseminating information about the benefits of these types of instruments.

The development of domestic bond markets is another key component of a strategy of safer sovereign finance. These markets hold the promise of providing a stable investor base for government debt and offsetting—at least to some degree—the risk of sudden stops and volatility in international markets. Moreover, domestic markets are a natural venue for debt denominated in domestic currency, and the benefits of a well-developed domestic currency bond market would also extend to the private sector.[4] There is the risk, however, that governments might attempt to capture the resources of institutional investors, such as pension funds, through regulation or moral suasion, which again underscores the importance of prudent fiscal policies in ensuring the success of any policy of encouraging the development of domestic markets.

THE ROLE OF THE INTERNATIONAL FINANCIAL INSTITUTIONS

In recent years, the international community has focused on the process of resolution of debt defaults with the widespread introduction of collective action clauses in debt contracts. But the *prevention* of debt crises has not made the same kind of progress. In this area, there is a great deal that the international financial institutions (IFIs) could do.

---

[4] Although several Latin American countries have placed some local currency issues internationally, the widespread international practice for emerging economies has been to issue local currency bonds in their domestic markets.

The IFIs could design workable, fast-disbursing credit facilities to offset rollover risks. Such facilities should work in much the same way as a central bank lends to domestic financial institutions, which is an effective deterrent to a possibly self-fulfilling run. Rather than limiting themselves to loans to governments, the IFIs could develop a strategy to respond to certain global emergencies more effectively by directly acting on international markets. Although this type of intervention has so far been outside the toolkit of the IFIs, a set of well-established rules could avoid any anticipated pitfalls.

The IFIs could also help make member countries' own efforts to prepare for emergencies more effective. In recent years, countries have attempted to gain a measure of protection against sudden stops by accumulating large international reserves. This is a generally expensive and inefficient self-insurance strategy. There have also been initiatives in Latin America and East Asia to gain efficiency and financial backing by partially pooling the reserves of several countries. The IFIs could assist in these efforts both at the technical level, refining operational methods and access rules, and by providing financial support. Moreover, as these initiatives are regional and risks are often regional by nature, there would be clear advantages to creating agreements that span several regions.

The IFIs also have an important new role to play as facilitators of reforms aimed at limiting the risk of sovereign finance. The IFIs can promote the development of markets for local currency instruments and new contingent debt instruments in various ways. The debt instruments used by governments today were mostly designed in an era preceding financial globalization, and there is room for improvement in widening the spectrum of instruments. The IFIs can provide assistance with the design of new instruments, and they can help to overcome the externalities and start-up costs of new markets and attract new investors, including by issuing their own debt securities with the contingencies promoted for country insurance.

Finally, the IFIs could change the nature of their own loans to member countries by offering a wide menu of domestic currency loans and contingent facilities and thus contribute to the dedollarization process.

I. STYLIZED FACTS

CHAPTER 1 | Introduction

A national debt, if it is not excessive, will be to us a national blessing.

—Alexander Hamilton (1755-1804)

The budget should be balanced, the treasury should be refilled, public debt should be reduced, the arrogance of officialdom should be tempered and controlled . . . lest Rome become bankrupt.

—Marcus Tullius Cicero (106-43, BC)

PUBLIC DEBT IS ONE OF THE MOST POWERFUL instruments of economic policy and, like a power tool, it can be used to efficiently achieve one's goals, but it can also cause severe injury.[1] Governments can issue debt to finance new investment in human and physical capital, to affect the use over time of a country's resources, to respond to cyclical downturns, or to meet the financing needs caused by exceptional events such as financial crashes or natural disasters. However, excessive public debt can also have long-lived negative consequences: it can create a burden on future generations, it may crowd out private investment, and it may increase a country's propensity for financial crises or inflation outbursts. Thus, it is not surprising that discussion on the causes and consequences of public borrowing was central in the economic debate even before Adam Smith officially gave birth to what is now called "economics."

In order to understand why countries borrow, it is useful to draw an analogy with the behavior of a family. Families borrow for essentially three reasons. First, they borrow to finance purchases that will yield services for an extended period of time. So, usually households borrow long term (with mortgages or college loans) to buy a house or finance an education, or borrow medium term (with car loans or consumer loans) to buy durable goods like automo-

---

[1] This report uses the terms "public debt" and "sovereign debt" interchangeably to define the total outstanding financial liabilities resulting from the public sector debt obligations of a country's government. Balassone, Franco, and Zotteri (2004) provide a concise survey of the history of the academic debate on the role of public debt.

biles or appliances. Along similar lines, governments borrow to fund long-term development projects, which could be either physical infrastructure (like roads and bridges) or human capital investment (like providing more schooling and better health services).

Second, households may decide to borrow in the face of a temporary negative shock. Suppose, for instance, that the head of a household is temporarily laid off from work but knows that he or she will resume employment with similar pay within a few months. Then, instead of drastically reducing living standards during the unemployment period, the household can smooth consumption by borrowing (probably short term) during the unemployment period. Alternatively, the household may suffer a large negative shock, like a costly health problem. In this case as well, it would not make much sense to finance all the expenses out of current income and would be optimal to borrow (probably at a longer-term maturity) to distribute these expenses over time. Along similar lines, a government may decide to borrow to maintain current spending without increasing taxes during periods of cyclical downturns or to finance the expenses brought about by natural or man-made disasters (such as hurricanes, earthquakes, or wars).

Finally, a household may decide to borrow to smooth consumption over time. Take, for instance, the case of a student who has just been accepted at a top medical school. This person will face several years of possibly no income (while studying) and then fairly low income (while in residency training), but after those years, this future doctor will presumably earn a relatively high income. Then, this person may decide that it is optimal to anticipate future consumption by borrowing during the study and residency years, and repaying once he or she takes a well-paid position as a medical doctor. Along similar lines, countries that expect to grow at a fast rate—perhaps because they have already started along a take-off stage of development—may decide to borrow to anticipate some of their consumption spending, effectively redistributing resources from future generations to the current one.

There are, however, several limitations to the analogy between households' and governments' borrowing decisions. First, while heads of a household may make some poor decisions, because they underestimate risks or suffer from myopia, for example, it is reasonable to assume that all their financial decisions aim at maximizing the family's welfare. In contrast, public policy decisions may be distorted by nonaltruistic politicians and special interest groups who are more concerned with their short-term objectives than maximizing social welfare. Politicians may worry only about their own popularity, which may increase in step with the size of the country's budget. So, when a household head decides to buy a new house, this is expected to be a good decision for the family as a whole. By contrast, when a politician decides to build a bridge in a particular region of his or her country, the true motivation may be to favor his or her own constituency or, even worse, to extract bribes from the companies that will build the bridge. The ability to issue public debt makes this problem worse, because it allows politicians to increase spending without immediately increasing taxes, and this may temper the resolve of citizens to monitor whether the additional spending is desirable. Furthermore, while personal debts cannot be inherited by future generations, which limits individuals' ability to borrow, large public debts are regularly passed on to future generations. This may be problematic, because future generations are not directly represented in the current decision-making process.

Second, households can often post appropriable collateral in order to borrow at more favorable terms and reduce credit risk, but this option is generally not available to sovereign borrowers, because legal recourse for attaching the sovereign's assets is limited. More generally, personal bankruptcy and the restructuring of government debt which is the equivalent of a sovereign bankruptcy procedure are governed by different legal structures and confer different legal rights on creditors.[2]

Third, countries have greater capacity to adjust their revenue (through taxation) than households and hence, when faced with the need to finance a given expenditure, they have available to them a broader set of options than an individual does.

Fourth, countries are large players in markets—at least in domestic ones—and hence the spillovers from a country's debt policy are likely to be much larger than any repercussion from decisions of individual households. For example, when a household borrows to smooth consumption in response to a large personal shock, there is no aggregate effect on the economy of the country where the household is located. But when a government increases its borrowing by a significant amount, it will probably cause an increase in interest rates, which will affect private borrowers and financial institutions directly, and almost every sector of the economy indirectly.

In short, like any individual, governments can use borrowing to improve the general welfare by financing long-lived investments and preserving living standards through periods of temporary hardship. But unlike those of individuals, government borrowing decisions may be distorted by political biases and fuzzy property rights, and governments' imposing size implies that mistakes and misdeeds will have far-reaching consequences.

DOES PUBLIC DEBT MATTER?

In order to analyze whether debt matters, it is useful to separate spending from financing decisions. A benevolent government that needs to decide whether to increase public expenditure will need to follow two steps. In the first step, the government needs to evaluate whether the social return on a given spending decision is higher than the cost incurred. In the second step, the government needs to choose whether it is better to finance the expenditure by issuing debt or increasing taxes.[3] The debate on whether debt matters should focus on this second step, rather than on whether the size and composition of public expenditure matters—a distinction that is often missed in public debates. Hence, this debate could also be framed in terms of a government's choice of increasing taxes and retiring debt or decreasing taxes and issuing new debt, for a given level of public expenditure.

So does debt matter? This seems to be a trivial question from today's perspective in Latin America and the Caribbean, but there is a 200-year-old result in economics known as "Ricardian equivalence" that states that under certain conditions, public debt does not matter.[4] More precisely, for any given level of expenditure, the decision regarding whether to finance the expenditure through debt or taxes is of no economic consequence. While

---

[2] Interestingly, it has been noted that personal bankruptcy has more in common with sovereign bankruptcy than corporate bankruptcy does (see Bulow, 2002).

[3] There are, of course, further decisions that involve the choice of the particular type of tax to be used or the structure of the debt to be issued.

[4] Incidentally, Ricardian equivalence is similar to one of the main theorems in corporate finance (the Modigliani-Miller theorem), which suggests that a firm's decision on whether to finance its activity by issuing debt or equity is irrelevant for the firm's value.

Ricardian equivalence holds only under a set of relatively restrictive assumptions, it is an important concept for at least two reasons. First, it is supported by a small but prominent set of economists. Second, and probably more important, a good grasp of the conditions under which Ricardian equivalence may hold is useful in understanding why it does not hold in most cases—in other words, why debt *does* matter.

WHEN PUBLIC DEBT IS IRRELEVANT: RICARDIAN EQUIVALENCE

Ricardian equivalence takes its name from the nineteenth-century British economist David Ricardo, who first noted that a government's debt-financed tax cut will lead to higher taxes in the future and hence it will only postpone, not reduce, a country's overall tax burden.[5] Aware of the unchanged tax burden, forward-looking individuals, rather than increasing consumption, will save all the additional income brought about by the tax cut to finance their obligation to pay future taxes. As a consequence, national saving, consumption, and economic growth will be unchanged by the government's tax cut. While this had been in the mind of economists since the work of Ricardo, the first full-fledged formal framework of Ricardian equivalence was developed in a seminal 1974 article by Robert Barro.[6]

Barro's formulation made it clear that there are three main necessary conditions for Ricardian equivalence to hold. The first necessary condition is the presence of forward-looking individuals characterized by intergenerational altruism. The argument goes as follows: one of the reasons why debt may matter is that it redistributes resources from future to current generations. However, Barro notes that people care about the well-being of their children and, as future generations are the children of the current generation (the argument applies, recursively, to grandchildren), people will incorporate future generations' welfare into their current consumption decisions, and hence debt will not lead to any intergenerational transfers.

A second necessary condition for Ricardian equivalence is the presence of perfect capital markets. As noted above, households with a rising income profile may choose to borrow when they are young and repay the debt when they are old. However, in the presence of imperfect capital markets, such households may be credit constrained and hence unable to borrow and consume as much as they would want when they are young. A cut in current taxes relaxes this constraint by increasing current disposable income and leads to higher consumption, in violation of Ricardian equivalence.

Finally, Ricardian equivalence holds in the presence of nondistortionary (lump sum) taxation. Barro himself in a 1979 article recognized that debt management matters when taxes are distortionary. Consider, for instance, a distortionary tax that reduces the incentives to work or invest, and assume that this distortion grows as the level of the tax increases.[7] In this case, textbook public finance shows that the policy that minimizes distortions is "tax

---

[5] This subsection draws from Elmendorf and Mankiw (1999), which provides a detailed description of Ricardian equivalence and also of the history of the idea.

[6] Interestingly, Barro did not refer to his theorem as "Ricardian equivalence"; it was a subsequent 1976 article by James Buchanan that recognized that the idea went back to Ricardo.

[7] For instance, in the presence of a 100 percent tax, nobody will work or invest, because everyone will know that all the income generated by their efforts will be appropriated by the government.

smoothing," which implies keeping tax rates unchanged over time.[8] As a consequence, any change in the tax-debt policy would have real effects and violate Ricardian equivalence.

WHEN PUBLIC DEBT MATTERS: THE CONVENTIONAL VIEW

Most economists and policymakers agree that Ricardian equivalence is unlikely to hold in practice and subscribe to what Elmendorf and Mankiw (1999) call the "conventional view" of public debt, which states that debt management has important effects both in the short and the long run.

According to the conventional view, a debt-financed tax cut has a positive effect on output in the short run and hence can be used to speed recovery from a recession. This positive effect requires two conditions. The first is that Ricardian equivalence does not hold, and hence the debt-financed tax cut leads to an increase in aggregate demand through higher household consumption. The second is that the economy is characterized by slow-moving prices and wages, and hence an increase in aggregate demand, rather than leading to an immediate jump in prices and wages, translates into higher output in the short run. The effect is different in the long run, when prices and wages are allowed to fully adjust to their equilibrium level. In this case, the available productive resources determine the level of output, and the debt policy described above will result in lower output, because it increases consumption and reduces saving, thus crowding out private investment and leading to lower capital accumulation.

WHAT IS THE STORY IN LATIN AMERICA AND THE CARIBBEAN?

While in developed countries the debate on the consequences of public debt has mostly focused on the trade-off between its expansionary effects in the short run and its contractionary effects in the long run, these are largely second-order problems in Latin America and the Caribbean, or in emerging markets more generally. The central issue in these countries is how to avoid the risks linked to macroeconomic volatility and financial crises.

Risky sovereign debt in an emerging economy also increases the cost of borrowing in international markets by private firms in those economies. The level of risk assigned to sovereign debt usually serves as a benchmark for the valuation of private debt in the country, and unlike in advanced economies, where sovereigns have the highest rating, sovereign ceilings make it difficult for private firms in emerging economies to borrow at lower rates than the sovereign. Thus, the negative spillovers of country risk are usually larger than the classic crowding-out effect emphasized in the literature that focuses on advanced economies.

Research focusing on developing and emerging market countries has also shown that higher levels of debt place substantial constraints on the conduct of an independent mon-

---

[8] Consider the following experiment: a country has an income of 100, a public expenditure of 30, a tax rate of 30 percent, and no debt. Suddenly, the government decides to push taxes to zero and finance expenditure by issuing debt that pays an interest rate of 10 percent. In the short run, economic conditions are likely to improve, because lower distortionary taxes will lead individuals and entrepreneurs to increase labor supply and investment. However, in the next period, the government will either need to push taxes to 63 percent (in order to retire the debt plus interest issued in the previous period and finance current spending) or permanently keep taxes at 33 percent and keep rolling over the debt. As distortions are increasing with the level of taxation, this increase in taxation will have a negative effect which is larger than the positive effect of the original tax cut.

etary policy. This is especially the case when most debt is denominated in foreign currency, and an accommodating monetary policy may lead to currency depreciations and substantial negative balance sheet effects (Hausmann, Panizza, and Stein, 2001; Calvo and Reinhart, 2002). But domestic currency debt is not problem free. High levels of domestic currency debt reduce a central bank's ability to credibly commit to a policy of low inflation because they generate the temptation to inflate the debt, and by lowering the central bank's credibility capital (which in most developing countries is not high to start with), they further limit the country's ability to conduct a countercyclical monetary policy. In fact, most hyperinflation episodes have been rooted in a combination of irresponsible fiscal and monetary policy and high levels of debt (Dornbusch, Sturzenegger, and Wolf, 1991).

On the positive side, while high levels of public debt constrain policy, moderate levels of debt in the form of liquid government bonds can nurture the development of the private bond market by providing a benchmark yield curve and improve the effectiveness of monetary policy by facilitating the central bank's open market operations. Therefore, public debt management can potentially play an important role in promoting the development of private domestic bond markets. This is particularly important in Latin America, which is characterized by small financial markets and excessive reliance on bank credit.

However, the most important effect of public debt in developing countries is that it makes them vulnerable to volatile capital markets and costly debt and financial crises. The design of policies aimed at reducing this vulnerability is the main theme of this report.

DEBT RISKS

Usually, the analysis of the risks of debt is framed in terms of debt levels. A conventional view in the literature is that higher levels of debt increase default risk, because the temptation to renegotiate the terms of the debt increases as the debt size (and thus the debt burden) goes up. Alternatively, the chance that an adverse shock to the economy (and hence to fiscal revenues) will deprive a government of the resources needed to service the country's debt rises in proportion to the country's level of indebtedness. However, recent research in the field has stressed the fact that, while important, debt levels are not the ultimate determinant of sovereign debt risk.

There is also evidence that debt levels are not crucial determinants of the perception of default risk, as measured, for example, by the credit ratings assigned by the international credit-rating agencies. A simple plot of debt levels against credit ratings illustrates the point, showing the weak correlation between the two variables. For instance, Figure 1.1 includes countries with high credit ratings (such as Belgium, Italy, and Japan) and debt levels well above 100 percent of GDP, and countries with similar debt levels but low, speculative grade credit ratings (such as Ghana, Jordan, and Jamaica). At the same time, there are countries with high credit ratings and negligible levels of debt (Luxembourg and Australia) as well as several countries with low debt and low credit ratings (Guatemala and Kazakhstan).[9] In the same vein, research on early-warning prediction of debt crises has failed to identify any mea-

---

[9] A formal statistical test shows that, with other factors controlled for, a 35 percentage point increase in the debt-to-GDP ratio would be associated with, at most, a one-notch decrease in credit rating (Eichengreen, Hausmann, and Panizza, 2005b).

Figure 1.1
Public Debt and Sovereign Rating (1995–2005)

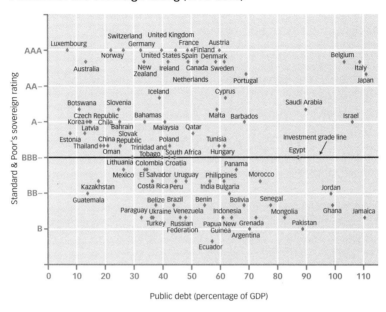

Sources: Jaimovich and Panizza (2006b) and Standard & Poor's.

sure of the level of public debt as a significant indicator of a high probability of a subsequent debt crisis (Manasse, Roubini, and Schimmelpfennig, 2003).

If debt levels do not matter that much, what are the drivers of the large differences among countries in perceived (and actual) credit risks? Three main factors explain these differences. The first has to do with the country's economic quality, the second relates to the country's political and institutional quality, and the third involves the government's debt quality.

With respect to the first factor, low- and middle-income countries characterized by limited diversification, high dependence on a few commodities, and high levels of income inequality tend to have a small and volatile tax base, which weakens their credit quality (IDB, 1995). With respect to the second factor, countries with unstable political systems tend to be characterized by policies with low levels of credibility (IDB, 2005b) and hence will not be trusted by either domestic or foreign investors, who will demand a substantial risk premium as a result. Finally, governments that have a risky debt structure—which depends on the country's economic structure but essentially means a high incidence of short-term and foreign currency debt—face situations where the level of debt suddenly jumps in response to a depreciation of the exchange rate or a change in investors' perception of country risk.

While this report largely focuses on this last factor, debt quality, it is important to note that the three factors listed above tend to be mutually reinforcing. Countries characterized by high levels of macroeconomic volatility will tend to have weaker political coalitions, which, in turn, will often be reflected in suboptimal policies that will further increase macroeconomic volatility. Furthermore, as high economic and political instability increases country risk, investors will provide intermittent lending, be reluctant to engage in long-term nominal contracts, prefer to lend either short term or in foreign currency, and thus further increase the risk generated by the debt, which, in turn, will increase economic and thus political instability.

This report attempts to take a broad view of the risks associated with sovereign debt. From the point of view of the creditor, sovereign debt risk (or country risk) refers narrowly to the risk that a sovereign will fail to honor the terms of its debt contract (for a discussion of risks from the creditor's point of view, see de la Torre and Schmukler, 2004b). The risk faced by the sovereign borrower, which this report labels the *risk of sovereign finance*, spans a broader set of concerns. The risk of sovereign finance comprises two distinct hazards: (1) the risk of a costly financial crisis resulting at least in part from turbulence in sovereign debt markets[10] and (2) the degree to which debt amplifies the consequences of an adverse shock and constrains domestic policies.

This suggests that debt quality is a major determinant of the risks of sovereign finance, with low-quality debt being associated with higher risk for any given debt level. But why do countries have different debt structures, and what can they do about it?

There are essentially two explanations for the poor quality of the debt structure of many countries (Borensztein et al., 2004). The first view postulates that countries' poor reputations and institutions (a bad credit record, poor institutional quality and contract enforcement, and a history of high deficits and inflation) account for prohibitively expensive currency and maturity premiums and motivate the use of short-term and foreign-currency-denominated debt. The second explanation stresses the lack of significant deep markets for better-quality instruments. For example, the ability to issue debt in domestic currency at a fair price may depend critically on the existence of a well-developed domestic bond market and a stable domestic investor base, which in turn becomes a strong constituency for fiscal prudence. The creation and growth of any financial market is fraught with externalities, and thus the absence of markets for high-quality instruments may be the result of historical accident and insufficient policy initiative.

Although sometimes one of these explanations is emphasized at the expense of the other, the two are not mutually exclusive. Overcoming institutional and credibility gaps and developing sound, deep markets should be the twin objectives of proactive debt management policies. These policies and these markets, perhaps aided by substantive reforms to the international financial architecture, can set Latin American countries free from the high-cost, high-risk trap and ensure a safer debt structure and more macroeconomic stability. This is the view subscribed to by the present report.[11]

---

[10] This often, but not always, involves a sovereign default. For instance, a debt problem was at the root of Mexico's 1995 financial crisis, although debt contracts were fully honored.

[11] This report focuses on the risks of sovereign finance and on mechanisms aimed at avoiding crises, rather than on crisis resolution and debt restructuring. Some excellent references on the latter topic are Eichengreen and Portes (1995), Roubini and Setser (2004), and Sturzenegger and Zettelmeyer (2006).

STRUCTURE OF THE REPORT AND MAIN FINDINGS

The report comprises five sections and an appendix. In addition to this introductory chapter, the first section describes *recent developments in debt and deficits in Latin America and the Caribbean and around the world*. Chapter 2 describes the evolution of public debt in Latin America and the Caribbean, focusing on both debt levels and debt composition. The chapter shows that public debt in Latin America and the Caribbean decreased in the early 1990s, increased in the second half of the 1990s, and decreased moderately over the last two years. All things considered, the average level of public debt in the region is now similar to that prevailing in the early 1990s. Changes in debt composition have been more substantial. In 1994, about 60 percent of the public debt of the largest countries in the region was external, and an even larger share was denominated in foreign currency. By 2004, the share of external debt had dropped to 40 percent, and that of foreign currency debt had declined to 45 percent. This is critically important, because until recently the focus of most analyses of public debt in developing and emerging market countries was on external debt, and statistics on domestic debt were—and in many cases still are—difficult to come by. One of the objectives of this report is to highlight and correct this bias. In fact, one of the contributions of this report is a new data set that describes debt levels and composition (including that of domestic debt) for several Latin American and Caribbean countries. The excessive focus on external debt has led some observers to conclude that all is well in Latin America and the Caribbean because public debt is decreasing. The complete story, however, is that the ongoing decline in external debt ratios is compensated for by an increase in domestic debt. In other words, the real change concerns debt composition, not debt levels. Does this change improve debt quality? While the shift towards domestically issued, domestic-currency-denominated debt should make the region more resilient in the face of balance sheet effects brought about by currency devaluation, it may do so at a cost if it leads to large currency premiums and a generally shorter debt tenor, factors that may resurrect the ghosts of high inflation and currency crises.

Chapter 3, which focuses on the main determinants of debt growth, documents a striking finding: recorded budget deficits play only a secondary role in explaining debt growth in developing countries. In Latin America and the Caribbean, in particular, recorded deficits account for only 5 percent of the variance in debt growth. The remaining 95 percent is explained largely by balance sheet effects due to real exchange rate adjustments and contingent liabilities. For example, in January 1999, Brazil's net debt-to-GDP ratio jumped to over 51 percent of GDP from only 42 percent one month earlier, the equivalent of an annualized deficit of 120 percent of GDP. The reason was the currency depreciation that followed the abandonment of the Real Plan. The Dominican Republic's debt ratio, which stood at about 25 percent of GDP at the end of 2002, more than doubled to 55 percent of GDP by the end of 2003, the equivalent of a 30 percent fiscal deficit for the year, as a result of an extremely costly banking crisis. This is not to say that deficits are not important (in fact, contingent liabilities are often the manifestation of poorly recorded past deficits), but it points out that while most of the discussion on the appropriateness of fiscal policy focuses on some deficit indicators, debt explosions are often due to something else, and this "something else" should be central in the policy debate.

The second section focuses on *external debt*. External debt has long been a prime source of financing for Latin American and Caribbean sovereigns. Chapter 4 reviews the history of sovereign lending to Latin America and the Caribbean over the past 200 years and shows that the region has been characterized by waves of capital flows, which are then followed by sometimes extended periods of default and limited or no access to foreign financing. Despite recurrent crises, poor institutions, and often explosive political environments, Latin America and the Caribbean kept promising—and occasionally delivering—high returns that attracted international investors again and again. The parallel with the modern Latin American and Caribbean sovereign bond market is striking.

Chapter 5 looks at the workings of the international debt market today and analyzes a number of its imperfections: sudden stops in capital inflows triggered by events sometimes far removed from Latin American and Caribbean economies but with strong bearing on global financial markets; contagion effects that spread a market panic to a whole group of countries in the same "asset class"; the volatility of emerging market premiums, which show a strong tendency to experience large spikes and subsequent reversals or "mean reversions"; the predominance of external factors as determinants of emerging market spreads; the risk of (and evidence for) self-fulfilling crises, in which a market panic causes a deterioration in economic conditions in the country that validates the run; and the role of sovereign credit ratings, which seem to follow market developments rather than lead them and spill over into private borrowers' credit standing. In addition, the chapter reviews recent developments that have resulted in global conditions very favorable to emerging market borrowers and discusses reasons to be optimistic—but cautious—about the durability of these conditions.

Chapter 6 analyzes the effects of official lending and describes the behavior of the multilateral development banks, a key component of sovereign finance in Latin America and the Caribbean, both for low-income economies with no market access and for middle-income emerging economies.[12] The chapter finds evidence that, unlike private flows to emerging economies, multilateral lending tends to be countercyclical and finds no evidence that non-concessional lending of multilateral development banks is politically influenced. The chapter presents evidence of a catalytic role of multilateral lending, as greater multilateral lending today tends to result in greater private lending tomorrow. The chapter also finds that, as bilateral lenders are subject to coordination problems which lead to inefficiencies in planning and monitoring projects, multilateral lending may play a coordinating role for individual bilateral lenders.

The third section focuses on *domestic debt markets*. Chapter 7 looks at the development of domestic bond markets. It shows that the region has relatively well-developed markets for government bonds, but extremely small private bond markets, and discusses different views on the nature of spillovers from public to private debt markets. The chapter suggests that, while a well-functioning market for government debt is probably a necessary condition for the development of a private bond market, there is a fine line between market

---

[12] In fact, the share of official lending in total public debt in the region was higher in 2004 than in the early 1990s, a trend that was partly reversed in 2005–2006 after Brazil and Argentina repaid their debt to the IMF and may be further undone by Mexico's planned repayment of its debt to the multilateral development banks.

development and crowding out. Hence, public issuers need to be careful to avoid saturating domestic demand for bonded debt.

Chapter 8 focuses on the role of institutional investors (pension funds, mutual funds, and insurance companies) in the development of local bond markets. It argues that a group of large and well-managed institutional investors plays a key role in the workings of domestic securities markets and discusses policies aimed at making government bonds attractive to institutional investors. However, the chapter also points out that institutional investors can become victims of their own success, as financially constrained governments may attempt to capture the resources of such investors through regulation and persuasion. Therefore, it is essential to have in place good institutional and regulatory frameworks aimed at reducing the risk that a government will pressure institutional investors to buy government bonds when it faces financial strains.

The fourth section deals with some of the *causes and consequences of debt*. Chapter 9 focuses on the political economy of debt, recognizing that political developments and institutions can cause government borrowing to deviate from its legitimate purposes. The chapter shows how self-interested politicians can transform public borrowing from a useful development tool into a mechanism that wastes public resources and generates vulnerabilities. The chapter also discusses possible institutional reforms aimed at limiting these problems.

Chapter 10 studies the complex relationship between debt and economic development. It shows that, while it is extremely hard to find, in empirical research, a clear relationship between public borrowing and economic growth, there is some evidence that limited levels of external debt are good for growth but high levels of debt can severely stunt economic development. The chapter also shows that public borrowing seems to be useful for increasing a country's investment in infrastructure but that excessive debt levels tend to have a negative effect on poverty-reducing social expenditure. As this last finding provides some evidence in support of the current debt relief initiative aimed at helping low-income countries reach the Millennium Development Goals, the chapter also surveys the existing literature on debt relief and finds that the evaluation of the effects of past debt relief initiatives is mixed.

Chapter 11 discusses debt sustainability using both standard methodologies and more recent approaches that explicitly take into account the structure of debt, macroeconomic volatility, and the full balance sheet of the public sector. In this light, the chapter shows that Latin America and the Caribbean made important progress in terms of debt sustainability coming out of the debt crisis of the 1980s. A comparison of several indicators of debt sustainability suggests that, on average, the current fiscal position in the region is better than that prevailing in the early 1990s. In line with one of the main messages of this report, the chapter points out that debt structure is often more important than debt levels and, although some progress has been made in reducing liability dollarization and in lengthening the maturity of domestic debt, vulnerability to balance sheet effects and rollover risk has not disappeared.

Chapter 12 focuses on the cost of sovereign default. The chapter argues that there is a disconnect between the theoretical literature and the empirical evidence on sovereign defaults and renegotiations. According to the theoretical literature, default events should occur in good times, when countries enjoy a strong financial position and do not anticipate the need of market financing in the near future. Defaults in such cases are strategic rather than bankruptcies of the kind that occur in the business world. There is little evidence, however, of strategic sovereign defaults' ever occurring, and time after time default events occur in situations in which a country has reached a condition that can be described as sovereign bankruptcy. In fact, the evidence suggests that policymakers tend to postpone the moment of reckoning and, as a consequence, the costs of debt crises are often incurred before, and not after, the moment of default. This does not imply per se that strategic, opportunistic defaults would go unpunished. On the contrary, the fact that strategic defaults are never observed probably reflects the recognition that they would be extremely costly.

The fifth section discusses the *risks of sovereign debt and policies aimed at reducing these risks*. Chapter 13 specifically delves into the risks of sovereign finance, focusing on the two main sources of vulnerabilities: debt denomination (foreign currency debt) and debt maturity (short-term debt). After discussing the possible risks arising from these characteristics of debt, the chapter analyzes whether there is a trade-off between foreign currency and short-term debt. Finally, the last chapter closes the circle by addressing the question that guides the present report: how can countries limit the risks of sovereign finance? The report emphasizes the benefits of prudent fiscal policy, sophisticated debt management, and large and sound domestic bond markets and elaborates on the benefits of innovative debt instrument design. However, these domestic efforts may not be sufficient to build a crisis-proof debt structure at a reasonable cost given the high exposure to external factors (real and financial) that characterizes the economies in the region. With this in mind, the chapter closes with a discussion of ongoing and proposed international initiatives aimed at limiting the negative influence of international financial volatility, an area where international financial institutions like the IDB have an essential role to play.

CHAPTER 2 | Public Debt in Latin America and around the World

It is a capital mistake to theorize before one has data. Insensibly one begins to twist facts to suit theories, instead of theories to suit facts.

—Sir Arthur Conan Doyle (1859-1930)

THE OBJECTIVE of this report is to analyze the relationship between public debt, economic development, and macroeconomic stability. A clear understanding of these issues requires comparable cross-country data on the level and structure of public debt, but the problem is that good data on public debt are hard to find.

The ideal data set on public debt would cover the level of debt and break the data down according to the characteristics of the instruments of which it is composed. This data set would include figures for both net and gross debt at the levels of the general government, central government, and subnational governments.[1] However, data on the level of debt alone would not be enough, because different types of debt generate different types of vulnerabilities. For instance, short-term borrowing in foreign currency is likely to be more dangerous (albeit less expensive) than borrowing by issuing long-term domestic currency contingent debt (for a discussion of these issues, see Borensztein et al., 2004). Therefore, one would like to have data describing the composition of public debt. These data should separate domestic and external debt, and then divide each category according to maturity (long term and short term), currency of denomination (domestic and foreign), and type of indexation (nominal, indexed to prices, indexed to the interest rate). Finally, one would like to have information on both the face value of debt and its net present value.

This would be a complete data set. In reality, one might need to be less ambitious. Despite the importance of accurate measures of the level and composition of public debt for both policy and research purposes, until recently there existed no data set on the composition (in terms of both maturity and currency) of public debt, and even data on the level of government debt had gaps.

---

[1] This would also require a list of the variables that are used in going from gross to net debt (so that the researcher could make sure that the definition of net debt is homogenous across countries).

Box 2.1 New Data Sets on Public Debt

The most widely used sources of macroeconomic data are the *International Financial Statistics* (IFS) published by the International Monetary Fund and the *World Development Indicators* (WDI) published by the World Bank. However, public debt data contained in these databases have many missing observations, limiting their usefulness for research that requires data on the stock of public debt.[a] Jaimovich and Panizza (2006b) show that even for the largest countries, IFS and WDI coverage of data on public debt is less than satisfactory. For instance, they consider 29 countries (the seven largest advanced economies, the five largest countries in the respective regions of Latin America and East Asia, and the three largest countries in each of Eastern Europe, the Middle East, South Asia, and Sub-Saharan Africa) and show that IFS and WDI have data on public debt for only 19 of these countries, and even for those countries the coverage is often incomplete. To address this issue, Jaimovich and Panizza (2006b) searched several publicly available sources of data on public debt and compiled a database that covers 89 countries for the 1991-2005 period and 7 other countries for the 1993-2005 period.[b] This is the first public debt database used in this report.

Although the Jaimovich-Panizza data set increases available data on public debt, it focuses on central government debt and provides no information on debt composition. The CLYPS database of Cowan, Levy Yeyati, Panizza, and Sturzenegger (2006) focuses on 22 countries in Latin America and the Caribbean and reports public debt data disaggregated by type of debt (external ver-

sus domestic, official versus private, bonds versus bank loans), currency composition, indexation maturity, and level of government.[c] This is the second public debt database used in this report (Box 2.2 discusses this data set in greater detail). While Jaimovich and Panizza (2006b) focus on central government debt, Cowan et al. (2006) focus on a wider definition of the public sector and hence tend to obtain higher debt ratios.

The data set assembled by Cowan et al. (2006) focuses on Latin America and the Caribbean and hence does not allow for comparisons across different regions of the world. Jeanne and Guscina (2006) assembled a data set which includes information on debt levels and composition for 19 emerging market countries located in Asia (7 countries), Latin America (6 countries), Eastern Europe (4 countries), and the Middle East (2 countries). This is the third public debt database used in this report.

---

[a] Data availability is particularly limited in regard to domestically issued public debt. Data on external public debt for developing countries are generally available from the World Bank's *Global Development Finance* (GDF) and the Bank for International Settlements, International Monetary Fund, Organisation for Economic Co-operation and Development, and World Bank Joint External Debt Hub (www.jedh.org).

[b] The data are available at http://www.iadb.org/res/pub_desc.cfm?pub_id=DBA-005.

[c] The data set includes information on currency composition for nine countries and information for term structure for eight countries. The data are available at www.iadb.org/res/pub_desc.cfm?pub_id=DBA-007.

Two data sets assembled for this report, and a third one assembled by researchers at the International Monetary Fund, partly address these issues by increasing the country and time coverage of data on the level of central government debt, and by stressing for the first time information on the composition of debt for several Latin American, Caribbean, and emerging market countries.[2] These data sets (described in Boxes 2.1 and 2.2) will be the main source of data used in this report. With these data at hand, this chapter will describe and characterize the evolution and the structure of public debt in Latin America and the Caribbean and compare Latin America and the Caribbean with other regions of the world.

PUBLIC DEBT IN LATIN AMERICA AND THE CARIBBEAN[3]

Figure 2.1 provides a bird's-eye view of the ratio of debt to GDP in the region

Figure 2.1
Public Debt in Latin America and the Caribbean
(*percentage of GDP*)

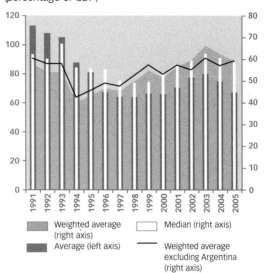

Source: Authors' calculations based on Cowan et al. (2006).
Note: Countries included: Argentina, Bahamas, Barbados, Belize, Bolivia, Brazil, Chile, Colombia, Costa Rica, Ecuador, El Salvador, Guatemala, Guyana, Haiti, Honduras, Jamaica, Mexico, Nicaragua, Panama, Paraguay, Peru, Trinidad and Tobago, Uruguay, and Venezuela.

and shows four different measures of aggregate indebtedness.[4] The dark bars report simple averages across countries and show that in the early 1990s, the region was characterized by very high levels of debt (above 100 percent of GDP). Debt decreased rapidly over the 1993–1997 period, bottoming out at 64 percent of GDP. The late 1990s and early years of this century were characterized by a wave of financial and debt crises (East Asia in 1997, Russia in 1998, Brazil in 1999, and Argentina in 2001), which led to a rapid increase in debt (from 64 to 80 percent of GDP over the 1998–2003 period). The unwinding of these crises was then associated with a decrease of approximately 12 percentage points during 2004 and 2005.

The declining trend of the early 1990s was mostly driven by debt reduction in a few countries with very high levels of debt. As a consequence, median values (the light bars) show a much less dramatic decline than the average values, decreasing from 62 to 49 per-

---

[2] However, the data sets do not include information on the net present value of public debt.

[3] This section is based on the CLYPS data set presented in Cowan et al. (2006).

[4] This chapter focuses on aggregate figures, while individual country data are reported in the appendix. Although CLYPS data end in 2004, Figures 2.1 and 2.2 report data for 2005, which were computed applying growth rates from Jaimovich and Panizza (2006b).

Box 2.2 The CLYPS Data Set

A new database compiled for this report is the CLYPS data set assembled by Cowan, Levy Yeyati, Panizza, and Sturzenegger (2006).[a] The apparently simple goal of measuring government debt in a comparable manner across countries requires important methodological definitions. The figure in this box provides a sense of the importance of methodological decisions by plotting different measures of the debt-to-GDP ratio in Mexico. Focusing on the year 2004, there are three data sets (those from Jaimovich and Panizza and ECLAC and the traditional definition of debt published by the Mexican authorities), spanning a range of between 23 and 36 percent of GDP for government debt. CLYPS data indicate a debt-to-GDP ratio of around 40 percent, and the "augmented" definition tracked by the Mexican government indicates a debt-to-GDP ratio of approximately 47 percent (the difference between CLYPS and the augmented definition is that CLYPS does not include debt issued by development banks and to guarantee the financing of infrastructure projects. These enormous differences (which mostly arise from the treatment of debt issued to rescue the banking system in 1995) apply to gross debt and hence do not even reflect differences that can arise from different netting methodologies.

The first methodological decision has to do with the level of government considered. This entails a decision on the inclusion or exclusion of subnational entities, the way in which central bank assets and liabilities should be handled, and the role of the liabilities of state-owned enterprises (SOEs). The general approach followed by CLYPS is to look at the consolidated central government and then, for countries with important subnational entities, report subnational debt separately. While ideally one would also wish to include the liabilities of SOEs, CLYPS does not include these liabilities on the grounds that counting the liabilities without an equivalent assessment of the net worth of SOEs seems inappropriate.

In some countries, a significant fraction of multilateral and external lending is assumed by the central bank and represents an outstanding obligation of the authorities; thus, the definition of consolidated central government adopted by CLYPS includes the liabilities of the central bank. Exceptions to this rule are the money base and liabilities issued by the central bank for the purpose of monetary intervention. A final methodological issue is the definition of external and domestic debt. The standard distinction focuses on the residence of the holders and defines external debt as those liabilities held by nonresidents.[b] While the resident/nonresident distinction is important for understanding the income effects of changes in the debt stock and for constructing measures of domestic and foreign wealth, this distinction is very difficult to make in prac-

cent of GDP over the 1991–1998 period. Over the 1998–2003 period, by contrast, median debt increased as rapidly as average debt.

The shaded area in Figure 2.1 reports a weighted average of the debt-to-GDP ratio. This gives relatively more importance to large countries because it is equivalent to computing tice, especially for traded bond debt. The distinction by debt holder is feasible only for countries whose stocks of marketable debt are negligible.[c] CLYPS adopts an alternative classification criterion based on who has legal jurisdiction over debt that has been issued. External debt comprises all liabilities issued under foreign legal jurisdiction, and domestic debt is debt issued under domestic governing law. This in turn determines the courts (that is, the legal system) where debt settlements and potential litigations are to be resolved. This aspect may be potentially relevant for debt analysis to the extent that it relates to the differing quality of local institutions and financial markets (see Cowan et al., 2006, for more details).

[a] This box is adapted from Cowan et al. (2006).
[b] This is the definition used in the *External Debt Statistics: Guide for Compilers and Users* jointly published by the Bank for International Settlements, Eurostat, International Monetary Fund, Organisation for Economic Co-operation and Development, Paris Club, United Nations Conference on Trade and Development, and World Bank. In fact, on page 7, the guide states, "Gross external debt, at any given time, is the outstanding amount of those actual current, and not contingent, liabilities that require payment(s) of principal and/or interest by the debtor at some point(s) in the future and that are owed to nonresidents by residents of an economy."
[c] IMF staff tried to estimate with very limited success the participation of nonresidents in

Public Debt in Mexico According to Different Definitions
(*percentage of GDP*)

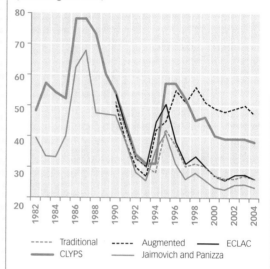

Sources: Authors' calculations based on Cowan et al. (2006), Jaimovich and Panizza (2006b), ECLAC, and IMF.
Note: CLYPS = Cowan, Levy Yeyati, Panizza, and Sturzenegger database.

the domestic capital market. "It is difficult to obtain complete data on the composition of investors in sovereign bonds. Unlike bilateral, multilateral or bank loans neither issuers nor other data gatherers publish comprehensive decompositions of commercial investors in EM [emerging market] sovereign debt. . . . A survey of 18 EM countries was carried out to obtain the composition of investors in domestic and externally issued debt. Only a handful of countries would provide detailed information on investor composition" (IMF, 2006d, 95-96).

the sum of total debt in Latin America and the Caribbean and dividing it by the total regional GDP. The weighted debt-to-GDP ratio, which reached a minimum of 40 percent in 1994, has been increasing since then, reaching 66 percent of GDP in 2003 and then dropping to 59 percent of GDP in 2005. The weighted-average data show two interesting patterns. First, the weighted average is always lower than the simple average, indicating that larger countries tend to have smaller debt.[5] Second, while the difference between the simple and weighted average was extremely large in the early 1990s, the two ratios have tended to converge in recent years because debt has been decreasing in small countries and increasing in large countries.

The last debt indicator reported in Figure 2.1 is the weighted debt-to-GDP ratio computed excluding Argentina from the sample (this is the solid dark line). This indicator isolates the aggregate measure from the influence of the sharp fluctuations in Argentina in the 2000s. The figure shows that dropping Argentina from the sample removes the local peak of 2003 and makes the pattern of debt smoother and more evident.

There are many ways to interpret the data reported in Figure 2.1. An optimistic observer would focus on the simple average measure and note that debt in 2005 is much lower than in 1991. This is likely to be a misreading of the data, however, because the large drop in debt is basically due to the behavior of two small countries (Guyana and Nicaragua) that in 1991 had debt levels above 500 percent of GDP and by 2005 had managed to bring debt down to the still considerable level of 150 percent of GDP. A more moderate optimist would focus on median values or the weighted averages and note that by 2005, debt was at about the same level as in 1991 and that these levels of debt compare well with those of several other regions (for instance, they are lower than those prevailing in the advanced economies). Such an optimist would think that this is a good outcome after a decade punctuated by a number of severe financial crises and high market volatility. This person's optimism would be further fueled by the decline in debt in the last two years and favorable changes in the composition of debt, as well as the fact that part of the previous debt increase resulted from the privatization of pension systems, which will be discussed below.

A callous pessimist, however, would note that debt has been generally rising since 1995, squandering the gains from the significant debt reduction achieved in the early 1990s. Such an observer would also note that, while the 1990s were punctuated by several crises, the 1980s (often referred to as the "lost decade") had been an even more traumatic period for Latin America and the Caribbean. The pessimist would also point out that part of the original debt reduction was due to the privatization process and that, having sold the family jewels, most Latin American and Caribbean countries are back where they were before privatization.[6]

Something on which optimists and pessimists are likely to agree, though, is that debt is still of significant magnitude in Latin America and the Caribbean and that good debt management must be a clear priority for the stability of a region which has been hit by devastating debt crises in the past.

One natural question is whether the patterns documented in Figure 2.1 are driven by valuation effects in the presence of foreign-currency-denominated debt. A way to partly address this issue is to adjust GDP for the currency composition of debt and isolate the

---

[5] Part (but not all) of this difference is due to the behavior of Nicaragua and Guyana, which have a small GDP and extremely high levels of debt (see appendix).

[6] Rough estimates suggest that over the 1990s privatization revenues were close to US$90 billion (about US$60 billion in Argentina, Brazil, and Mexico alone). Back-of-the-envelope calculations suggest that without these privatizations, average debt would have been 5 percent of GDP higher than that reported here.

changes in debt over GDP due to apprecia-tions or depreciations of the real exchange rate.[7] Adjusting for valuation effects due to changes in the real exchange rate mitigates but does not change the upward trend in debt in the 1995–2005 period. This adjustment also shows that the recent slight decrease in debt is partly due to the real appreciation faced by several coun-tries in the region (Figure 2.2).

The level of market access is an im-portant dimension that may affect trends in the level of debt and its composition across countries, and the 24 countries used to compute the averages of Figure 2.1 can be divided into two subgroups. The first consists of emerging market countries with access to the international capital market, and the second consists of countries with no access or only limited access. The next sections discuss sepa-rately trends in those two groups.[8]

Figure 2.2
Importance of Denominator
(*percentage of GDP*)

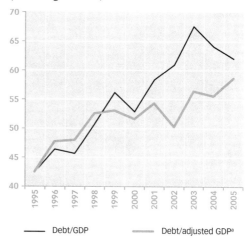

Source: Authors' calculations based on Cowan et al. (2006).
Note: Countries included: Argentina, Barbados, Bolivia, Brazil, Chile, Colombia, Costa Rica, Honduras, Mexico, Panama, and Peru.
[a] GDP adjusted by currency composition.

Emerging Market Countries

As the emerging market group comprises the largest countries in the region, the behavior of the weighted average of debt over GDP for these countries is basically identical to that of the weighted average for the whole sample of countries. Figure 2.3 describes the composition of total debt in emerging market countries, breaking it down into external debt owed to official creditors (such as the International Monetary Fund, the Inter-American Development Bank, the World Bank, and bilateral creditors), external debt owed to private creditors (bondholders and banks), and domestic debt.[9] It shows that official debt remained fairly stable at about 10 percent of GDP and that private external debt also remained more or less constant, ranging between 13 and 16 percent of GDP (with a spike of 18 percent of GDP in 2003). As a conse-quence, there is no clear trend in external debt.[10] The increasing trend in debt is entirely the

---

[7] This is done in the following way. Let *GDPCO* be GDP in U.S. dollars, measured at a constant exchange rate (using 1995 as a base, which does not affect the trend in the ratio). Let *ADJ GDP* denote adjusted GDP and be computed ac-cording to *ADJ GDP = d * GDPCO + (1 − d) * GDPCU*, where *d* is the share of total public debt denominated in foreign currency and *GDPCU* is GDP in U.S. dollars measured at the current exchange rate. This measure is available only for 11 countries which have a sufficiently long series on debt composition by currency.

[8] There are several possible definitions of emerging market countries. This report defines as "emerging market" all the countries which are included in the JPMorgan Emerging Market Bond Index Global. IMF (2003a) uses a similar classification but includes Costa Rica in the sample of emerging markets. The Bahamas is not included in either group because, as a high-income offshore financial center, it is in a group by itself.

[9] See Box 2.2 for details on the definition of external debt used in this report.

[10] To be precise, there is a slight U-shaped pattern, with external debt dropping by approximately five percentage points between 1991 and 1997 and then increasing in the following seven years.

Figure 2.3
Composition of Public Debt in Emerging Latin American Economies
(*percentage of GDP*)

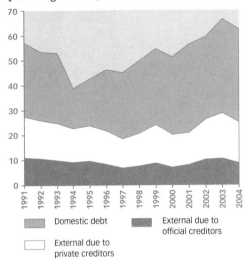

	Domestic debt		External due to official creditors
	External due to private creditors		

Source: Authors' calculations based on Cowan et al. (2006).
Note: Countries included: Argentina, Brazil, Chile, Colombia, Ecuador, El Salvador, Mexico, Panama, Peru, Uruguay, and Venezuela.

Figure 2.4
Composition of Public External Debt in Emerging Latin American Economies
(*percentage of GDP*)

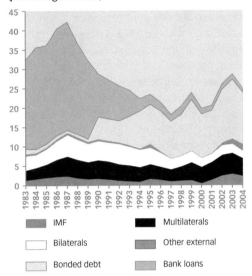

	IMF		Multilaterals
	Bilaterals		Other external
	Bonded debt		Bank loans

Source: Authors' calculations based on Cowan et al. (2006).
Note: Countries included: Argentina, Brazil, Chile, Colombia, Ecuador, El Salvador, Mexico, Peru, Uruguay, and Venezuela.

result of the increase in domestic debt, which rose from 16 percent of GDP in 1994 to 37 percent of GDP in 2004.

Data on external debt are available for a longer period and show a visible downward trend in debt ratios, which fell from a peak of 42 percent in 1987 to 25 percent of GDP in 2004 (bottoming out at about 18 percent in 1997). Data on the composition of external debt show that lending by the IMF and other multilaterals has hovered around 5 percent of GDP (or 20 percent of external debt), with peaks during the Mexican, Brazilian, and Argentine crises (Figure 2.4). Bilateral lending has, instead, become progressively less important, falling from a peak of 6 percent of GDP in 1987 to 2 percent of GDP in 2004. Borrowing from private sources (comprising bank and bonded debt) has fallen sharply from a peak at 30 percent of GDP in 1987 to about 16 percent of GDP in 2004. The debt instruments shifted from mostly bank loans in the 1980s to mostly bonds in the 1990s, after the Brady Plan debt-restructuring operations resuscitated the market for emerging market bonds, which had largely died out in the interwar period (see Chapters 4 and 5). The result of a decreasing amount (in terms of GDP) of external debt owed to private lenders and a constant amount of external debt owed to official lenders is that the relative share of official debt has been increasing. While financing from international financial institutions represents a small fraction of international capital

Box 2.3 Original Sin

Eichengreen and Hausmann (1999) defined original sin as "a situation in which the domestic currency is not used to borrow abroad or to borrow long-term even domestically" (330). According to this definition, there are two components of original sin: an international component (the domestic currency is not used to borrow abroad) and a domestic one (the domestic currency is not used to borrow long-term even domestically).[a]

Eichengreen, Hausmann, and Panizza (2005a, 2005b) focus on the international component of original sin. They start from the observation that, in 1999-2001, 85 percent of the $1.3 trillion in outstanding securities placed in international markets by countries that do not issue one of the five major currencies was denominated in these five currencies. Next, they use three indices to quantify international original sin and find that these indices are associated with lower credit ratings, lower exchange rate flexibility, and higher volatility of GDP growth and capital flows. They study the determinants of international original sin and find that good policies are a necessary but not a sufficient condition for redemption from original sin and that the only vari-

able that is robustly correlated with original sin is country size.

Research on the domestic component of original sin has been limited by the difficulty of finding data on the currency and maturity composition of domestic debt. Hausmann and Panizza (2003) were able to collect data for a small sample of countries and show that, unlike international original sin, domestic original sin is associated with past bad policies, especially inflationary history. Their main index of domestic original sin is defined as

$$DSIN3 = 1 - \frac{\text{Domestic Currency Fixed Rate Domestic Debt}}{\text{Total Domestic Debt}}$$

Successive work by Mehl and Reynaud (2005) and Jeanne and Guscina (2006) confirms the link between policies and original sin and also shows that, while very important for Latin America, domestic original sin is not as pervasive as international original sin (see Figure 2.6).

---

[a] For a criticism of the original sin research agenda see Goldstein and Turner (2004). For a rebuttal see Eichengreen, Hausmann, and Panizza (2003).

flows (including private borrowing and foreign direct investment), it still accounts for a significant share of the stock of external public debt in the largest Latin American countries.[11]

The currency composition of public debt appears to be especially important for this group of countries. The literature on "original sin," liability dollarization, and currency mismatches has argued that countries with long-term domestic currency debt tend to have a safer debt structure than countries with short-term foreign currency debt (Box 2.3). Basically all external debt issued by Latin American and Caribbean emerging markets is denominated

---

[11] As these data cover only the period through 2004, they do not capture the recent repayments to the IMF by Argentina and Brazil and to the IDB and the World Bank by Mexico.

Box 2.4 Recent International Bond Issues in Domestic Currency

Until very recently, virtually all debt issued in international markets by Latin American countries was denominated in foreign currency.[a] At the end of 2003, Uruguay issued a global bond denominated in real pesos (and indexed to inflation), and in 2004 Uruguay issued another domestic currency bond, this time in nominal pesos. Colombia launched nominal peso issues in 2004 and 2005. In 2005, Brazil issued a large bond (close to US$1.5 billion) with a long maturity and denominated in nominal *reais* (see table on the facing page). In the corporate and financial sector, the Mexican oil company Pemex, several Brazilian banks (Votorantim, Unibanco, Banco do Brasil, Bradesco, and Santander Banespa) and two Brazilian corporations (Eletropaulo and Telemar) have been able to float bonds denominated in domestic currency abroad as well. Furthermore, Unibanco has issued a real Eurobond linked to the Brazilian inflation rate.

These bonds are reasonably long term and often have low spreads. In Colombia's November 2004 issue, primary spreads were 20 to 50 basis points below those on com-parable domestic bonds (Tovar, 2005). In Brazil's government bond case, the international issue was a 10-year-maturity, fixed rate instrument, with a yield some 250 basis points below comparable domestic law yields. International investors may find *reais* bonds issued under New York governing law and settled in U.S. dollars more attractive as a result of their lower risk of capital controls and other taxes (Amato, 2006).

While these are welcome steps, there are some factors that may limit the enthusiasm for these new issues. First, it may be argued that there are two ways to induce investors to hold domestic currency bonds. One way is to issue abroad in domestic currency, and the other is to promote the entry of local investors into the domestic bond market (this is the strategy followed by Mexico). It is possible that in Brazil and Colombia the government decided to tap the international market because of regulations that restricted the entry of foreign investors into the local bond market, and it is not clear whether this strategy is superior to the one adopted by the Mexican authorities (Tovar,

in foreign currency, while about two-thirds of domestic debt is denominated in nominal (i.e., not indexed to prices) domestic currency. Nevertheless, several local currency bonds have been issued in international markets over the past two years. While this is an interesting widening of financing options for Latin American and Caribbean countries, these issues are still too small to affect the aggregate figures, and it is not clear whether they are part of a developing trend or merely temporary factors (see Box 2.4). Those recent issues notwithstanding, there is a fairly close relationship for the time being between legal jurisdiction and the currency denomination of government debt issues.[12]

[12] This probably results from a combination of some degree of home bias on the part of investors and differential currency preferences between residents and nonresidents (see Levy Yeyati, 2004). This domestic-external market distinction is in line with the evidence that past debt dedollarization experiences have been driven by a deepening of the domestic markets (Bordo, Meissner, and Redish, 2005) and that original sin is negatively correlated with the size of domestic financial markets (Eichengreen, Hausmann, and Panizza, 2003).

Issuance of Government Domestic Currency Bonds in International Markets

	Argentina		Brazil		Colombia		Uruguay		Total	
Year	Number of bonds	US$ million	Number of bonds	US$ million	Number of bonds	US$ million	Number of bonds	US$ million	Number of bonds	US$ million
1997	3	1,500							3	1,500
2001	1	931							1	931
2003							1	290	1	290
2004			1	100	1	500	1	250	3	850
2005			1	1,483	1	325			2	1,808
Total	4	2,431	2	1,583	2	825	2	540	10	5,379

Sources: Borensztein, Eichengreen, and Panizza (2006b) and Tovar (2005).

2005). Second, there may be doubts over whether international investors' current appetite for local currency instruments is permanent. In particular, expectations of falling local interest rates and appreciating currencies cannot continue forever. Ample liquidity has made for unusually favorable conditions for emerging economies on global markets; if central banks continue to drain that liquidity and there is a flight to quality on the part of investors, it is not clear that an appetite for Latin American bonds will in fact survive (see Borensztein, Eichengreen, and Panizza, 2006b).

[a] Argentina issued three peso bonds in 1997 and another peso bond in the wake of the 2001 crisis, but until 2003, no other Latin American country had entered this market.

The recent evolution of debt in emerging Latin American and Caribbean economies shows a tendency towards "onshorization" (that is, substitution of domestic for external debt) and "dedollarization" (substitution of domestic currency debt for foreign currency debt), as depicted in Figure 2.5. This is in line with the correspondence between market of issuance and currency denomination noted above. For example, although there are important exceptions in individual cases, domestic debt in foreign currency is fairly small, and foreign debt in domestic currency is still insignificant as of 2004 for the aggregate of emerging Latin American and Caribbean economies. This onshorization process has resulted in a large increase in nominal (that is, nonindexed) local currency debt, which rose from 20 percent of GDP in 1996 to 30 percent of GDP in 2004, and also in debt indexed to the local CPI, which more than doubled over the 1996–2004 period to reach 6 percent of GDP.

Figure 2.5
Currency Composition of Public Debt in Emerging Latin American Countries (*percentage of GDP*)

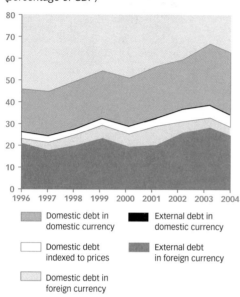

Domestic debt in domestic currency

Domestic debt indexed to prices

Domestic debt in foreign currency

External debt in domestic currency

External debt in foreign currency

Source: Authors' calculations based on Cowan et al. (2006).
Note: Countries included: Argentina, Brazil, Chile, Colombia, Mexico, Panama, Peru, Uruguay, and Venezuela.

Figure 2.6
Domestic Original Sin in Latin America and Other Emerging Regions

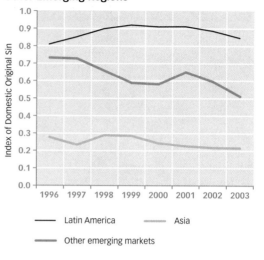

Latin America   Asia

Other emerging markets

Source: Authors' calculations based on Jeanne and Guscina (2006) data set.
Note: Original sin is measured as share of domesic debt which is short term, denominated in foreign currency, or indexed to prices or the interest rate. "Latin America" includes Argentina, Brazil, Chile, Colombia, Mexico, and Venezuela. "Asia" includes China, India, Indonesia (from 1998), Korea, Malaysia, Philippines, and Thailand. "Other emerging markets" includes Czech Republic, Israel, Hungary, Poland, Russia, and Turkey.

While this switch towards more domestic currency debt is a positive development, the problem is that a large fraction of domestic debt issued in local currency tends to be either short term or indexed to the short-term interest rate. In 2003, only 15 percent of total domestic public debt was fixed rate, long term, and denominated in domestic currency (up from 9 percent in 1999), indicating that "domestic original sin" (as defined by Hausmann and Panizza, 2003) is still a problem in Latin America, and to an even larger degree than in the rest of the emerging world (Figure 2.6).

Countries with Limited Market Access

Countries that have limited access to the international capital markets are characterized by high levels of debt but do not show the increasing trend which the sample of emerging market countries has followed over the past 10 years. In fact, public debt in this group of countries decreased until 1997 and then remained stable at a level of about 80–90 percent of GDP (about 60 percent if the weighted average shown in Figure 2.7 is considered).

A decomposition of the evolution of total debt shows that over the 1991–2004 period, these countries halved their debt with official creditors (from 53 to 25 percent of GDP), maintained a low level of debt with private external creditors, and doubled the amount of debt issued in the domestic market (from 14 to 27 percent of GDP). Almost by definition, this group of countries has a composition of external debt which is very different from that of the emerging market group (Figure 2.8). On average, 80 percent of external debt is owed to official creditors, but there have been large swings in the share of debt held by private creditors. In the early 1980s, about one-third of external debt was owed to private creditors, mostly in the form of syndicated bank loans. The importance of this source of financing decreased substantially (both in relative and in absolute value) over the 1984–1997 period, reaching a minimum of 11 percent of total external debt (corresponding to 3.6 percent of GDP). Access to the international credit market picked up over the 2000–2004 period, however, and by 2004 about 25 percent of the external debt of this group of countries was owed to private creditors, mostly in the form of sovereign bonds in line with the evolution of global financial markets. There have also been large changes in the composition of official debt. Bilateral creditors were extremely important in the 1980s, but their share in total external debt continuously decreased over the 1990–2004 period, from 50 to about 20 percent of total external debt. Over the same period, the multilateral development banks became increasingly important and, by 2004, they accounted for more than 50 percent of the total external debt of this group of countries.

One important consideration is that the debt figures reported above are likely to grossly overstate the debt burden for several of the countries that are characterized by a large share of

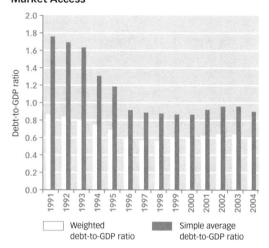

Figure 2.7
Public Debt in LAC Countries with Limited Market Access

Source: Authors' calculations based on Cowan et al. (2006).
Note: Countries included: Barbados, Belize, Bolivia, Costa Rica, Guatemala, Guyana, Honduras, Jamaica, Nicaragua, and Paraguay.

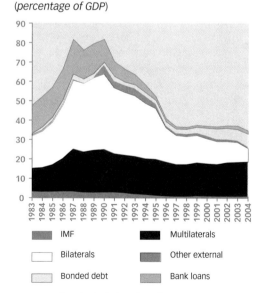

Figure 2.8
Composition of Public External Debt in Latin American and Caribbean Countries with Limited Market Access
(*percentage of GDP*)

Source: Authors' calculations based on Cowan et al. (2006).
Note: Countries included: Belize, Bolivia, Costa Rica, Guatemala, Guyana, Honduras, Jamaica, Nicaragua, and Paraguay.

concessional debt. In the sample of countries with no market access, the net present value of total external debt was about 77 percent of book value; by 2004, the net present value had decreased to about 68 percent of book value.[13]

Gross versus Net Debt

Many countries compute a measure of net debt to obtain a more accurate measure of their level of indebtedness. Net debt measures subtract holdings of debt by some public entities, and sometimes they also deduct holdings of financial assets by the public sector. One problem with official statistics on net debt is that different countries use different methodologies to compute net debt. Although each of these different netting strategies is probably the most appropriate for the individual country that uses it, as a group they produce figures on net debt that are difficult to compare across countries (Box 2.5 describes the methodology used by the Brazilian authorities, which is clearly spelled out in various publications).

In order to obtain statistics on net debt that are comparable across countries, this report follows the methodology outlined in Cowan et al. (2006) and considers two definitions of net debt. The first definition (Net Debt 1) subtracts from gross debt the holdings of government debt by the central bank. As the central bank submits its profits to the government, interest payments by the treasury to the central bank will eventually return to the treasury. Thus, holdings of government paper by the central bank are not really a liability of the consolidated public sector.[14]

The second definition (Net Debt 2) is obtained by subtracting international reserves from Net Debt 1. Although widely done, the netting of reserves is conceptually more debatable. The main role of international reserves is to support the functioning of the foreign exchange system. In a fixed exchange rate system, central bank reserves need to be available for purchases by the private sector if there is net demand for them. Under such a system, if the private sector has a net external surplus, the resulting accumulation of international reserves will show up as a reduction in the government's Net Debt 2 measure, when in fact it is simply the counterpart to the accumulation of assets by the private sector. In a (managed) floating exchange rate system, the central bank has more latitude to supply foreign reserves to the market, but in emerging market economies, central banks typically hold significant international reserves in order to intervene when market conditions require. Aggregate data show that over the 1991–2004 period, the difference between Gross Debt and Net Debt 1 averaged 3 percent of GDP, reaching a maximum of 6 percent of regional GDP in 1996. The difference between Gross Debt and Net Debt 2, however, is much larger. Over the 1991–2004 period, this difference averaged 11 percent of regional GDP. Reserves were lower in the early

---

[13] In the emerging market sample, the net present value is almost identical to the book value (over the 2000–2004 period the difference ranged between 2 and 7 percent). The difference between book value and net value was computed using data from the World Bank's *World Development Indicators*.

[14] As the money base is not included in gross debt, the methodology used in this report does not deduct the holdings of government paper by the central bank that build up the domestic credit counterpart to the money base (see Cowan et al., 2006, for more details). Similarly, as the debt issued by state-owned banks and state-owned enterprises is not included in the gross debt figures used in this report, public debt held by state-owned banks and state-owned enterprises is not netted out.

Box 2.5 Net Debt in Brazil

Brazil's official figures for net debt differ substantially from the ones used in this report. This large difference is almost completely driven by different netting methodologies.[a] The purpose of this box is to illustrate the procedure used by the Brazilian authorities to calculate net debt (for a similar discussion, see Martner and Tromben, 2004a).

In calculating net debt, Brazilian authorities subtract from gross debt a series of assets that can be used to redeem gross debt. These assets include both liquid assets that can be used to repay short-term debt and less-liquid assets. The rationale for including the latter class of assets is that they can be used to redeem debt with longer maturity (Goldfajn and Refinetti Guardia, 2003). The table below lists the main assets used by the Brazilian authorities in their calculation of net debt. Deposits in the social security system, tax collected but not

yet transferred to the treasury, and demand deposits of the federal, state, and local governments (including government deposits in the central bank) are among the most liquid assets that are included. Over the 2000-2005 period, these liquid assets ranged between 5.6 and 8.3 percent of GDP and mostly consisted of deposits. Liquid assets are, however, only about one-third of the debt that is netted out by the Brazilian authorities. Longer-term assets like the Worker Support Fund (FAT) and investment in several other public funds are part of the larger share of the less-liquid assets netted out by the Brazilian authorities' methodology.

------

[a] One reason that the data are not identical has to do with the denominator (rather than the numerator) of the debt-to-GDP ratio. The Brazilian authorities sometimes use a "valorized" definition of GDP which may yield figures substantially different from those reported in IMF statistics (see IMF, 2003a).

Gross and Net Debt in Brazil (percentage of GDP)						
	2000	2001	2002	2003	2004	2005
Total net debt	**48.8**	**52.6**	**55.5**	**57.2**	**51.7**	**51.6**
Liquid assets						
Deposits of the social security system	0.1	0.1	0.1	0.1	0.1	0.0
Tax collected and not transferred	0.1	0.1	0.0	0.1	0.0	0.0
Deposits (all levels of government)	5.4	6.4	6.0	5.8	5.9	8.3
Total liquid assets	5.6	6.6	6.1	6.0	6.0	8.3
Less-liquid assets						
Investment in financial funds and programs	2.5	2.7	2.2	4.2	3.7	3.8
Worker Support Fund (FAT)	4.4	4.9	4.8	5.5	5.5	6.0
Other government credit	1.1	1.2	1.5	2.2	2.2	2.0
Credit with public enterprises	2.1	2.4	1.1	1.7	1.2	1.6
Total less-liquid assets	10.1	11.2	9.6	13.6	12.6	13.4
Other	0.2	0.2	0.1	0.3	1.7	1.5
Gross debt	**64.6**	**70.6**	**71.4**	**76.9**	**71.9**	**74.8**

Source: Authors' calculations using data from Central Bank of Brazil.

1990s but increased rapidly in the mid-1990s, reaching a peak of 15 percent of regional GDP in 1996. Interestingly, the data show that there is no difference in reserve accumulation between small and large countries.

Implicit versus Explicit Debt: What Happens When Countries Privatize Their Pension Systems?

All measures of debt discussed so far have focused on explicit debt. Several countries, however, have unfunded public pension systems, which constitute a large implicit liability. In the past decade, many Latin American countries have transformed their social security systems from public, pay-as-you-go systems to private capitalization systems. The transition between these two types of systems typically involves an increase in explicit government debt, as the last generation of the pay-as-you-go system is still collecting pension payments, but younger generations have moved to the private system and do not contribute to the public social security system. Thus, the analysis of trends in public debt accumulation may net out the result of the pension system transition, although debt accumulated on account of the transition is conceptually indistinguishable from debt accumulated for any other reason. Ideally, one would like to have a measure of debt that includes pension obligations. However, the actual value of implicit liabilities is virtually impossible to assess, because the government maintains the option of diluting them by introducing legal changes such as reducing benefits or tightening eligibility conditions.

As an alternative to adding actual pension obligations to obtain a grand total for the debt level in every country, debt could be made comparable across countries by subtracting the value of the reduction in implicit liabilities in those countries which have privatized their pension systems. How can this be done? In the simplest case of pension system privatization, the pay-as-you-go system was completely shut down at the time of reform, with obligations to those who were participating in the system recognized by issuing bonds which were then deposited in private pension funds. Thus, the value of those compensation bonds would be a natural estimator of the reduction in the implicit liabilities faced by the government. Gross Debt would show a sizable increase at the time of the reform, which would be equal to the increase in assets managed by private pension funds, and a Net Debt measure could be constructed by subtracting pension fund holdings from Gross Debt.[15]

The treatment of pension reforms that did not change the status of current pensioners but only changed the relationship with the younger generations is more complicated. These reforms usually were implemented by eliminating the tax obligations on the current workers, who were then able to use those resources to build up private assets. As before, the question is, by how much does this pension reform reduce government liabilities at each point in time? If the cash flows into and out of the system are balanced, it seems reasonable to assume that what has been accumulated in pension funds is equivalent to the value of liabili-

---

[15] This is the case of Chile, where Bonos de Reconocimiento (Recognition Bonds) made explicit the benefits owed to retirees at the time of privatization. In this way, rather than continuing to pay benefits through the social security window, the government honored its social security obligations by servicing this newly issued debt. Subtracting the value of recognition bonds is a sensible way to correct for what would otherwise be an overstatement of the overall liabilities of the government (Cowan et al., 2006).

Figure 2.9
Gross and Net Debt in 2004
(*percentage of GDP*)

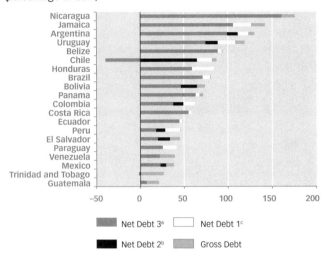

Net Debt 3[a]   Net Debt 1[c]

Net Debt 2[b]   Gross Debt

Source: Authors' calculations based on Cowan et al. (2006).
[a] Net Debt 2 minus assets of private pension funds.
[b] Net Debt 1 minus international reserves.
[c] Gross Debt minus cross-holding of government debt by the central bank.

ties that will not have to be honored by the government in the future, and therefore this amount provides an estimate of the reduction in the government's implicit liabilities resulting from the pension privatization scheme.[16]

This suggests another definition of net debt (Net Debt 3), this one being equal to Net Debt 2 minus assets of private pension funds. In the early 1990s, Net Debt 3 was basically identical to Net Debt 2, but after the pension reforms of the mid-1990s, private pension funds grew very rapidly. By 2004, assets of private pension funds were above 7 percent of regional GDP, generating a substantial wedge between Net Debt 2 and Net Debt 3. Correcting for pension privatization, however, does not alter the fact that Latin American public debt has been on an increasing trend since the mid-1990s.

While the netting methodology discussed above has some desirable properties, it is far from problem free. A first problem with the methodology is that if pension fund investments perform better than expected, the assets accumulated in the pension funds end up being greater than would have been necessary to guarantee the payments made by the old system, and this netting strategy will overcompensate for the drop in implicit liabilities brought about by the pension reform. This can be a sizable problem. Figure 2.9 decomposes Gross Debt into the three definitions of Net Debt discussed above and shows that the correction is substantial for countries with relatively large private pension systems (like Bolivia, Colombia, Peru, and El Salvador) and enormous in the case of Chile, where the assets of private pension funds are larger than Gross Debt, yielding a negative level of Net Debt (−40 percent of GDP).

---

[16] This assumption has several useful properties. If the government finances with debt all the revenue shortfall from the reform and forces the pension funds to purchase all of this debt, then a measure of Net Debt that subtracts pension fund holdings from Gross Debt will not change with privatization, capturing the fact that there has not been any reduction in net obligations. However, if the reform is financed with other taxes, then there is a net reduction in future government liabilities which will be captured in this measure of Net Debt and missed in conventional measures.

Box 2.6 Accounting for Pension Obligations in Retirheaven and Retirhell

Consider the following two hypothetical countries. Retirheaven is a country with a generous policy for its retirees and a pay-as-you-go pension system that guarantees each worker over the age of 65 a pension. Retirhell is, in contrast, a country which has no public pension system. Also assume that the two countries have exactly the same explicit public debt: 50 percent of GDP. This figure correctly captures the indebtedness of Retirhell but underestimates the obligations of the government of Retirheaven. Now, suppose that Retirheaven privatizes its pension systems and makes implicit liabilities explicit by issuing recognition bonds which are then deposited into private pension funds. Also, assume that these recognition bonds amount to 10 percent of GDP, pushing public debt in Retirheaven to 60 percent of GDP.

What is the best way to measure post-reform debt? As regards gross debt, public debt in Retirheaven is higher than public debt in Retirhell, but focusing on this measure would suggest that the pension reform led to a sudden deterioration of Retirheaven's fiscal situation, which is not correct, because total debt (implicit plus explicit) in Retirheaven has not changed. The netting strategy applied in the CLYPS database considers total debt in Retirheaven to be equal to that in Retirhell, which is also not correct. However, CLYPS's net debt measure leads to the correct conclusion that nothing has really changed in Retirheaven.

A second issue is that the implicit future debt generated by public pay-as-you-go systems is of a different nature than the explicit debt issued to finance the transition. In particular, pension obligations are easier to dilute and are implicitly indexed to GDP, but explicit debt is often expressed in nominal or real terms (sometimes in foreign currency) and is more difficult to restructure in the event of insolvency.[17]

A third problem is that countries may differ in their systems for providing support to retired workers (Box 2.6). The example in Box 2.6 makes it clear why the most accurate measure would be for countries to report their implicit liabilities linked to unfunded pension obligations. Only in this case would debt levels be truly comparable both across countries and within countries across time. Given the complexities involved in estimating these liabilities, this is a possible area for technical assistance by the international financial institutions, which could help their member countries to develop and implement a standard methodology for calculating and reporting these liabilities.

---

[17] It may also be argued that a country's government does not necessarily walk away from all its implicit pension-related obligations by privatizing the pension system. In particular, if a low return (or failure) of the private pension funds generates lower-than-expected pension benefits, then the government may be forced to step in and supplement the private pensions. The same is true if people undercontribute to the private pension system and expect to be taken care of by the government anyway. The methodology outlined above implicitly controls for these possibilities, because low contributions to or poor performance of pension funds will be reflected in lower assets of pension funds, and hence a smaller correction from Net Debt 2 to Net Debt 3.

HOW DO LATIN AMERICA AND THE CARIBBEAN COMPARE WITH THE REST OF THE WORLD?

Are the patterns documented in the previous section part of a global trend or are they limited to Latin America? Simple averages that include 94 countries show that Sub-Saharan Africa, the Middle East and North Africa, and South Asia are the regions with the highest levels of public debt. Latin American and Caribbean countries have intermediate levels of debt, which are not much higher than those of the advanced economies and higher than levels of public debt in East Asia and Eastern Europe and Central Asia (Figure 2.10). While public debt in Latin America displayed U-shaped behavior, public debt in East Asia increased substantially (going from 36 to 52 percent of GDP) between 1991 and 2005 (the period under observation in the figure). Public debt also increased (but at a slower pace) in South Asia and decreased in the Middle East and North Africa.

Weighted averages yield a different picture in terms of both levels and trends (Figure 2.11). As two large economies (Japan and Italy) have high levels of debt, weighting by GDP substantially increases the debt ratios of the advanced

Figure 2.10
Public Debt around the World (simple averages)
(*percentage of GDP*)

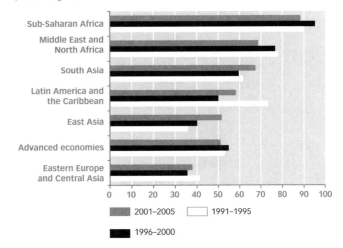

Source: Authors' calculations based on Jaimovich and Panizza (2006b).

Figure 2.11
Public Debt around the World (weighted averages)
(*percentage of GDP*)

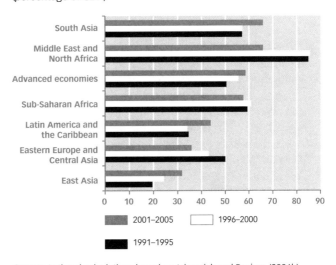

Source: Authors' calculations based on Jaimovich and Panizza (2006b).

Figure 2.12
Evolution of Public Debt in Crisis-Prone Regions (weighted averages)
(*percentage of GDP*)

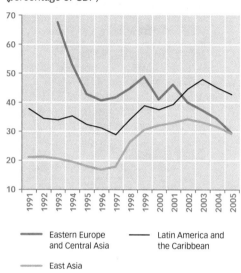

Eastern Europe and Central Asia — Latin America and the Caribbean

East Asia

Source: Authors' calculations based on Jaimovich and Panizza (2006b).

Figure 2.13
Foreign Currency Domestic Public Debt as a Percentage of Total Domestic Public Debt

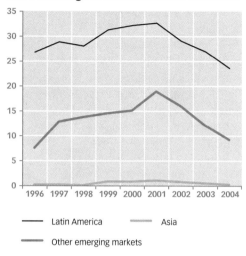

Latin America — Asia

Other emerging markets

Sources: Authors' calculations based on Cowan et al. (2006) for Latin America and Jeanne and Guscina (2006) for other emerging markets and Asia.
Note: "Latin America" includes Argentina, Brazil, Chile, Colombia, Mexico, Peru, Uruguay, and Venezuela. "Asia" includes China, India, Indonesia (from 1998), Korea, Malaysia, Philippines, and Thailand. "Other emerging markets" includes Czech Republic, Israel, Hungary, Poland, Russia, and Turkey.

economies, which become similar to those of countries located in Sub-Saharan Africa. At the same time, weighting by GDP gives less importance to countries like Nicaragua and Guyana (small economies with high debt ratios) and reduces the average debt ratios for Latin America and the Caribbean. As a consequence, the weighted debt-to-GDP ratio in Latin America is much lower (by about 15 percentage points) than that of the advanced economies.

As East Asia, Eastern Europe and Central Asia, and Latin America were at the center of the main debt and financial crises of the late 1990s, it is interesting to compare the evolution of central government debt in these three regions (Figure 2.12). Eastern Europe, which started with high levels of debt (68 percent of GDP in 1993), showed a net decrease in debt over the 1993–1996 period, an increase in debt around the Russian crisis of 1998 (with another spike in 2001), and then a sustained decrease in debt, which reached 29 percent of regional GDP in 2005. East Asia shows the opposite trend. Debt was low and decreasing in the early 1990s (20 percent of GDP in 1991 and 17 percent in 1996) but increased rapidly after the crisis of 1997, reaching 34 percent of regional GDP in 2002. Since 2002, debt has been decreasing again, reaching 29 percent of regional GDP in 2005. In Latin America and the Caribbean, in contrast, debt has been constantly increasing over the 1997–2003 period. The resolution of the Argentine crisis and the current appreciation of several Latin American currencies have helped to reverse this trend since 2003, but debt still was 13 percent of GDP higher than in the other two regions as of 2005.[18] Even though debt in this region is now decreasing and it is hard to tell what will happen in the future, the series of crises that affected the region seem to have had a ratcheting effect, with debt stabilizing at a higher level after each crisis, a pattern that does not seem to characterize East Asia and Eastern Europe and Central Asia.

Latin America and the Caribbean is different from other emerging regions not only in terms of debt levels but also in terms of debt composition. Figure 2.6 presented some evidence in this direction by showing that Latin America is characterized by high levels of domestic original sin. Interestingly, the region does worse than the rest of the world in two of the three components of domestic original sin. Focusing on currency composition, while in Asia basically all domestic public debt is denominated in domestic currency, Latin America has high levels of domestic debt denominated in foreign currency (about twice as high as the levels prevailing in other non-Asian emerging market countries) (Figure 2.13). Focusing on maturity, Latin America has a larger share of short-term debt than Asia, and its share of short-term debt is only marginally smaller than that prevailing in other emerging market countries (Figure 2.14). Focusing on indexation, more than 60 percent of debt issued in Latin America is indexed either to prices or to the short-term interest rate, which is twice as high as the average for the non-Asian emerging market countries and about six times the Asian average (Figure 2.15).

Figure 2.14
Short-Term Domestic Public Debt as a Percentage of Total Domestic Public Debt

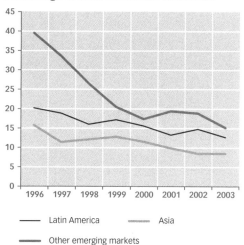

Source: Authors' calculations based on Jeanne and Guscina (2006) data set.
Note: "Latin America" includes Argentina, Brazil, Chile, Colombia, Mexico, and Venezuela. "Asia" includes China, India, Indonesia (from 1998), Korea, Malaysia, Philippines, and Thailand. "Other emerging markets" includes Czech Republic, Israel, Hungary, Poland, Russia, and Turkey.

THE CROSS-COUNTRY PICTURE

Latin America and the Caribbean is far from being a homogeneous region, and a better understanding of the level, evolution, and composition of public debt in the region requires a closer look at country-level data. Such a closer look immediately reveals that there is a large dispersion in the levels of debt (Table 2.1). Focusing on the 1990–2004 average, there were

---

[18] As explained in Box 2.1, the data for Latin America and the Caribbean are not identical to those of Figure 2.1, because Figure 2.12 uses central government data from Jaimovich and Panizza (2006b), while Figure 2.1 uses general government data from Cowan et al. (2006). The main difference is that the data in Figure 2.12 do not include the cost of rescuing the Mexican financial system (see the figure in Box 2.2) and hence show a decreasing debt ratio over the 1995–1997 period.

Figure 2.15
**Domestic Public Debt Indexed
to Prices or Interest Rate as a Percentage
of Total Domestic Public Debt**

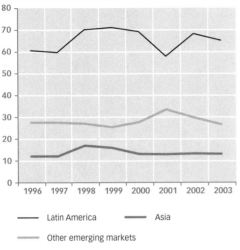

Latin America ——— Asia

Other emerging markets

Source: Authors' calculations based on Jeanne and Gus-
cina (2006) data set.
Note: "Latin America" includes Argentina, Brazil, Chile,
Colombia, Mexico, and Venezuela. "Asia" includes China,
India, Indonesia (from 1998), Korea, Malaysia, Philippines,
and Thailand. "Other emerging markets" includes Czech
Republic, Israel, Hungary, Poland, Russia, and Turkey.

four countries with levels of public debt
well below 40 percent of GDP and four
countries with levels of debt that were 100
percent of GDP or higher. There are also
large differences in the evolution of debt.
Broadly speaking there are three groups
of countries: (1) 11 countries in which debt
over GDP in the 2000–2004 period was
lower than in the first half of the 1990s;
(2) nine countries in which debt over GDP in
the 2000–2004 period was higher than that
prevailing in the early 1990s; and (3) three
countries with constant debt ratios.[19]

The first group includes several small
Central American countries and three of
the seven largest countries in the region.
Over the 1990–2004 period this group of
countries had an average debt ratio close
to 90 percent of GDP (this would drop to
60 percent of GDP if Nicaragua and Guyana
were excluded from the sample) and, on
average, reduced its debt by more than 30
percent. The second group includes most
of the English-speaking countries located
in the Caribbean and, like the first group,
three of the seven largest countries in the
region. Over the 1990–2004 period, this group of countries had an average debt ratio of approximately 60 percent of GDP and experienced a nearly 75 percent increase in debt. The
third group of countries (which includes Bolivia, Costa Rica, and Mexico) also had an average
level of debt close to 60 percent of GDP.

There is also a considerable degree of heterogeneity across countries in the composition
of public debt. There are 7 countries in which more than 50 percent of public debt is issued
domestically and 14 countries in which most public debt is external. Chile is the country with
the largest share of domestic debt, and Belize, Paraguay, and Honduras are the countries
with the highest shares of external debt (Figure 2.16). Interestingly, the share of domestic
debt does not seem to be correlated with the overall level of financial development. Countries such as Uruguay and Chile have similar levels of financial development but large differences in the share of domestic public debt. There is instead a strong correlation between the
share of domestic debt and income per capita (Figure 2.17), but here as well the correlation
is far from perfect. Argentina and Uruguay are among the countries with the highest income

---

[19] The Dominican Republic would probably be included in the second group, but data for the early 1990s are not avail-
able. The appendix discusses country studies in detail, and Chapter 3 focuses on the determinants of debt growth.
The ranking of countries by debt-to-GDP ratios does not change significantly according to the debt measure used.
The correlation between Gross Debt and Net Debt 2 is well above 90 percent.

Table 2.1 Summary Statistics for Total Debt to GDP (1990-2004)

Country	Mean	Maximum	Minimum	Standard deviation	Coefficient of variation	Minimum year	2000-2004/1991-1995	
Chile	0.38	0.69	0.21	0.15	0.39	2004	0.63	
Ecuador	0.79	1.18	0.49	0.22	0.28	2004	0.69	
El Salvador	0.48	0.60	0.34	0.08	0.17	1999	0.76	
Guatemala	0.23	0.42	0.17	0.07	0.30	1998	0.75	
Guyana	3.34	6.38	1.79	1.64	0.49	2004	0.40	Declining debt to GDP
Honduras	1.00	1.29	0.79	0.19	0.19	2001	0.69	
Nicaragua	3.38	6.85	1.76	1.93	0.57	2004	0.38	
Panama	0.84	1.27	0.65	0.21	0.25	1998	0.68	
Peru	0.70	1.07	0.48	0.19	0.27	1997	0.65	
Trinidad and Tobago	0.48	0.67	0.25	0.12	0.25	2004	0.57	
Venezuela	0.45	0.64	0.27	0.13	0.30	2000	0.63	
Group average	**1.10**	**1.91**	**0.66**	**0.45**	**0.32**		**0.62**	
Argentina	0.60	1.43	0.29	0.40	0.68	1994	2.79	
Bahamas	0.33	0.38	0.25	0.04	0.12	1990	1.12	
Barbados	0.66	0.81	0.54	0.08	0.12	1990	1.13	
Belize	0.58	0.94	0.44	0.18	0.30	1994	1.79	Increasing debt to GDP
Brazil	0.66	0.89	0.37	0.17	0.27	1995	1.37	
Colombia	0.41	0.66	0.26	0.14	0.35	1994	2.03	
Jamaica	1.05	1.52	0.72	0.25	0.24	1994	1.47	
Paraguay	0.32	0.52	0.20	0.10	0.32	1997	1.68	
Uruguay	0.59	1.24	0.36	0.31	0.52	1996	2.30	
Group average	**0.58**	**0.93**	**0.38**	**0.19**	**0.32**		**1.74**	
Bolivia	0.72	0.80	0.64	0.05	0.07	1997	0.95	
Costa Rica	0.59	0.83	0.54	0.08	0.13	1993	0.97	No clear pattern
Mexico	0.43	0.57	0.31	0.09	0.20	1994	0.99	
Group average	**0.58**	**0.73**	**0.49**	**0.07**	**0.13**		**0.97**	
LAC average	**0.84**	**1.41**	**0.54**	**0.30**	**0.29**		**1.13**	

Source: Authors' calculations based on Cowan et al. (2006).

per capita, but they also have intermediate levels of external debt. In fact, the relationship between the share of foreign currency debt and the level of development is driven in part by the behavior of several low-income countries that are characterized by a large share of official debt (which is all external). By contrast, market size as proxied by total GDP seems to be an important factor explaining the size of the domestic debt component of government liabilities (Figure 2.18).[20]

Figure 2.16
Domestic Debt as a Percentage of Total Debt
(average, 2000–2004)

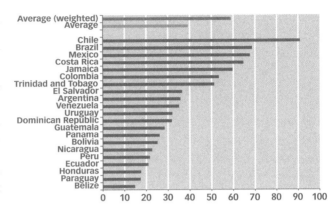

Source: Authors' calculations based on Cowan et al. (2006).

In regard to the creditor side, the data show that most of Latin America's public debt is either official or bonded.[21] As a generalization, emerging market countries tend to borrow by issuing bonds, and countries that have limited market access tend to use official debt. But even these subgroups are far from being homogenous. In the emerging market group, the share of bonded debt goes from 38 percent (Peru) to 97 percent (Chile). At the same time, this group also includes countries with a substantial share of official debt; in 2004, for example, Peru, Ecuador, El Salvador, and Uruguay owed more than 40 percent of their debt to official creditors. In the group of countries with limited market access, the share of official debt ranges from 16 percent (Costa Rica) to 81 percent (Paraguay) of total debt.

Another source of heterogeneity is the currency and maturity composition of domestic debt. Almost 100 percent of external debt is in foreign currency (there have, however, been recent cases of issues in domestic currency, as described in Box 2.4), but there are large differences in the degree of "dollarization" of domestically issued public debt, ranging from less than 2 percent in Mexico and Nicaragua to 80 percent in Uruguay. Focusing on maturity, over the 2000–2004 period short-term debt (defined as debt with maturity shorter than one year) was particularly important in Brazil and Uruguay and less important in Colombia and Peru.

Data on maturity and currency composition can be combined to provide a global picture of public sector vulnerability. De la Torre and Schmukler (2004a) argue that dollarization and short-termism are alternative ways of coping with aggregate price risk. So, while several countries have made substantial progress in reducing their reliance on foreign-currency-denominated domestic debt, governments might be substituting short-term debt for dollarization (see Chapter 13 for a discussion of these issues).

---

[20] In a horse race regression, the effect of size (total GDP) dominates that of the level of development (GDP per capita).

[21] There is only one country (Belize) in which bank debt is the main source of financing, and there are three countries in which bank debt is close to 10 percent of gross debt (Costa Rica, the Dominican Republic, and Colombia).

SUMMING UP

In the past, most emerging market crises have been external debt crises. As a consequence, the analysis of emerging market sovereign finance has focused on the external component of public debt. That this component of debt is now lower than in the early 1990s is often mentioned in support of the fact that Latin American policymakers are now adopting more prudent fiscal policies and as a reason for the current optimism regarding the prospects of the Latin American and Caribbean economies. A different picture arises, however, when total debt (external plus domestic) is considered. While past analyses may have exaggerated the importance of the difference between debt issued abroad and debt issued domestically, globalization of international capital markets is making this distinction even less important. At the time of the Argentine crisis of 2001, for instance, it became clear that a large amount of debt issued under international law was in the hands of Argentine residents. At the same time, it is now becoming increasingly common for foreign investors to enter local markets and buy domestically issued debt directly. For instance, in 2004 foreign investors bought 80 percent of the domestic long-term bonds issued by the Mexican government (Castellanos and Martínez, 2006).

While the fact that several countries in the region are substituting domestically issued debt for external debt does not necessarily mean that the next crisis will be a domestic debt crisis, it does mean that policymakers and the international financial institutions ought to develop instruments to monitor potential new sources of vulnerability. This need notwithstanding, it is extremely hard to obtain timely data on the level and composition of domestic debt in Latin America, and the international financial

Figure 2.17
Ratio of Domestic Debt to Total Debt and GDP per Capita
(*average for 2000–2004*)

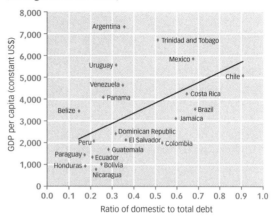

Source: Authors' calculations based on Cowan et al. (2006).

Figure 2.18
Ratio of Domestic Debt to Total Debt and Country Size
(*average for 2000–2004*)

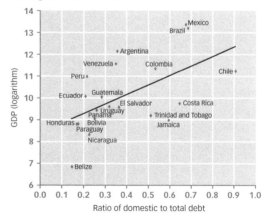

Source: Authors' calculations based on Cowan et al. (2006).

institutions often overlook the role of domestic debt (until recently, most IMF Article IV consultation reports did not include any information on the level, let alone the composition, of domestic public debt). This chapter documents a first attempt to assemble a data set that can keep track of such vulnerabilities, but more work needs to be done in this direction. Fortunately, countries now realize that disseminating timely and accurate information can have positive effects on market confidence, lowering their borrowing costs and reducing the probability of sudden stop episodes and, hence, are taking actions aimed at improving their data dissemination strategies.[22] In this sense, the IDB-sponsored Group of Latin American and the Caribbean Debt Management Specialists (LAC Debt Group) is playing a key role in the development of a common platform for the dissemination of public debt data in the region.

A final message of this chapter has to do with the role of official debt (Chapter 6 discusses multilateral debt in greater detail). It is often claimed that the relative importance of official lending has declined markedly (see, for instance, Meltzer, 2000) and hence multilateral development banks are becoming irrelevant. This may be true if official lending is compared with total international private capital flows. However, in Latin America and the Caribbean official lending remains a significant component of sovereign finance. In 2004, 73 percent of external public debt and 40 percent of total public debt of Latin American and Caribbean countries with limited market access was owed to official creditors. But heavy reliance on official finance is not limited to this group of low-income countries. In the same year, 34 percent of external public debt and 14 percent of total public debt in Latin American and Caribbean countries with market access was owed to official creditors. These figures are higher than those prevailing in the early 1980s and similar to those prevailing in the early 1990s. This unambiguously indicates that official lending still plays an important role in Latin American and Caribbean sovereign finance.

---

[22] The relationship between data quality and borrowing costs is documented by Cady and Pellechio (2006) and Wallack (2005). Calvo (2005b) shows that contagion episodes can arise from the actions of uninformed investors.

CHAPTER 3 | How Does Debt Grow?

EVERY TIME there is a debt crisis, policymakers, investors, and the international community ask the same question: "How did debt in country X get to be so high?" The purpose of this chapter is to answer that question by describing and quantifying some of the factors that lead to debt accumulation in emerging economies. Essentially there are two factors that determine debt growth. The first factor is the budget deficit, and the second is an unexplained residual entity called "stock-flow reconciliation."

These two components of debt growth display some characteristics that are surprising, indeed. Specifically, quantification of the stock-flow reconciliation shows that, contrary to what is commonly thought, this is not a residual entity of limited importance, but often a key determinant of debt explosions. The discussion of stock-flow reconciliation is somewhat technical, but its key message should be clear: although most of the policy debate focuses on measured deficits, there is a large share of change in debt that cannot be explained by the deficit, and a better understanding of this "unexplained part of debt" is key to preventing debt crises.

With respect to the behavior of the component of debt accumulation, the chapter investigates the determinants of cross-country differences in the cyclicality of the budget deficit. The findings in regard to this cast doubt on the conventional wisdom. In particular, the chapter shows that the use of appropriate statistical techniques challenges the standard finding that fiscal policies are countercyclical in developed countries and procyclical in developing countries. Again, this seemingly technical discussion has important policy implications, as it may lead to the devising of policies that could reduce the high income and consumption volatility that characterizes most developing countries.

SOME SIMPLE DEBT ARITHMETIC

The answer to the question "How do countries get into debt?" may seem trivial.[1] Anyone who has taken even the most basic economics course knows that countries accumulate debt whenever they run a budget deficit (i.e., whenever public expenditures are greater than revenues) and reduce their debt when they run a budget surplus. In fact, the standard Economics 101 textbook debt accumulation equation states that the change in the stock of debt is equal to the budget deficit (for those who like equations, this can be expressed as $DEBT_t - DEBT_{t-1} = DEFICIT_t$) and that the stock of debt is equal to the sum of past budget deficits.

---

[1] This section draws on Campos, Jaimovich, and Panizza (2006).

However, anyone who has worked with actual debt and deficit data knows that the equation presented above rarely holds and that debt accumulation can be better described as the sum of deficit plus an unexplained residual. Formally, this can be written as

$$DEBT_t - DEBT_{t-1} = DEFICIT_t + SF_t,$$

where SF_t measures the stock-flow reconciliation, a cumbersome name that comes from the fact that this residual entity reconciles the deficit, which is a variable measured over a period of time (i.e., a "flow" variable), with debt, which is a variable measured at a given moment (i.e., a "stock" variable).

Clearly, the textbook equation is a good approximation for debt accumulation only if one assumes that SF_t is not very large. In fact, the stock-flow reconciliation is often considered to be a residual of little importance. Is it really the case that the stock-flow reconciliation doesn't play a major role? Should policymakers not worry about stock-flow reconciliations and just focus on the deficit? One of the main findings of this chapter is that the stock-flow reconciliation does matter and that policymakers do need to take account of it.

Before moving to a systematic analysis of the stock-flow reconciliation, it is useful to consider three examples. In December 1998, Brazil's net debt-to-GDP ratio stood at approximately 42 percent of GDP, but by January 1999 this ratio had surpassed 51 percent of GDP. Could the Brazilian government have run a deficit of almost 10 percent of GDP in just one month? This seems highly improbable.

Likewise, in 2001 Argentina's debt-to-GDP ratio stood at just above 50 percent of GDP, and by 2002 the country's debt was well above 130 percent of GDP. Conversely, in 2004 Argentine debt totaled 140 percent of GDP, but by the end of 2005 the country's debt had fallen to 80 percent of GDP. Was it truly possible for the Argentine government to run a deficit of 80 percent of GDP in one year and a surplus of 60 percent of GDP less than two years later?

Uruguay presents a third case that is puzzling at first glance. In March 2002, Uruguay's debt-to-GDP ratio was 55 percent, yet by the end of 2003 the country's debt had soared to 110 percent of GDP. Could the Uruguayan authorities have run a deficit of 55 percent of GDP in less than two years?

These jumps in debt were clearly not due to standard budget deficits. In the case of Brazil, the sudden jump in debt resulted from the currency devaluation that followed the abandonment of the Real Plan. In the case of Uruguay, debt surged because of both a currency devaluation (which led to an increase in the debt-to-GDP ratio of approximately 40 percentage points) and the resolution of a banking crisis (which had a cost of approximately 18 percent of GDP). In the case of Argentina, the causes are similar but even more complex (see Box 3.1).

Campos, Jaimovich, and Panizza (2006) express the stock-flow reconciliation in terms of GDP and show that, on average, the change in debt explained by stock-flow reconciliation is 5 percent of GDP (Figure 3.1), clearly a residual of no small importance! The highest values for this reconciliation are in Sub-Saharan Africa (almost 9 percent of GDP), Latin America and the Caribbean (above 7 percent of GDP), and the Middle East and North Africa (7 percent of GDP). These high values may be driven by a few episodes (due to either exceptional events or measurement errors) with very large values for stock-flow reconciliation. There are in fact some observations in which this residual entity is well above 200 percent of GDP. The green bars in Figure 3.1 report average values of the stock-flow reconciliation obtained by dropping the top and bottom 2 percent of the distribution of this variable. As the figure shows, extreme values are irrelevant for the advanced economies and East Asia and the Pacific but are important for other regions. Excluding outliers substantially lowers the averages for the Middle East and North Africa, Latin America and the

Figure 3.1
The Stock-Flow Reconciliation
(*percentage of GDP*)

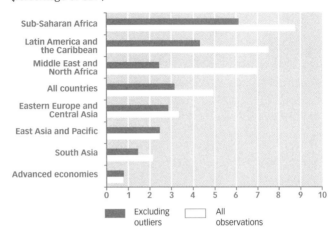

Source: Campos, Jaimovich, and Panizza (2006).

Caribbean, and Sub-Saharan Africa, but the last two regions remain the ones with the highest average stock-flow reconciliations (4 and 6 percent of GDP, respectively). Considering the whole sample of countries, the figure shows that excluding extreme values brings the average stock-flow reconciliation to 3 percent of GDP. This is much lower than in the sample with outliers but still a substantial figure indicating that, in the average country year, debt grows three percentage points of GDP faster than is implied by the budget deficit.[2]

Another way to assess the importance of the stock-flow reconciliation is to divide both sides of the equation discussed at the beginning of this chapter by GDP and use it to estimate the following statistical model:

$$d_{i,t} = \beta * def_{t,i} + \alpha_i + \varepsilon_{t,i},$$

where $d_{i,t}$ is the change in debt divided by GDP,[3] $def_{t,i}$ is deficit over GDP, α_i is a country-specific parameter (this parameter controls for the fact that the data come from different sources, that countries have different levels of debt, and that they use different methodologies for computing debt and deficit), and $\varepsilon_{t,i}$ is the error term of this statistical model, which should be interpreted as the stock-flow reconciliation. If the stock-flow reconciliation is

---

[2] The presence of large stock-flow reconciliations is also discussed by Martner and Tromben (2004a), IMF (2003a), and Budina and Fiess (2004).

[3] Formally, $d_{i,t} = \left(\dfrac{D_t}{Y_t} - \dfrac{D_{t-1}}{Y_t} \right) = \left(\dfrac{D_t}{Y_t} - \dfrac{D_{t-1}}{Y_{t-1}(1+g)} \right),$

where D is the level of debt, Y measures GDP, and g measures GDP growth.

Box 3.1 Debt Explosions in Argentina

In Argentina, as in most other countries, debt statistics are recorded on a cash basis rather than on an accrual basis.[a] As a consequence, new debt is registered when a bond is issued and not when the liability is generated. This difference is important in understanding debt evolution in Argentina, where each round of macroeconomic turmoil has generated hidden liabilities that showed up in official statistics several years later. These "skeletons in the closet" are among the main determinants of the difference between deficit and change in debt.

In the late 1970s most of Argentina's public debt was external and was owed to official creditors and foreign banks. After the default of 1988, the country's debt was restructured, and foreign bank loans were transformed into Brady bonds. In the late 1980s and early 1990s, domestic debt figures began to increase as hidden liabilities were recognized. One of the first actions that led to the explicit recognition of past liabilities was the Bonex Plan, which had the objective of resolving a banking crisis by compensat-

ing individuals who were not able to access their demand deposits. This plan takes its name from the fact that depositors were forced to exchange their demand deposits for a 10-year bond called "Bonex 89."

Around the same period, there were several court rulings that forced the Argentine government to give refunds to pensioners and pay off past debts to suppliers. These liabilities were consolidated through the issuance of bonds called "Bocones." In the following years more Bocones were issued to finance hidden liabilities (for instance, to compensate victims of state terrorism during the country's dictatorship).

In 1994, Argentina implemented a reform of the pension system, moving from a pay-as-you-go system to a capitalization system. This led to another increase in debt because, unlike the explicit liabilities used to finance the transition, future liabilities of the pay-as-you-go system were not explicitly recognized in public debt.[b]

The financial crisis of 2001-2002 led to a large real devaluation and a drop in the

unimportant, the estimation of the above equation should fit the data well and yield a value of β close to one. Figure 3.2 shows the results obtained estimating the above equation using the sample without outliers. The diagonal line in the figure indicates the value of β and shows that this parameter takes a value slightly greater than one. The position of the points gives a graphical representation of the "goodness of fit" of the statistical model. Points that are close to the line indicate observations for which the data fit the model well, and points that are far away from the line indicate observations for which the data fit the model poorly. As the figure shows, there are large cross-country differences. In the case of advanced economies, the points tend to be close to the line, indicating a relatively good fit. However, in Latin America and the other developing countries, the points are far away from the line, indicating that in these countries deficits do not do a good job of explaining the change in debt.

A more precise measure of goodness of fit is the statistical model's R^2. This statistic measures the share of variance of the dependent variable ($d_{i,t}$) which is "explained" by the dollar value of GDP. As most of Argentina's debt was denominated in foreign currency, the devaluation and economic crisis led to a sudden jump in the debt-to-GDP ratio (bonds issued under foreign law tripled their value in terms of GDP). The "pesification" of domestic law debt denominated in foreign currency led to a debt reduction of approximately US$20 billion.[c] As the new pesified bonds were indexed to inflation, part of the savings brought about by the pesification was compensated for by an increase in the interest payment resulting from higher-than-expected inflation (the cost of inflation is estimated at approximately US$9 billion). However, balance sheet effects were not the only reason for the debt explosion that followed the crisis. In fact, the authorities again started issuing domestic bonds (called "Boden") to compensate the financial system, depositors, government employees, and pensioners. The federal government also rescued the provinces by issuing Bodens to retire the various provincial currencies that were circulating during the crisis and by issuing a 16-year bond called a "Bogar" (amounting to approximately 6 percent of GDP) to consolidate the domestic debt of the provincial governments.

The outcome of the debt renegotiation concluded in January 2005 implied a net present value "haircut" of approximately 70 percent (corresponding to approximately US$60 billion or 30 percent of GDP).[d] This, together with robust economic growth, reversed the explosive trend in debt documented above by reducing the debt-to-GDP ratio from approximately 1.3 in 2003-2004 to approximately 0.8 in 2005.

---

[a] This box draws from Fernández et al. (2006).
[b] See Chapter 2 for a discussion of these issues.
[c] In February 2002, domestic law debt denominated in foreign currency was "pesified" at an exchange rate of 1.4 pesos per dollar and transformed into peso bonds indexed to the price level.
[d] This does not include holdouts, which are estimated at US$18 billion plus past-due interest.

independent variables (in this case $def_{t,i}$). An R^2 value of one indicates a perfect fit with the independent variables, explaining the totality of the variance of the dependent variable, whereas an R^2 value of zero indicates that there is no relationship between the dependent and the explanatory variables. Figure 3.3 displays the R^2 values obtained by estimating the equation described above for different subsamples of countries. It shows that when all countries are pooled together, the R^2 value is just above 0.07, indicating that deficits explain less than 8 percent of the change in debt (and the stock-flow reconciliation more than 90 percent)—a very poor fit for an equation which is often considered to be an identity.[4]

---

[4] Campos, Jaimovich, and Panizza (2006) also ran separate regressions for the 58 countries for which they had at least 15 years of data. They found that β had average and median values of approximately 1 and ranged between −1.8 (Zaire) and 5.9 (Rwanda). The regressions' R^2 had an average value of 0.32 and a median value of 0.25 and ranged between 0.007 (Egypt) and 0.87 (Italy). There were only 4 countries (all developed) with a value for R^2 above 0.8 and 16 countries (11 of them developed) for which the R^2 value was higher than 0.5.

Figure 3.2
Deficit and Change in Debt

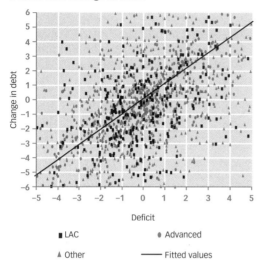

Source: Campos, Jaimovich, and Panizza (2006).

Figure 3.3
Debt and Deficit: Goodness of Fit

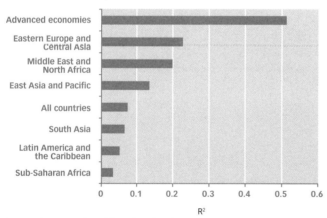

Source: Campos, Jaimovich, and Panizza (2006).

As the figure shows, the region with the poorest fit, according to the model, is Sub-Saharan Africa. In this group of 29 countries, the deficit explains only 3 percent of the variance of the change in debt. In the cases of Latin America and the Caribbean (25 countries) and South Asia (5 countries), the deficit explains between 5 and 6 percent of the variance of the change in debt. The developing region with the best fit is Eastern Europe and Central Asia (15 countries), for which the deficit explains 23 percent of the variance of the change in debt. Only in the advanced economies (24 countries) does the deficit explain more than one-quarter of the within-country variation in the change in debt, but even in this case, the regression can explain only half of the variance of the dependent variable, suggesting that the stock-flow reconciliation is as important as the deficit in explaining changes in debt.[5]

It is also interesting to explore whether the difference between deficit and change in debt is associated with debt growth. In other words, is the stock-flow reconciliation one of the main determinants of debt explosions? A look at the relationship between the growth rate of debt over GDP and the ratio of deficit to change in debt shows that for countries with relatively low levels of debt growth (below 5 percent per year), the deficit explains between 70 and 80 percent of the change in debt. However, when debt

---

[5] Of course, these statistics exaggerate the situation, because measurement errors and some mismatches between the level of government at which the debt and deficit are measured would always generate values for R^2 smaller than one. Still, it remains surprising that these R^2 values are so small.

starts growing at a faster rate, the share of debt explained by the deficit drops dramatically. When annual debt growth reaches 10 percent of GDP, the deficit explains less than 40 percent of the change in debt.

Most of the preceding discussion has focused on the change in debt divided by GDP rather than on the growth of the debt-to-GDP ratio. The first concept focuses on changes in debt without considering the effect of nominal GDP growth, while the second focuses on the change in debt relative to the change in GDP.[6] While the difference between these two measures may seem to be a technical one, both are useful concepts. The first makes it possible to estimate precisely the difference between deficit and change in debt without the need to isolate the effects of GDP growth and inflation. The second allows debt growth to be decomposed and the relative contributions of each of its determinants to be evaluated. Furthermore, it is the variable commonly used to assess fiscal sustainability.

Figure 3.4 focuses on the second measure and decomposes the growth of the debt-to-GDP ratio into five components: inflation, real GDP growth, stock-flow reconciliation, interest expenditure, and primary deficit (the last two components add up to the total deficit).[7] Inflation and GDP growth are the main mechanisms of debt reduction (there is also a small positive effect of primary surpluses in Latin America, the advanced economies, and East Asia, and a larger effect of this variable in the Caribbean), and the effect of inflation dominates that of real GDP growth in every region

Figure 3.4
Average Decomposition of Debt Growth in Different Regions of the World
(*average, 1970–2003*)

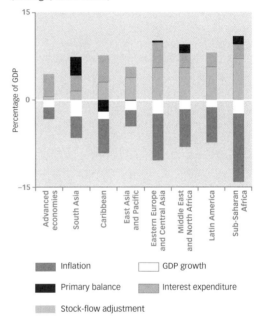

Inflation   GDP growth

Primary balance   Interest expenditure

Stock-flow adjustment

Source: Campos, Jaimovich, and Panizza (2006).

---

[6] Consider, for instance, a country that in year 1 has a public debt of $90 million and a GDP of $90 million and in year 2 has a public debt of $105 million and a GDP of $100 million. The change in debt over GDP is 15 percent ((105 – 90)/100 = 0.15), but the change in the debt-to-GDP ratio is only 5 percent ((105/100) – (90/90) = 0.05). As nominal GDP growth is usually positive, the change in debt divided by GDP is usually larger than the growth of the debt-to-GDP ratio.

[7] The decomposition takes the following form:

$$\frac{DEBT_t}{Y_t} - \frac{DEBT_{t-1}}{Y_{t-1}} = \frac{PD_t}{Y_t} + i\,\frac{DEBT_{t-1}}{Y_{t-1}(1+g)} - (gr + \pi)\,\frac{DEBT_{t-1}}{Y_{t-1}(1+g)} + \frac{SF_t}{Y_t},$$

where the first term on the right-hand side of the equation is the contribution of the primary deficit, the second term is the interest bill, the third term is the contribution of nominal growth (which can be split into real growth and inflation), and the last term is the stock-flow reconciliation.

of the world.[8] The effect of inflation is particularly large in Sub-Saharan Africa, Eastern Europe and Central Asia, the Middle East and North Africa, and Latin America. In the advanced economies and the Caribbean, interest payments are the main determinant of debt accumulation, and in South Asia, the budget deficit (primary balance plus interest payment) is the main determinant. In all other regions of the world, the stock-flow reconciliation is the key determinant of debt accumulation. In Latin America, for instance, the total deficit adds up to 2.4 percent of GDP, wheareas the stock-flow reconciliation equals 5.5 percent of GDP.

Figure 3.5 decomposes debt growth for Mexico and six South American countries and shows that in four of these countries, the stock-flow reconciliation is the main determinant of debt growth. The exceptions are Brazil, Colombia, and Mexico, where the main determinant of debt growth is interest payments (in Mexico, the amounts for interest payments and the stock-flow reconciliation are basically the same). All the countries, with the exception of Colombia, have primary surpluses, which are a substantial source of debt reduction in Brazil and Chile. Only in Chile is real GDP growth a substantial source of debt reduction, and in fact inflation is the main source of debt reduction in all seven countries. Figure 3.6 repeats the experiment for five countries located in Central America and the Caribbean. Although in three countries (The Bahamas, Costa Rica, and Guatemala) the deficit (again, primary balance plus interest payment) is the main determinant of debt growth, in two of them (Guatemala and Costa Rica), the stock-flow reconciliation is nevertheless an important determinant of debt growth (representing 30 and 90 percent of the deficit, respectively). Panama has a primary surplus but large interest payments, which dominate the stock-flow reconciliation as a main determinant of debt growth (which, however, remains an important factor). In El Salvador, the stock-flow reconciliation is the main determinant of debt growth. Focusing on the factors that contribute to debt reduction, inflation is the main determinant of debt reduction

Figure 3.5
Decomposition of Debt Growth in Mexico and South America
(*average, 1990–2003*)

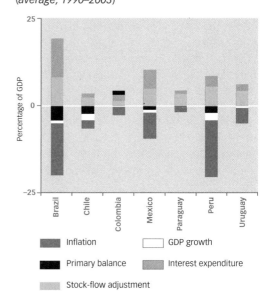

Source: Campos, Jaimovich, and Panizza (2006).

---

[8] Inflation is an important component of debt reduction because it is one of the main drivers of *nominal* GDP growth (see the decomposition in the previous footnote). However, inflation can only reduce nominal debt. This is why investors located in countries with a history of high inflation tend to protect themselves by holding debt denominated in foreign currency or indexed to prices or interest rate.

in Costa Rica, El Salvador, Guatemala, The Bahamas, and Panama. Figure 3.7 decomposes debt growth year by year by aggregating data for the seven largest Latin American economies (Argentina, Brazil, Chile, Colombia, Peru, Mexico, and Venezuela). As expected, the stock-flow reconciliation is shown to have a tendency to be very large at the time of crisis or just after a crisis. In particular, it was very high in the two years that followed the Tequila crisis (1995–1996), the year of the Russian crisis (1998), and the year of the Brazilian devaluation (1999) and reached epic levels at the time of the Argentine crisis (2002–2004). Interestingly, the stock-flow reconciliation was basically zero (or even negative) in tranquil years like 1997 or 2005.[9]

IS IT POSSIBLE TO EXPLAIN WHAT DRIVES THE UNEXPLAINED PART OF DEBT?

Having documented that there are large differences between deficits and changes in debt, it is interesting to explore the determinants of these differences. Campos, Jaimovich, and Panizza (2006) use a statistical model that tries to explain the determinants of the stock-flow reconciliation using three groups of variables.[10]

The first set of variables aims at capturing balance sheet effects due to the interaction of currency depreciations and the presence of foreign currency debt.

---

[9] There are two reasons for the substantial negative stock-flow reconciliation in 2005: the resolution of the Argentine default, and the consequent debt cancellation and real appreciation that characterized several large countries.

[10] They also control for inflation and real GDP growth.

Figure 3.6
Decomposition of Debt Growth in Central America and the Caribbean
(*average, 1990–2003*)

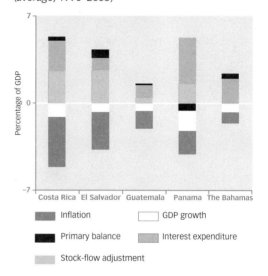

Source: Campos, Jaimovich, and Panizza (2006).

Figure 3.7
Decomposition of Debt Growth in Seven Largest Latin American Economies

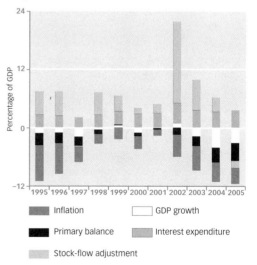

Source: Authors' calculations based on data from Campos, Jaimovich, and Panizza (2006).

Figure 3.8
Determinants of Stock-Flow Adjustment

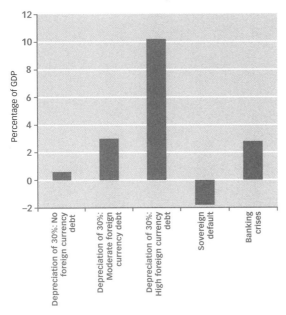

Source: Campos, Jaimovich, and Panizza (2006).

The idea is that currency devaluations should lead to large stock-flow reconciliations in countries with high levels of foreign currency debt. Figure 3.8 plots the main results and shows that this prediction is supported by the data. The figure shows that, assuming a real depreciation of 30 percent (not an uncommon event in some developing countries), in countries with no foreign currency debt, the depreciation has basically no effect on the stock-flow reconciliation (less than 1 percent of GDP and not statistically significant). In countries with moderate levels of foreign currency debt, a similar devaluation leads to a difference between deficit and debt of approximately 3 percent of GDP. Finally, in countries with high levels of foreign currency debt (i.e., the top third of the distribution), a 30 percent depreciation is associated with a stock-flow reconciliation equal to 10 percent of GDP.[11]

The second set of variables attempts to capture the effect of the resolution of sovereign default episodes. As default episodes result in partial debt cancellation (e.g., Sturzenegger and Zettelmeyer, 2005a, show that recent defaults implied "haircuts" that ranged from 13 to 73 percent of outstanding bonded debt), they should be associated with negative stock-flow reconciliations. In fact, Figure 3.8 shows that defaults are associated with a negative stock-flow reconciliation of approximately 2 percent of GDP.

The last explanatory variable explores the role of banking crises. These are important events, because they generate a series of contingent liabilities and other off-balance-sheet activities that can translate into debt explosions (see Box 3.1). In fact, the statistical model of Campos and her colleagues shows that the average banking crisis is associated with a stock-flow reconciliation of almost 3 percent of GDP.

While these are interesting results that suggest that building a safer debt structure and implementing policies aimed at limiting the creation of contingent liabilities are key to avoiding debt explosions, it is important to note that the variables discussed explain only

---

[11] Note that the use of yearly data may put excessive weight on the importance of balance sheet effects. This is because exchange rate overshootings amplify balance sheet problems in the short run, but the appreciation that follows the overshooting may lead to a reduction of debt. Hence, in the long run, recorded deficits may be a more important determinant of debt behavior than in the short run.

20 percent of the variance in the stock-flow reconciliation (country-specific factors explain another 30 percent of this variance).[12]

There are two possible reasons why the statistical model described above does such a poor job of uncovering the determinants of the unexplained part of debt. The first has to do with the fact that measurement errors that lead to an underestimation of the deficit are more important in some countries than in others. This is probably related to the fact that developing countries have less transparent accounting and budgeting systems, which make it possible to hide some liabilities. This is consistent with the findings of Aizenman and Powell (1998), who suggest that governments have incentives to misreport public expenditure and that this comes back to haunt them as debt is subsequently reassessed.

The second possible reason for the limitations of the statistical model is that the importance of contingent liabilities that lead to debt explosions varies across countries and that the controls included in the statistical exercise described above do not capture all the possible sources of contingent liabilities. One variable that is likely to be important, for example, but that is not included in the analysis is the effect of court decisions that force a government to make payments that it has not budgeted for (see Box 3.1 for the role of courts in Argentina and Chapter 9 for a discussion of how courts may affect the budget).[13]

HOW SHOULD DEFICITS MOVE, AND HOW DO THEY MOVE IN REALITY?

As noted in the first chapter of this report, most economists agree that a sound fiscal policy should exhibit countercyclical behavior. By running deficits in bad times and surpluses in good times, countries can smooth consumption, reduce the volatility of output, and minimize tax distortions. But the benefits of countercyclical policies are not limited to their welfare effects in terms of stabilization of the business cycle. Such policies can also be an effective strategy for limiting the growth of public debt.[14] This is because in the presence of procyclical fiscal policies, a stable debt ratio would require expenditure cuts (or tax increases) during recessions, and such adjustments are extremely difficult to implement. As a consequence, procyclical fiscal policies may contribute to snowballing budget deficits and debt levels that are eventually resolved with debt crises, high inflation, or outright default.[15]

If procyclical policies are so bad and countercyclical policies so good, one would expect all countries to adopt countercyclical policies. However, this does not seem to be what actually happens. Gavin and Perotti (1997) compare the main characteristics of fiscal policy in Latin America and the advanced economies and find that, while in the latter group of countries, policies tend be countercyclical, Latin America is characterized by procyclical

---

[12] Furthermore, Campos, Jaimovich, and Panizza (2006) show that their model does a much better job of explaining positive stock-flow reconciliations than negative ones.

[13] Another key difference among countries is in the size of regional governments, which is often not well captured by the data used in this statistical exercise.

[14] Not everyone agrees with this statement. Gordon and Leeper (2005), for instance, argue that countercyclical fiscal policies lead to higher levels of debt.

[15] This statement requires a qualification, however. Procyclical policies do not, by their design, necessarily result in debt accumulation, but they may end up doing so because it is is extremely difficult to run large surpluses during recessions. So procyclical policies often tend to be asymmetrical: expansionary during good times and not contractionary during bad times (see Hercowitz and Strawczynski, 2004).

Figure 3.9
Cyclicality of Budget Balance

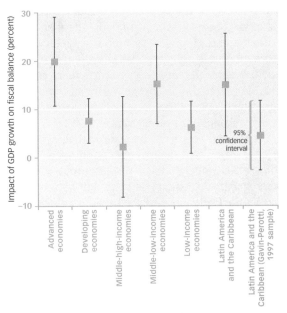

Source: Jaimovich and Panizza (2006).

fiscal policies. In particular, Gavin and Perotti use a statistical model that estimates how GDP growth affects a country's fiscal balance and find that in advanced economies, when a country's GDP grows by 1 percent, its budget surplus grows by approximately 0.4 percent. In Latin America, in contrast, they find that there is basically no correlation between GDP growth and changes in the budget balance. They argue that the lack of a positive relationship between growth and a country's fiscal balance suggests that discretionary fiscal policies are procyclical because, in the absence of such a procyclical response, a country's fiscal balance would automatically be positively correlated with growth.

Figure 3.9 updates the estimations of Gavin and Perotti (1997), with the blocks showing the point estimates and the vertical bars the respective 95 percent confidence intervals. The first block shows that in advanced economies, a 1 percentage point increase in output growth is associated with an increase in the fiscal surplus of 0.2 percentage points (an effect smaller than what Gavin and Perotti found, but still large and statistically significant). The second block focuses on developing countries and shows that, while the relationship between GDP growth and fiscal balance is still positive and significant, the point estimate indicates a much lower elasticity than that of industrial countries. In this case, a 1 percentage point increase in output growth is associated with an increase in the fiscal surplus of 0.08 percentage points. The next three vertical bars split the sample of developing countries into three subgroups and show that developing countries are far from uniform in regard to the way the fiscal balance responds to GDP growth.

The first group (middle-high-income economies) consists of 18 emerging markets.[16] In this group of countries, there is no significant correlation between GDP growth and fiscal balance. In fact, this is the group of countries with the lowest level of countercyclicality. The second group includes 25 middle-low-income countries (see Kaminsky, Reinhart, and Végh, 2005, for a full list of countries); in these countries the correlation between GDP growth and the budget balance is about three-quarters of the level found in the advanced economies

---

[16] These are Argentina, Botswana, Brazil, Chile, Costa Rica, Gabon, Korea, Lebanon, Malaysia, Mauritius, Mexico, Oman, Panama, Saudi Arabia, Seychelles, Trinidad and Tobago, Uruguay, and Venezuela.

but still large, positive, and statistically significant. The third group focuses on low-income economies; here the correlation between GDP growth and fiscal balance is lower, but still larger than in the emerging market countries and significantly greater than zero.

The last two vertical bars in Figure 3.9 focus on Latin America and the Caribbean. The first of these two vertical bars uses the largest possible sample of countries and, contrary to the findings of Gavin and Perotti (1997), shows a positive and statistically significant correlation between output growth and changes in the budget balance. The last vertical bar restricts the sample to the 13 countries (mostly emerging markets) used by Gavin and Perotti and confirms their result of a low and not statistically significant correlation between output growth and changes in the budget balance. This suggests that Gavin and Perotti's finding was driven by the behavior of Latin American emerging markets and that Latin America is not different from other developing regions of the world, where procyclicality is higher in emerging market countries.

While the foregoing discussion has confirmed that there are large differences between the degree of fiscal procyclicality in developing and advanced economies, it has also shown that there are large differences within the sample of developing countries and that one should allow for heterogeneous effects when trying to estimate the degree of fiscal cyclicality in this group of countries. But lumping together different types of developing countries is not the only problem with standard analyses of the difference in procyclicality between developing and advanced economies. There is also a problem with the variable that is usually used to measure the cyclicality of fiscal policy. Kaminsky, Reinhart, and Végh (2005) criticize the use of the budget balance to measure cyclicality and argue that procyclicality should be studied by looking at the behavior of public expenditure.[17] According to their definition, countercyclical policies would be associated with a negative correlation between GDP growth and the growth rate of government expenditure, while procyclical policies would be associated with a positive correlation between these two variables.[18]

Figure 3.10 focuses on the cyclicality of public expenditure and shows that in advanced economies, there is no correlation between output growth and expenditure growth (an observation consistent with an acyclical policy) and that in developing countries there is a strong and statistically significant correlation between output growth and expenditure growth (an observation consistent with procyclical policies).[19] As in Figure 3.9, the group of middle-low-income countries is the one with the lowest procyclicality, but in Figure 3.10 the coefficient remains high and statistically significant for all subgroups of developing countries. In fact, Figure 3.10 shows that the various groups of developing countries have similar levels of procyclicality and that not only are the coefficients statistically significant, but they are also large. The point estimates are close to one, suggesting that a 1 percent increase in output growth almost fully translates into a 1 percent increase in government spending (in other words, the share of government expenditure in GDP remains constant).

---

[17] This is basically because revenues are directly influenced by GDP growth and any fiscal indicator that is expressed as a ratio of GDP is also directly influenced by GDP growth (see Kaminsky, Reinhart, and Végh, 2005, for more details).

[18] Alesina and Tabellini (2005) suggest that the distinction here is mostly semantic. In particular, while most authors define as countercyclical a policy that holds constant the tax rate and discretionary spending as a fraction of GDP over the cycle, Kaminsky, Reinhart, and Végh (2005) define such a policy as acyclical.

[19] Again, the blocks measure the point estimates and the vertical bars represent 95 percent confidence intervals.

WHY PROCYCLICALITY?

So, everyone seems to agree that, when measured in the proper way, fiscal policies are countercyclical (or, at worst, acyclical) in the advanced economies and procyclical in developing economies. By why is this so? Do policymakers in the advanced economies know something that policymakers in developing countries do not know? In other words, is this different behavior on the part of policymakers due to incompetence, or does it reflect deeper economic problems? The literature has suggested two classes of explanations for this situation. The first is based on capital market imperfections and borrowing constraints and the second on voracity effects and political distortions.[20]

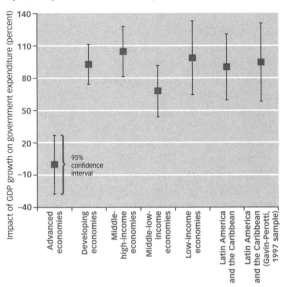

Figure 3.10
Cyclicality of Government Expenditure

Source: Jaimovich and Panizza (2006a).

Gavin and Perotti (1997) argue that developing countries find it hard to follow a countercyclical policy because, more often than not, they lack access to credit during recessions.[21] Consider, for instance, the case of a commodity exporter (which many developing countries are). If commodity exports are part of the collateral backing up a country's sovereign debt, the value of the collateral moves together with the price of the commodity, and when the price of the commodity falls, the risk of default increases. As a consequence, the interest rate increases as well and, in some cases, it becomes so high that the country will be virtually prevented from accessing international capital markets. The opposite occurs when the commodity price increases. In such a situation, conducting a countercyclical policy would require the country to issue debt when it is expensive to do so and to retire debt at times when it is cheap to borrow (Rigobón, 2006). The bottom line is that policymakers located in developing countries would like to implement countercyclical fiscal policies, but they cannot do so because they cannot finance fiscal deficits during difficult economic times.

---

[20] A third possible explanation, which is still being developed at the time of writing, is that procyclicality occurs because fiscal spending converges over time to a desired spending level determined by long-run fundamentals and that the speed of convergence increases with the distance between desired and actual spending. In this setting, procyclicality is generated by the fact that convergence is faster during booms than during recessions, suggesting that governments in economies with postponed public consumption are hard pressed to spend whatever windfall they receive almost immediately (Galiani and Levy Yeyati, 2003).

[21] Riascos and Végh (2003) also emphasize market incompleteness.

There are three questions that arise from this explanation. The first is: why is this not a problem for the advanced economies? The standard answer is that these countries do not face this sort of problem because they have small country risk premiums. As a consequence, the procyclicality of their interest rates is negligible. This suggests that any explanation of the procyclical behavior documented above needs to take into account the *precarious creditworthiness* of developing countries. Clearly, this gives rise to another question: why is precarious creditworthiness a problem for developing countries and not the advanced economies, when the latter often have much higher debt ratios? Chapter 12 focuses on this issue and shows that precarious creditworthiness is a greater problem for developing countries partly because they have smaller governments, more volatile sources of revenues, and a more dangerous debt structure. The third question has to do with lack of self-insurance: why do developing countries not avoid borrowing in bad times by saving in good times and creating a stabilization fund? The answer is that they often try to do so, but stabilization funds are problematic because they tend to be very expensive (see Chapter 14 for a discussion of this problem) and they can be easily expropriated by politicians. This problem is related to the second class of explanations for procyclical policies, one based on political rather than market failures.[22]

Tornell and Lane (1999) describe voracity effects that arise in the presence of various interest groups that compete for a share of tax revenues and treat the country's resources as a common pool. The presence of such groups will generate procyclicality because when there is a positive shock to the country's resources, no group will be willing to moderate its claims on the increased resources, as it knows that the saved resources will be appropriated by another group. Talvi and Végh (2005) use a model that assumes that fiscal surpluses will generate political pressures for wasteful public spending. In order to avoid this wasteful public expenditure, a benevolent social planner will adopt a procyclical fiscal policy by decreasing taxes during booms (and hence avoiding the accumulation of surpluses) and increasing taxes during recessions. Alesina and Tabellini (2005) show that the political pressure for higher spending assumed by Talvi and Végh (2005) represents optimal behavior in the presence of a situation that combines voters with imperfect information on the level of government borrowing and corrupt politicians who can appropriate part of tax revenues for their own consumption. Alesina and Tabellini's empirical analysis is consistent with the main predictions of their model and shows that procyclicality is positively correlated with corruption.

IS IT PROCYCLICALITY OR REVERSE CAUSALITY?

None of the explanations previously discussed takes into account one of the first things that one learns in economics: correlation does not imply causation.[23] While it is uncontroversial to state that the correlation between GDP growth and either the budget balance or government expenditure is consistent with procyclicality in developing countries and coun-

---

[22] Chapter 9 focuses on the political economy of debt and deficit.

[23] This statement is unfair to Gavin and Perotti (1997), who list reverse causality as one of the possible explanations for their findings. However, they argue that reverse causality is only part of the story.

tercyclicality in the advanced economies, these correlations do not prove that policymakers located in developing countries do adopt procyclical policies. This could be a case of what economists call "reverse causality."[24]

Box 3.2 discusses this problem in greater detail and shows that, if shocks to the growth rate of government expenditure are larger than shocks to GDP growth, any attempt to estimate the effect of GDP growth on expenditure growth may end up capturing the opposite relationship (i.e., the effect of expenditure growth on GDP growth). Therefore, the standard finding of procyclical policy in developing countries and countercyclical policy in the advanced economies could be due simply to the fact that in the advanced economies, GDP growth shocks dominate shocks to expenditure growth (a situation like the one depicted in panel B of the figure in Box 3.2), and in developing countries, expenditure growth shocks dominate GDP growth shocks (a situation like the one depicted in panel C of that figure).[25]

While reverse causality is a serious problem, if it were possible to find a variable that has a direct effect on GDP growth and no direct effect on the fiscal account, then it would still be possible to estimate the cyclicality of fiscal policy even in the presence of reverse causality (Box 3.2). Jaimovich and Panizza (2006a) argue that the average growth rate of a country's trading partners has these properties and reproduce standard estimations of the relationship between fiscal policy and growth using this variable as an "instrument" for GDP growth.[26] Figure 3.11 reports the results. It shows that once reverse causality is controlled for, fiscal policy in the advanced economies becomes clearly countercyclical (the coefficient is negative and statistically significant). In developing economies, instead, the coefficients are often negative (the exception is the middle-high-income countries, for which the coefficient is close to zero) but not statistically significant, indicating that fiscal policy is either countercyclical or acyclical. This is an intriguing result suggesting that procyclical policies capture only part of the story in regard to the factors that lead to high volatility in emerging market countries.

---

[24] A brief illustration of the reverse causality problem is useful. Suppose a social scientist wanted to test the hypothesis that going to the hospital makes people sick by looking at the health status of a randomly selected group of people. The social scientist would probably find a positive correlation between the probability of being sick and the number of visits to the hospital. It would, however, be wrong to use this evidence to claim that going to the hospital makes people sick. It is very likely that the causality goes in the opposite direction: sick people tend to go to the hospital more often! The causality issue is very important because, in Rajan and Zingales's (2003c) words: "Correlation is the basis for superstition, while causality is the basis for science" (109). A statistical technique that can address the causality issue is the instrumental variables method (Box 3.2).

[25] Rigobón (2005) presents preliminary evidence that this explanation might be accurate. Rigobón notes that developing countries tend to be commodity producers, and the behavior of their budget balances is often directly linked to commodity prices. As increases in terms of trade lead to increases in government revenues, they are likely to increase expenditure as well.

[26] Gali and Perotti (2003) adopt a similar instrumenting strategy to study the cyclical behavior of fiscal policies in the Euro Area.

SUMMING UP

While the fiscal policy debate focuses on deficits, most debt explosions have little to do with *measured deficits* but arise from contingent liabilities often associated with past policies or with inherent vulnerabilities in a country's debt structure. While this finding has several important policy implications, it is important to start with what it *does not* imply. It does not imply that politicians should not worry about deficits. The statement above emphasizes *measured deficits* because debt explosions are often associated with past deficits which were not appropriately accounted for (see Box 3.1) as a result of extrabudgetary activities. So, a first policy suggestion is

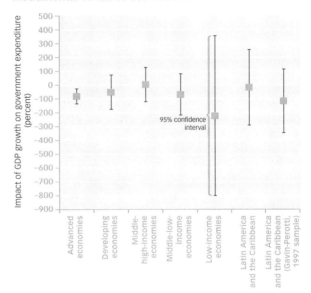

Figure 3.11
Cyclicality of Government Expenditure: Instrumental Variables Estimations

Source: Jaimovich and Panizza (2006a).

to build better accounting systems that make it possible to keep track of liabilities as soon as they are incurred.[27] But the findings of this chapter cannot be due only to measurement error associated with bad public accounting. If they could, positive and negative error would wash out, and there would be no evidence that a country's change in debt is systematically higher than its deficit. Hence, there is something that induces politicians and bureaucrats to hide actual deficits and create "skeletons in the closet" which will then be associated with successive debt explosions (Aizenman and Powell, 1998). Hence, another policy implication is to expand the definition of budget tracked by the authorities and explicitly include in a country's budget several of the items that are now off-budget. The market seems to know that these are important issues, and there is evidence that countries with better and more transparent accounting tend to have not only better fiscal results (Wallack, 2004), but also lower financing costs (Wallack, 2005; Cady and Pellechio, 2006).

However, poor accounting and implicit liabilities are not everything. The chapter shows that debt structure is extremely important. The usual arrangement, in which deficits are decided in the political arena and debt management is left to technocrats who often have the explicit objective of minimizing the cost of borrowing, may generate perverse incentives

---

[27] It would also be ideal (albeit very difficult) to have an accounting system that keeps track of implicit liabilities (like those arising from an unfunded pension system or a poorly capitalized banking system).

Box 3.2 "Identifying" the Cyclicality of Fiscal Policy

The cyclical behavior of fiscal policy[a] can be assumed to follow the equation

$$EG = \alpha + \beta YG + \varepsilon, \qquad (1)$$

where EG is the growth rate of public expenditure, YG is the growth rate of GDP, ε is a shock to expenditure growth, and α and β are two parameters. The sign of β will determine the cyclicality of fiscal policy, with $\beta > 0$ being associated with a procyclical fiscal policy and $\beta < 0$ with a countercyclical fiscal policy.

Now, it is necessary to note that public expenditure is also likely to affect GDP growth (which is exactly why countercyclical policies can stabilize income). Such a relationship between expenditure growth and GDP growth can be described by the following equation:

$$YG = a + bEG + u, \qquad (2)$$

where EG and YG are defined as before, u is a shock to GDP growth, and a and b are parameters, with b capturing the effect of expenditure on GDP growth. Standard Keynesian arguments suggest that b should be positive.[b]

Panel A of the figure that appears on the opposite page is a graphical representation of these two equations. The EE line plots equation (1) under the assumption of countercyclical fiscal policy (i.e., $\beta < 0$), and the YY line plots equation (2) under the assumption that $b > 0$. Note that if the two lines do not move (i.e., if the shock parameters

ε and u do not change), the only thing that the econometrician can observe is the intersection between the two lines (point A), and hence she will be unable to estimate either equation. What happens if the lines move?

Panel B shows what happens when equation (2) moves a great deal and equation (1) moves very little (i.e., when the variance of u is larger than the variance of ε). In this case, the econometrician will observe the nine points labeled $B1$-$B9$, and by fitting the best line that passes through these points, she will be able to estimate an equation for the EE line (i.e., equation (1)).

Panel C, in contrast, shows what happens when equation (1) moves a great deal and equation (2) moves very little (i.e., when the variance of u is smaller than the variance of ε). In this case the econometrician will observe the nine points labeled $C1$-$C9$, and by fitting the best line that passes through these points, she will be able to estimate an equation for the YY line (i.e., equation (2)).

Panel D shows the case in which both equation (1) and equation (2) move a great deal. In this case, the econometrician will observe points $D1$-$D9$, and she will not be able to estimate either of the two equations. In a nutshell, this is the "identification" problem that arises in the presence of simultaneous equations (or reverse causality).

There are statistical techniques that, if certain conditions are satisfied, make it possible to estimate systems of equations similar to the one described above. One of these techniques is called the "instrumental

The Identification Problem

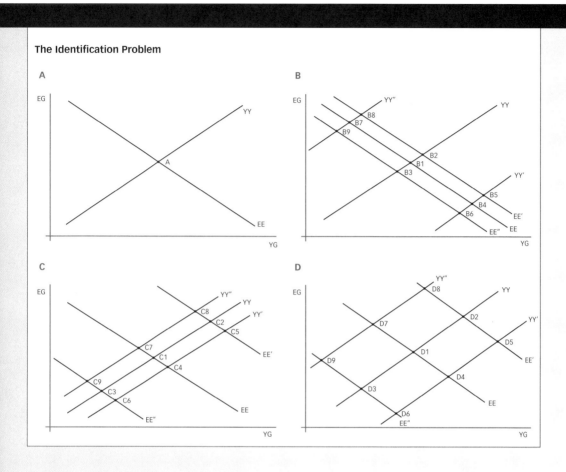

variables method." This method requires a third variable (an "instrument") that shifts one curve without affecting the other. Suppose, for instance, that an econometrician is interested in estimating the fiscal policy function described in equation (1). Then she would need an instrument for *YG*. Such an instrument should have two key characteristics: (1) it should be correlated with *YG*, and

(2) it should have no effect on *EG* except the one that occurs through *YG*.

_____

[a] For a more technical discussion of these issues see Rigobón (2003, 2005).
[b] The literature on non-Keynesian effects suggests that *b* could also be negative (see Alesina et al., 2002). In any case, the sign of the parameter does not affect the discussion in this box.

towards issuing too much low-cost, high-risk debt. Policymakers should be aware of the cost-safety trade-off and, by recognizing that more costly debt may have a desirable insurance component, internalize this trade-off in their decision on the costs of financing a given deficit (this would lead to setting technocrats' incentives in terms of both the cost and risk of debt). It is a welcome development that several emerging market countries are indeed moving in this direction.[28]

What should one make of the results suggesting that the difference in fiscal procyclicality between developing countries and the advanced economies is not as strong as previously thought? Again, one should start by highlighting what the findings of this chapter do not imply. They do not imply that the previous findings that the correlations between fiscal outcomes and GDP are different in developing countries and the advanced economies are wrong. In fact, the chapter presents strong evidence in support of those findings. What the chapter questions is the mechanism that drives this difference in correlations. While the previous literature has suggested that this difference was driven by differences in fiscal policy (possibly due to different constraints faced by policymakers in developing and advanced economies), this chapter offers a potential alternative explanation: that part of the difference might be due to differences in the exogenous shocks faced by the two groups of countries. Understanding more on the causes of these different correlations is extremely important, because if they are due to differences in policies, then any solution to the procyclicality problem should focus on removing the constraints (due to either political or market imperfections) that lead policymakers to adopt procyclical policies. However, if they are due to the different nature of the shocks faced by developing countries, then any effort aimed at reducing procyclicality should be aimed at determining the main drivers of these different shocks.

---

[28] IMF (2006d, Box 3.2) discusses debt management in six emerging market countries (including Brazil and Mexico) and shows that debt managers in these countries are indeed asked to minimize financing costs while maintaining low levels of risk.

CHAPTER 4 | History of Sovereign Debt in Latin America

THE LATIN AMERICAN BOND MARKET IN HISTORY: 1820–1913

More than any other region, Latin America provides an expansive historical experience on the contribution to economic development of foreign capital in general and sovereign debt in particular.[1] Latin America is the only part of the formerly colonial periphery with two centuries of post-independence historical experience. Once free from Iberian rule, Latin American countries rapidly embraced the use of global capital markets to finance their public debt (and, increasingly, their private sector debt as well). Perhaps surprisingly, their former colonial status per se does not explain why they had not previously enjoyed this option; debt in British colonies would come to be held by a variety of creditors in the nineteenth century, particularly in the semiautonomous dominions. In Latin America, however, tight Iberian control and immature international financial markets had foreclosed the option of external financing from sources other than Spain and Portugal.

Independence opened the door to external finance starting in the 1820s. Over the next one hundred years, foreign capital flows arrived in four great waves—punctuated by defaults, crises, and periods of near autarky. With the outbreak of World War I, global bond issuances came to an abrupt halt, and they would not restart for Latin American countries until the 1990s. This chapter reviews the historical record of Latin American sovereign debt from 1820 to 1913 and highlights some important parallels between the course of events in the nineteenth century and today.

First Wave

In the 1820s, the newly independent governments of Latin America approached the burgeoning international capital markets of London and Amsterdam. Funding was sought to establish security and infrastructure, and on a smaller scale the private sector went in search of development finance. British investment dominated the first wave.

In 1822, government bond issues with a face value of £3.65 million were floated by Colombia, Chile, Peru, and the fictitious "Poyais" (see Box 4.1); in 1824, there were new issues by Colombia and Peru, plus Buenos Aires, Brazil, and Mexico, to the tune of £10.4 million; and in 1825, Peru (yet again), along with Brazil, Mexico, Guadalajara, and Central America, issued bonds for a further £7.1 million. Sold at an average discount of almost 25 percent, these £21

---

[1] This section draws heavily on della Paolera and Taylor (2006).

Box 4.1 The State of Poyais

Although all Latin American bonds were risky investments in the 1820s, European investors' interest was so high and information so sketchy that even a fictitious country, Poyais, managed to place bonds. In 1823, a Scottish swindler, Gregor Mac-Gregor, claiming to be the "Cazique" of Poyais, described a thriving European colony in Central America endowed with rich gold mines. He managed to issue bonds, exchange Poyaisian dollars for pounds sterling, and even encourage immigration to the alleged settlement.

Of course, the attempted colonists did not find the capital city of "Saint Joseph" or the rich gold mines while trekking through a plague-infested, isolated tract of jungle. MacGregor sold similar certificates and other Poyaisian material in both Britain and France during the 1820s and 1830s. Despite the evident fraud, he was never convicted of any crime and eventually retired to Venezuela.

Source: Scottish Executive News (2004).

million in government bonds realized on net only £16 million for the borrowers. As investors soon discovered, these issues were at best risky, and at worst (in the case of Poyais) a fraud. When fiscal burdens escalated with the wars of independence and subsequent civil wars, the unseasoned sovereign borrowers soon found themselves with no means to service their debts, and a wave of defaults ensued. As a result, all Latin American bond issues were in default by 1827 (Rippy, 1959; Marichal, 1989; Stone, 1977).

New loans were not extended to the region until the defaults were resolved and political and economic stability seemed more assured, a process that took years and, in some cases, decades (Table 4.1). Of the various 1820s sovereign issues that quickly failed, only the Brazilian default was quickly resolved, in 1829, and most remained in default for decades, with restructuring attempts frequently subject to failure as well. Here was a seemingly clear case in which reputation mattered: the bad debtors paid for their defaults by being excluded for a long period from the financial markets (Lindert and Morton, 1989; Tomz, 2001).

Second Wave

Starting in the 1850s, there was a marked renewal of interest in Latin America in the London capital markets, directed both at government bonds and at new private (especially railroad) investment. By 1880, these new investments had grown into a sizable stock that dwarfed the previous boom in the 1820s, and by then a total of £179 million was outstanding to Britain, £123 million in government bonds (69 percent) and £56 million in private enterprise debts (Table 4.2). The new surge in investment was driven in large part by a global trade boom from the 1850s until the onset of the Great Depression of the 1870s. More exports and imports meant more revenues (principally from customs duties) that governments could use to amortize loans. These new debts constituted a major increase in leverage for the public sector

Table 4.1 Default History of Latin American Government Bonds Issued in the 1820s

Borrower	Principal owed (pounds)	Resolution (if any)
Brazil	21,129,000	Arrears on interest paid and service resumed in 1829.
Mexico	6,400,000	Refinancing in 1831 to cover principal and arrears on interest. Quickly defaulted on. New refinancing in 1837. More defaults and re-funding. Resolved 1864.
Costa Rica	13,608	Inherited share of Central American confederation debt. Principal paid off in 1840, but not arrears on interest.
Chile	1,000,000	Arrears on interest paid and service resumed in 1842.
Peru	1,816,000	Arrears on interest paid and service resumed in 1849. Default in 1876.
Colombia (New Granada)	3,375,000	Inherited 50% share of Gran Colombia debt. Principal and arrears paid off by new loan in 1845. Default in 1850. Principal and arrears paid off by new loan in 1861.
Venezuela	1,923,750	Inherited 28.5% share of Gran Colombia debt. Principal and arrears paid off by new loan in 1841. Default in 1847. New arrangements and further defaults then followed.
Ecuador	1,451,259	Inherited 21.5% share of Gran Colombia debt. Principal paid off by new loan in 1855. Arrears cancelled in exchange for land warrants and Peruvian bonds. Default in 1868.
Guatemala	68,741	Inherited share of Central American confederation debt. Principal and arrears paid off by new loan in 1856.
Buenos Aires	1,000,000	Resumed service in 1857.
El Salvador	27,217	Inherited share of Central American confederation debt. Paid off 90% of debt in 1860, but balance not until 1877.
Honduras	27,217	Inherited share of Central American confederation debt. Principal and arrears paid off by new loan in 1867.
Nicaragua	27,717	Inherited share of Central American confederation debt. Paid off 85% of debt face value in 1874.

Source: Rippy (1959, 26–28).
Note: Poyais is omitted.

Table 4.2 British Investments in Latin America at the End of 1880

(*pounds sterling*)

Country	Total	Private enterprise	Government bonds	Government bonds in default (year)
Argentina	20,338,709	9,105,009	11,233,700	n.d.
Bolivia	1,654,000	n.d.	1,654,000	1,654,000 (1875)
Brazil	38,869,007	15,808,905	23,060,102	n.d.
Chile	8,466,521	701,417	7,765,104	n.d.
Colombia	3,073,373	973,373	2,100,000	2,100,000 (1874)
Costa Rica	3,304,000	n.d.	3,304,000	3,304,000 (1874)
Cuba	1,231,600	1,231,600	n.d.	n.d.
Dominican Republic	714,300	n.d.	714,300	714,300 (1872)
Ecuador	1,959,380	135,380	1,824,000	1,824,000 (1868)
Guatemala	544,200	n.d.	544,200	544,200 (1876)
Honduras	3,222,000	n.d.	3,222,000	3,222,000 (1872)
Mexico	32,740,916	9,200,116	23,540,800	23,540,800 (1866)
Nicaragua	206,570	206,570	n.d.	n.d.
Paraguay	1,505,400	n.d.	1,505,400	1,505,400 (1874)
Peru	36,177,070	3,488,750	32,688,320	32,688,320 (1876)
Uruguay	7,644,105	4,124,885	3,519,220	n.d.
Venezuela	7,564,390	1,161,590	6,402,800	n.d.
Other	10,274,660	10,274,660	n.d.	n.d.
Total	179,490,261	56,412,255	122,978,006	71,097,020

Source: Rippy (1959, 25, 32), with corrections.
Note: n.d. = no data.

and a test of governments' creditworthiness after three decades of "financial hibernation." A total of 50 major foreign loans were negotiated from 1850 to 1873, most of them in London, and a few in Paris and other European markets (Marichal, 1989).

But the extension of credit to sovereigns was more selective in the second wave as compared to the first—investors avoided riskier locations and started to follow the signals given by the few countries that had shown some dedication to debt service. With respect to sovereign loans, Brazil had worked harder than other countries to honor debts and was duly rewarded with the largest share of the new flows. Other countries took longer to re-establish their creditworthiness. Argentina did not fully resolve internal disputes and old debts until the 1860s, and only then were new loans negotiated. Paraguay borrowed in London in 1871, and Uruguay and Bolivia could do likewise in 1872 (the first Bolivian issue in 1864 had failed). Chile floated issues in 1858, 1865, 1866, 1867, 1870, and 1873 totaling £8.5 million. Costa Rica, Guatemala, and Honduras all issued nonrefinancing debt (new net inflows) at the peak of the investment boom from 1867 to 1872 (Rippy, 1959; Marichal, 1989).

As might be expected, risk premiums paid by countries varied over a wide range. Good risks like Brazil or Chile could float loans with 5 percent coupons at a price of 80 or 90, for a yield of under 6 percent, and Peru could offer approximately the same yields. Argentine coupons ran to 6 or 7 percent, and the issues sold at around 90, while Costa Rica floated 6s and 7s and sold them for about 70. But war-torn Paraguay had to offer 8s and Honduras 10s, and these bonds still could not be sold for more than 80 (Marichal, 1989).

But a global macroeconomic and financial crisis was stirring yet again, and a second wave of defaults spread over the region in the 1870s. By the end of 1880, of the £123 million in British capital invested in Latin American government bonds, more than £71 million (58 percent) was in default (see Table 4.2). Some of these loans had been ill-conceived in the first place, and some were again tainted by fraud. But even legitimate loans in the larger republics ran into servicing problems as the global depression spread.

Credit conditions suffered. A much wider global debt crisis was under way of which Latin America was only a small part: by 1876 fifteen non-European nations had defaulted to the tune of £300 million. Global capital flows again ground to a halt, and irate bondholders chased down the insolvent republics long into the 1880s. Settlements were again drawn out, and defaulting governments were shut out of new borrowing during negotiations and often for many years beyond.

Third Wave, Crash, and Fourth Wave

An even bigger borrowing boom began in the 1880s as global economic activity, and especially trade, recovered. Defaulting governments gradually straightened out their fiscal problems and sought access to credit again. The overall flows were massive, and by the end of 1890 total British investments in the region were about £425 million, more than double the 1880 total. Of this, £194 million was held in government bonds, now for the first time surpassed by a slightly higher amount, £231 million, in securities issued by private enterprises (Rippy, 1959).

The regional distribution of the new wave of investment favored those countries that prospered the most in the new trade boom. In the 1880s, capital inflows were concentrated in just five countries: 37 percent in Argentina, 17 percent in Mexico, 14 percent in Brazil, 7 percent in Chile, and 5 percent in Uruguay. Government loans were even more skewed, with 60 percent of all new loans going to Argentina and Uruguay. Economic divergence was starting to be seen: foreign capital—which sought out the most profitable investment, the most dynamic economies, and the most creditworthy countries—played a part in furthering economic divergence in the region (Marichal, 1989).

Foreign capital could have helped some countries accelerate their development, a clear gain. But open capital markets required greater fiscal discipline, could quickly punish the guilty for their inconsistent policies, and could even hurt innocent bystanders through volatility over the business cycle and contagion during periodic crises. As financial development and monetization in Latin American economies grew in the late nineteenth century, the consequences of government-induced macroeconomic crises became deeper and more far reaching. With any increase in the probability of default, sovereign spreads widened and the capital market tightened. Domestic banks found themselves in distress, and a credit crunch followed that squeezed local borrowers. Whereas government defaults in the 1820s and 1870s could bypass premodern economic modes of production that relied more on retained profits and less on financial intermediation, by the 1890s the region's more modern economies risked more-resounding economic crises after a default. The major crises in the 1890s for two large capital recipients, Argentina and Brazil, illustrate these new financial risks.

The first crisis occurred in Argentina—arguably the world's first example of a modern "emerging market" crisis, combining debt crisis, bank collapses, maturity and currency mismatches, and contagion. Argentina's bold development strategy of the 1880s rested on a highly leveraged parastatal banking sector, which borrowed in gold and lent in pesos. When the economy faltered and the fiscal gap widened, it was covered by means of printing money, which broke the exchange rate peg and unleashed inflation. A generalized financial and banking crisis ensued, and stabilization and debt restructuring took the better part of a decade. Foreign capital flows dried up, and a global recession contributed to a delayed recovery (della Paolera and Taylor, 2001).

A second crisis followed in Brazil. Political and economic instability was high in the 1890s following the proclamation of the republic: the country was adjusting to the abolition of slavery, the gold standard had been abandoned, and inconsistent monetary and fiscal policies had the presses printing money at full speed. The currency steadily devalued, by a factor of 3.5 from 1890 to 1898, adding to the domestic costs of debt service. Default was put off for a time but was unavoidable in 1898–1900, and again in 1902–1909. By then, the real economy was in deep recession, having never really recovered from the financial instability of the early 1890s (Cardoso and Dornbusch, 1989; Fishlow, 1989; Triner, 2001).

The root cause of these crises looks familiar. Both Argentina and Brazil had increased their government debt levels at a fast pace as a result of persistent and large deficits, a reflection of the inability of the governments to balance the books and set out a sustainable fiscal path. Eventually a debt ceiling was reached, and markets were unwilling to roll the debt over one more time. Both countries paid a high price during the messy cleanups that followed. Argentina's national debt service was backstopped by rollovers agreed to by the 1891 Rothschild Committee, but at such a punitive interest rate that the deal had to be renegotiated almost immediately that same year. Brazil's 1898 funding loan, another Rothschild product, had harsh adjustment conditions attached to it.

The global capital market quickly recovered from the crisis of the 1890s, although countries badly affected, most notably Argentina, took longer to recover. However, compared to the 1870s boom and bust, this one was not associated with widespread default in the region, but rather a more general and global increase in country risk that slowed foreign capital flows for the better part of a decade. Inflows to Argentina and Uruguay were sluggish in the 1890s, but in other countries in the region, the tap was still open.

WHY WAS LATIN AMERICA THE FAVORITE OF THE MARKETS?

Latin America played a prominent role as recipient of capital flows in the nineteenth century. Between 1880 and 1913 the region received about one-quarter of total British foreign capital flows (Table 4.3). Yet many countries in the region were involved in military and political conflicts, had weak institutions, and showed serious inconsistencies in applying sound fiscal and monetary policies. What accounts for this market preference?

Investment Needs and Savings Scarcity

In the nineteenth century, global capital followed closely a textbook pattern of flowing from advanced, capital-rich countries to less-developed, capital-scarce economies (see Figure

Table 4.3 Cumulative Gross Capital Flows from Britain to Latin America, 1880-1913

(millions of pounds)

Type	Country	1880	Share (%)	To 1890	Share (%)	To 1900	Share (%)	To 1913	Share (%)	Growth rates (%)		
										1880–1891	1890–1901	1900–1914
Private	Argentina	9	3	78	10	102	10	257	12	24	3	7
	Brazil	10	3	29	4	40	4	90	4	11	3	6
	Chile	1	0	12	2	18	2	32	2	28	4	4
	Cuba	1	0	3	0	6	1	20	1	8	7	10
	Mexico	4	1	19	2	27	2	64	3	17	4	7
	Peru	2	1	5	1	6	1	11	1	10	1	5
	Uruguay	5	2	12	2	14	1	20	1	9	2	3
	These seven	32	11	157	20	212	20	494	24	17	3	7
	All countries	296	100	770	100	1,064	100	2,065	100	10	3	5
All	Argentina	21	3	132	10	160	9	332	10	20	2	6
	Brazil	22	4	56	4	74	4	166	5	10	3	6
	Chile	8	1	22	2	33	2	60	2	11	4	5
	Cuba	1	0	3	0	6	0	26	1	8	7	13
	Mexico	5	1	26	2	39	2	80	3	18	4	6
	Peru	27	4	30	2	30	2	37	1	1	0	2
	Uruguay	7	1	20	1	23	1	30	1	11	2	2
	These seven	90	15	289	22	365	20	732	23	12	2	6
	All countries	599	100	1,334	100	1,812	100	3,203	100	8	3	4

Source: Stone (1999).

4.1). In Latin America, government financing accounted for a large fraction of overall capital inflows, because public sector needs were closely correlated with the level of investment demand in the country as a whole. The case of transport infrastructure is a typical example of the strong complementarity between private and public sector investment. When the railroads were publicly operated, lending was directed via government borrowing. But even when they were privately owned, construction of railroads was often accompanied by significant public expenditure: related infrastructure, guarantees and subsidies, and so on. The same was true of ports, canals, and other large transportation-related projects. Latin American countries had very different investment needs in the nineteenth century, and this certainly affected their *overall* need to draw on foreign capital inflows, and infrastructure-led public borrowing in particular. As noted above, foreign financing of railways was a dominant category of foreign capital flows in this period (Twomey, 2000).

Financing needs also came about as a result of the insufficiency of domestic savings and the underdevelopment of domestic financial markets. For example, Davis and Gallman (2001) find that in the "settler economies," the British dominions generally had more advanced financial systems than Argentina, a finding consistent with the account of della Paolera and Taylor (2003). In the Argentine case, penetration by foreign banks, many of them branches of London banks, brought the country to the doorstep of the deep and liquid British financial markets. In this type of setting, foreign financial development can substitute for—and thus crowd out—domestic financial development. This effect was probably at work in many less-developed economies, within and beyond the British Empire, before 1914.

Figure 4.1
Foreign Capital in Rich and Poor Countries: Then versus Now

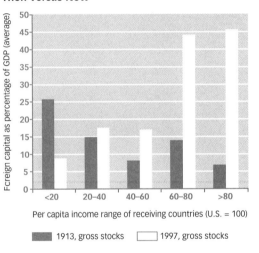

Per capita income range of receiving countries (U.S. = 100)

■ 1913, gross stocks   □ 1997, gross stocks

Source: Obstfeld and Taylor (2003).

In addition, in many Latin American countries savers were rather scarce for demographic reasons. Taylor (1992) made the argument for Argentina, but it applies to many other countries too. In many developing countries then, as now, fertility and population growth rates were very high. The standard life cycle argument would predict that such countries would tend to save less, as compared to countries with a more mature population with greater numbers in high-saving midlife cohorts. Taylor and Williamson (1994) show how these effects could explain a fair portion of the capital flows from Britain to the settler economies before 1914. The small size of the domestic financial markets was an additional reason pushing governments to borrow from abroad.

Policies, Institutions, and Reputations

Sovereign risk premiums, the spread over the market's benchmark bond yield (in those days the British consol), also varied significantly across countries and over time, as seen in Figure 4.2. In extreme cases, countries suffered complete market exclusion, typically as a result of unresolved past defaults. What drove risk premiums? A considerable body of research in recent years has explored this topic, and the answers have focused on policies (adherence to the gold standard, fiscal balance), political and institutional factors (wars, colonial linkages), and reputations (the history of defaults and their resolution).[2]

There is evidence that sovereign borrowers received a lower risk premium when they adhered to the gold standard, which has been interpreted as the equivalent of a "seal of approval" on policies (Bordo and Rockoff, 1996). Because countries needed to maintain sound policies to operate a credible commitment to the gold standard, this automatically reassured bondholders of a country's creditworthiness. The risk premium fell by an estimated 40 or more basis points upon adoption of the gold standard (Obstfeld and Taylor, 2003).

Gold was a highly relevant policy issue for the Latin American countries because they were generally among the weakest countries maintaining gold standard adherence. What was it about the region's economies that made it so difficult for them to stick to a hard monetary regime? Volatility seems to be the answer. The Latin American economies seem to have been more susceptible than any other group of countries to extreme fluctuations in public debt-to-GDP ratios. The region's governments engaged in big run-ups in debt levels during periods of easy credit, which halted suddenly during tighter times or after a default/repudiation episode. Latin American countries were burdened with considerable fiscal volatility, either because their tax revenues were volatile (owing, for example, to trade volatility and terms-of-trade shocks affecting customs revenue) or because spending was volatile (owing, for example, to wars and military spending caused by internal or external political instability). Moreover, governments' propensity to use external borrowing was sometimes fed by institutional weakness of a different sort: governments pursuing short-run prosperity for political gain. Whatever the origin, it is clear

Figure 4.2
Country Risk, 1870–1914: External Bond Spread over British Consol, Latin America versus 11 Core Countries and British Empire Bonds

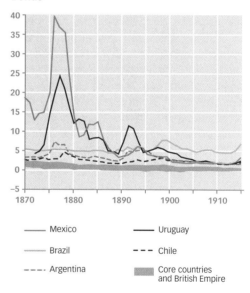

— Mexico   — Uruguay

— Brazil   --- Chile

---· Argentina   ▨ Core countries and British Empire

Source: Taylor (2003).

---

[2] The most comprehensive coverage of this topic is in Mauro, Sussman, and Yafeh (2006).

that Latin American governments lived in a more fiscally volatile world and witnessed more dramatic fluctuations in their debt positions than countries elsewhere in either the core or the periphery.

Military conflicts involving the sovereign borrower, both civil wars and inter-state wars, were often behind episodes of insolvency, especially in the turbulent period immediately following national independence. Furthermore, wars often meant going off gold, worsening the deterioration in creditworthiness. In fact, political and institutional determinants were so unfavorable in the region that it is not clear how most parts of Latin America could have been expected to attract large-scale capital inflows. Spain and Portugal did not establish colonies that were characterized by good political and economic institutions. Power was concentrated in privileged elites, democracy never flourished, and property rights and the rule of law were weak (except where needed to protect the elite). Although these flaws persisted after independence, the region did manage to sustain strong economic growth in the nineteenth century and hence became attractive to foreign capital, except where the worst political and institutional failures could not be contained.

It is fair to say that Latin America's post-independence experience remains relatively neglected in the theories currently in vogue that stress the importance of colonial-times institutions. Despite their weak institutions, countries in the region enjoyed respectable economic growth and capital market access. Although defaults were undoubtedly higher than in the British Empire group, the region still managed to attract significant capital flows despite higher default risks. The returns must have outweighed the risks in the eyes of the investors. Colonial origins did not doom the region to failure, at least up to 1914.

Nonetheless, frequent episodes of default were a major factor influencing the cost and availability of foreign financing for Latin America in this period. The crises of the 1820s and 1870s started to cement in investors' minds the untrustworthiness of Latin American sovereign borrowers, a reputation that was to expand in the years ahead and that persists even to this day.

According to Tomz (2001), of the 77 government defaults from 1820 to 1914, 58 (75 percent) involved Latin American countries. Compared to other periphery countries, the economic potential and sovereign independence of the region obviously encouraged this outcome: the potential for high returns favored more borrowing ex ante, and independence from empire gave more freedom to default ex post. Another factor may have been a relatively modest cost for a soiled reputation, according to some estimates. Studies put the penalty for default at about 100 basis points for a full default and 50 basis points for partial defaults (Obstfeld and Taylor, 2003; Ferguson and Schularick, 2006; see Chapter 12 for a discussion of the cost of default). Figure 4.3 shows the incidence of sovereign default in the region from 1820 to 1940, and the fraction of years that debtors spent in default status is impressive: 38 percent on average.

CHARACTERISTICS OF THE HISTORICAL SOVEREIGN BOND MARKET

In the nineteenth century, sovereign bonds typically had a very long maturity. Their maturities averaged more than 20 years, while in the current globalization period of the 1990s and 2000s, the issue of Eurobonds by emerging market sovereigns was at maximum maturities of 7 to 10 years. Also, in the 1870–1913 period, early redemption clauses were the norm in the

structuring of public debt issues. These were the so-called
"lottery clauses," allowing partial repayment and conversion
on bonds whose numbers were
drawn randomly at specified
moments.[3] This implies that
the international capital markets of the nineteenth century
(notably, the London market)
offered favorable conditions
to debtor countries, allowing
them to refinance and swap
long-term debt instruments
for comparable instruments at
lower interest or coupon rates
to exploit favorable liquidity
conditions, perhaps more easily than in the modern market.

Most of the sovereign

Figure 4.3
Latin America: Periods in Default, 1825–1940

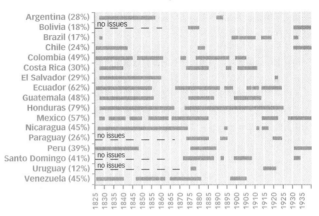

Sources: Taylor (2003); default data from Tomz (2001); issue dates from
Marichal (1989).
Note: Percentage of years in default shown in parentheses. Poyais is
omitted.

bonds floated by Latin American countries in the period were denominated in foreign currency or in terms of gold (or else had "gold clauses," allowing the creditor to choose to be
paid in gold). Moreover, Latin American countries, especially Brazil and Argentina, also issued domestic debt with gold clauses. Although this was fairly common practice in emerging
markets at the time, the acute credibility problems created by monetary and fiscal policies
in Latin American countries left them with little choice in the matter (Bordo and Meissner,
2005).

In terms of seniority, a notable difference between international markets then and those
today was that in many debt issues, export revenues and tax revenues were earmarked as
collateral to guarantee servicing of the debt. This granted some public bonds an explicit
seniority over other bonds of the same type and issued by the same national political entity.
Most bond issues in current times include "negative pledge" clauses that prevent the selective use of collateral. In the same vein, "sharing" clauses, which prevent selective default on
certain bonds, were not used very often in the nineteenth-century market.

A country's cost of borrowing was closely associated with its track record. "Seasoned"
borrowers could expect to pay much lower spreads than debtors with poor reputations. But
the difference narrowed or disappeared during good times, times of abundant liquidity and
solid performance in the global economy, as emphasized by Tomz (2001). During the first
wave of lending (the 1820s), the Latin American economies were new borrowers par excel-
lence, and spreads were around 350 basis points. In the second wave of the 1870s, the market attached reasonable premiums to seasoned borrowers and to countries that had settled
past defaults or were new entrants, but the proven "lemons" or junk bonds were trading at
an average yield of 27 percent.

---

[3] Because bonds sometimes traded above par, investors who "won" lotteries in those cases actually lost money.

The high cost of capital in the first wave might have been associated with the building up of reputation for the early borrowers, but in addition, genuine asymmetric-information problems were surely quite acute during the 1820–1870 period. Paucity of information, in fact, was a major issue, especially until the second wave in the 1870s. In the 1820s there were in London several important newspapers which compiled quite sophisticated data on bond pricing and volumes traded and also reported on the political and economic news of different countries. *The Colonist, Common Sense, The Times,* and *Course of Exchange* followed Latin American debt closely during the first wave on a daily basis until the generalized defaults of 1826–1827. Della Paolera and Taylor (2006) collected data on a substantial portion of the sovereign bonds outstanding for the six years 1822–28 and constructed a Latin American bond composite index that is quite comparable to the current Emerging Markets Bond Index (EMBI) (Figure 4.4).

During the second wave, by contrast, news was much more widely available. Information on macro variables such as outstanding debt per nation, trade flows, fiscal positions, population, railway construction as a proxy for investment, and prices and quotations of sovereign bonds was readily available from additional sources such as *Investor's Monthly Manual, The Economist, Palmer's Index,* and the *Annual Reports of the Corporation of Foreign Bondholders,* which was created in the mid-1860s as an association of British investors holding bonds issued by the emerging economies.

Defaults and Their Resolution

The major Latin American nations in the wave of the 1820s—Brazil, Chile, Mexico, Peru, Gran Colombia, the Federation of Central America, and the Province of Buenos Aires (which seceded in the 1820s from the Argentine Confederation)—all defaulted between 1826 and 1828. All of these borrowers had issued their sovereign bonds in the early 1820s, but by the mid-1830s, they had started renegotiating and settling their debt situations. Their situations were completely regularized no later than the 1870s, with arrangements that capitalized interest and amortization arrears. Although repayment was often very delayed, in this first wave there were no cases of outright repudiation.

In between the two waves, for the period 1850–1873, the approximate total of outstanding foreign loans to Latin America was £140 million—but 45 percent of this stock was simply devoted to refinancing the defaults of the 1820s. Later, after the crisis of 1873, which saw a massive fall in the price of commodities, eight Latin American countries defaulted, but most of them restructured in the 1880s, with the exception of Honduras, which was in a perennial situation of default and was one of the few cases in which gunboat diplomacy was applied (in 1905–1907). Hence, most countries were in some sense willing to restructure their debts and resume service when they could take advantage of renewed liquidity in global capital markets. Interestingly enough, in the cases of both Chile (a span of 18 years of outright default) and Argentina (a period of 16 years of outright default and 13 years of a unilateral partial-repayment scheme), debt restructuring did not include *any* debt relief or principal reduction schemes. In the case of Brazil, the most significant principal owed, about £21 million, went into default by the mid-1820s, but default was short lived, and already as early as 1829, arrears on interest were paid and service resumed normally (again, see Table 4.1).

In the period of the 1880s and 1890s Argentina alone was the recipient of 30 percent of all foreign loans to Latin America, followed distantly by Brazil, with 14 percent of total foreign loans inflows to Latin America. It is no surprise, then, that when Argentina started to reveal by the end of 1890 that it would have problems servicing its foreign debt, a panic arose in London, and means were sought to avoid a contagion in the event of an Argentine default. This event became famously known as the Baring Crash of 1890–1891. To avoid an across-the-board default by Argentina, the Bank of England coordinated a rescue operation in January 1891 that involved a syndicate of merchant banks providing a "standby" loan of £15 million, a "6 percent funding loan," to cover the full service of the external debt over three years for the

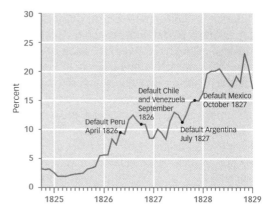

Figure 4.4
London Latin American Bond Market in the 1820s: Composite Yield Index Using Coupon-Price Ratio

Source: della Paolera and Taylor (2006).
Note: Index comprises Argentina (Buenos Aires), Brazil, Colombia, Chile, Mexico, and Peru.

Argentine bonds. This arrangement, known as the "de la Plaza–Bank of England agreement," also included very harsh conditionality measures. Yet, in spite of the stabilization reform efforts, it became clear in 1892 that the package had failed to put debt service onto a sustainable path. The *real* yield at which the funding loan was floated was 16 percent at a time of recession, when the debt-to-GDP ratio rose from 72 percent to 91 percent. A debt forgiveness package was proposed by J. J. Romero in 1893 to a committee of creditors headed by the House of Rothschild, leading to a successful resolution (della Paolera and Taylor, 2001, 106–117). Argentina's "Romero Agreement" of 1893 stated that, between 1893 and 1898, the Argentine government would pay half the level of original debt service envisaged in the de la Plaza–Bank of England agreement, then from 1898 onwards, it would pay the full level of debt service, and finally from 1901, the government would begin to amortize principal on the national sovereign bonds. Therefore, the Argentine bonds were never technically in default, but they avoided default only through two sequential restructuring operations. It is important to note here that some provincial and municipal Argentine bonds had been in default since 1891 and that the federal government would assume those obligations, some as late as 1898. Argentina could float new bonds again only in 1901, so the country was effectively without access to international financing for almost a decade.

AFTER THE COLLAPSE

In the space of the next few decades, the integrated global markets for goods, capital, and labor that had been built over the course of the long nineteenth century were effectively destroyed. The outbreak of World War I led to capital controls and the collapse of the gold standard under inflationary war-financing policies. The core European countries, and Britain in particular, were no longer in any position to export capital to the developing world. The center of the world capital market gradually shifted from London to New York, but the American capacity to supply funds to the rest of the world did not fill the void left by the British. There was considerable distress in the region in the wartime years: Brazil defaulted again, for example, as did Uruguay and revolutionary Mexico, but Argentina did not, despite a brutal recession. The 1920s were a period of marked improvement for Latin American borrowers, notwithstanding the still-uncertain outlook in the world economy. By late in the decade, capital flows to the region seemed to be on their way to recovering their previous shine, but this was soon to change.

In the 1930s, the situation grew gloomier. The Great Depression reached its lowest point from 1929 to 1933. Capital controls and competitive devaluations became widespread. Nearly all Latin American countries also adopted capital controls in this decade, most fell in default of their external debts, and several attempted to maintain multiple exchange rates, which gave rise to active parallel markets in foreign currency. Despite these unfavorable conditions, some countries remained engaged with capital markets as best they could in the 1930s. A small few, notably Argentina, did not default, and they were rewarded with favorable access to new trickles of capital in the late 1930s. Others continued engaging with creditors to renegotiate debts, perhaps hoping for a resumption of global flows. Many governments managed to shrink their debt burden through secret buybacks of their own debt at the deep discount that was offered by the secondary market. Through buybacks, unilateral offers to creditors, or renegotiation, several countries achieved substantial debt concessions. In this decade, at least, default had little stigma attached to it—almost every bank, enterprise, or country was afflicted by it. Reputations could be rebuilt, then, but as it would turn out, another war and a new backlash against global finance would soon render efforts in this direction moot, and no significant capital flows would be seen again in the region for three or four decades.

From the 1940s to the 1980s, the constraints on global capital markets were to fluctuate, but not until the 1990s did financial globalization appear to regain prominence again, and even then, on a more modest scale than in the nineteenth century. Virtually no foreign capital flowed from rich to poor countries for most of the period after World War II. And when capital flows resumed in the 1970s and 1980s, they tended to favor areas other than Latin America. Foreign direct investment provides a sharp example. In 1914, and similarly in 1938, Latin America accounted for about 55 percent of world stock of inward foreign investment in developing countries, but by the year 1990, the region accounted for only 37 percent (Twomey, 2000). Asia has gained significant market share, but the major destination of gross flows from advanced economies is now to other advanced economies.[4] With the resumption of capital flows, major debt crises have again swept over the region in a manner eerily reminiscent of the experiences from the 1820s to the 1930s. Sovereign debt exploded in the 1970s in the form of bank loans, in the context of the global growth slowdown and the recycling of the so-called petrodollars of newly rich creditors in the Organization of the

---

[4] The decline in importance of foreign direct investment (FDI) for the Latin American economies is dramatic. In 1914, the stock of FDI was estimated to be the equivalent of 270 percent of GDP, while by 1990, after a modest recovery, it amounted to only 47 percent (Twomey, 2000).

Petroleum Exporting Countries (OPEC). International bank lending to Argentina, Brazil, and Mexico doubled from 1979 to 1981. In 1982 a default crisis engulfed these countries and many others in the region and elsewhere on the periphery. A recession in the global economy, high interest rates, weak commodity prices, and overborrowing led to another familiar scenario. Renegotiations and an orderly working out of this debacle took almost a decade, during which the door to financial markets was temporarily shut once again and the region endured more political and economic turmoil.

CHAPTER 5 | The International Emerging Bond Market Today

FROM THE DEBT CRISIS TO THE NEW BOND MARKET

THE TWO WORLD WARS, the Great Depression, and the end of the first era of globalization witnessed a long hiatus in private international lending to developing countries. When such lending resumed in the 1970s, the traditional bond instrument was replaced by syndicated loans from international banks. With the advent of the Eurodollar market, "money center" banks created syndicates to make international loans to middle-income countries. This activity received a big impetus when the surpluses of the oil-exporting countries started to increase liquidity among the banks. At the same time, developing countries' demand for external financing was growing in step with their trade deficit, and international financial institutions and policymakers from the largest industrial countries seemed to encourage recycling of oil surpluses to allow an easier adjustment to the oil price shock in the global economy.

The syndicated bank loans of the 1970s were mostly short or medium term, at variable interest rates, and denominated in U.S. dollars. It was a period of high inflation and low, even negative ex post real interest rates, in the context of high export prices and strong global demand for the products of most developing countries. But the nature of the loans meant that borrowing countries were assuming essentially all the risks if the conditions prevailing at the time of the loans changed. Indeed, when real interest rates turned highly positive and the world economy slowed down at the end of the decade, borrowing countries began to face serious debt sustainability problems, especially those that had been more profligate during the period of abundant liquidity in international markets.

The public statement by the finance minister of Mexico, in August 1982, that Mexico was unable to service its debts marked the end of a wave of capital inflows. In the following months and years, most other large borrowers followed suit and defaulted on their debt obligations in one way or another. The debt crisis that ensued had serious economic consequences. In the borrowing countries, it created the need to make huge adjustments to budget deficits and external current accounts; in many countries the difficulty of implementing these adjustments resulted in high inflation or hyperinflation. Domestic economies fell into deep recessions, while private investment collapsed and remained depressed for years under the weight of a "debt overhang" that would persist for years. (Chapter 10 describes the debt overhang problem.)[1]

---

[1] The literature on the debt crisis of the 1980s is very rich. Useful retrospectives are to be found in Cline (1995) and Dooley (1995); an interesting collection of papers that provides an overview of issues and ideas at the beginning of the resolution of the crisis is Husain and Diwan (1989).

The debt crisis of the 1980s also had a substantial impact in the financial markets of the advanced economies. Some of the largest banks in the United States and other developed countries were holding sizable amounts of the defaulted debt, and heavy losses on developing country debt threatened their financial soundness. At least four of the largest U.S. banks had exposures on loans to Latin American countries that exceeded their total capital. Although the situation was a little less extreme, several major banks in the United Kingdom, Canada, and Japan were likely to become insolvent if claims on Latin American sovereigns had become worthless.

In that environment, the solution to the debt crisis became difficult and protracted. It involved bilateral negotiations between debtor governments and creditor committees representing the main banks, but it was strongly influenced by the policies and initiatives of the international financial institutions and the governments of the advanced economies. In the end, a new strategy was announced by U.S. Secretary of the Treasury Nicholas Brady in March 1989 that provided official incentives, through IMF and World Bank loans, for agreements to restructure debts into bonds with significant write-downs of the claims. The objective—which the strategy proved successful at achieving—was to bring debtor countries back into sustainable positions without causing destabilizing financial losses to the creditor commercial banks.

THE RISE OF THE EMERGING MARKET ASSET CLASS

The restructuring of sovereign debts of developing countries under the Brady Plan marked the return to bond financing for Latin America and emerging markets more generally. The first operation was the Mexican debt restructuring in 1990, and it was followed by similar operations in 20 other countries in the following years. The deals exchanged new Brady bonds for defaulted syndicated bank loans. Some of the bonds preserved the value of the principal but carried significantly discounted coupons ("par" bonds), while others carried coupons more in line with market interest rates but discounted the face value ("discount" bonds). Many of the bonds also had some form of enhancements in the form of partial guarantees or "value recovery rights" (VRRs) which offered extra payments if certain economic conditions were met. (Box 5.1 discusses the VRRs included in these deals.) The guarantees typically consisted of collateral in the form of zero-coupon U.S. Treasury bonds which would cover part of the payments in case of default on the Brady bonds (see Box 10.2).

By the early 1990s, an active market for the new Brady bonds was in full swing. Supported by strong—if sometimes fickle—investor appetite, sovereigns in Latin America and other emerging markets began to issue Eurobonds and global bonds in the 1990s, which started to displace the original Bradys and now dominate the markets.[2] In fact, most countries preferred to replace their Brady bonds with bonds of other types because they felt that the origin of the Bradys in the restructuring of defaulted loans was a reminder of a tainted past, and certain features—such as partial guarantees—that were introduced to facilitate an

---

[2] A Eurobond is an instrument denominated in a currency different from that of the country in which the bond is issued. The first Eurobond (issued in 1963) was a dollar-denominated instrument issued in Luxembourg by an Italian company. Global bonds, in contrast, can be denominated in the currency of the country that issues the bonds and can be simultaneously offered on several markets.

Box 5.1 Value Recovery Rights in Brady Bonds

Many Brady deals included a "sweetener" for the creditor banks in the form of value recovery rights (VRRs). Payments on VRRs were contingent on favorable conditions for the debtor countries, especially in regard to exports. The general principle was that, if the debtor country's terms of trade or economic conditions improved, creditors could also benefit from these improvements by receiving additional payments. For example, Mexico's and Venezuela's VRRs were contingent on the international price of oil (in the case of Mexico, on a combination of price and export volumes), and Costa Rica's, Bulgaria's, and Bosnia-Herzegovina's were contingent on either the growth rate or the level of GDP reaching a certain value (see World Bank, 2004a).

Although the VRRs included in these deals became a marginal part of the emerging debt market, their inclusion was a valuable experience on the road to creating contingent debt instruments. Some of the lessons from this experience stem in fact from design flaws in some of the VRRs. For example, instruments with low market value failed to attract much investor interest because the small—and likely illiquid—market did not justify the cost of learning how to value the instrument. This was the case, for example, with VRRs that were well "out of the money" at issue because the conditions under which the payments associated with

them would take place were not likely to be met until many years later. Similarly, interest was very slight when the formula that determined the payoff amount was unnecessarily complicated, as this also raised the cost of getting the instrument on the radar screens of investors.

Another important lesson involved the convenience of making VRRs detachable from the main bond with which they were associated, such that they could be traded as separate financial instruments, as was the case with Mexico's VRR. Bonds that had VRRs attached to them were of a different nature than the rest of the bonds issued by the same country and detracted from the desirable feature of offering a full, liquid yield curve for the country's debt. Market participants value the liquidity of a financial instrument and the possibility of trading along a complete curve of different maturities, and this results in lower spreads. As bonds with VRRs did not contribute to the yield curve, they detracted from the effort to offer the fullest yield curve possible. Similarly, bond markets found the partial guarantees that were included in some of the Brady bonds to be an obstacle to developing a clean, transparent yield curve. In fact, Brady bonds started to be quoted and traded stripped from their collateral; this stripping could be achieved by selling short the corresponding U.S. Treasury bond.

agreement with creditor banks were proving unattractive to current bond investors. Of the total global volume of $175 billion in Brady bonds that was issued, just over $10 billion remain in circulation now, after buybacks (including some ongoing operations), amortizations, and some new defaults and restructurings that have occurred in the past few years. Latin American countries have been the most active in buying back or exchanging their Brady debt, and their share of these instruments has fallen sharply (Table 5.1).

Table 5.1 Brady Bonds: Original Amounts and Outstanding Balances

(US$ billion)

Country	Year of issue	Issued		Outstanding (March 2006)		
		Face value	Percentage of total	Face value	Percentage of total	Retired (percent)
Latin America		**143.1**	**81.8**	**3.9**	**36.4**	**97.3**
Argentina	1993	24.8	14.2	0.0	0.0	100.0[a]
Brazil	1994	51.3	29.3	0.0	0.0	100.0[b]
Costa Rica	1990	0.6	0.3	0.0	0.0	100.0
Dominican Republic	1994	0.5	0.3	0.4	3.7	20.0
Ecuador	1995	6.3	3.6	0.0	0.0	100.0
Mexico	1990	35.6	20.4	0.0	0.0	100.0
Panama	1996	2.9	1.7	0.9	8.4	69.0
Peru	1996	4.2	2.4	2.0	18.7	52.4
Uruguay	1991	1.1	0.6	0.0	0.0	100.0
Venezuela	1990	15.8	9.0	0.6	5.6	96.2
Other countries		**31.8**	**18.2**	**6.8**	**63.6**	**78.7**
Bulgaria	1994	4.6	2.6	0.0	0.0	100.0
Croatia	1996	1.5	0.9	0.0	0.0	100.0
Ivory Coast	1997	2.0	1.1	2.0	18.7	0.0
Jordan	1993	0.7	0.4	0.0	0.0	100.0
Morocco	1990	2.8	1.6	0.7	6.5	75.7
Nigeria	1992	2.1	1.2	1.4	13.1	33.3
Philippines	1990	3.9	2.2	1.0	9.3	74.4
Poland	1994	7.1	4.1	1.2	11.2	83.1
Russia	1993	6.4	3.7	0.0	0.0	100.0
Slovenia	1996	0.2	0.1	0.0	0.1	95.5
Vietnam	1997	0.5	0.3	0.5	4.7	0.0
Total		**174.9**	**100.0**	**10.7**	**100.0**	**93.9**

Source: Authors' calculations on the basis of data from JPMorgan and Bloomberg databases and IMF, *Global Development Finance.*
[a] There is still about $300 million in defaulted Brady debt that has not been exchanged.
[b] Including the announced buyback operation.

The retirement of the Bradys is in fact a sign of the strength of the emerging economies' sovereign bond market, which has grown to significant proportions in global capital markets. According to Bank for International Settlements figures, total outstanding international sovereign emerging debt reached about $450 billion in 2005, of which Latin American debt accounted for about $240 billion. The emerging economies total represents almost one-third of the global supply of international government bonds (Table 5.2). The international debt securities of corporations and financial institutions in emerging economies are fast approaching the level of government bonds and reached almost $390 billion in 2005. Nonetheless, Latin America accounts for a much lower share of private borrowing than of government borrowing in international markets. The share of emerging markets in world private bonds is also lower but still amounts to 9 percent. Emerging markets have a much smaller share of the market for bonds issued by financial institutions (Table 5.3).

Figure 5.1
Turnover in Emerging Market Bonds

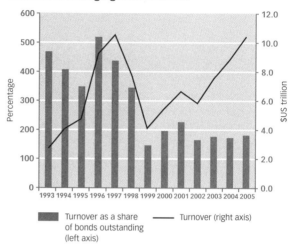

Turnover as a share of bonds outstanding (left axis)

Turnover (right axis)

Sources: Turnover data from Trade Association for the Emerging Markets database and outstanding bonds data from Bank for International Settlements database.
Note: Country ratios are weighted by the outstanding amounts of international bonds of each country.

The global market is active and liquid for the sovereign bonds of most Latin American countries. EMTA (the Trade Association for the Emerging Markets, an industry association based in New York with broad membership among market participants) has been surveying its members and compiling data on secondary market trading of emerging market bonds since 1993. Trading in such bonds was relatively light in the early years when the instruments were still new and the investor base was starting to develop. Subsequently, trading reached frantic levels during 1997–1998, in the context of a series of financial crises and unsettled conditions in many financial markets (Figure 5.1). Turnover in Latin American issues tends to be higher than that in issues from other regions, reflecting in part large holdings of Latin American, and in particular Mexican, paper by international investors who are members of EMTA.

In assessing the volume of emerging market debt in global markets, it is noteworthy that the distinction between international and domestic debt has become increasingly blurred. Not all holders of international bonds are international investors, nor are all the holders of domestic debt residents of the country issuing the debt. In fact, residents of countries that are emerging markets tend to be active participants in the global debt markets of their countries, acquiring securities either in domestic exchanges or through international accounts.

Table 5.2 Outstanding International Government Debt Securities

(US$ billion)

Country	1993	1996	1999	2002	2005 Amount	2005 Percentage
Advanced economies	311.1	429.9	413.9	524.5	957.7	68.1
United States	0.2	0.4	3.9	3.1	3.2	0.2
Emerging markets	110.1	228.0	311.1	383.5	449.4	31.9
Latin America and the						
Caribbean	75.4	166.1	207.8	231.4	243.0	17.3
Argentina	18.2	42.0	64.2	79.5	69.4	4.9
Brazil	1.0	45.8	47.0	54.0	62.9	4.5
Chile	0.3	0.0	0.5	2.0	3.5	0.2
Colombia	0.4	1.9	5.6	10.7	13.1	0.9
Costa Rica	0.6	0.6	0.9	1.6	2.1	0.1
Dominican Republic	0.0	0.5	0.5	1.0	0.4	0.0
Ecuador	0.0	6.0	6.2	4.0	4.2	0.3
Mexico	36.1	50.5	59.9	50.9	47.5	3.4
Trinidad and Tobago	0.3	0.3	0.6	0.7	0.7	0.0
Uruguay	1.1	1.5	2.3	3.9	5.1	0.4
Venezuela	17.4	17.1	15.2	14.4	20.6	1.5
Africa and Middle East	4.6	7.7	13.7	20.9	29.0	2.1
Asia and Pacific	10.8	13.3	25.1	35.5	46.1	3.3
Europe	19.3	40.9	64.5	95.7	131.3	9.3
Total	421.2	657.9	725.0	908.0	1,407.1	100.0

Source: Bank for International Settlements database.
Note: Data are from September of each year.

And international investors are increasingly entering domestic debt markets (see Chapter 7). Although there are no reliable data for estimating a breakdown of bondholders by residence, there is broad anecdotal evidence that holdings of emerging market government bonds by residents of the issuing country are indeed significant. For example, surveys conducted in connection with the 2005 Argentine debt restructuring suggested that institutional and individual residents of Argentina held as much as 75 percent of the country's outstanding global sovereign debt in 2001–2002.[3]

---

[3] This estimate comprises the debt restructured in "Phase 1" in November 2001, which had a face value of about $24 billion and was entirely held by residents of Argentina, largely banks, and "more than 50 percent" of the remaining approximately $80 billion in face value that was estimated by the Argentine authorities to be held by Argentine institutions and individuals. See http://www.mecon.gov.ar/download/financiamiento/canje_deuda_nov01.pdf and http://www.argentinedebtinfo.gov.ar/documentos/road-show-cwg-oct-03.pdf, page 10.

Table 5.3 Outstanding International Private Debt Securities

(US$ billion)

Country	1993	1996	1999	2002	2005 Amount	2005 Percentage
		Corporate issuers				
Advanced economies	494.5	477.0	643.9	1,083.7	1,371.6	91.0
Emerging markets	29.6	65.8	108.1	111.7	135.3	9.0
Latin America and the Caribbean	18.8	30.8	50.7	45.5	41.8	2.8
Argentina	2.1	6.5	11.6	8.3	3.8	0.3
Brazil	3.5	7.9	12.2	11.4	9.8	0.7
Chile	0.3	2.0	3.6	5.3	7.2	0.5
Colombia	0.2	0.3	0.3	0.3	0.9	0.1
Costa Rica	0.0	0.1	0.0	0.0	0.1	0.0
Mexico	10.5	12.2	21.5	19.4	19.0	1.3
Venezuela	2.3	1.9	1.0	0.5	0.3	0.0
Total	524.1	542.8	752.0	1,195.4	1,506.9	100.0
		Financial institutions				
Advanced economies	843.0	1,509.7	3,298.9	6,081.4	10,364.9	97.6
Emerging markets	37.3	81.5	120.9	130.3	253.0	2.4
Latin America and the Caribbean	15.9	30.2	39.8	47.2	63.7	0.6
Argentina	1.3	2.9	3.6	1.6	1.6	0.0
Brazil	4.2	13.9	16.5	24.2	34.4	0.3
Chile	0.0	0.1	0.6	0.6	0.4	0.0
Colombia	0.1	1.1	1.4	0.8	0.8	0.0
Mexico	10.3	11.5	11.6	14.5	23.6	0.2
Peru	0.0	0.1	0.2	0.2	0.2	0.0
Uruguay	0.0	0.1	0.4	0.3	0.3	0.0
Venezuela	0.1	0.3	5.3	4.6	1.8	0.0
Total	880.3	1,591.2	3,419.8	6,211.7	10,617.9	100.0

Source: Bank for International Settlements database.
Note: Data are from September of each year.

SUDDEN STOPS AND CONTAGION

Although the renewed access to the global financial market since the 1990s has contributed to investment and budget smoothing for the public sector, the availability of financing and the spreads paid on emerging markets' bonds have displayed a high degree of volatility, as was the case in the previous golden era of bond financing (1870–1914) described in Chapter 4.[4] High volatility may be a pervasive feature of these instruments, and the reason for this

---

[4] For a comparison of emerging market spreads now and then, see Mauro, Sussman, and Yafeh (2002).

may be that the fundamental economic factors that underlie the creditworthiness of sovereigns in emerging economies are themselves highly volatile. For example, in many cases, government revenues are highly dependent on commodity export prices and economic growth, which are subject to large swings over time. If government debt is largely denominated in foreign currencies, the volatility of the exchange rate will also result in large changes in the relative value of debts and the creditworthiness of the sovereign. In addition, investors face a more difficult challenge in trying to assess the creditworthiness of a sovereign than that of a private firm. In the latter case, equity prices and debt-to-equity ratios provide precise information that helps to make the valuation of debt more precise. There are no comparable market instruments to help in the valuation of sovereign debt. Moreover, should a default occur, the recovery value of government bonds is harder to predict, because the framework for sovereign debt restructuring is less well defined than is the case with private borrowers.

The structure of the market and the cost of obtaining and updating information have been contributing factors to market volatility as well. When debt instruments of a given country represent a small share of an investor's portfolio, there will be a tendency to rely on general information (like current market trends) and to pay less attention to the subtle details of the current economic conditions in that country, especially when information is costly to acquire and changes frequently. Calvo and Mendoza (2005) show that in this situation, a slight change in expectations may bring about a sharp and unexpected portfolio repositioning, sudden stops in capital flows, contagion to seemingly unrelated countries, and generally higher market volatility.

Thus, frequent sudden stop episodes have been the distinctive element of the modern international bond market for emerging economies (Calvo, 1998). Sudden stops are periods of market panic in which the valuation of bonds seems to be well below economic fundamentals. For example, a spread of 1,500 basis points would imply a probability of default of almost 66 percent within one year, and almost 90 percent within three years, in a typical 10-year bond configuration.[5] These seem to be excessively pessimistic prospects. Sudden stops may be associated with a global event or with a financial crisis breaking out in one of the emerging economies, but they have the tendency to result in virtual market closures and significant jumps in spreads for several or all emerging countries. A plot of the spreads implicit in JPMorgan's Emerging Market Bond Index Global (EMBIG) starkly highlights four major sudden stop episodes: the Tequila crisis, the Russian–Long-Term Capital Management (LTCM) crisis, the aftermath of the September 11 terrorist attacks in the United States, and the uncertainty associated with the election of President Luiz Inácio Lula da Silva in Brazil and with the Enron and other corporate fraud cases in the United States (Figure 5.2).[6]

Another sign of the intense turbulence that has affected emerging economies' debt markets is the high degree of correlation among different countries. It is also telling that this correlation has increased sharply during periods of distress (or sudden stops). This "contagion" effect was particularly strong during the Tequila and the Russian-LTCM crises and

---

[5] This assumes a recovery value of 75 percent and a U.S. Treasury yield of 4 percent.

[6] Long-Term Capital Management was a hedge fund whose collapse led to large losses for other financial institutions and resulted in severely disruptive conditions in global financial markets, including emerging economies' bond markets.

generated considerable debate over the extent to which it was justified by fundamental economic conditions or was purely the result of runs by irrational speculators (see, for example, Forbes and Rigobón, 2000). It is true that the underlying risks that affect emerging economies are somewhat related, in part because economies in the same region tend to maintain close trade and investment linkages with one another. Intraregional trade is more important in East Asia, where it accounts for close to one-half of total trade, than in Latin America, where it amounts to roughly 15 percent. The trade linkages are also indirect. For example, Mexico and some East Asian economies are competitors as exporters to the same third markets. Thus a crisis in East Asia, for example, that results in large currency depreciations would make the East Asian economies more competitive and have a negative effect on Mexico.

Figure 5.2
Emerging Markets and Latin American Spreads

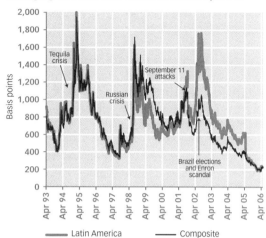

Source: Authors' calculations based on JPMorgan database from Bloomberg database.
Note: Spreads are a combination of EMBI and EMBI Plus. The Latin America index comprises the four largest debtors: Argentina, Brazil, Mexico, and Venezuela. Weights are adjusted to consider the structural break resulting from the Argentine default.

It is perhaps telling that for the sudden stop event in which contagion was the strongest, the Russian devaluation and domestic debt default of 1998, it is impossible to identify important linkages to Latin America running through trade, investment, or any other fundamental factor in the real economy. The direct and indirect relation of Russia with Latin American economies is insignificant. The overall share of Russia in the global economy is very small. And yet the Russian event triggered a large spike in emerging market bond spreads (see Figure 5.2). This event, and the contagion phenomenon more generally, raised considerable concern within the international community because, if crises are easily transmitted within and between regions, the ability of official international financial institutions to respond by providing liquidity support diminishes significantly. In fact, the consequences of the Russian crisis were so widespread that they reached some of the advanced markets themselves, with the most notorious casualty being LTCM.

There is broad consensus that the Russian contagion operated through financial markets. The financial channels of contagion are varied and subtle. The most obvious possibility is a direct connection, that is, residents of one country holding large amounts of sovereign debt or other financial assets in another country. Direct financial links, however, tend not to be very important among emerging economies. One notable exception may be the links involving Argentina and Uruguay, which resulted in a massive propagation of the Argentine financial crisis of 2001–2002 to its neighbor. A more common channel is through "common creditors" such as banks or international investors that hold claims in different emerging markets. Banks, for example, can react to losses in one emerging market economy by adopting a more conservative strategy and reducing their exposure in other emerging market economies where they have loans or investments. There may also be a more mechanical effect triggered by declines in asset prices. Leveraged investors face margin calls when their asset prices fall, which may force them to reduce their positions in other markets. Mutual funds may benchmark their returns against an emerging market bond index comprising bonds from many countries and may not want to deviate much from the index composition, or they may be constrained by their investment mandates from doing so. This means that they need to sell the whole emerging markets asset class when they want to reduce their exposure to one country.

The structure of information that is behind investors' decisions is a more subtle way in which problems in one country can be transmitted to others. Monitoring and understanding economic and political developments in each individual emerging economy involve significant costs. They may require consulting experts, and with conditions changing rapidly, the consultations would have to be frequent. At the same time, an individual emerging country may represent only a small part of a particular investor's portfolio, especially for a class of investors who are not dedicated to the emerging economies segment of the market. Under these conditions, two types of investors are likely to emerge: informed investors, who are specialists in emerging economies, and uninformed investors, who prefer to follow the actions of informed investors, as can be read from signals such as price changes and market developments. The resulting information structure is likely to generate overreaction of market prices and contagion to other emerging markets (see Calvo, 2005a, and Calvo and Mendoza, 2005). The propagation of the sellout can be further magnified when compensation of fund managers implies stiff penalties for underperforming relative to the market average; in such a case, managers have strong incentives to "herd" together. It becomes quite risky to deviate from the trends that other investors are following (see Rajan, 2005b).

The tendency toward contagion seems to have abated recently. In particular, the Argentine default of 2001 and market concerns about the outcome of the Brazilian presidential election in 2002 did not generate widespread spillovers to other borrowers. In fact, the correlations among sovereign bonds are now broadly the same as the correlations among the high-yield borrowers from different industrial sectors of the U.S. economy. Figure 5.3 calculates the average six-month correlation between all the pairs of indices of high-yield debt corresponding to 30 economic sectors, as well as the average correlation between pairs of emerging market sovereigns. As the figure shows, although correlations between emerging markets were much higher until 1999—and especially during the Tequila and the Russian-LTCM crises—they are now broadly the same as those between high-yield bonds of different industries in the United States.

The durability of the recent decline in contagion does not seem to be assured, however. In recent years, liquidity in international financial markets has been high, and this may account for across-the-board strong performance of assets. If conditions change, with the rise in interest rates in advanced markets, for example, there may be a selling off of emerging market securities and a reappearance of the contagion phenomenon. Although there is very partial and fragmented information about the positions of different classes of investors, there is no reason to believe that the structure of financial links among countries has changed substantially from what they were during past contagion episodes. In Latin America, there appear to be increases in the share of domestic institutional investors among holders of sovereign debt. Domestic institutional investors are believed to provide a stable source of demand, either by choice or to comply with existing regulations. Among international investors, highly leveraged participants like hedge funds are gaining market share, as are less specialized investment funds—the so-called crossover investors. At a more fundamental level, the low level of contagion in the most recent crises and market runs may have been a response to the fact that they had been well anticipated (Didier, Mauro, and Schmukler, 2006). Crisis episodes in Argentina and Turkey in the past few years developed gradually, and indicators such as forward exchange rates showed clear signs of anticipation months before the crises came about. Gradually developing, broadly expected crises are well understood even by the least-informed groups of investors and are not likely to generate unexpected margin calls for highly leveraged investors. This means that the requisite conditions for contagion were not prominent in recent episodes.[7]

Figure 5.3

Average Correlations among Sovereign Emerging Market Bonds and Industrial Sector Indices of U.S. High Yield Bonds

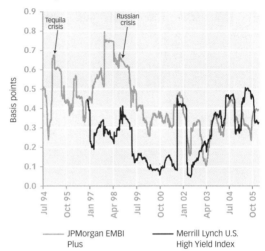

Source: Authors' calculations based on JPMorgan and Merrill Lynch databases from Bloomberg database.
Note: Figure plots the average six-month correlation in 78 country pairs of the JPMorgan EMBI Plus and 465 sector pairs of the Merrill Lynch U.S. High Yield Index. Correlation coefficients are based on daily returns of indices.

GLOBAL FINANCIAL MARKETS AND SELF-FULFILLING CRISES

The above characterization of the modern international sovereign bond market implies that global financial conditions are a substantial determinant of the borrowing costs of emerging economies. Investors' risk appetite is of course unobservable per se, but the evolution of some financial variables can provide a rough indicator of market sentiment. One variable that is commonly associated with the market attitude towards risk is the Chicago Board Options Exchange Volatility Index (VIX), which is an index of the volatility of the U.S. stock market implicit in the prices of various option contracts. Loosely speaking, higher values

---

[7] The contagion to Uruguay of the debt and financial crisis in Argentina in 2001–2002 is a special case. Although the financial linkages between the two countries were well known, there was an element of surprise in this event. Previous situations of financial distress in Argentina had caused inflows into the Uruguayan banking system from Argentine savers looking for safer alternatives, but the severity of the financial crisis caused the opposite effect on this occasion.

Figure 5.4
Emerging Market Bond Index and Chicago Board Option Exchange Volatility Index

———— Chicago Board Option Exchange Volatility Index (VIX) (right axis)

———— Emerging Market Bond Index (EMBI) (left axis)

Sources: Bloomberg database and Standard & Poor's (2006).

of the VIX imply that these options are more expensive. Because options are contracts that permit investors to hedge against large changes in the underlying asset (the U.S. stock market in this case), investors are willing to pay higher prices to obtain such protection in periods when expected volatility is higher. Figure 5.4 depicts the VIX and the Emerging Market Bond Index (EMBI) and illustrates their high correlation with one another, especially since the 1998 global financial turmoil. A similar picture obtains if one uses the spread on high-yield—or "junk"—bonds in U.S. markets as a proxy for risk aversion.

In this vein, several empirical studies have measured the importance of the risk appetite of fixed income investors and liquidity conditions in U.S. markets for the spreads of Latin American and other emerging markets over risk-free interest rates. Risk appetite is typically measured as the VIX or a high-yield index. Market liquidity is measured by the U.S. Treasury bond yield; a lower yield indicates an easier monetary stance by the Federal Reserve Board and thus more abundant liquidity in financial markets. A recent study (González Rozada and Levy Yeyati, 2006) puts the combined effect of these two global factors at about 30 percent of the total variability of emerging market spreads throughout the 1990s and at over 50 percent for the period 2000–2005. In addition to these two external factors, the contagion effect arising from events like the Mexican and Russian crises, which are controlled for separately, add considerable weight to the impact of global factors during periods of international turmoil. The effect of global financial conditions does not dissipate when longer time horizons are considered for their relationship with sovereign spreads, and in fact, it becomes stronger. This means that improving creditworthiness, for example, by reducing deficits and introducing needed reforms, has a somewhat limited effect on the risk premium that must be paid, even if global conditions are free from any major financial crisis.[8]

The temporary nature of changes in the level of financial variables can be measured by calculating their level of "mean reversion." Mean reversion measures the tendency of financial returns that are temporarily very high or low to return to average levels rather than continue to be high or low. Mean reversion would characterize a market in which bubbles, that is, divergences between market and fundamental values, often emerge, but beyond

---

[8] On the influence of global factors on emerging market yields, see also Calvo and Talvi (2005), Grandes (2003), Herrera and Perry (2002), and particularly García Herrero and Ortiz (2005).

some limit they are eliminated by market forces (Poterba and Summers, 1988). Most studies of mean reversion have focused on looking for the presence of bubbles in the stock market. Given that bonds have a maturity date and a well-defined principal value at that point, it is not possible to have a rational bubble. Just before maturity, the price of the bond cannot deviate from its principal (discounted by a small time factor), and since that value is known, so is the price of the bond a little before that, etc. Because of this, a rational bubble can never get started, in contrast to the case of open-ended securities like equity. Mean reversion in EMBI spreads would be consistent with the story that panics or sudden stops drive spreads well above fundamental values and that periods of euphoria or exuberance tend to narrow spreads excessively.

In fact, the EMBI tends to return fully to previous levels within 24 months of any sudden stop. This feature seems to be exclusive to emerging bond markets, as it is largely absent from other bond markets in the United States and is much lower in equity markets. For example, U.S. equities, as measured by the Standard & Poor's 500 index, have been found to display a certain degree of mean reversion, but this is 10 times smaller in magnitude than the EMBI's mean reversion. High-yield (junk) bonds in the United States show virtually zero mean reversion. The magnitude of the mean reversion found in the EMBI using various specifications of the length and nature of the statistical procedures is quite high—about 10 times the level found in studies of the U.S. stock market—and takes place over periods which are significantly shorter (see Borensztein and Valenzuela, 2006).

As documented in various studies, the dynamics of the emerging bond market seem to be quite different during tranquil periods and during periods of market distress. When this feature is allowed for in calculating mean reversion, a strong contrast emerges. Periods of tranquility tend to persist, while periods of turbulence show a much stronger tendency to be reversed. The same is true when the technique is applied to other bond indices such as those for high-yield bonds. Interestingly, the periods of tranquility and turbulence that the model identifies for these different indices do not always coincide, as shown in Table 5.4. The Tequila effect in 1994–1995 and the Asian crisis in 1997 did not affect high-yield markets in the United States, but the Russian crisis of 1998 did. Similarly, the NASDAQ crash in 2000 did spread to the emerging bond market (in addition to its impact in U.S. markets) but did not very significantly affect many Latin American countries on an individual basis.

Volatility and contagion are a reason for concern because they may become a bigger problem than temporary high spreads and liquidity shortages. It is possible for negative expectations to become "self-fulfilling," and what started as a more or less unwarranted market run may create a dislocation in a country's domestic economy that seriously impairs the country's repayment ability. This may happen because the international market "closure" may trigger high domestic interest rates and sharp exchange rate depreciations, especially if the country's debt is short term and international reserves are not plentiful. These may have a large negative impact on the domestic economy, especially when the banking system is vulnerable to such shocks. Sometimes, the policy response may result in deeper crises, such as when the government resorts to general deposit freezes to protect the weakest institutions, with devastating effects on economic activity. The result is that the creditworthiness of the country will be severely impaired, as the recession hurts government revenues and the burden of debt soars with the cost of bank rescue operations and the effect of the exchange rate depreciation. An initially unwarranted panic has thus

Table 5.4 Periods of Turbulence in Different Markets and Their Associated Events

Associated event	Date	U.S. high yield	EMBI	EMBI Brazil	EMBI Mexico	EMBI Venezuela
Iraqi invasion of Kuwait	1990:08	1990:08-1991:01				
Tequila crisis	1994:12		1995:01-1995:03	1995:01-1995:03	1995:09-1995:11	
Asian crisis	1997:10		1997:11	1997:11	1997:11	1997:11
Russian crisis	1998:08	1998:06-1998:10	1998:08-1998:09	1998:08-1998:09	1998:08-1998:09	1998:07-1998:09
Brazil devaluation	1999:01			1998:12-1999:01		
U.S. stock market crash	2000:12	2000:03-2000:12	2001:07	2001:04-2001:07		
September 11 attacks	2001:09	2001:06-2001:10				
U.S. stock market crash	2002:10	2002:06-2002:10				
Lula elected president	2002:10			2002:05-2002:10		

Source: Borensztein and Valenzuela (2006).

resulted in a real insolvency problem (see Calvo, Izquierdo, and Talvi, 2005, and the discussion in Chapter 11).

CREDIT RATINGS

Low credit ratings can be an important determinant of high cost and unreliable access to international bond markets. There is a fairly close relationship between the credit rating assigned to a bond by the main rating agencies and the spread over U.S. Treasury bonds that the issue pays in the markets. Although, as will be shown below, the direction of influence may run both ways—namely, an increase in spreads may sometimes prompt the rating agencies to downgrade a sovereign—there is no doubt that a bond's credit rating is an important factor in the consideration of most investors. Moreover, the rating determines the asset class in which a security is included, and this determines the group of investors that may consider including it in their portfolios. Typically, an "investment grade" rating—with which the agencies signal a security that has a low risk of going into default—qualifies an asset to be part of the portfolio of many institutional investors like insurance companies and pension funds. Some of these investors are required by regulations or their own charters or policies to restrict their holdings to investment grade issues. Thus, a sovereign that obtains an investment grade rating gains not only more favorable spreads but also a broader and more stable investor base and market access.

Emerging market economies started to seek credit ratings in the 1990s, when they started to issue bonds in the global markets once again. Before the 1990s, Standard & Poor's rated only a dozen sovereigns, almost all of them in the top (AAA) rating category. Similarly, Moody's had rated only 11 countries up to 1980, and all of them were in the investment grade range.[9] This means that there is a fairly short experience with sovereign ratings for use in observing their evolution, especially compared with the century-long corporate ratings (Moody's, 2003).

Although the ratings of some Latin American sovereigns have improved steadily in recent years, most countries still have not achieved good ratings. In fact, the broad distribution of credit ratings, shown in Table 5.5, has hardly improved since mid-2000, which is the point at which the emerging market asset class had recovered from the Russian-LTCM turbulence and had not yet been hit by another major global shock. As of June 2006, only two countries in Latin America enjoyed an investment grade rating: Chile and Mexico.

One reason why credit ratings are important is that there is a close relationship between credit ratings and spreads. Figure 5.5 displays that relationship for sovereigns, U.S. firms, and firms in emerging economies on September 1, 2005. The steeper slope of the sovereign spreads curve tends to hold regularly. It may perhaps reflect, at the low credit ratings end, the expectation of a longer and more uncertain recovery process in the case of sovereign

---

[9] Prior to the 1990s, the only "ratings" data available for emerging economies are those assigned by *Institutional Investor (II)*. *II* is a financial publication that rates sovereigns, on the basis of surveys of investors and analysts, on a scale that is broadly consistent with that of the credit-rating agencies. It is noteworthy, however, that *II*'s ratings are only a survey measure, while the rating agencies provide a professional service to bond issuers, and their ratings are a factor in investment mandates and capital requirements. Nevertheless, some studies have focused on *II* ratings (see Reinhart, Rogoff, and Savastano, 2003, and Ul Haque et al., 1996).

Table 5.5 Sovereign Ratings in Latin America

Country	2000	2003	2006
Investment grade (AAA to BBB-)	Chile	Chile	Chile
	Uruguay	Mexico	Mexico
Some uncertainty (BB+ to BB-)	Argentina	Colombia	Brazil
	Bolivia	Costa Rica	Colombia
	Colombia	El Salvador	Costa Rica
	Costa Rica	Guatemala	El Salvador
	El Salvador	Panama	Guatemala
	Mexico	Peru	Panama
	Panama		Peru
	Peru		Venezuela
High risk (B+ to B-)	Brazil	Bolivia	Argentina
	Dominican Republic	Brazil	Bolivia
	Paraguay	Dominican Republic	Dominican Republic
	Venezuela	Uruguay	Paraguay
			Uruguay
Speculative (CCC+ to D)	Ecuador	Argentina	Ecuador
		Ecuador	
		Paraguay	
		Venezuela	

Source: Standard & Poor's (2006).
Note: Data as of July of each year.

defaults. The figure suggests that sovereign ratings have a sizable impact on the cost of borrowing. At lower rating levels, a single-notch downgrade may represent 50 basis points in spread.

Although the rating agencies claim that their success in predicting sovereign defaults is comparable to that in predicting corporate defaults (Moody's, 2003), there have been some conspicuous cases of misjudgment. In the Asian crises, the rating agencies were criticized for reacting too late (Adams et al., 1998), and later for overreacting, most notably in the case of Korea (Reisen and von Maltzan, 1999; Huhne, 1998). Famously, Uruguay maintained an investment grade rating until early 2002, even after a financial crisis had already erupted in Argentina and even in Uruguay itself. Only months later, Uruguay had no option but to restructure its sovereign debt. In determining sovereign ratings, the credit-rating agencies look at a five-year horizon, evaluate a number of economic and political factors, and make a qualitative and quantitative assessment of the government's financial prospects. Yet Cantor and Packer (1996) find that eight variables explain more than 90 percent of the variance in sovereign ratings assigned by both Moody's and Standard & Poor's: per capita income, GDP growth, inflation, fiscal balance, current account balance, debt-to-export ratio, an indicator variable of advanced economy, and an indicator variable of default since 1970. And in fact, one variable (GDP per capita) explains 80 percent of the cross-country variance in credit ratings.

There is, however, no consensus among researchers on the failings of the rating agencies. Some studies have claimed that the agencies aggravate financial crises by being excessively procyclical in their ratings (Ferri, Liu, and Stiglitz, 1999). More recent research, however, concludes that ratings are in fact too sticky rather than excessively procyclical (Mora, 2004). Although cases such as Uruguay in 2002 are extreme, precipitous declines in the agencies' estimation of countries' creditworthiness are not rare. Table 5.6 shows that rating agencies' perceptions of sovereign creditworthiness can change quickly. Leaving aside the case of Venezuela, the top panel of the table displays 13 cases of defaults. In almost half of these cases (six), the rating was closer to investment grade than to default just one year before the default.[10] The *Institutional Investor* ratings of the 1980s, displayed in the bottom panel of the table, give an even starker picture. One year prior to the occurrence of default, over 90 percent of the ratings were closer to investment grade than to default. In fact, in almost 40 percent of the cases, the rating was the equivalent of investment grade in the rating agencies' scales.

There is some evidence that changes in ratings are themselves influenced to some degree by movements in spreads. Event studies show that spreads start to widen weeks before the announcement of a downgrade in ratings (Figure 5.6). In fact, there seems to be no change in spreads in the days following the announcement. In the case of upgrades, spreads also tighten weeks before the announcement, but the effect is smaller than in the case of downgrades. In part this may result from the agencies' reacting more slowly to the same news as the market, which could be expected to be the case. It is also possible that

Figure 5.5
Bond Spread by Credit Rating
(*basis points*)

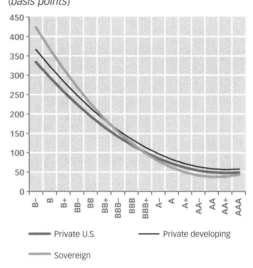

Private U.S.   Private developing

Sovereign

Source: Borensztein, Cowan, and Valenzuela (2006).
Note: As of September 1, 2005. Fitted curves are obtained via quadratic trend.

---

[10] In the case of Venezuela, the 2005 default corresponds largely to an oversight on the part of the government of a payment on an oil-price-linked bond clause that took a little too long to be corrected. Although the country did receive a "selective default" rating briefly, there was never the expectation that Venezuela would attempt to restructure the terms of its debt.

Table 5.6 Foreign Currency Sovereign Credit Ratings before Defaults

		Rating before default[a]	
Country	Year of default	One year	Two years
Rating agencies[b]			
Dominican Republic	2005	19	13
Venezuela	2005	16	17
Grenada	2004	13	13
Uruguay	2003	12	10
Nicaragua	2003	15	15
Paraguay	2003	15	15
Moldova	2002	17	16
Indonesia	2002	16	21
Argentina	2002	13	12
Ukraine	2001	17	16
Indonesia	2000	17	16
Ecuador	1999	16	14
Pakistan	1999	17	14
Russian Federation	1999	13	13
Institutional Investor[c]			
Jordan	1989	13	13
Paraguay	1986	13	13
South Africa	1985	9	9
Egypt	1984	14	11
Tanzania	1984	18	18
Brazil	1983	10	10
Chile	1983	10	9
Morocco	1983	14	13
Nigeria	1983	10	9
Peru	1983	12	11
Philippines	1983	12	12
Uruguay	1983	12	12
Argentina	1982	9	7
Dominican Republic	1982	15	14
Ecuador	1982	12	13
Mexico	1982	6	5
Panama	1982	12	11
Venezuela	1982	7	6
Pakistan	1981	16	15
Poland	1981	13	10
Romania	1981	10	9

Source: Based on Borensztein, Eichengreen, and Panizza (2006a).

[a] The rating agencies' and *Institutional Investor*'s scales were converted to a numerical scale from 1 to 22, with 1 being the highest rating and 21 the lowest nondefault rating. A rating of 10 is the lower bound for "investment grade" status.

[b] Foreign currency rating of long-term debt.

[c] Selected government defaults and reschedulings of privately held bonds and loans from Sturzenegger and Zettelmeyer (2005a).

Figure 5.6
Events Study: Rating and Outlook Changes

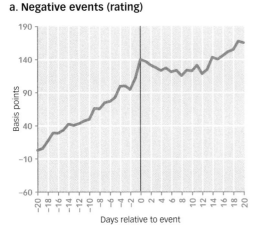

a. Negative events (rating)

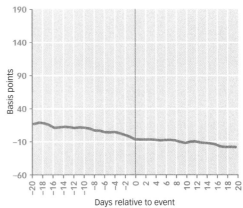

c. Positive events (rating)

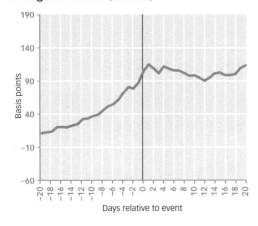

b. Negative events (outlook)

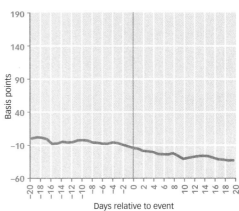

d. Positive events (outlook)

Source: González Rozada and Levy Yeyati (2006).

the movement in spreads reflects to some extent the market expectation of a downgrade or upgrade by the credit-rating agencies. However, the same anticipation of spreads holds in the case of announcements of changes in the credit outlook for a country. This type of announcement indicates that the rating agencies are studying a possible change in rating, a sort of early warning to limit the element of surprise if eventually the agencies decide to change the rating of a borrower. Thus, outlook changes should be more difficult to predict from the market than changes in rating, yet spreads tend to move just as much before changes in rating outlook as well. This suggests that the ratings actions of the agencies are themselves influenced by the market prices of a sovereign's debt as well (see González Rozada and Levy Yeyati, 2006)

Another important cost of a low sovereign credit rating arises from its significant influence on the ratings achieved by private companies and banks in the country in their international borrowing. Up to 1997, the rating agencies applied a "sovereign ceiling" to the ratings assigned to private borrowers, which meant that no firm in a particular country could obtain a rating higher than that of the sovereign. Although the policy has been progressively relaxed, sovereign credit risk continues to be a key consideration in the assessment of the credit standing of banks and corporations. The main argument is that governments facing a situation of financial distress or default may force private sector defaults by imposing exchange controls and other restrictive measures. Although, post-1997, the sovereign rating is no longer an absolute ceiling, the influence of the sovereign rating is still significant. Borensztein, Cowan, and Valenzuela (2006) show that over the past 10 years, 79 percent of emerging market corporations received a rating lower than the sovereign, 15 percent received the same rating as the sovereign, and only 5 percent received a rating higher than the sovereign. In banks, 88 percent of the sample received a rating lower than the sovereign, 10 percent received the same rating as the sovereign, and just 2 percent received a rating higher than the sovereign. The study concludes that, after indicators of creditworthiness of the firms and macroeconomic conditions in the country are controlled for, sovereign ratings are a significant factor affecting private ratings and can imply an onerous burden for private borrowers in emerging markets. On average, a two-notch slip in sovereign rating implies roughly a one-notch decrease in private ratings. For banks, the effect is even larger. For a prime corporation operating in the average emerging market economy, this effect can add 100–200 basis points to the cost of borrowing. The effect varies across countries and time, as there is a stronger effect in developing countries and prior to 1998. It is also asymmetrical: sovereign downgrades have a somewhat stronger impact than upgrades, while the impact of changes in sovereign rating on private ratings is stronger if the private rating was approaching the sovereign ceiling in the previous period.

Has Volatility Abated?

Emerging market spreads have been on a downward trend in the past few years. As of May 2006, the EMBI was at an all-time low since its inception in the 1990s. With modest financing needs—thanks to strong fiscal positions—governments have an easy time finding willing investors for their new placements. Under these favorable conditions, governments have been able to begin improving the profile of their obligations and increasing the share of domestic-currency-denominated instruments, which for the first time are also attracting the interest of international investors. Private corporations and banks in Latin America are also coming to international debt markets in record numbers. Although market volatility and spreads increased in May 2006 under the perception that U.S. interest rates were going to be raised more than previously expected, the increase in emerging market spreads was modest compared to that in previous similar episodes. Has market dysfunctionality been cured, or is this only another temporary period of calm before the next storm breaks?

Whether the current favorable trends will constitute a durable change depends on the nature of the forces supporting the current environment. Has there been a change towards a more stable investor base for emerging markets? Is the increase in investors' appetite for local currency instruments a reflection of a desire for portfolio diversification or merely the response to a temporary profit opportunity? Have fiscal policies and debt management policies in Latin America benefited from the lessons of the turbulent 1990s, and have critical vulnerabilities been reduced?

There are some signs that the environment has changed so as not to be conducive to sudden stops. Policies have strengthened in the Latin American countries, indicating that the experience of past crises has not been in vain. Against the backdrop of strong economic performance, primary surpluses have increased significantly in many countries, supporting a reduction in debt-to-GDP ratios and improving solvency positions. Countries hold much larger reserves than a decade

Figure 5.7
Current Account Balances in Latin America

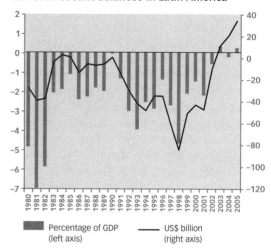

Percentage of GDP (left axis)   US$ billion (right axis)

Sources: World Bank, *World Development Indicators*, and IMF, *International Finance Statistics*.
Note: "Latin America" comprises Argentina, Brazil, Chile, Colombia, Costa Rica, Dominican Republic, Ecuador, El Salvador, Mexico, Panama, Peru and Uruguay.

ago and less short-term debt, which reduces their external financing needs and allows them to be better prepared to face unexpected shocks. The region is also taking advantage of favorable terms of trade and strong foreign demand and showing a steady improvement in current account balances (Figure 5.7). Argentina, Brazil, and especially Venezuela are enjoying large current account surpluses. (Venezuela is excluded from the calculations underlying the figure because its current account surplus of 20 percent of GDP makes it a significant outlier.) Although many firms and economic sectors may still be dependent on foreign financing, a current account surplus in a country implies, in principle, that the country as an aggregate could satisfy all of its financial needs domestically.

There is also some evidence of a progressive process of learning in which investors are increasingly able to better assess risks on the basis of fundamentals and differentiate countries on a firmer basis. It should be recalled that when the emerging bond market came into existence in the 1990s, economic information was harder to come by and often less accurate. Some of the most important currency crises of the 1990s came as complete surprises, in part owing to the lack of information—or the presence of inaccurate information—on the level of international reserves. Today, much more economic and financial information is available about each country, and governments make an effort to disseminate it through investor relations offices and other means of communication. This helps investors better assess risks and differentiate among countries.

The increasing sophistication of investors is also reflected in their demand for local currency instruments, inflation-linked bonds, and the recently issued Argentine GDP-linked unit. Since 2003 three Latin American countries (Brazil, Colombia, and Uruguay) have placed domestic-currency-denominated government bonds on foreign markets for the first time. In the private sector, several Brazilian and Mexican banks and corporations, among others, have been able to float bonds denominated in domestic currency abroad as well (see Box 2.4). These bonds are in local currency, as noted, and are reasonably long term (they mature between 2010 and 2016). These are very important first steps toward creating a more resilient profile of external debt. The question is whether they can be followed with further issues and at costs that do not make them prohibitive. Entrenched expectations of inflation and weak creditor rights (a combination of weak contract enforcement and the presence or expectation of capital controls) have often resulted in high risk premiums on domestic-currency-denominated debt, and governments have often turned to foreign currency borrowing because of the high cost of borrowing in domestic currency.

Attracting international investors to domestic currency instruments may provide the opportunity to lower the steep cost of such instruments and extend their maturity. In Colombia's November 2004 issue, primary spreads were 20 to 50 basis points below those on comparable domestic bonds (Tovar, 2005).[11] In Brazil's case, the international bond was a 10-year-maturity, fixed rate instrument, and the government simply does not have recourse to this kind of financing in the domestic market on a reliable basis. Domestically placed Brazilian *reais* bonds are typically floating rate instruments that adjust with the overnight rate; the yield on Brazil's international bond was 13 percent, while the overnight interest rate has fluctuated between 16 and 20 percent in Brazil, over the past two years. International investors may find *reais* bonds issued under New York governing law and settled in U.S. dollars more attractive as a result of their lower risk of being subject to capital controls and other taxes (Amato, 2006).

There are also increasing opportunities for countries to issue new types of instruments that provide a measure of insurance against various risks that affect their economies. The active market that is developing on the Argentine GDP-linked unit is one indicator of such opportunities. Small amounts of this type of instrument were issued before, most notably in many Brady deals, but generally failed to attract any trading interest. But investor interest in this type of instrument seems to be on the rise, as also shown by some more exotic instruments. Recently, the World Food Program, a UN agency, sold futures on Ethiopian rains, effectively obtaining an insurance policy that pays the agency a sum of money in case of drought. In this way, the agency has access to liquid funds to distribute among farmers faster than is possible through traditional aid channels.[12] In another interesting example, pension funds in England have sold "longevity bonds" that insure them against an increase in their liabilities arising from demographic changes. And Mexico has issued "catastrophe" bonds that provide coverage in case of earthquakes of large magnitude in the most affected areas. It should be noted, however, that investor willingness is only half of the requirement for developing country insurance instruments. Political problems and the relative complexity of the operations tend to be serious obstacles. Commodity prices, for example, have a major impact on the economies of many emerging countries; although futures markets are fairly

---

[11] Uruguay did not benefit from lowering borrowing costs on international markets, presumably because its issue took place under the difficult conditions of a debt restructuring.

[12] *New York Times*, March 7, 2006.

available at certain maturities, countries have nonetheless made little use of them (Chapter 14 discusses these issues).

It is believed that the investor base in emerging market bonds has been widening since 2003 to include a broader group of dedicated investors, such as retail investors from Asia and Middle Easterners with "petrodollars." Investors such as pension funds and insurance companies have also been in a process of broadening their portfolios by incorporating new asset classes, and now it seems to be the turn of emerging market debt. These "strategic accounts" are believed to follow a buy-and-hold policy and thus provide a more stable source of demand. These developments may contribute to reducing market volatility for two reasons. First, a more diverse investor base would contribute to stability, because investors who follow similar strategies tend to react in the same way to news of economic shocks. Second, investors with a longer horizon are more likely to focus on the economic fundamentals in the borrowing countries rather than chasing current trends.

But there are also reasons to be cautious in interpreting the current situation too favorably. For starters, the improvement in fundamentals, while noticeable, is quite difficult to characterize empirically. In particular, while economic fundamentals are undoubtedly stronger throughout the region, their strength is in great measure due to external factors, such as terms-of-trade improvement and growth in the global economy, as well as abundant liquidity and relatively high investor risk appetite. Indeed, a large fraction of the decline in spreads (and yields) can be attributed to these positively correlated global drivers rather than to more robust improvements in economic fundamentals.

In fact, the current level of the EMBI spreads appears to be lower than could be predicted based on current conditions, applying a fairly standard model to explain spreads (Figure 5.8). Using a set of standard variables measuring macroeconomic conditions in the borrowing country and a few variables that characterize the situation of global financial markets, the model predicts spreads as indicated by the shaded area in the figure.[13] Actual spreads have been significantly lower than predicted over the past three years, by as much as 200 basis points. Furthermore, if one assumes that favorable global conditions will not prevail and that global variables will have values equal to their sample average instead of current values, the discrepancy is even larger (Figure 5.9). While the model used for this exercise has not been tested extensively and no claim is made about its predictive accuracy, it does represent a fairly standard approach to explaining spreads. A similar exercise that was conducted in 1996 also found that spreads were "excessively" low, and this was just months before the Asian crises (Cline and Barnes, 1997).

In this context, some question whether the policy framework has improved to take full advantage of favorable external conditions. If the current confluence of high export prices, strong demand in the global economy, and low interest rates were to alter for the worse, there would be no guarantee that Latin American economies could meet such a challenge without difficulty.

---

[13] The domestic variables used in the regression are international reserves, inflation, the current account deficit, external debt, total public debt, openness of the economy, fiscal deficit, and recent appreciation of the real exchange rate. The external variables used in the regression are an index of volatility in financial markets (the VIX), the spread on U.S. high-yield bonds, the interest rate on U.S. Treasury bonds, and the terms of trade.

As for the widening of the international investor base, it has been noted that, in addition to strategic investors, hedge funds—whose assets have grown exponentially in recent years—seem to be gaining in importance in emerging market debt markets. Hedge funds pursue investment strategies to take advantage of market anomalies and in the process contribute to making such anomalies smaller, which should be considered a positive factor for market stability. But hedge funds usually hold highly leveraged positions. This implies that, in a downturn, they may need to liquidate their holdings immediately, which may turn a market downturn into a full-fledged crisis. Memories of the impact of LTCM's collapse in the altered markets of the post-Asian and Russian crises certainly suggest caution in regard to large hedge fund activity.

More generally, there may be doubts as to whether international investors' current appetite for local currency instruments is permanent and whether corporations will follow where governments lead. Ample liquidity has made for unusually favorable conditions for emerging economies on global markets; if central banks continue to raise interest rates and drain that liquidity and there is a flight to quality on the part of investors, it is not clear that an appetite for Latin American bonds will in fact survive.

The massive growth in credit derivatives has introduced a new element that can change the nature of bond markets in ways that are still not fully understood. Credit default swaps (CDSs), for example—securities that insure against the event of default in an underlying bond—have grown to the point that, although direct data do not exist, such

Figure 5.8
Predicted and Actual Spreads, Latin America and the Caribbean

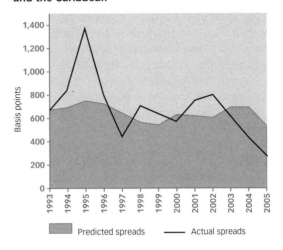

Source: Authors' calculations based on JPMorgan database from Bloomberg database.

Figure 5.9
Predicted and Actual Spreads with Average External Conditions, Latin America and the Caribbean

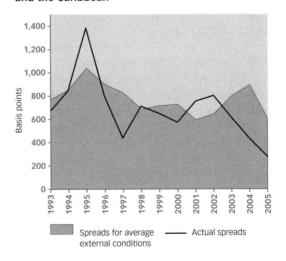

Source: Authors' calculations based on JPMorgan database from Bloomberg database.

credit derivatives have been estimated to amount to about 50 percent of the face value of emerging markets' international debt securities.[14] The purchaser of CDSs pays an annual premium to the seller and, in the case of default, can sell the underlying bond and receive the full face value from the insurance provider. But the buyer of the CDS does not need to own the bond, and thus this derivative instrument provides a simple, low-cost method of "shorting" a bond. If an investor has a negative view of the debt of a certain borrower, he or she can purchase CDSs on the underlying bond. If the investor's expectations prove correct, the spreads on the underlying bond will widen, and the annual rate on the CDS will likewise increase. The investor can sell the position for a profit at that point or enter an offsetting CDS transaction, assuming the opposite side this time. This means that the volume of credit derivatives could increase out of proportion to the existing underlying bonds and that tracking who is assuming what risks may become very difficult for a financial markets regulator. At the other end, the seller of insurance can take a highly leveraged position by obtaining a rate of return comparable to that of the underlying bond but without needing to disburse the money that would have been necessary to buy the bond.

The sharp growth in the CDS market could be a positive development in providing for a better risk distribution and more complete markets. Institutions like banks or other investors can more easily adjust the degree of exposure that they wish to have against certain credit risks. But with a relatively new and complex instrument—the CDS market on U.S. corporate debt, for example, did not take off until the late 1990s—there is always the risk that some investors will take large positions without understanding them very well and that a shock may cause the market to unravel. A scenario could arise in which conditions turn unexpectedly for the worse in the underlying country, and institutions that have taken highly leveraged positions will incur large losses that they may be unable to absorb.

---

[14] The IMF reports rough estimates in the range of US$300–500 billion in face value CDSs, while the outstanding stock of international debt securities—public and private—of emerging economies is just above US$800 billion (IMF, 2006c).

CHAPTER 6 | The Role of Multilateral Lending

SOVEREIGN DEBT OWED TO PRIVATE CREDITORS grew substantially over the 1990s, but official debt (multilateral and bilateral lending) remains significant—and constitutes more than 40 percent of the total sovereign external developing country sovereign debt (Figure 6.1).[1] Moreover, multilateral debt, which accounts for 28 percent of total developing country sovereign external debt, remains important not only for its sheer size, but also because different theories regarding the role of official creditors, and multilaterals in particular, suggest that their influence extends well beyond the cash they provide. Hence, while it is a commonplace to note the declining market share of multilaterals in capital flows, they remain important players for sovereign debt management.

Multilateral lenders consist of the International Monetary Fund, the World Bank, the regional development banks (RDBs, which include the Inter-American Development Bank), and other smaller institutions. The multilaterals each have different mandates in accordance with their charters or articles of agreement, and this affects their lending policies. For example, the IMF's mission of supporting adjustment to external payments imbalances should imply a specific pattern of lending flows, heavily influenced by the external financial position of its member countries. The World Bank seeks to enhance development in lower-income countries and to eradicate world poverty, and thus its flows should be determined by longer-term strategies and to a lesser extent by current financing needs. The RDBs each have a particular set of objectives closer in spirit to those of the World Bank. The World Bank Group and RDBs including the IDB also lend to the private sector, an area

Figure 6.1
Structure of Developing Country Public External Debt

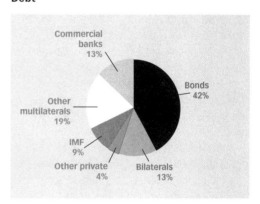

Source: World Bank, *Global Development Finance*.

---

[1] This figure is for 2004, using the *Global Development Finance* definitions for long-term public sector debt, including IMF lending. Concessional lending is excluded. Naturally, multilateral financing is even more important in those countries that do not have market access and in which concessional finance is more significant.

which is growing in importance, but the majority of the business of most multilateral development banks remains sovereign lending.[2]

Multilateral lenders offer concessional finance and aid as well as finance at nonconcessional rates—although in general these rates are still lower than market rates paid on commercial debt. Concessional finance is offered to countries in accordance with particular conditions related to per capita income and the level of national development. Official lending also includes bilateral lending through national development agencies such as the United States Agency for International Development (USAID), the United Kingdom's Department for International Development (DFID), and Germany's Kreditanstalt für Wiederaufbau (KfW) and Deutsche Investitions- und Endtwicklungsgesellschaft (DEG). The majority of this debt is concessional in nature. However, bilateral lending also includes government-guaranteed loans extended by export credit agencies such as Hermes (Germany), Companía Española de Seguros y Créditos a la Exportación (CESCE, Spain), Coface (France), and the United States Export-Import Bank. Lending by these agencies may be nonconcessional. For example, export credit guarantees granted by these institutions to developing country governments or to private borrowers with official backing are included in sovereign lending and may be on nonconcessional terms.

BROAD TRENDS IN SOVEREIGN EXTERNAL DEBT

Total long-term developing country sovereign external debt (excluding that financed by the IMF) rose sharply during the 1990s but since the late 1990s has been flat at about $1 trillion (Figure 6.2) (see Chapter 2 for a discussion of the evolution of external debt in Latin America). Sovereign external debt held by private creditors in the 1980s was largely held by commercial banks, but through the 1990s, in part as a result of the Brady restructurings and then through subsequent new issues, debt in the form of bonds grew substantially. Bonds only represented some 6 percent of sovereign debt owed to private creditors in 1989 but now represent as much as 46 percent of total sovereign external long-term nonconcessional debt.[3]

At the same time, within nonconcessional debt it is notable that multilateral debt has increased relative to bilateral debt in recent times. In 1991, bilateral nonconcessional debt accounted for about 20 percent of total debt, and it reached a peak of about 25 percent in 1994–1995 with the financial support offered to alleviate the Mexican crisis. It has now fallen back to about 14 percent. Multilateral debt represented only 11 percent of the total in 1984, was about 18 percent of the total in 1991, and has now risen to about 21 percent of the total. In the last decade or so, then, multilateral debt has lost market share relative to private debt but has gained it relative to bilateral debt, and the net effect has been if anything a slight rise in market share (the trends are roughly identical when Latin America is considered, as op-

---

[2] In fact the European Bank for Reconstruction and Development is the only multilateral that principally lends to the private sector.

[3] In this chapter, whether or not debt is external is defined by residence, in keeping with the GDF definitions, and hence the definition in this chapter is different from the one used in Chapter 2. The idea here is to compare multilaterals (which by definition are nonresidents of the countries to which they lend) and nonresident private sector agents.

Figure 6.2
External Sovereign Debt Stocks

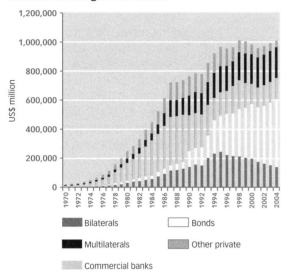

US$ million

- Bilaterals
- Multilaterals
- Commercial banks
- Bonds
- Other private

Source: World Bank, *Global Development Finance*.

posed to all developing countries; see Chapter 2).

Country recipients of multilateral finance are highly concentrated. The top 10 recipients accounted for 58 percent of the stock of multilateral lending as of 2004. However, these countries also accounted for about 69 percent of recipient GDP. But within this group there are very different cases. China, for example, accounts for 30 percent of recipient GDP but only 7.4 percent of the stock of multilateral lending.[4] And India accounts for 13 percent of recipient GDP and only 3.5 percent of multilateral lending. By contrast, the remaining 8 countries in the top 10 account for 47 percent of multilateral lending but only 25 percent of recipient GDP.[5] While these 8 countries then appear to account for a disproportionate amount of multilateral debt stocks according to this measure (and China and India too little), it is interesting to note that they also account for 51 percent of external private sector lending to recipient sovereigns.

Considering Latin America specifically, the concentration of multilateral finance mirrors the size of recipient economies more closely. The largest seven economies in the region accounted for 90 percent of recipient GDP and received 80 percent of the stock of multilateral lending as of 2004. Chile is something of an exception, accounting for 4 percent of recipient GDP but receiving only 1 percent of multilateral lending. The stock of multilateral financing also mirrors closely that of external private financing, with the seven largest economies accounting for some 87 percent of total private external lending to the region.

Figure 6.3 illustrates the importance of multilateral financing in Latin America (panel a) and the importance of concessional finance within multilateral finance (panel b) as of 2004. Panel (a) shows that the World Bank tends to provide a large share of lending to the large countries in the region, and the RDBs concentrate more on the smaller countries. For the largest seven countries, the World Bank provides 39 percent of multilateral finance, ranging from 9 percent in Venezuela to 56 percent in Mexico.[6] For the smaller Latin American and Caribbean countries, the World Bank's average market share of multilateral lending is 24 percent, with the range from 4 percent in Barbados to 51 percent in Haiti.

---

[4] GDP at "long-term" exchange rates (purchasing-power parity) is used here; this makes China an even larger economy in terms of total recipient GDP.

[5] The other 8 countries are Argentina, Brazil, Colombia, Indonesia, Mexico, Peru, Russia, and Turkey.

[6] This is a simple average; a weighed average would yield a larger value.

Figure 6.3
Multilateral Debt Composition for LAC

a. Multilateral debt
(percentage of total external debt)

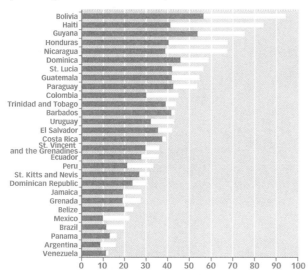

b. Multilateral concessional debt
(percentage of total multilateral debt)

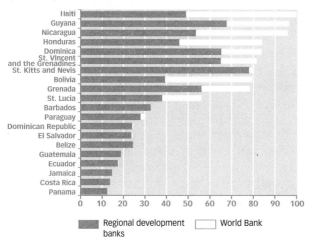

Source: World Bank, *Global Development Finance*.
Note: Data refer to 2004 stocks. Countries are ordered by nonconcessional multilateral debt as a share of total external debt (panel a) and by concessional multilateral debt as a share of concessional plus nonconcessional debt (panel b). "Regional development banks" include the IDB and other multilateral and intergovernmental agencies.

Multilateral finance is particularly important for the poorer countries of the region, including Bolivia, Haiti, and Guyana, and less important for countries such as Venezuela, Argentina, Panama, Brazil, and Mexico. And for those countries in which multilateral finance is particularly important, concessional finance tends to be an important component of multilateral lending. In fact, total concessional finance (to all developing countries) increased considerably over the 1980s and jumped further in 2003 to reach the current stock of about US$450 billion (Figure 6.4). Note that the majority of concessional finance comes from bilateral donors—about 62 percent in 2004—although multilaterals have been gaining market share. In 1990, bilaterals accounted for about 75 percent of the stock of concessional financing, and the figure was 80 percent in 1980. As Figure 6.5 shows, in Latin America, concessional finance peaked in dollar terms in 1995 at just under US$40 billion. Again, multilaterals have increased their market share considerably vis-à-vis bilaterals since the early 1990s, with that share reaching 44 percent in 2004 (debt relief may affect these figures significantly).[7]

There is a small literature on the multilaterals and official lenders more generally. A survey of Econlit (a comprehensive elec-

---

[7] The issue of debt relief is discussed further in Chapter 10.

Figure 6.4
Concessional Lending by Bilaterals and Multilaterals to All Developing Countries

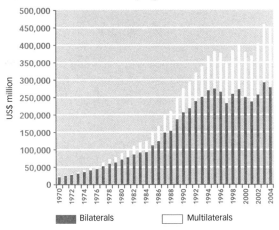

■ Bilaterals ☐ Multilaterals

Source: World Bank, *Global Development Finance*.
Note: Concessional debt is defined as loans with an original grant element of 25 percent or more.

Figure 6.5
Concessional Lending by Bilaterals and Multilaterals in LAC

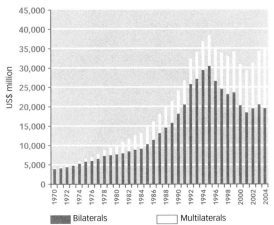

■ Bilaterals ☐ Multilaterals

Source: World Bank, *Global Development Finance*.
Note: Concessional debt is defined as loans with an original grant element of 25 percent or more.

tronic catalogue of papers published in economic journals) reveals some 924 references to the IMF from 1969 to the present; about 52 percent of all references to the international financial institutions are about the IMF.[8] However, the catalogue contains only 100 references in all to the regional development banks. In fact, there is almost no research on what makes multilateral lenders different or special or on how they may differ from private lenders or bilateral lenders.[9] And hence from this point on, the chapter focuses on multilateral lenders, specifically the multilateral development banks, excluding IMF lending.

DIFFERENCES BETWEEN MULTILATERAL AND PRIVATE LENDERS

What makes multilateral lending different from private lending? First and foremost, multilaterals and private sector lenders have different objectives. The private sector is motivated by profits, whereas multilateral lenders have a general objective of promoting development and social welfare in the countries that borrow from them. This may lead multilaterals to lend more in support of development projects, to lend in riskier environments, and to lend more in hard times relative to private lenders. This characterization also supports the view that multilaterals may act countercyclically, while it is likely that private lenders would be procyclical (Ratha, 2001).

---

[8] There are some 782,000 references in Econlit, so the papers on the IMF account for about 0.1 percent.

[9] The International Financial Institutions Research Site (www.wellesley.edu/Economics/IFI) is a useful resource for literature on multilaterals.

Second, it has been argued that multilateral lending has a greater potential to become a victim of political influence than does private lending. Most multilaterals are governed by boards of directors controlled by the richest countries.[10] This composition may be reflected in lending priorities. Barro and Lee (2005) suggest that IMF loan frequency is affected by country voting rights in the IMF and the alignment of countries with the United States in terms of voting patterns in the UN assembly and trade patterns. This analysis is extended in Bobba (2004), which also finds support for politics in IMF lending. Faini and Grilli (2004) argue that the pattern of World Bank and IMF lending is affected by shareholders' commercial relations.

Third, from the standpoint of the borrower, multilateral loans may be considered more costly in terms of red tape and conditionality (when the borrower sees the latter as a burden) but cheaper in terms of the interest rate charged. Borrowing from a multilateral generally involves detailed discussions about the intended use of the funds, conditions regarding promised economic reforms or other matters, and extended negotiations on many details of both the loan and possibly the macroeconomic environment.[11] On the other hand, a bond may have a higher interest rate than a loan from a multilateral, and while there are certainly administrative and legal costs associated with a bond issue that have to be paid, these may be less demanding in terms of time of senior officials. As a consequence, when countries have access to relatively inexpensive private funds, for example, in periods of abundant global liquidity, officials may prefer to borrow from the private sector, but when conditions are less favorable and private sector interest rate spreads rise, the additional red tape and conditionality is worth enduring to obtain the lower costs associated with borrowing from multilaterals. In the limit, in times of severe market dislocation, multilateral funds may be the only ones available.

Fourth, it has been argued that an important difference between a private lender and a multilateral is the structure of information (Rodrik, 1995). Information problems have been stressed as explanations of both excessive private lending and sudden stops and—potentially—enhanced sensitivity to fundamentals on the part of private lenders.[12] A close relative to these information issues is coordination problems between individual lenders. This may give rise to such crises as multiple equilibria phenomena, as in the classic models of bank runs. Multilaterals may be presumed to be exempt from such behavior.

A fifth difference is seniority. Multilateral institutions enjoy the status of a preferred creditor, which grants them legal priority over private creditors. (Note that this does not extend, in general, to bilateral official loans.) The interaction between official and private debts in times of debtor distress is, however, a complex one, as official loans are usually made available at such times, while short-term private financing may be withdrawn (Jeanne and Zettelmeyer, 2001; Demirgüç-Kunt and Fernández-Arias, 1992).

---

[10] Exceptions include the IDB and Andean Development Corporation (CAF).

[11] Conditionality may act similarly to covenants in a private sector loan contract, potentially increasing the probability of repayment, or promoting the development agenda of the multilateral—perhaps solving a political coordination problem in the recipient country or allowing reform to take place where reform involves up-front costs and longer-run payoffs.

[12] See Kletzer (1984) on the possibility of lending booms (and busts) and Calvo (1998) and Calvo and Mendoza (2000) on enhanced sensitivity to fundamentals.

The preceding discussion suggests that multilateral and private flows are likely to affect each other. An attractive feature of multilateral lending is that it may be catalytic, namely, that it may provide incentives for private investors to lend to the country as well. Rodrik (1995) suggests that multilaterals may have better information on the economic fundamentals in a particular borrowing country and rationalizes their lending as "putting their money where their mouth is." In the absence of such lending, statements from the multilaterals regarding the good health of a particular economy may not be considered credible. Multilateral lending is then seen as a signal to enhance the generally poor information available to private lenders.[13] An alternative view that has not been explored in the existing literature is that causality may run in the opposite direction. That is, private flows may affect the amount of multilateral flows that follow in later years. Two theories that support this alternative are as follows. The first is that a negative effect of private flows on multilateral flows could be due to the fact that countries that obtain ample private finance graduate from multilateral lending and hence should see the share of multilateral lending in total lending diminish over time. A second theory, which would instead predict a positive correlation between private and multilateral flows, might be that countries attract private flows precisely because they have enacted reforms that also attract multilateral interest. A third, more political view might be that countries that are borrowers on private markets, and hence are highly integrated into world financial markets, have greater negotiating power or have become "too big to fail" and hence also attract more multilateral financing, especially when times are hard.

MODELING MULTILATERAL LENDING

The foregoing discussion suggests a set of interesting questions: do multilaterals lend to the same countries as the private sector, and if not, what might explain the differences? Is multilateral lending explained by economic variables: do countries graduate from multilateral lending such that private lending is a substitute for multilateral, or are the two lending sources complements, and does multilateral lending decline as GDP per capita rises? Is multilateral lending pro- or countercyclical, and does GDP per capita matter for nonconcessional multilateral lending? Is multilateral lending influenced by political factors? What happens to multilateral lending when countries default? In times when countries have access to private finance, does demand for multilateral lending decline as world interest rates fall?

The group of four graphs in Figure 6.6 illustrates multilateral and private flows to developing countries worldwide over two time periods. Panel (a) illustrates that multilateral flows rose substantially after 1976 as per capita GDP growth fell, reaching a peak in 1983 when per capita growth fell to a low of just over 1 percent in developing countries. Panel (b) shows a similar pattern in the 1990s. Multilateral flows rose in 1992 and peaked in 1993, while per capita GDP growth fell to a low in 1992 and then recovered strongly beginning the next year. In the remainder of the 1990s, growth remained high and multilateral flows low, although

---

[13] However, using a panel vector autoregression framework, Powell, Ratha, and Mohapatra (2002) find mixed evidence that multilateral flows (IMF plus World Bank plus RDBs) stimulate private flows. A second catalytic role of multilaterals might be to coordinate private sector lenders. Morris and Shin (2003) and Corsetti, Pesenti, and Roubini (2001) focus on the potential role of the IMF in this regard. Mody and Saravia (2003) attempt to test whether there is evidence of IMF programs' being catalytic. They find that there is no general evidence in favor of a catalytic effect but that if an IMF program is extended before fundamentals have deteriorated too much, and if reform looks likely, then IMF programs may spur private sector lending.

there is substantial volatility in the series. At the end of the time series depicted in the panel, in 2003, per capita GDP growth picks up again, and multilateral flows fall.

Panels (c) and (d) of Figure 6.6 illustrate private sector sovereign lending flows over the period. As the panels show, private flows are much more procyclical than multilateral flows in the same period. In the period covered in panel (c), private flows fall sharply as growth falls, although they do not pick up as growth recovers, surely reflecting the fact that many countries, especially in Latin America, were in default over this period. In panel (d), covering the 1990s, private flows rose strongly as growth increased. Going beyond this graphical analysis is complicated by the dynamic nature of loans, as a loan extended in one year has consequences for future flows and for future stocks. Fernández-Arias and Powell (2006) use dynamic panel techniques designed to handle this dynamic nature. Their main findings in regard to the factors influencing patterns of multilateral financing can be summarized as follows (Figure 6.7):[14]

Figure 6.6
Multilateral and Private Sovereign Debt Net Flows

a. Multilateral flows (1976–1989)

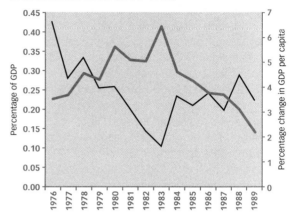

b. Multilateral flows (1990–2003)

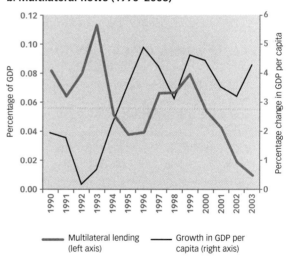

▬▬ Multilateral lending (left axis)   ▬▬ Growth in GDP per capita (right axis)

---

[14] In Fernández-Arias and Powell's study, the dependent variable (or variable that the regressions attempt to explain) is the stock of multilateral lending, and the explanatory variables include the stock of private sector lending as a percentage of GDP, economic variables such as growth and the fiscal deficit, and political variables such as whether a particular recipient country is politically aligned with the United States, measured using voting patterns in the UN General Assembly. The short-term U.S. interest rate is included as a measure of world liquidity, and a variable is also defined to indicate whether a particular recipient country is in default with private creditors. The great advantage of using panel techniques is the ability to control for factors that are common across time for a single country (so-called country fixed effects) and factors that are common across countries for a single moment in time (known as time effects). See Fernández-Arias and Powell (2006) for technical details. In brief, the analysis employs the Blundell-Bond estimator, which estimates a system including an equation in levels and a second equation in first-differences, instrumenting variables that are considered endogenous.

c. Private flows (1976–1989)

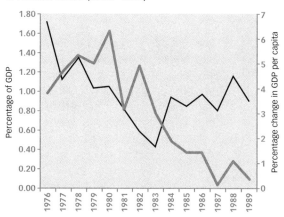

d. Private flows (1990–2003)

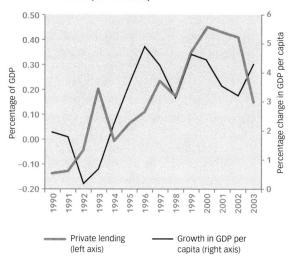

Private lending (left axis)

Growth in GDP per capita (right axis)

Source: World Bank, *Global Development Finance*.

1. Lower per capita GDP growth is associated with larger multilateral lending, suggesting that multilaterals' financing flows are countercyclical.
2. There is some mild support for the notion that countries that are more politically aligned with the United States receive a higher share of multilateral loans as a percentage of GDP, but the coefficient is only marginally statistically significant.
3. There is no support for the idea that closer economic ties to the United States bring about higher multilateral lending.
4. Countries that receive more private sector lending also receive more multilateral finance.[15] Hence, there is no evidence of "graduation" in these estimates, in the sense that the results indicate that multilateral lending and private lending have been complements, rather than substitutes.
5. The coefficient on the indicator for being in default is highly significant, suggesting that countries in default, and hence lacking access to private markets, receive more multilateral finance.
6. In nondefault periods, when U.S. interest rates rise, countries appear to draw more multilateral financing, indicating that when countries do have access to private markets, the opportunity cost of borrowing on such markets becomes an im-

[15] While it is likely that countries that attract private sector funding by implementing reforms such as privatization attract both forms of finance at the same time, the econometric technique controls for this possible channel and does not support such an explanation. A second interpretation is that countries with large private loans outstanding have more bargaining power or are considered "too big to fail" and hence attract greater multilateral finance.

Figure 6.7
Explaining Multilateral Lending

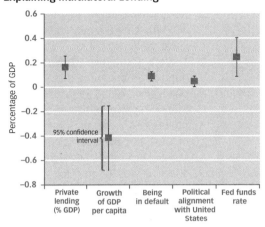

Source: Authors' calculations based on data from World Bank, *Global Development Finance.*
Note: Blocks indicate the estimated long-run marginal effects of one additional unit of independent variable (horizontal axis) on dependent variable (multilateral lending (% GDP)).

Figure 6.8
Differences between Multilateral and Private Lending

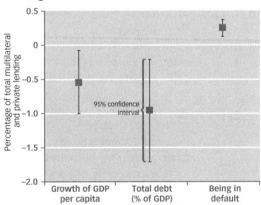

Source: Authors' calculations based on data from World Bank, *Global Development Finance*.
Note: Blocks indicate the estimated long-run marginal effect of one additional unit of independent variable (horizontal axis) on dependent variable (difference between multilateral disbursements (% GDP) and private disbursements (% GDP)).

portant determinant of the choice of financing source. As world interest rates fall, countries borrow less from multilaterals.

The preceding analysis provides salient information about patterns in multilateral lending, but it still does not answer the question, how is multilateral lending different from private lending? If multilaterals behave like private creditors, then the explanatory variables should affect both sources of lending in the same way. Any deviation from such a pattern would then be suggestive of a differential effect of the explanatory variables. To filter out commonalities, Fernández-Arias and Powell (2006) conduct an analysis of the *difference* in lending shares of private and official creditors. Figure 6.8 illustrates the main results. The negative coefficient on the indicator of GDP growth suggests that multilaterals are more countercyclical than private creditors in their lending. There is also a negative coefficient on total external debt, indicating that as debt rises, multilaterals tend to lend less than the private sector. However, the positive coefficient on the private default variable indicates that multilateral financing is made available when countries do not have access to private creditors.[16]

---

[16] An intriguing result not illustrated in the figure is that multilateral amortizations appear with a positive sign, whereas those involving the private sector appear with a negative one. This suggests that multilateral disbursements (relative to private) rise when multilateral amortizations increase but decrease relative to private when private amortizations rise. It is also found that countries obtain more multilateral finance relative to private when the fiscal balance is more negative (higher deficit) or inflation is higher, but these effects are not significant

ARE MULTILATERALS CATALYTIC?

If multilaterals have an information advantage over smaller, uncoordinated private lenders, multilateral lending may provide a "seal of approval" type of signaling effect (Rodrik, 1995). Fernández-Arias and Powell (2006) test this idea by examining whether private lending flows are affected by multilateral flows and a set of other explanatory variables (Figure 6.9).[17] They find evidence that multilateral flows do indeed crowd-in private flows. The lagged multilateral flow variable in their study is statistically significant with a positive coefficient, although the significance level varies in alternative specifications. One possibility is that the positive coefficient arises from waves of privatization or liberalization reforms and hence higher inflows of both private and multilateral money. However, introducing indicator variables for such effects does not change the results, and the indicators themselves are not significant. Growth also has a positive coefficient, suggesting that private flows are procyclical, and being in default has a negative coefficient, highlighting the previously discussed differences with respect to multilaterals. Overall, Fernández-Arias and Powell's conclusion is that the catalytic effect of multilateral flows on private lending flows is robust to alternative specifications. Naturally, the result is open to different interpretations; three possibilities are (1) the story advanced by Rodrik: that multilaterals have superior information and signal good housekeeping; (2) that multilaterals actually promote reforms (that are not picked up in other variables in the regression), enhancing the investment climate; and (3) that multilaterals facilitate private sector lending through other channels, for example, by improving infrastructure and the availability of human capital.

Figure 6.9
Multilateral Catalytic Effect

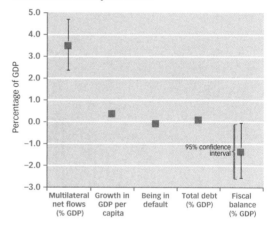

Source: Authors' calculations based on data from World Bank, *Global Development Finance*.
Note: Blocks indicate the estimated long-run marginal effect of one additional unit of independent variable (horizontal axis) on dependent variable (private net flows (% GDP)). Confidence intervals that are too narrow to be displayed meaningfully are not shown.

In sum, the empirical results show that there are indeed significant differences between multilateral (nonconcessional) flows and private flows. There is evidence that the private

---

[17] These variables include GDP growth, total external debt, GDP per capita, fiscal deficit, and an indicator for being in default with private sector creditors. They also include country fixed effects and time effects to control for other nonobservable variables common for particular countries and across time, respectively. Variables are included as a percentage of GDP or in logarithms to ensure appropriate scaling. An indicator variable for banking crises was also employed in some specifications. Note that this analysis differs from the one discussed in the previous section because of the different dynamic lag structure (for example, in the regression used for this analysis, contemporary multilateral flows are not included).

sector is procyclical, whereas multilaterals are countercyclical, with respect to recipient country growth. Multilaterals tend to increase their exposure during periods when a borrowing country is in default, when private sector flows are reduced. Recipient countries tend to reduce their borrowing from multilaterals when world interest rates are low and increase them when these rates rise. There is only weak and not particularly robust evidence that politics affects multilateral lending. There is evidence that multilaterals catalyze private sector flows.

DIFFERENCES BETWEEN MULTILATERAL AND BILATERAL LENDERS

Total official development assistance (ODA) to developing countries grew rapidly over the 1970s and 1980s and then stabilized in the mid-1990s, with a slight falloff at the end of that decade, followed by another increase in the early 2000s (Figure 6.10). Bilateral aid is an important component of ODA, as more than 70 percent of the total consists of bilateral aid from 22 OECD countries. Development assistance is less important for Latin America relative to other regions, although it is important for some individual Latin American countries.[18] Again the majority of development assistance (about 75 percent of the total) offered to Latin America comes from bilateral sources.

Rodrik (1995), in considering the question of why multilateral lending exists, asks what would drive a creditor country to lend through the intermediary of a multilateral rather than directly to a recipient country. He suggests that multilaterals may have a comparative advantage over individual countries in establishing and monitoring appropriate *condi-*

Figure 6.10
Official Development Assistance to Developing Countries

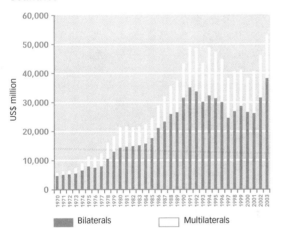

Bilaterals ▨   Multilaterals ▢

Source: OECD (2005).
Note: Total official development assistance includes grants or loans to countries and territories included in Part I of the OECD Development Assistance Committee's List of Aid Recipients (developing countries).

tionality. This is important because recent research suggests that the macroeconomic policy environment in a country may be important for making aid to that country effective.[19] Multilateral loans also enjoy a preferred creditor treatment that bilateral loans do not receive. Moreover, a country may attempt to selectively default on one bilateral, hoping that relations

[18] Over the last five years, Nicaragua received ODA valued at 2.5 percent of GDP, Bolivia 2.2 percent, and Honduras 1.9 percent.
[19] On conditionality, see, for example, Hopkins et al. (1997). On aid and growth, see, for example, Burnside and Dollar (2000) and Easterly (2003).

with others will not be affected. The Paris Club, although only an informal group, attempts to avoid these problems by reaching consensus among creditor nations.

The issue of coordination among bilateral lenders is also an important consideration. It is likely that $1 million in aid administered through one agency will be more effective than the same sum administered through 20 agencies. The 20 agencies might suffer problems in coordinating project preparation and planning, in monitoring the use of money extended, or in monitoring projects themselves. If several agencies support a single project, it clearly makes sense to aggregate many functions rather than duplicate them. These arguments suggest that multilaterals may have an advantage in simply coordinating aid from a wide set of bilateral donors and also suggest that aid may be more effective in countries that have only one or two donors.

It could be argued that politics may be more important for bilateral lending decisions than for multilateral lending decisions or that politics may affect bilateral lending in a different way from multilateral lending. Alesina and Dollar (2000), for example, compare bilateral concessional flows to private FDI flows, arguing that the former are driven more by politics and the latter more by economics. A bilateral lender may face the choice of lending out of its own resources to a political ally versus the possibility of harnessing the greater resources of many bilaterals, through the medium of a multilateral lender, but perhaps seeing its particular interest diluted.

Figure 6.11 sorts OECD donors in terms of total aid extended and describes the determinants of their allocations of bilateral aid. As the figure shows, the United States is the largest donor among the OECD countries, accounting for about 23 percent of total aid from those countries over the period considered here. The other large donors are Japan (20 percent of total aid), France (13 percent of total aid), Germany (11 percent of total aid), and Great Britain (5 percent of total aid).

The figure divides the determinants of bilateral aid into four categories: economic ties, political ties, colonial connections, and GDP per capita. The bars in the figure illustrate the importance of each factor in assigning each donor's aid to recipient countries (see Powell and Bobba, 2006, for details).[20]

The figure indicates that some donors extend significant percentages of aid to ex-colonies (France, Great Britain, and Portugal), countries with economic ties (Australia, Portugal, New Zealand, and Greece, and to some extent, the United States and Japan), and countries with political ties (Greece, New Zealand, and Switzerland). The data suggest that the United Kingdom, Holland, Italy, Canada, Sweden, Norway, Denmark, Belgium, Finland, and Ireland extend more financing to poorer countries (as measured by GDP per capita), with the United States, Japan, Spain, and Greece extending less assistance to poorer countries according to

---

[20] The bars depicting "Economic ties" give the percentage of the donor's aid that is extended to recipient countries that have a value on the "Economic ties" measure that ranks them above the 75th percentile on that measure among all recipients of aid from that donor for the sample period. The bars depicting "Political ties" show the percentage of the aid extended by the donor to recipient countries that have a value on the "Political ties" measure that ranks them above the 75th percentile on that measure among all recipients of aid from that donor for the sample period. The bars depicting "GDP per capita" show the percentage of the aid extended by the donor to recipient countries whose GDP per capita ranks below the 25th percentile on that measure among all recipients of aid from that donor for the sample period. And the bars that depict "Colonies" show the percentage of the donor country's aid that is extended to ex-colonies of that donor country over the sample period.

Figure 6.11
Characteristics of Bilateral Aid: Indications of Donor Preferences

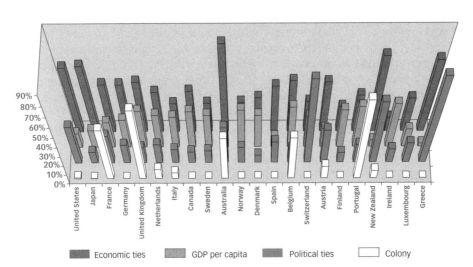

Source: Authors' calculations based on data from OECD (2005); IMF, *Direction of Trade Statistics*; and UNCTAD and Bank for International Settlements databases.
Note: Order of donors is in terms of total aid granted. Bars for "Economic ties," "Political ties," and "Colony" show, as a percentage of total aid, the amount of aid extended by a particular donor to recipients where there are economic, political, and colonial connections, respectively, with that donor. Bars for "GDP per capita" measure donors' attitude toward giving aid to poorer countries.

this measure. The observations on colonial connections and to a lesser degree on political ties support the conclusions of Alesina and Dollar (2000).

Powell and Bobba (2006) compare the behavior of multilateral and bilateral aid flows, and while they control for a large set of variables, they focus their analysis on two variables. The first is a measure of political ties, and the second is an index that captures whether aid is given by many donors or is extended by only a few. In order to build an index of political ties for multilaterals, Powell and Bobba (2006) add, across donors, the log of their measure of political ties between each recipient and donor, with weights that consider the voting power of that donor within a particular multilateral institution.[21] The authors use the Herfindahl index to measure the concentration of bilateral aid to each country.[22]

---

[21] Let T_{ij} be the variable representing political ties between donor i and recipient j and q_{mi} the quota of each donor i in multilateral m, and let D be the total number of donors; the variable representing the connection between the particular multilateral, m, and recipient j is then computed as

$$T_{mj} = \sum_{i=1}^{D} T_{ij} * q_{mi}.$$

Hence the explanatory variables reflect the relevant characteristics of donors, and in the case of multilaterals, aggregation, with the donor's voting power in a particular multilateral used as a proxy for its influence in that multilateral.

[22] The Herfindahl index has a value of one if a country has only one bilateral donor; as the number of donors increases, the index falls, eventually tending to zero if many donors extend only a tiny amount of aid each.

Figure 6.12
Bilateral versus Multilateral Aid Allocation

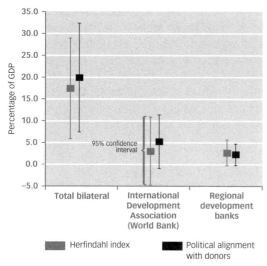

Source: Authors' calculations based on OECD (2005) data.
Note: Blocks indicate the estimated marginal effect of one additional unit of independent variable (Herfindahl index or political alignment with donors) on dependent variables (alternately, multilateral aid net flows (% GDP) or bilateral aid net flows (% GDP), horizontal axis). Herfindahl index is defined as sum of squares of lending shares of donors' aid to each recipient.

Figure 6.12 illustrates Powell and Bobba's (2006) main findings and shows that political ties are very important for bilateral lending and also that where bilateral aid is concentrated in only a few donors, recipients tend to receive more aid.[23] However, the effect of politics is much smaller and often not statistically significant for the multilaterals, including the International Development Association (the concessional arm of the World Bank), and even less important for the regional development banks. Powell and Bobba (2006) also find that the Herfindahl index is not significant for multilaterals.

The interpretation is that bilateral aid may be more subject to political influence relative to multilateral aid and that a lack of donor coordination (where there are many bilateral donors) may result in donors' restricting aid, presumably because their aid is less effective or because they are less confident that the aid extended goes where it is intended. Multilateral aid does not appear to suffer from the same problems, suggesting that multilaterals may help to resolve coordination problems, but perhaps at the cost of diluting a bilateral donor's particular interests.

MULTILATERALS: CONCLUDING COMMENTS

What makes multilateral development banks different when it comes to sovereign lending? This question in fact may be decomposed into two parts: first, what makes multilaterals different from private lenders with regard to nonconcessional lending, and second, what makes multilateral lending different from bilateral lending when it comes to concessional lending and in particular, official development assistance? The chapter shows that there are significant differences between the two types of lenders in both respects.

First, based on a direct test of whether multilaterals are similar in behavior to private sector lenders, there is evidence that multilaterals are more countercyclical and that multilaterals are particularly helpful when countries are starved of liquidity by global markets.

---

[23] There is no evidence of the importance of economic ties, but Powell and Bobba do find that colonial ties are important (these results are not illustrated in the figure).

Second, there is evidence that multilateral flows are catalytic in that they appear to lead to higher future private sector flows.

Finally, there are broad differences between multilateral and bilateral lenders when it comes to concessional financing and specifically to aid flows. Multilateral aid flows are less affected by political or colonial ties or political alignment, whereas bilateral flows do tend to be affected by these factors. There is also evidence that bilateral flows are larger where they are more concentrated in a few donors. A potential interpretation of this last result is that many bilateral lenders face a problem in terms of coordinating aid. Countries with many bilateral donors receive less aid in total. Intermediating aid through the multilaterals may resolve the problems of donor coordination, but at the cost of diluting the interests of a particular donor.

CHAPTER 7 | The Dawn of the Domestic Bond Market

DEVELOPING BOND MARKETS and enhancing the capacity of public and private sector borrowers to issue long-dated, domestic-currency-denominated debt securities is high on the policy agenda in several emerging market countries.[1] Crises in Mexico in 1995 and Argentina in 2001 and in various East Asian countries in 1997–1998 demonstrated the danger of disruptions to the supply of bank credit when other sources of finance are underdeveloped. The short tenor of bank loans, itself a consequence of the tendency for banks to fund themselves with demandable debt, meant that even where financial institutions continued to operate, borrowers finding themselves unable to roll over their maturing obligations might experience a credit crunch. Access to bond markets came to be seen as an essential "spare tire" (Greenspan, 1999).

Yet the development of a well-functioning bond market presupposes extensive infrastructure, including well-developed accounting, legal, and regulatory systems, payments and settlements systems, rating agencies, and networks of brokers to sell bonds. It requires rigorous disclosure standards and effective governance of corporations issuing publicly traded debt securities. It presumes the existence of well-established companies whose operations and credit standing are well known and that are large enough to defray the non-negligible fixed costs of placing a bond issue. These are not preconditions that can be fulfilled overnight. Rather, they are by-products of the larger process of economic and financial development, which is why even in the advanced countries, bond markets historically have been late to develop.[2] As long as some of these developmental preconditions remain unfulfilled, borrowers may prefer to tap the more extensive and efficient bond market infrastructure that exists in the major financial centers. Or they may find it easier to borrow from banks, which rely on long-term relationships with their clients to obtain information and

---

[1] This section and the next two draw from Borensztein, Eichengreen, and Panizza (2006a, 2006c).

[2] Although governments in the advanced economies were able to place bonds with domestic investors, albeit sometimes only bonds of very short maturity indexed to the exchange rate or denominated in foreign currency, the situation facing corporations was different. Prior to the 1980s corporate bond markets were essentially nonexistent outside the United States (IMF, 2005a). In Japan, the bond market grew rapidly from the second half of the 1980s as a restrictive regulatory environment gave way to widespread liberalization, in turn precipitating institutional innovation. The "Big Bang" reforms of the mid-1990s facilitated further growth even in the face of a stagnant economy (IMF, 2002b). In Europe, corporate bond markets remained small, reflecting the continent's traditional dependence on bank finance. This changed with the advent of the single market, which intensified competition in the financial sector, especially following the advent of the euro in 1999, suggesting that exchange rate risk and problems associated with the small scale of national markets may have played a role (Eichengreen, 2000; Nierop, 2005).

enforce repayment, thereby enabling them to circumvent imperfections in the information and contracting environments.

At the time of the crises that hit several emerging market countries in the 1990s, bond markets of sorts already existed, of course. But even in good times, the ability to issue in local markets was limited to large, well-known entities, and during crises they provided little relief. The yield on new issues skyrocketed. Worse still, market access and liquidity evaporated just when they were needed most. Low secondary market liquidity prevented investors from rebalancing their portfolios, and the illiquidity of the secondary market, which depressed retail demand, in turn limited the ability of potential issuers to place bonds on the primary market. In addition, the appetite of foreign investors seemed to be limited to issues denominated in dollars or other hard currencies, a fact that created further difficulties in bad times when the exchange rate had a tendency to depreciate. This hardly seemed like even a functional spare tire at a time when market conditions seemed to demand a set of high-performance all-weather radials.

Bond markets are not important only in times of crisis. Even during tranquil times, a well-working corporate bond market can help firms to obtain long-term finance and lower their financing costs and can enhance overall microeconomic efficiency. Developing a domestic bond market is likely to be particularly important for meeting the credit needs of small and medium-sized enterprises (SMEs). While global underwriters are interested only in relatively large issues, which are beyond the means of smaller borrowers, local markets are better positioned to acquire and process the information needed to evaluate the creditworthiness of SMEs.

The conclusion drawn from the 1990s crises by policymakers in several emerging market countries was that drastic action was needed to enhance the access of governments and, in particular, private corporations to bond finance. The Financial Stability Forum, the World Bank, the Inter-American Development Bank, the Asian Development Bank, and the Organisation for Economic Co-operation and Development all studied what emerging markets could do to develop local markets. Their key recommendations were for emerging markets to strengthen macroeconomic policies to provide a stable setting for both borrowing and lending, to improve corporate governance to ensure that firms would borrow prudently, to strengthen financial disclosure requirements to enhance the ability of potential bondholders to make prudent investment decisions, to encourage the growth of institutional investors to enhance diversification opportunities and reduce transaction costs, and to solidify bond market infrastructure generally by creating efficient clearing and settlement, credit enhancement, and custodial facilities.

Emerging markets have made important efforts in these directions. Yet the results have been disappointing. Domestic bond markets have grown only slowly. Liquidity is scarce, and turnover rates remain low. Notwithstanding the commentary surrounding the recent surge of funds into emerging markets, foreign participation in local bond markets, corporate bond markets in particular, remains quantitatively limited (with a few prominent exceptions like Mexico).

These disappointing results are rationalized in two (not necessarily incompatible) ways. First, institutions and policies remain weaker in emerging markets than in advanced countries, and there is no quick fix to this problem. Like it or not, eliminating the institutional and policy deficiencies slowing the development of deeper and more liquid bond markets is a difficult and time-consuming process. Second, emerging market countries seeking to develop their bond markets are handicapped by the small size of both their firms and their economies. Market depth and liquidity require a certain minimum efficient scale which is particularly hard to achieve in small countries. This country size effect is amplified by the fact that most emerging market countries tend to have small firms which cannot afford the fixed costs linked to issuing bonds. Related to this is the fact that emerging markets are not first movers in the competition for global market share; there already exist deep and liquid markets in the leading global financial centers. From the point of view of liquidity and transaction costs, it is therefore more attractive for issuers and investors from emerging markets to transact in the major global markets than it is for foreign investors to transact in emerging markets.

THE EVOLUTION OF THE DOMESTIC BOND MARKET

There are different ways to describe the evolution of the Latin American domestic bond market. One way is to scale outstanding bonds by GDP (Figure 7.1). By this measure, the advanced economies have the largest bond markets, followed by East Asia, Latin America, and Eastern Europe and Central Asia. While the Latin American bond market is not much smaller than that of East Asia (35 versus 45 percent of GDP), there are large differences in composition. Latin American local markets are heavily skewed toward government bonds, while in East Asia fully half the outstanding stock is made up of issues of financial institutions and corporations.

This situation looks different if bond market capitalization is instead scaled by the size of the domestic financial system (proxied by M2) (Figure 7.2). In Latin America, evidently, it is financial sectors generally and not merely bond markets that are underdeveloped. This suggests that the growth of bond markets should be viewed as an organic part of the process of financial market development, and that countries will develop deep and liquid markets in debt securities only once they have succeeded in reducing the larger obstacles to financial development. Indeed, there are good reasons to think that banking systems and bond markets develop together, as they have prerequisites in common. In both cases confidence requires a reasonable level of information disclosure. In turn, mandating disclosure may require regulation by a supervisory agency or securities commission. The development of both a bond market

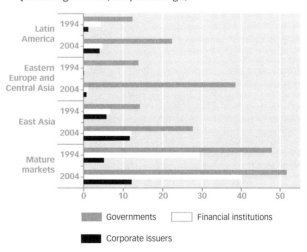

Figure 7.1
Domestic Bonds
(*percentage of GDP, simple average*)

Governments   Financial institutions

Corporate issuers

Source: Bank for International Settlements.

Figure 7.2
Domestic Bonds
(*percentage of M2, simple average*)

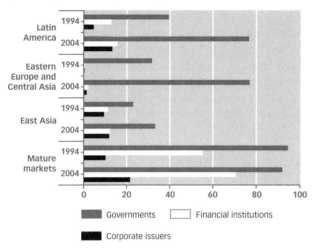

Source: Bank for International Settlements.

and a sound banking system requires strong creditor rights and an effective system of corporate governance so that small creditors can be assured of being dealt with fairly. In both cases, confidence may require macroeconomic stability, so that depositors and investors do not fear that the value of their claims will be inflated away, and strong creditor rights, so that they are confident that they will be treated fairly in the event of a debt or banking crisis. There are in fact strong complementarities between bond finance and bank finance, and bond market development should not be seen as an alternative to the development of an efficient banking system but rather as part of the same organic process (Box 7.1).

The sequencing involved in this view is rather different from the traditional one in which bank finance develops first because the information and contracting environments are highly imperfect. In such a setting, according to the traditional model, banks in long term relationships with their clients have a comparative advantage in bridging information gaps, enforcing repayment, and reorganizing problem loans. Bond markets develop only later, once an economy has acquired strong institutions of information disclosure, corporate governance, insolvency reorganization, and so forth. Recent research (e.g., Rajan and Zingales, 2003b) suggests that the actual sequencing of external finance, starting with banks and moving to bond markets and finally equity markets, is not so clear-cut in reality. It differs in different times and places. While not denying the special role of banks in the kind of imperfect information and contracting environment that is characteristic of many emerging markets, the perspective presented here suggests that the development of banking systems does not just precede the development of bond markets; rather, the two are complementary processes.

Clearly, there is also the danger that an imperfectly competitive banking system, in which financial institutions use their incumbency advantage and market power to slow the development of securitization and disintermediation, can retard the growth of the bond market. It may do so by limiting access to the payment system and supporting the maintenance of regulations that increase the cost of underwriting and issuance.[3] The actual situation on the ground appears to vary considerably. The IMF (2002b) observes that banks in Thailand

---

[3] See Schinasi and Smith (1998), Rajan and Zingales (2003a), and Eichengreen and Luengnareumitchai (2004) for theory and evidence.

have been able to place barriers in the way of bond issuance in an attempt to limit competition from the bond market. In Chile, the Latin American country with the most active corporate bond market, fully 26 investment banks have been active in underwriting and helping to place domestic debt securities. But it is an exception to the rule. Whereas 20 different commercial and investment banks act as lead underwriters in Brazil, three of them account for 90 percent of issues. The case is similar in Mexico, where three large banks dominate the underwriting and selling side of the market. In a number of East Asian countries, a handful of underwriters similarly dominate the market.

Not only do the Latin American bond markets tend to be small, but they also lag along a number of other

Figure 7.3
Composition of Bonds Issued during 2000–2005

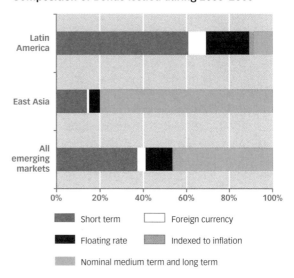

Source: Borensztein, Eichengreen, and Panizza (2006a).

dimensions, not just when compared with those in the advanced economies, but even when assessed relative to those in other emerging economies. For instance, the duration of issues on Latin American markets remains relatively short. The region has made some progress here, but in terms of, say, the share of bonds with a residual maturity of less than one year, it still compares unfavorably with emerging East Asia, much less with the advanced economies. The majority of issues on Latin American markets have floating rates, and investors demand that interest rates be indexed to inflation or the exchange rate, in contrast to emerging East Asia, where fixed rates are the norm and indexation is virtually nonexistent. About 80 percent of all bonds issued in East Asia between 2000 and 2005 (weighted by value) had a maturity longer than one year and no indexation, whereas the comparable figure for Latin America was less than 10 percent (Figure 7.3). With the exception of a few benchmark issues, turnover rates remain relatively low in Latin America, leaving markets relatively illiquid. And regional markets are still disproportionately dominated by government bonds.

THE DEVELOPMENT OF THE DOMESTIC BOND MARKET: WHAT DO THE DATA SAY?

One way of systematically comparing the determinants of bond market development is to use aggregate data for a cross-section of countries and series of years to estimate the determinants of bond market capitalization. Borensztein, Eichengreen, and Panizza (2006a) use annual data for 43 countries over the 1995–2004 period and show that a limited number of observable policy variables and country characteristics explain some 70 percent of the difference in bond market capitalization between Latin America and the advanced economies.

Box 7.1 Bonds versus Banks

One frequently expressed concern is that bond markets may crowd out banks. However, empirical work focusing on both OECD and emerging market countries finds that bond market development and bank lending are positively correlated (Jiang, Tang, and Law, 2001), and there is also some evidence that bond markets do act as a "spare tire" (albeit only a semi-inflated one) providing some limited offset to reductions in bank lending (Hawkins, 2002). In several countries, banks are major holders of both corporate and government bonds and act as managers for retail investors.[a] Furthermore, banks play a key role in the development of the bond market by securitizing their loans and by acting as underwriters (i.e., guaranteeing that a given issuance of corporate bonds will be fully subscribed) and credit enhancers (i.e., guaranteeing part of the payment of corporate bonds).

From a theoretical point of view, there are interesting interactions among the corporate and government bond markets and bank lending. Bolton and Freixas (2006) study the determinants of the composition of sovereign bonds, corporate bonds, and bank financing in a general equilibrium model of an emerging market economy characterized by a shortage of capital, weak debt enforcement institutions, and potential government overborrowing which may expose the country to sovereign default. In their model, bank financing is more flexible because banks have better information and can show forbearance towards a firm that has liquidity, or even solvency, problems. For the same reason bank monitoring is more costly to the firm and imposes more conditions. Bonds do not have the same flexibility but have a lower cost. The implication is that firms that are less likely to fail will prefer bonds.

Next, Bolton and Freixas (2006) introduce the role of the government and show that the presence of such a big player

This same handful of observable variables also explain 90 percent of the difference between the two in the development of the market for the bonds of corporations and financial institutions. This means that if it were possible to take these country characteristics and replace their average values for Latin America with their average values for the advanced economies, the two regions would have private bond markets of similar size.

In the real world, of course, growing bond markets is not so easy. Improvements in policies and institutions take time to work their effects. In addition, the statistical analysis shows that one-quarter of the difference in bond market capitalization between advanced economies and Latin America is due to small country size and the general level of economic development. Another 15 percent of the difference is related to geography and historical factors like the origin of the legal code. Another 15 percent is attributable to the underdevelopment of the financial system, something that again takes time to correct. More easily manipulated policy variables like the exchange rate regime, the presence or lack of capital controls, the level of public debt, bank concentration, and banking spreads are all statistically significant in the empirical analysis but play a smaller role in explaining the difference between the lowers the cost of issuing bonds (because of economies of scale) but also positively affects the probability of a banking crisis if the government defaults. The banking crisis is characterized as a run on deposits which leads to bank failures and also triggers bankruptcies in firms with bank debt, thus increasing the risk of bank debt. In this sense, the bond market does act as a spare tire, because it helps isolate firms from sovereign default risk and the associated banking crisis. Hence, introducing the government leads to an additional benefit arising from the presence of a bond market. Besides the standard effect of providing lower cost of financing to the safest firms, the presence of a bond market isolates these firms from the cost of a banking crisis. Therefore, the benefits of creating such a market are higher in emerging markets than in the advanced economies, which have lower risk of facing a banking crisis. The other side of this coin is that when a larger

fraction of firms start using bond finance, the government realizes that the cost of a banking crisis has been lowered and it assumes more risk (by overborrowing), increasing the probability of default.

An alternative is securitization. With this form of financing, firms keep the flexibility of bank financing but are immune from banking crises. However, transaction costs increase, because firms need to pay both bank fees and bond issuance cost. A result of this setup is that the firms that are least likely to fail issue bonds, the weakest firms use bank loans, and those that are in the middle go for securitized bank loans.

------

[a] This may generate a conflict of interest if the bank is also a lender to the company issuing the bonds. As the bank is likely to have an information advantage, it may induce a firm to issue bonds to repay its bank loans and promote these bonds among its own customer base (this is what Italian banks have been accused of doing in the recent Cirio and Parmalat defaults).

development of the bond markets of advanced economies and that of the bond markets of Latin America. This should not be taken to mean that policies and institutions do not matter (in fact about 20 percent of the difference in the size of bond markets in Latin America and the advanced economies is due to macroeconomic stability, investor protection, and lower cost of enforcing contracts), but it is a reminder that there are no shortcuts. The same policies that are necessary for economic development in general are also necessary for the development of domestic bond markets.

SIZE DOES MATTER

As there are significant fixed costs associated with underwriting, publicizing, and distributing a bond issue, and as secondary market liquidity will be greater where there exist a large number of bonds and bondholders, potential market size is an important factor limiting the issue of bonds. This provides a rationale for the traditional Latin American strategy of also relying on international markets, where the fixed costs of issuance are lower and liquidity is higher. At the same time, it provides an obvious rationale for Asian efforts to integrate national markets into something resembling a single regional market, so that the size of the regional economy rather than that of the national economies is the constraint on market growth (Boxes 7.2 and 7.3).

If perceived lack of demand (perhaps because of low saving rates) is what is holding Latin America back from developing bond markets, one possible strategy is to encourage the participation of investors from outside the region. However, foreign investors are most inclined to take positions in countries with larger bond markets (Brazil, for example)—where the costs of closing out positions are least—that is to say, where liquidity is already the greatest. Brazilian authorities have sought to capitalize on this interest by retiring foreign debt from the market and replacing it with domestic currency (interest-rate- and inflation-indexed) issues. Mexico, where foreign participants are reported to hold more than 50 percent of the government's 10-year bonds and more than 80 percent of its 20-year bonds, has sought to take advantage of foreign participation by issuing exclusively on the domestic market.

To be sure, there is also a foreign demand for "exotics," or the less-liquid bonds of smaller countries, but this phenomenon is quantitatively limited; for most investors, the limited liquidity of exotics, together with the lack of hedging instruments and the fixed costs of obtaining information about issue quality, currency risk, withholding tax regimes, and so on in smaller markets, limits foreign demand.

This raises the possibility that the globalization of bond markets, and the growing participation of foreign investors in Latin America's local markets in particular, may be encouraging a bifurcation between the region's larger and smaller markets by further enhancing the already greater liquidity of the larger markets while having little discernible impact on their smaller counterparts. Similarly, it may be enhancing the liquidity of government bond markets relative to corporate bond markets. This may encourage smaller countries in the region to borrow by issuing global bonds in extraregional financial centers as an alternative to developing their domestic markets. But that in turn may further limit the development and liquidity of local markets and further discourage foreign participation.[4] On the other hand, one can argue that international issues are useful for familiarizing foreign investors with a country's situation and its debt instruments and that domestic and international issues are complements rather than substitutes.

THE MARKET FOR DOMESTIC GOVERNMENT BONDS

Simple averages based on a sample of 18 Latin American and Caribbean countries show that over the 1990–1994 period, domestic government bonds were around 16 percent of GDP, ranging between 2 percent of GDP in Bolivia and 74 percent of GDP in Chile (Table 7.1). By 2000–2004, the share of domestic bonds in GDP had grown to 24 percent, ranging from 6 percent in Guatemala to 78 percent in Jamaica. While there are 14 countries in which the share of domestic debt increased by more than five percentage points between 1990–1994 and 2000–2004, there are only two countries with a substantially decreasing share of do-

---

[4] The literature on whether foreign listing of equity claims discourages domestic trading of the same stocks points in this direction (Levine and Schmukler, 2006).

Table 7.1 Size of Domestic Bond Market

Country	Domestic bonds/GDP			Domestic bonds/public debt		
	1990–1994	1995–1999	2000–2004	1990–1994	1995–1999	2000–2004
Emerging markets in Latin America						
Argentina	0.15	0.09	0.31	0.37	0.25	0.31
Brazil	0.22	0.37	0.55	0.56	0.71	0.68
Chile	0.74	0.58	0.49	0.79	0.93	0.91
Colombia	0.08	0.11	0.27	0.29	0.32	0.45
Dominican Republic	n.d.	n.d.	0.16	n.d.	n.d.	0.30
Ecuador	0.05	0.09	0.13	0.05	0.13	0.21
El Salvador	0.04	0.03	0.14	0.08	0.06	0.32
Mexico	0.14	0.23	0.26	0.35	0.45	0.67
Panama	0.14	0.09	0.13	0.13	0.12	0.18
Peru	n.d.	0.06	0.07	n.d.	0.12	0.16
Uruguay	0.18	0.15	0.19	0.40	0.38	0.21
Venezuela	n.d.	0.05	0.13	n.d.	0.15	0.35
Mean	*0.19*	*0.17*	*0.24*	*0.34*	*0.33*	*0.40*
SD	*0.21*	*0.17*	*0.15*	*0.24*	*0.28*	*0.24*
Nonemerging markets in Latin America						
Belize	0.07	0.07	0.07	0.14	0.14	0.09
Bolivia	0.02	0.07	0.18	0.02	0.11	0.25
Costa Rica	0.18	0.26	0.27	0.28	0.46	0.48
Guatemala	n.d.	n.d.	0.06	n.d.	n.d.	0.28
Honduras	0.15	0.10	0.14	0.13	0.11	0.18
Jamaica	0.17	0.38	0.78	0.19	0.42	0.58
Nicaragua	0.09	0.23	0.44	0.02	0.11	0.23
Paraguay	0.05	0.06	0.07	0.20	0.24	0.17
Trinidad and Tobago	0.21	0.22	0.17	0.36	0.44	0.51
Mean	*0.12*	*0.17*	*0.24*	*0.17*	*0.25*	*0.31*
SD	*0.07*	*0.12*	*0.23*	*0.12*	*0.16*	*0.17*
All Latin America						
Mean	*0.16*	*0.17*	*0.24*	*0.26*	*0.30*	*0.36*
SD	*0.16*	*0.14*	*0.19*	*0.20*	*0.23*	*0.21*
East Asia						
Mean	*0.16*	*0.15*	*0.27*	*0.44*	*0.48*	*0.63*
SD	*0.18*	*0.12*	*0.09*	*0.26*	*0.29*	*0.22*
Other emerging markets						
Mean	*0.35*	*0.29*	*0.39*	*0.50*	*0.59*	*0.65*
SD	*0.44*	*0.22*	*0.24*	*0.33*	*0.27*	*0.28*
Advanced economies						
Mean	*0.42*	*0.47*	*0.48*	*0.76*	*0.79*	*0.87*
SD	*0.24*	*0.23*	*0.28*	*0.19*	*0.16*	*0.15*

Sources: Cowan et al. (2006) for Latin America; Bank for International Settlements database and Jaimovich and Panizza (2006b) for all other.

Note: "East Asia" includes China, Indonesia, Malaysia, Philippines, Singapore, South Korea, and Thailand. "Other emerging markets" includes Czech Republic, Hungary, India, Lebanon, Pakistan, Poland, Russia, Slovakia, South Africa, and Turkey. "Advanced economies" includes Australia, Austria, Belgium, Canada, Denmark, Finland, France, Germany, Greece, Iceland, Ireland, Italy, Japan, Netherlands, New Zealand, Norway, Portugal, Spain, Sweden, Switzerland, United Kingdom, and United States. n.d. = no data available.

Box 7.2 Strategies for Developing the Bond Market, East Asia versus Latin America

It is useful to distinguish five classes of policy initiatives for developing bond markets: (1) efforts to strengthen financial and legal systems, (2) investments in building dedicated market infrastructure, (3) steps to encourage the participation of institutional investors, (4) measures to encourage the participation of foreign investors, and (5) extranational initiatives. How do Latin America and East Asia compare in regard to these policy initiatives?

Strengthening financial and legal systems. Here East Asia is in the lead. While there are wide variations in measures of legal infrastructure in regard to investor and creditor protection, Latin America tends to fare poorly in terms of both. In both cases, the highest-ranked Latin American country (Chile) has values that are lower than the Asian average. The principal East Asian countries also do better than their Latin American counterparts in terms of measures of financial transparency. With the exception of Mexico and Peru, every Latin American country for which the International Accounting Standards Committee provides information on financial transparency ranks behind each and every Asian country for which these data are available.

Investment in dedicated market infrastructure. Both regions have come a long way in the development of requisite infrastructure to support a bond market. By 2002, 88 percent of Latin American countries had created a capital market supervisory authority; 91 percent had established custody arrangements; and 92 percent had invested in a clearing and settlement process. All countries in the region had put modern trading systems in place (de la Torre and Schmukler, 2004b). The same is true of all the middle- and high-income countries of East Asia, but not of their lower-income counterparts. At the same time, several Asian countries have taken exceptional steps to enhance the transparency of the secondary market. Malaysia has established a bond information dissemination system in which dealers are required to enter price and volume information within 10 minutes of a trade. The Thai Bond Market Association requires traders to report over-the-counter trades within three minutes and distributes their information to members four times daily. The Korea Security Dealers Association requires dealers to report their transactions within 15 minutes via its information distribution system and then posts these data to its website on the same day. Indonesia now plans to move in the same direction by establishing an autonomous bond-pricing agency. Initiatives to disseminate information on the secondary market in Latin America are less ambitious.

Encouraging participation by institutional investors. Latin American countries have long had generous pension and retirement systems. The privatization of these systems in recent years has thus created a large constituency of institutional investors with an appetite for locally issued bonds, especially government bonds (Chapter 8). In Asia, in contrast, social security systems have historically been underdeveloped, encouraging households to rely on high saving rates to prepare for retirement. But state provident funds have strong demands for fixed income securities to match their annuity profiles.

Encouraging foreign participation. This is where the differences between the strategies followed by the two regions are most pronounced. The Latin American economies are proceeding on a country-by-country basis, each seeking to enhance the efficiency of market infrastructure, the predictability of transactions, and the transparency of regulation. Each country is, in effect, competing with its neighbors for foreign investors. East Asian countries, in contrast, are moving as a group, not just upgrading arrangements, but also harmonizing institutions and regulation within the region and creating not only national investment vehicles attractive to foreign investors, but also regional investment vehicles like the Pan Asia Bond Index Fund (see Box 7.3). In principle, both approaches have advantages. Latin America's decentralized approach allows countries with the desire to do so to move ahead quickly, while East Asia's collective approach applies peer pressure to those apt to lag behind. The Latin American approach promises an immediate payoff to countries that succeed in implementing ambitious reforms, but it threatens to run up against limits of minimum efficient scale. That is, even if a small Central or South American country succeeds in creating one of the world's most efficient corporate bond markets and in encouraging high levels of foreign investor participation, the small size of the country, its firms, and its market means that it will still lack the liquidity and low costs of larger markets, given that bond issuance and trading are subject to strongly increasing returns to scale. For its part, the Asian approach is likely to be slower because consensus must precede reform. But it promises to deliver an integrated regional bond market and thus to relax the constraint of insufficient scale.

Extranational initiatives. Another difference between the two regions is that several Latin American countries have sought to relax the constraint of small market size and the difficulty of quickly strengthening investor and creditor rights by facilitating the efforts of domestic entities to borrow as well in the major international financial centers. Latin America continues to look to global markets. East Asia, in contrast, has sought a regional solution to these problems. Of course this characterization paints the contrasting strategies with a broad brush; the reality is more complex, especially in Latin America, where, as highlighted above, a much lower level of coordination is observed.

Source: Based on Borensztein, Eichengreen, and Panizza (2006c).

Box 7.3 The Asian Bond Fund

The Asian Bond Fund 2 (ABF2) initiative seeks to expand market size by developing a pan-regional bond index, the Pan Asia Bond Index Fund (PAIF), and a passively managed mutual fund operated by private sector managers and designed to track the index. Unlike the Asian Bond Fund 1 (ABF1), the mutual fund is open to further subscription by private investors and, whereas under ABF1 the participating central banks invested in the dollar bonds of sovereign and quasi-sovereign issuers, under ABF2 they are investing in local currency issues.[a] The index is designed to provide a benchmark structure for tracking pan-Asian performance; the idea is that investors will find it more attractive to purchase a security that represents claims on a basket of regional bonds, which will enable them to take bets on the regional economy while diversifying away idiosyncratic national risk (however, ABF2 also entails the establishment of a series of national bond funds). The global custodian for PAIF and the single market funds has established a region-wide custodian network linking up all eight countries that participate in the fund, and it is hoped that this model will give a boost to the integration of national markets.

A constraint on exporting this model is that it requires the elimination of restrictions on the participation of foreign investors. Thus, to facilitate development of the initiative, Malaysia had to liberalize access to its markets for PAIF portfolio managers, and PAIF was given permission by the Chinese government to invest in both exchange traded bonds and interbank traded bonds and to freely repatriate the proceeds.[b] Countries like Brazil and Colombia would have to relax their restrictions on foreign participation for this model to be emulated in Latin America.

But the most serious limitation of this model is that the regional bond funds in question are all concentrating on sovereign and quasi-sovereign securities. According to Leung (2006, 74), "it is believed that the experience gained can still shed some light on the development of corporate bond markets in Asia." Presumably this does not mean that central banks will invest directly in portfolios of corporate securities in some future Asian Bond Fund 3, but rather that private sector managers, impressed by the performance of PAIF, will be moved to create a similar index of corporate securities.

---

[a] The Asian Bond Fund (ABF), launched in June 2003, was designed to catalyze the growth of Asian bond markets by allocating a portion of the reserves of regional central banks to purchases of government and quasi-government securities. The initial $1 billion of investments, known as ABF1, was devoted to Asian sovereign and quasi-sovereign issues of dollar-denominated bonds.
[b] China continues to apply various limits on investment in such bonds and repatriation of interest and principal, but it is not clear that these will remain viable now that a window has been opened for PAIF.
Source: Based on Borensztein, Eichengreen, and Panizza (2006c).

mestic government bonds in GDP: Chile and Trinidad and Tobago.[5] Note that this trend is not unique to Latin America; the share of domestic bonds in GDP also increased in emerging economies elsewhere over the same time period and in the advanced economies.

It is not clear, however, whether the trends documented above are due to the behavior of total public debt or to its composition. Simple averages for all countries for which data are available show that the share of domestic bonds in total public debt has increased substantially (going from 26 percent in 1990–1994 to 36 percent in 2000–2004), suggesting that the increase in the amount of domestic financing is due to a composition effect (i.e., the amount of domestic government bonds has grown more than total public debt), an observation consistent with the experience of East Asia, the other emerging markets, and the advanced economies. Here, however, Latin American countries can be divided into two groups. In the first group (which includes Argentina, Belize, Paraguay, and Uruguay), the share of government bonds in total debt has decreased, indicating that the increase in domestic government bonds (or the constant level, in the case of Belize) is due to higher levels of debt and not to a shift towards increased domestic debt. In the second group of countries, indeed, there is an increase in the share of domestic government bonds in total public debt, a sign that these countries have adopted a strategy aimed at developing the domestic market and reducing their reliance on international capital markets.

Interestingly, in the early 1990s several Latin American countries had small and shrinking domestic government bond markets, but the Tequila crisis that hit the region in early 1995 played a key role in the development of domestic bond markets (Cowan and Panizza, 2006).[6] The financial turmoil that followed the postcrisis Mexican devaluation deprived several countries of access to the international capital market and forced them to rely on the domestic market.[7] Under normal circumstances, countries probably would have quickly reverted to international borrowing, but the series of financial crises that followed the one originating in Mexico led to discontinuous access to the international capital market and convinced policymakers of the importance of developing a reliable domestic source of financing.

In fact, a cursory look at the development of Latin American government bond markets illustrates that a crisis, either domestic or international, is often the event that kick-starts a country's domestic bond market.[8] The most striking case is Chile, where the large amount of outstanding government bonds (mostly issued by the central bank) is the legacy of the banking crisis that hit the country in the early 1980s.[9] Mexico and Uruguay started issuing domes-

---

[5] As the table shows, in Chile the ratio fell from 74 to 49 percent of GDP (in 2001, the Chilean authorities decided to issue some international sovereign debt, not because they needed the financing, but because they wanted to provide a benchmark for private issuers), and in Trinidad and Tobago the ratio declined from 21 to 17 percent of GDP. There were also small decreases (about 1 percent of GDP) in Honduras and Panama.

[6] Pension reforms are another important element; see Chapter 8.

[7] This may not have been the case in Brazil, where the bond market may have originated from a shift in the way the government finances itself (from inflation to bond issuance), and the development of the domestic bond market was probably an outcome of the Real Plan and the country's desire to limit the extent of dollarization.

[8] This is not the case exclusively for Latin America. Bordo, Meissner, and Redish (2005) show that several former British colonies started developing their domestic markets when external events (like World War II) prevented them from accessing international capital markets.

[9] Caprio and Klingebiel (2003) estimate that over 1982–1985, the Chilean government spent 42 percent of GDP to resolve the banking crisis. In several countries the central bank is forbidden to issue bonds (in Colombia, the central bank was the main issuer until 1991, but then a law was enacted prohibiting the central bank from issuing bonds). Under the convertibility regime that previously existed, the Argentine central bank could not issue bonds, but this institution is now becoming an important issuer in the market for short-term bills.

Figure 7.4
a. Currency Composition of Domestic Public Debt, 1997

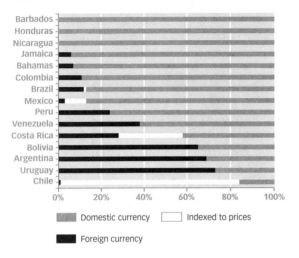

Source: Cowan et al. (2006).

b. Currency Composition of Domestic Public Debt, 2004

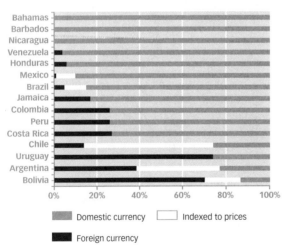

Source: Cowan et al. (2006).

tic government bonds after the debt crisis of early 1982 prevented them from accessing the international capital market. In the case of Argentina, the government bond market started in 1990–1991, when the government issued several bonds to consolidate central bank debt to the commercial banks and to consolidate existing liabilities in regard to pensioners, suppliers, and victims of the country's military regime. Most of these earlier issues were thus compulsory. Debt and domestic bonds became less important as soon as the Argentine government gained access to the international capital market after successfully restructuring its defaulted international bank loans (Fernández et al., 2006).

Besides changes in levels, there have also been changes in the composition of domestic debt in Latin America and the Caribbean. Focusing on the 1997–2004 period, there are five countries (Argentina, The Bahamas, Brazil, Mexico, and Venezuela) that substantially reduced the share of their domestic debt indexed to foreign currency by substituting for it either domestic currency debt or debt indexed to prices (Figure 7.4).[10] There are also six countries (Barbados, Bolivia, Costa Rica, Nicaragua, Peru, and Uruguay) with a more or less unchanged share of foreign currency debt over the period, and four countries (Chile, Colombia, Honduras, and Jamaica) with an increasing (but still small) share of foreign currency debt.

---

[10] Some countries, however, substantially increased the share of debt indexed to the interest rate.

Focusing on maturity, there are four countries in the region (Argentina, Brazil, Colombia, and Mexico) that lengthened the maturity of their domestic debt over the same period (Figure 7.5 plots the share of domestic debt with maturity less than one year), four countries (Barbados, Chile, Nicaragua, and Uruguay) with a more or less unchanged maturity over the period, and one country (Peru) with an increasing share of short-term government bonds (and thus a shortening maturity).

Two problems with the measures of debt structure highlighted above is that they do not capture the share of debt indexed to the short-term interest rate and that they do not highlight possible trade-offs between currency and maturity risk, as countries that issue more debt in nonindexed domestic currency may have debt with shorter maturities (see Chapter 13 for a discussion of this trade-off).

PRIVATE ISSUERS

A survey covering six Latin American countries (Argentina, Brazil, Chile, Colombia, Mexico, and Uruguay) showed that five of these countries had no private domestic bond market whatsoever at the beginning of the 1990s (Cowan and Panizza, 2006).[11] This is despite the fact that regulatory reforms allowing or fostering bond issuance had been carried out in several of these countries during the 1980s.[12]

Figure 7.5
a. Maturity Composition of Domestic Debt, 1997

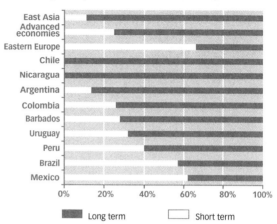

Sources: Bank for International Settlements and Cowan et al. (2006).
Note: In the case of Uruguay, data are for the year 2001.

b. Maturity Composition of Domestic Debt, 2004

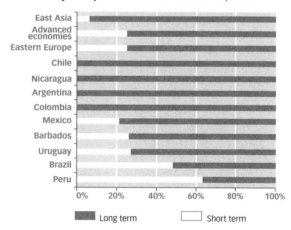

Sources: Bank for International Settlements and Cowan et al. (2006).

---

[11] This is also the case in Peru (Choy, 2002). This section and the next are based on Cowan and Panizza (2006).

[12] In Argentina corporate bonds (*obligaciones negociables*) were authorized in 1988 (Fernández et al., 2006). Brazil carried out several reforms aimed at developing the domestic financial system in the 1980s, although commercial paper rules were not passed until 1991 (Leal and Carvahal-da-Silva, 2006). The regulatory changes carried out in Chile after the financial crisis of 1982 are described by Braun and Briones (2005). Mexico authorized bonds in 1982 (Castellanos and Martínez, 2006).

Figure 7.6
Private Domestic Bond Issuances
(*percentage of GDP*)

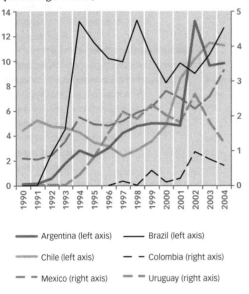

— Argentina (left axis)   — Brazil (left axis)

····· Chile (left axis)   – – Colombia (right axis)

– – Mexico (right axis)   ▬ ▬ Uruguay (right axis)

Source: Cowan and Panizza (2006).

Macroeconomic instability is partly to blame for this lack of development. Argentina and Brazil had hyperinflation episodes in the early 1990s, while in Mexico and Uruguay, inflation fell below 100 percent per year only as late as 1989 and 1992, respectively.[13] Chile, on the other hand, has enjoyed relative macroeconomic stability since the mid-1980s. In 1990, outstanding corporate bonds in Chile amounted to close to 5 percent of GDP. Colombia is something of an outlier along this dimension: despite broad macroeconomic stability in the 1980s, the private bond market failed to develop in the country.

Despite their similar starting points, private bond markets in these countries followed different paths during the 1990s (Figure 7.6). Issuance in Argentina started in earnest in 1991, following the reduction of inflation brought about by the convertibility plan and a tax reform that leveled the playing field between bank and bond finance, and continued until the recession of 1998. The market for Mexican bonds has grown more or less continuously since 1990 following stabilization of inflation in the late 1980s. New regulation introduced in 2001 has led to renewed growth in recent years. The Uruguayan bond market had a brief period of growth after 1994, until a series of corporate scandals led to reduced issuance and stagnation. Brazil experienced the fastest bond market growth among these countries, but this was concentrated in the years immediately following the reduction in inflation brought about by the Real Plan. Starting from basically nothing in 1990, the stock of private bonds in Brazil reached more than 10 percent of GDP by 1994 and fluctuated between 8 and 13 percent of GDP over the 1994–2004 period, then rose markedly, with the increase sparked by a new wave of issuance in 2005 (four times the level of 2004), with leasing companies being the most active market participants.

Once again Colombia is an outlier in the sample. Private bond market growth there has been slow and erratic, so that even by the end of the decade, outstanding private bonds remained below 1 percent of GDP. The evolution of the private bond market in Colombia stands in stark contrast to high levels of growth in the country's public debt sector, leading to concerns that government debt may be crowding out the private market (Aguilar et al., 2006).

---

[13] Braun and Briones (2005) find that inflation and budget deficits have a negative impact on the maturity of bonds. Burger and Warnock (2004) find that inflation volatility negatively affects the capitalization of local bond markets.

In Chile, the initial level of bond market capitalization was higher than in the other five countries, but the country experienced no bond market growth until the late 1990s. Several factors may explain the recent private bond market growth in Chile (Braun and Briones, 2005). The first relates to monetary policy—and in particular to the extreme spike in short-term interest rates brought about by the defense of the peso in 1998. This increase in short-term rates (and the associated credit crunch) made long-term nonbank financing increasingly attractive. A second and related explanation suggests that the closure of the international financial markets, combined with a large stock of institutional assets, jump-started the corporate bond market in Chile (Cifuentes, Desormeaux, and González, 2002). If the effects are permanent, then this would be another case in which a negative shock leads to the development of the domestic bond market. The third explanation suggests that the increase in private bonds was due to the market space vacated by falling Chilean public debt in this period.

Despite this recent growth, the stock of private debt in most of these countries remains low. In four of the six countries considered, private bond markets remained below 5 percent of GDP in 2005. The two exceptions are Brazil and Chile, in which outstanding private bonds were above 10 percent of GDP in 2005. In any case, these values are considerably lower than the averages of East Asia and the advanced economies (28 and 70 percent of GDP, respectively).

Besides differing in trends and levels, bond markets in the six countries covered also differ in the characteristics of the instruments issued (Table 7.2). Nominal debt is still rare in the region, with most countries issuing debt indexed to prices (Argentina and Chile), to the interest rate (Brazil), or to the dollar (Argentina and Uruguay). In this sense, the bond market mimics the maturity and indexation structure of other forms of corporate finance in the region: short and/or dollarized in the cases of Argentina, Brazil, and Uruguay (Kamil, 2004).

Furthermore, there does not appear to be a clear movement in the private sector towards "safer" forms of debt ("safer" from the perspective of the borrower, that is), such as debt indexed to prices and nominal debt. Mexico is the sole exception. In Mexico, the share of private nominal bonds has increased significantly in recent years, in line with developments in the government bond market. However, dollarization of private and government bonds has taken different tracks in Argentina. Despite falling shares of dollar-denominated government bonds, dollarization of private debt has remained high, even though new issuance and extensive rescheduling in 2002 and 2003 allowed ample opportunities for restructuring.

Where the six countries do coincide is in the type of firm that issues debt. Four out of the six case studies carry out a detailed firm-level analysis of the determinants of issuing bonds. Broadly speaking, the case studies find that large firms, with higher than average leverage, more tangible assets, and higher profitability, are more likely to issue bonds. A cursory look at the data shows that bond markets in Latin America are characterized by a small number of large firms issuing sizable bonds. This suggests that there are large fixed costs associated with bond issuance. The fact that many firms are "repeat issuers" (as suggested by the smaller number of firms than issues) points towards the existence of two forms of fixed costs: those related to becoming an issuer (disclosure costs, required accounting changes, etc.) and those related to each specific issuance (underwriting fees, etc.). These high issuance costs may be one explanation for the importance of alternative debt instruments in some of the countries considered, such as the checks of deferred payment that have become an increasingly common form of financing for firms in Argentina.

Table 7.2 Composition of Domestic Government Bonds

| Country | Year | Percentage of government domestic bonded debt | | | | | | Percentage of GDP |
		Foreign currency	Prices	Interest rate	Nominal	Short term[a]	Long term[a]	Total
Argentina	1994	65.82	0.00	0.00	34.18	0.00	100.00	7.90
	2000	89.66	0.00	0.00	10.34	15.52	84.48	11.60
	2005	28.05	71.29	0.00	0.66	0.00	100.00	30.30
Brazil	1990	0.00	0.00	86.86	13.14	13.14	0.00	6.50
	1994	44.27	32.11	22.04	1.58	1.58	76.38	10.10
	2000	4.95	2.33	67.76	24.95	26.67	5.57	27.50
	2005	0.58	15.35	54.29	29.78	18.38	27.34	51.90
Chile	1990	0.00	83.72	16.28	0.00	0.00	83.72	68.40
	1994	0.00	85.78	14.22	0.00	0.00	85.78	56.10
	2000	0.00	74.38	25.62	0.00	0.00	74.38	50.80
	2004	0.00	92.08	7.92	0.00	0.00	100.00	34.90
Colombia	1995	0.00	0.00	0.00	100.00	0.00	100.00	4.60
	2000	7.14	20.18	0.00	72.68	0.00	100.00	15.30
	2005	0.99	20.42	0.00	78.59	2.69	97.31	29.10
Mexico	1990	2.30	9.29	41.79	46.63	48.40	9.81	21.80
	1994	54.94	16.56	4.86	23.64	78.58	16.56	12.10
	2000	0.00	11.29	54.68	34.02	22.80	22.52	14.00
	2005	0.00	5.01	43.07	51.92	16.74	40.19	21.60
Uruguay	1990	92.80	0.00	0.00	7.20	58.90	41.10	23.60
	1994	98.31	0.00	0.00	1.69	40.68	59.32	12.00
	2000	96.81	0.00	0.00	3.19	9.57	90.43	9.40
	2005	71.72	26.90	0.00	1.38	20.00	80.00	14.60

Source: Cowan et al. (2006).
[a] As a share of total domestic debt.

The importance of issuance costs is confirmed by the results of a set of firm-level surveys which show that a sizable fraction of firms that used to issue bonds but no longer do so identify "high emission costs" and "emission requirements" as the main reasons for no longer issuing bonds. Moreover, firms surveyed usually state that minimum size, information requirements, and lengthy procedures make bonds less attractive as a source of financing vis-à-vis bank financing. At the same time, bonds dominate banks in terms of maturity and interest rates.

The importance of market size in these case studies is consistent with the cross-section results of Borensztein, Eichengreen, and Panizza (2006a) and Eichengreen and Luengnaruemitchai (2004), who find that country size is one of the few variables that has a systematic effect on the size of the private bond market. Interestingly, Borensztein, Eichengreen, and Panizza (2006a) show that size matters when bond stocks are scaled both by GDP and by a measure of broad financial development, indicating that in larger countries bond markets not only are larger but are also relatively more important within the financial system.

The obvious question, therefore, is whether the fixed issuance and disclosure costs that make bonds attractive only to a small group of large firms are particularly high in the region. Domestic issuances are more than twice as expensive in Uruguay as in Mexico. More importantly, in both Brazil and Chile, issuance costs for debt placed offshore are lower than the domestic costs (Table 7.3). Considering the higher relative prices of nontradable goods in the United States, this suggests space for significant reductions in the average costs of issuance in Latin America. It is an open question whether the cost differences are due to the existence of fixed costs in market infrastructure (and should therefore diminish as bond markets expand) or are due to differences in regulation and financial market structure that would lead to higher costs for a given size of total issuance.

Do bond markets in the region provide an alternative to bank financing for firms in the region? Not always. For a start (and as discussed above) bond markets remain small in most countries surveyed in this chapter. Furthermore, in many countries, private bond issuance is dominated by financial sector firms for whom bonds provide an alternative to demand deposits, time deposits, CDs, etc. This is particularly true in Mexico and Uruguay, where more than 80 percent of private sector bonds are issued by the financial sector. The upside of this is that smaller firms can potentially tap longer-term credit through financial intermediaries. In Brazil, for instance, about 70 percent of the volume consists of issues by leasing companies and is associated with long-term financing through leasing of fixed assets.

Furthermore, even if expensive and underdeveloped, domestic markets are likely to be the only way in which small and medium-sized enterprises can access the bond market. A sample of 22 emerging market countries shows that the median issue is US$17 million on the domestic market but $100 million on the international market (Table 7.4). Data for a sample of six Latin American countries show an even more striking difference: the median value of domestic issuances is $22 million and that of international issuances is $175 million. A way of focusing on the segment of the market relevant to SMEs is to look at the lowest decile of the distribution. In this case, the mean and median are both roughly $1.5 million for domestic issues but about $5 million for international issues. Again, the difference is even more striking in Latin America, where mean and median values for domestic issuance are about $0.6 million but those for international issuance are well above $40 million. This is consistent with the notion that SMEs in a position to borrow and service only relatively small amounts

Table 7.3 Total Issuance Costs for Issues of US$100 Million

(percentage of issue size)

	Brazil	Chile	Mexico	Uruguay[a]
Domestic debt	2.39	2.74	1.18	2.88
Domestic equity	4.39	1.62	3.93	n.d.
International debt	2.22	2.22	2.22	n.d.

Sources: Zervos (2004) and de Brun et al. (2006).
Note: n.d. = no data.
[a] Denotes cost of issuing a bond with a value of US$50 million.

of debt may be able to place issues on domestic markets even when they are locked out of international markets owing to their small scale (Borensztein, Eichengreen, and Panizza, 2006c).

Asset-backed securities are a fairly new family of financial instruments in Latin America, but their presence has been growing rapidly in the past two or three years, and they show interesting potential. The instruments include mainly securities that enable firms and financial institutions to securitize their receivables, mortgage-backed securities, and commercial paper. Several countries are creating the legal framework that permits the development of this type of instrument. In Brazil, the development of mortgage-backed securities (*certificado de recebíveis imobiliários,* or *CRIs*) and receivables investment funds (*fundos de investimentos em direitos creditórios,* or *FIDCs*), with impetus from the central bank and the securities and exchange commission, was a significant step in widening the market. Issues of these two instruments grew by 250 percent in 2005 and amounted to the equivalent of US$4.5 billion. Argentina is an interesting example in which asset-backed securities provided something of a spare tire for the ailing banking sector in recent years. The securitization of receivables (*fideicomisos financieros*), especially consumer credit and agricultural export revenues, and a form of commercial paper (*cheques de pago diferido*) grew strongly in recent years. The issue of *fideicomisos,* in particular, more than tripled in 2005, although the volume was still a fairly modest US$1.7 billion.

Asset-backed securities, if successfully implemented, may address two of the issues that hold back private bonds in Latin America. First, the legal and institutional requirements for exercising creditor rights are simpler for asset-backed securities because the assets are backed by collateral—such as property or a vehicle—and foreclosing should be less complicated than going through bankruptcy proceedings, as would be required in the case of unsecured corporate bonds. While effective and speedy recourse to the legal system still imposes requirements for institutions that may not be available everywhere, the bar is set lower for asset-backed securities. Second, the problem of small firm size can be circumvented by pooling a large number of firms in a structured security. Banks can use their superior expertise in selecting credits and can avoid carrying an excessive volume of correlated risk credits on their books. Especially in cases where banks have been very conservative in lending, asset-backed securities can be an effective instrument for increasing financial intermediation and investment in Latin America.

The international financial institutions can play a role in promoting securitization. Just to give one example, the IDB's Private Sector Department has provided guarantees to the Brazilian Securities Mortgage Instruments Warehouse Facility and is planning to conduct further operations based on future cash flow securitization.

Table 7.4 Issue Size for Domestically and Internationally Issued Corporate Bonds

(US$ million)

	Average	Median	5th percentile	10th percentile	Bottom decile Average	Bottom decile Median	Number of bonds
			Domestic bonds				
All emerging markets	47.8	17.4	1.5	3.4	1.5	1.4	13,624
Latin America	65.7	21.7	0.6	1.5	0.7	0.6	4,081
			International bonds				
All emerging markets	167.5	100.0	5.5	10.0	5.5	5.0	1,787
Latin America	216.0	175.0	45.0	65.0	42.0	45.0	395

Source: Borensztein, Eichengreen, and Panizza (2006a).

INTERACTIONS BETWEEN THE GOVERNMENT AND PRIVATE BOND MARKETS

The presence of a liquid market for government bonds can benefit the corporate bond market in terms of providing the necessary infrastructure for trading, producing information about the future path of interest rates, and providing a benchmark curve. However, bigger is not always better, as the benefits related to the creation of pricing and hedging instruments can be eliminated if the government crowds out private borrowers (McCauley and Remolona, 2000).

Empirical analyses of the relative costs and benefits of having a large domestic government bond market yield mixed results. Eichengreen and Luengnaruemitchai (2004) find no significant impact of the size of the government bond market on the development of the private bond market and conclude that this may be because the benefits in terms of liquidity and market infrastructure balance the costs in terms of crowding out. It is not obvious, however, how this crowding out would work. While a higher level of government debt may crowd out private investment through its effect on interest rates, it is less clear why the method of financing should matter. In fact, crowding out would require the assumption that private investors are willing to allocate a fixed share of their portfolio to bonded debt.

Borensztein, Eichengreen, and Panizza (2006c) use bond-level data for a sample of 16 emerging market countries to determine whether the level of public debt versus its composition has a differential effect on the development of the private bond market. They find that, with total public debt controlled for, having a large domestic bond market is associated with longer maturity and lower spreads of corporate bonds and that, with the share of domestic government bonds controlled for, higher levels of total public debt are associated with

Figure 7.7
Domestic Government Bonds and Corporate Bonds:
Regression with Country and Year Fixed Effects

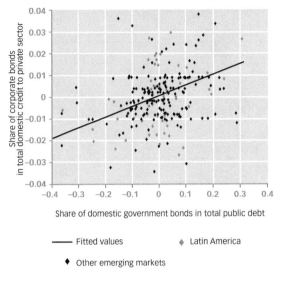

Share of domestic government bonds in total public debt

——— Fitted values   ♦ Latin America

♦ Other emerging markets

Sources: Bank for International Settlements, and World Bank, *World Development Indicators*.

shorter maturity and higher spreads of corporate bonds.[14] This suggests that crowding out comes from the level of public debt and not from its composition. A simple way to check the crowding out versus market development hypothesis is to compare the evolution of the composition of government debt with that of private debt. Figure 7.7 shows that the share of domestic government bonds in total public debt is positively correlated with the share of corporate bonds in total domestic credit to the private sector.[15] This finding goes in the same direction as the results of Borensztein, Eichengreen, and Panizza (2006c) in suggesting that, for a given level of public debt, the higher the share of domestic financing, the greater the development of the private bond market.[16]

A set of surveys aimed at determining whether institutional investors value the benefits of a larger government bond market found that investors in Chile, Colombia, Mexico, and Uruguay tended to agree with the idea that a large stock of public debt is important for the development of the corporate bond market, while investors in Brazil tended to disagree with this statement. There also seems to be agreement on the fact that having a yield curve is a crucial element for having the ability to price corporate bonds. The same surveys also found that government and corporate bonds seem to be competing in the portfolio of institutional investors located in Uruguay and to some extent Mexico, but this is not the case in Brazil, Chile, and Colombia (Cowan and Panizza, 2006).

What about spillover effects from the composition of public debt to that of private debt? As discussed above, there is no clear pattern emerging from the countries surveyed

---

[14] These results are in line with Dittmar and Yuan's (2006) finding that emerging markets' issuances of new sovereign bonds in international markets lower the spreads of existing corporate bonds.

[15] The figure is a partial plot of a regression that controls for country and year fixed effects. The sample includes only emerging markets but excludes Turkey and Argentina in 2002–2004 and Korea, Malaysia, and Thailand in 1997–1998. Including these outliers, however, would not alter the basic message of the correlation plotted in Figure 7.7.

[16] Developments in Chile do not seem to fit this stylized fact, because falling public bonds in the late 1990s coincided with rising private bond stocks. An alternative explanation is that private bond market development is less related to the stock of public bonds than to liquidity at different maturities in the public bond market. There is therefore a nonlinear relationship between government bond size and the development of the private bond market. Below the minimum level needed to sustain liquidity, increasing the size of the stock of government bonds has a positive effect on private development. After this level is reached, additional public bonds will either have no effect (as long as total public debt is constant) or lead to crowding out of private debt.

by Cowan and Panizza (2006). Whereas in Mexico, "safer" public bond debt has been accompanied by "safer" private bonds, this has not been the case in other countries. This is not surprising, as the relationship between private and public debt structure is complex. On the one hand, having a CPI-indexed or a nominal yield curve for public debt should make pricing of similar types of private debt easier. On the other hand, debt currency and maturity is the outcome of insurance transactions against various idiosyncratic risks (inflation, real exchange rate, real interest rate, etc.) between suppliers and demanders of credit. Changes in risk aversion or in the expectations regarding these shocks may be different in the public and private sectors. Take, for instance, the case of Argentina and assume that the reduction of foreign currency public debt came from an increased awareness in the public sector of the risks of this form of debt. This being the case, the government would then be willing to pay the higher interest charged on peso debt—which in the Argentine case specifically took the form of larger present value of payment in the negotiations in regard to defaulted debt. Nothing guarantees, however, that the private sector experiences the same shift in demand for safer debt. Indeed, seeing a government balance sheet with larger nominal debt may actually make investors more concerned about opportunistic government behavior and therefore demand more dollar debt contracts rather than fewer.

THE IMPORTANCE OF HAVING THE RIGHT PLUMBING

While there is an extensive literature that focuses on the relationship between market development and macroeconomic stability, much less is known about the role of market microstructure in emerging market countries (Madhavan, 2000). Economic theory often takes a view of financial markets as a black box that absorbs information and produces an optimal allocation of capital and pricing of risk. Microstructure theory tries to move away from this black box description and emphasizes that institutional features and trading mechanisms (often referred to as the plumbing of the market) are important determinants of market efficiency. According to this view, microstructure plays a key role in determining liquidity, efficiency, trading costs, and volatility (Glen, 1994). Politics also plays a role in determining microstructure, and if primary dealers manage to "capture" the state treasury, microstructure can become a source of rent and inefficiencies (Kroszner, 1998). This section briefly reviews some issues related to market microstructure, but it does not focus on issues related to the development of market infrastructure (such as depository and settlement facilities).[17] Furthermore, the section concentrates on the microstructure of the market for government bonds and hence does not discuss issues like corporate governance and the establishment of local credit-rating agencies, which are more relevant for the development of corporate bond markets.[18]

One way in which microstructure can affect market *liquidity* (i.e., the capacity for buying or selling without delay and with a minimum effect on prices) is through the decision on whether to trade through continuous or periodic auctions. The former system has the benefit of giving participants continuous access to the market, but the latter system has the benefit of bunching transactions together and hence increasing the depth of the market.

---

[17] For a detailed discussion, see IMF and World Bank (2003).
[18] For an excellent survey of these issues, see Luengnaruemitchai and Ong (2005).

Execution risk is often high in newly developed markets, which are often thin and illiquid, a situation that makes periodic markets preferable. Continuous auctions are preferable, on the other hand, in well-developed markets with a large number of participants. Debt managers can also improve liquidity in secondary markets by issuing a smaller number of security types and hence reducing the fragmentation of their own debt stock. Here as well, however, there are trade-offs. While having a small number of securities may be good for volatility purposes, it does reduce authorities' ability to issue instruments with different types of indexation and maturity.

Microstructure can have an effect on market *efficiency* (i.e., the idea that prices incorporate all available information) in that it affects the type of information available to investors. Take, for instance, the decision on whether a given security should be traded on an organized exchange or intermediated by dealers in decentralized over-the-counter (OTC) markets. Organized exchanges have advantages in terms of transparency and price discovery and hence tend to be positively associated with market efficiency. However, OTC markets are less institutionally complex, can provide immediate liquidity under uncertain market conditions, are cheaper to manage (because they require less-demanding clearing and settlement systems), and, having lower fixed costs, may dominate organized exchanges when markets are small.[19] While most countries trade government bonds on the OTC market, several Latin American countries also use organized exchanges (Table 7.5).

Price discovery on the primary market may also depend on the type of auction used to allocate government bonds. There are essentially two types of auctions used for this purpose: discriminatory price auctions (also called American or Yankee auctions) and uniform price auctions (also called Dutch auctions). In the first type of auction, securities are sold to each primary dealer at the bidding price quoted by that dealer. In a uniform price auction, in contrast, all successful bidders pay the same price (usually the lowest among those offered by the successful bidders). In theory, Yankee auctions should lead each dealer to pay its reservation price; in practice, though, dealers know that they might be subject to the "winner's curse," and this may induce them to underbid. In fact, there is some evidence that Dutch auctions may increase revenues (Bartolini and Cottarelli, 1997), and the U.S. Treasury has now moved to uniform price auctions. The problem is that Dutch auctions may also lead to collusion, especially in markets with a small number of primary dealers. In practice, Argentina, Chile, Colombia, and Peru use Dutch auctions, Brazil and Venezuela use Yankee auctions (Venezuela exclusively, Brazil predominantly), and Mexico uses both Dutch and Yankee auctions depending on the type of security (Table 7.5). Kroszner (1997) suggests that Dutch auctions are superior to Yankee auctions but that the latter increase the value of primary dealers' privileged information. As a consequence, discriminatory price auctions often result in a hidden transfer to the primary dealers.

Governments can also increase the efficiency of the market for government bonds by disseminating pre-trade and post-trade information. One way to improve the transparency of the primary market is to publish an issue calendar and make information about the auction

---

[19] This does not explain why most U.S. bonds are traded OTC. In fact, Biais and Green (2005) argue that this is mostly an accident of history and that retail investors would benefit if trading of these bonds were to move to an organized exchange.

Table 7.5 Structure of Latin American Government Bond Markets

	Type of primary auction	Secondary market	Bid-ask spread (basic points)	Daily turnover (US$ million)
Latin America				
Argentina[a]	Dutch	Stock exchange and OTC	20	60
Brazil	Mostly Yankee	Mostly OTC but also exchange	1–5	2,500
Chile	Dutch	Mostly OTC but also exchange	5	200
Colombia	Dutch	Exchange at Banco de la República	40[b]	1,900
Mexico	Yankee and Dutch	OTC	5–10	25,000
Peru	Dutch	OTC	n.d.	80
Venezuela	Yankee[c]	OTC[c]	100–200[c]	200
Other emerging markets				
Czech Republic[b]	Yankee	Stock exchange and OTC	20	100
Hong Kong	Yankee	OTC	4	2,500
Hungary	Yankee	OTC	10–20	350
India	Dutch	OTC	1–2	700
Indonesia	n.d.	OTC	25–100	Low
Korea	Dutch	OTC	1–5	10,000
Malaysia	Yankee	OTC	2–5	200
Philippines	Yankee	Exchange	3–50	40
Russia	Yankee	OTC	5–20	70
Saudi Arabia	n.d.	n.d.	20	Low
Singapore	Yankee	OTC	3–5	1,000
Slovak Republic	Yankee	OTC	10–20	Low
South Africa	Dutch	OTC	2–5	1,600
Taiwan	Dutch	OTC	5–20	1,600
Thailand	Yankee	OTC	5–10	300
Turkey	Yankee	OTC	10–20	1,000
United States				
United States[b]	Yankee	OTC	3–6	1,215,000

Source: JPMorgan (2006), except as otherwise noted.
Note: OTC = over the counter; n.d. = no data available.
[a] Central bank securities.
[b] Source of data is Mohanty (2002).
[c] Source of data is JP Morgan (2002).

outcome public.[20] Mohanty (2002) surveys 17 emerging market countries and shows that 14 of them (all in Mohanty's survey except Colombia, the Philippines, and Peru) have an issue calendar.

One matter on which there is no agreement concerns the role of primary dealers. These are dealers designated by the authorities to be the intermediary between debt managers and investors. Primary dealers are usually granted bidding privileges and special credit lines but are required to guarantee that auctions are fully subscribed and to act as market makers in the secondary markets. While the presence of primary dealers can help in providing a regular source of liquidity and information for debt managers, some markets may be too small to warrant the participation of this type of agent (IMF and World Bank, 2003), and these agents may end up capturing the regulator and extracting excessive rents (Kroszner, 1997). There is less disagreement, on the other hand, on the importance of having a set of market makers and on the fact that these agents need to have instruments (such as forwards, futures, and swaps) that allow them to hedge against interest rate risk (IMF and World Bank, 2003). Another important element for market development is the presence of related markets. The existence of a repo (repurchase agreement through which dealers "lend out" securities that they have in their inventories) market, for instance, is key for the development of the market for government bonds because it allows dealers to maintain the high level of inventories that is necessary to make two-way quotes (IMF and World Bank, 2003).

Microstructure can also affect *trading costs*. There are essentially two types of costs related to trading a security: fixed costs (commissions and taxes) and the difference between the price received for a sale and that paid for a purchase (the bid-ask spread). In markets with a small number of market makers, bid-ask spreads will tend to be high for at least two reasons. The first relates to the substantial risk absorbed by this small number of agents taking positions for the whole market. The second relates to the fact that the low level of competition is likely to generate monopoly rents. While one might think that a system with a large number of market makers (or an organized exchange with no market makers) should be preferable in terms of having lower spreads, there is a possible trade-off, because once they are deprived of their monopoly rents, some agents may decide to stop acting as market makers, and this could lead to liquidity problems (especially in small markets). Hence, market makers should not extract too much rent from their role, but authorities should recognize that market making entails both liquidity and interest rate risks, and hence they need to make sure that this activity is profitable for the intermediaries. Brazil, Chile, and Mexico have tight bid-ask spreads (close to those prevailing in the United States and in other emerging market countries with low spreads), but the bid-ask spreads in Argentina, Colombia, and Venezuela are wider (substantially so in the case of the latter two countries), as shown in Table 7.5. It is important to note that, besides microstructure, one of the key determinants of bid-ask spreads is market size (Figure 7.8).

Finally, microstructure is related to market *volatility* (i.e., the size and frequency of price changes that do not reflect changes in the fundamental value of an asset). Circuit breakers

---

[20] The publication of an issue calendar helps participants to formulate their bidding strategy and shows the government's commitment to accepting the auction's result. Publishing detailed information on the auction results increases investors' confidence in the process. One possible drawback of publishing an issue calendar is that this limits the government's flexibility in managing its funding needs (Mohanty, 2002).

and price limits that interrupt trading whenever prices exceed a given threshold are the most common mechanisms for limiting volatility. The benefit of such mechanisms is that they force investors to have a "cooling-off" period and allow them to absorb new information and price the security at its fundamental value. The problem is that these mechanisms reduce liquidity and may slow the convergence of an asset to its fundamental value.

While the above discussion has clarified the importance of market microstructure, it has also highlighted that there are no one-size-fits-all solutions and has indicated that systems that may work well in the presence of large markets may not work as well in the small markets that characterize a number of Latin American and Caribbean countries. Furthermore, the ideal microstructure of markets characterized by a large number of retail investors is likely to be different from that of markets characterized by relatively small numbers of sophisticated institutional investors.

Figure 7.8
Daily Turnover and Bid-Ask Spread

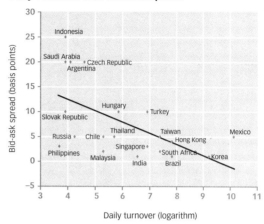

Source: Authors' calculations based on data from JP Morgan (2002, 2006).

SUMMING UP

This chapter has shown that Latin America tends to have relatively well-developed markets for government bonds but extremely small private bond markets. The question is whether this contrast is likely to be short lived or enduring. If the problem leading to small private bond markets in Latin America is that years of budget deficits have led to excessive government bond issuance that has crowded out private bond issuance, then many years of primary fiscal surpluses may have to pass before the "overhang" of government bonds is worked down. If it is that Latin America's history of macroeconomic and financial instability limits investors' demand to debt securities with interest rates indexed to inflation or the exchange rate, then many years may have to pass before stronger policies leading to reduced volatility will produce a demand for longer-term issues. If perceptions of imperfect corporate governance and unreliable contract enforcement currently render investors reluctant to hold corporate bonds at any price, then some time may have to pass before the relevant reforms begin to create a significant demand. If in smaller Latin American and Caribbean countries the local market's lack of scale is the obstacle to spreading the fixed cost of an issue and enhancing secondary market liquidity, then reasonable questions can be raised as to whether this obstacle can ever be overcome. Or maybe these estimates are overstated; maybe the relevant reforms will succeed in producing deeper and more liquid bond markets in short order. In sum, the question is: how long will it take for Latin America and the Caribbean to develop deep and liquid bond markets?

CHAPTER 8 | Institutional Investors and the Domestic Debt Market

WHILE A DOMESTIC INSTITUTIONAL investor sector is a fundamental component of well-developed financial markets, the presence of one can be a mixed blessing in some emerging markets, in which governments are often financially strained and look for "captive" investors with whom to place their debt.[1] In particular, governments can be tempted to obtain financing from institutional investors through moral suasion or by twisting regulations in situations in which market access by normal means becomes scarce. Scarcity of financing in a country may arise from concerns about the soundness of its public finances. If those concerns are well founded, the government's use of institutional investors to obtain financing will allow the country's debt to grow, and the eventual debt crisis to become more severe, while the losses that institutional investors eventually suffer may compromise the whole financial system. Conversely, a financing shortage in a country may arise from disruptions in the country's financial markets, with little justification in terms of economic fundamentals. This may be the result of poorly informed investors reacting as a "herd" and magnifying a small financial disturbance. In such a case, local institutional investors with better information and longer investment horizons can help increase stability in the market.

A group of large, well-managed institutional investors is the anchor of many advanced domestic capital markets. Complex problems generally arise when a country's domestic capital market is still relatively small, and when governments have large debts and are subject to frequent liquidity shortages.

THE GROWTH OF INSTITUTIONAL INVESTORS

Institutional investors are an important source of financing for central governments. In 2000, pension funds, insurance companies, and mutual funds held about one-quarter of total central government debt in emerging markets. By 2005, the share of government debt held by these institutional investors had grown to almost one-third of total central government debt (IMF, 2006b).

Although institutional investors are critically important for the functioning of a country's domestic government debt market, they are not a homogenous group with similar investment objectives. On the contrary, different types of institutional investors follow their own investment guidelines, and as a result the demand for government bonds ranges from short-

---

[1] This chapter draws on Kiguel (2006).

term treasury bills to long-term instruments. Pension funds and life insurance companies have a predictable funding flow and fairly predictable liabilities for long periods of time. As a consequence, they have a long-term planning horizon and look for assets that generate a stable flow of real income. By contrast, mutual funds and investment companies focus on the current market value of their portfolios, which is their main indicator of performance. Moreover, as they could face redemptions from shareholders at almost any time and are required to mark all their assets to market, they pay close attention to the liquidity of the financial instruments in which they invest.

Banks are different from standard institutional investors because of the nature of their liabilities. As they have short-term deposits that are fixed in nominal terms and are redeemable on demand, banks differ from mutual funds (which also have short-term liabilities but whose value fluctuates with the market value of their assets) and from insurance companies and pension funds, which face long-term liabilities.

The growth in the assets held by institutional investors has been remarkable in all segments of the global economy (Figure 8.1). In the advanced economies, the assets of pension funds and mutual funds increased from approximately 80 percent of GDP in 1997 to 112 percent of GDP in 2003.[2] Institutional investors are less important in emerging markets, but the growth of their assets in these markets has been very rapid as well, from 18 to 30 percent of GDP over the 1997–2003 period. In the mid-1990s, Latin American institutional investors held assets equal to approximately 10 percent of regional GDP, and hence their assets accounted for a much smaller share of GDP than those of average institutional investors in the emerging markets. Over the 1997–2003 period, the size of the assets held by Latin American institutional investors grew faster than that of institutional investors located in other emerging markets and, by 2003, the aggregate assets of Latin American institutional investors were almost identical in size to those of institutional investors in the emerging markets. This rapid growth in the asset size of Latin American institutional investors was mainly due to the creation of private pension funds that took place in many Latin American countries in the mid-1990s.

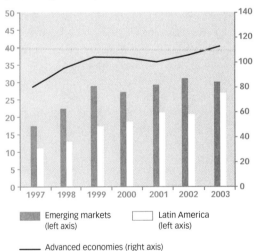

Figure 8.1
Assets of Mutual Funds and Pension Funds
(*percentage of GDP*)

Emerging markets (left axis)
Latin America (left axis)
Advanced economies (right axis)

Source: IMF (2004b).

---

[2] If insurance companies are added to these figures, the size of the assets held by institutional investors reaches 160 percent of GDP in 2003. The advanced economies with the largest amounts of assets held by institutional investors are the United States and the United Kingdom, followed by France and Canada. Germany and Spain have relatively small institutional investors (Kiguel, 2006).

Table 8.1 Assets of Institutional Investors

(percentage of GDP)

	Insurance companies	Pension funds	Mutual funds and investment companies	Total
Advanced economies	45.40	50.40	47.20	143.00
Argentina	4.60	12.00	1.00	17.60
Brazil	2.80	14.80	28.40	46.00
Chile	19.90	59.10	8.80	87.80
Colombia	1.00	10.30	23.30	34.60
Mexico	1.70	5.80	5.80	13.30
Peru	2.20	11.00	n.d.	n.d.
Latin American average	**5.37**	**18.83**	**13.46**	**39.86**

Sources: Kiguel (2006); for Brazil, Associação Brasileira Das Entidades Fechadas de Previdencia Complementar (ABRAPP), available at http://www.abrapp.org.br.
Note: All data are for 2003, with the exception of data for insurance companies, which refer to 2002. n.d. = data not available.

In the advanced economies, pension funds and insurance companies have traditionally been the largest institutional investors, although the amounts invested by investment companies (essentially, a variety of mutual funds) have recently been growing at a faster pace. The relative importance (in terms of total assets) of the different types of institutional investors varies from country to country. Insurance companies are relatively more important in the United Kingdom and in Japan, and pension funds in the United Kingdom, while investment companies prevail in the United States.

Within Latin America, the countries with the largest presence of institutional investors are Chile and Brazil (Table 8.1). Chile was the first country in the region to privatize its pension system, and the assets of its institutional investors now amount to 88 percent of GDP (with pension funds managing assets equivalent to 60 percent of GDP). In Chile, insurance companies grew together with pension funds, primarily because they provide both retirement income and life insurance to pension fund contributors. Mutual funds, though much smaller, still hold almost 9 percent of the Chilean GDP in assets under management. In Argentina, pension funds are the largest group of institutional investors, with assets amounting to 12 percent of GDP, while insurance companies manage assets equivalent to 5 percent of GDP, and mutual funds hold assets representing only 1 percent of GDP. Brazil is a unique case, as mutual funds are the largest institutional investors in that country, and their assets represent almost 30 percent of GDP.[3] Asset holdings of mutual funds are also substantial in Colombia, where they are equivalent to 23 percent of GDP, more than twice the amount managed by pension funds.

---

[3] Brazilian mutual funds work mainly as money market funds and hold primarily government debt.

PENSION FUNDS

The development of the pension fund industry in Latin America is relatively recent. In most Latin American countries, the industry started to grow in the mid-1990s as a result of the creation of private pension fund management companies when these countries started to move from pay-as-you-go pension systems to fully funded pension schemes. On average, the advanced economies tend to have larger pension funds than Latin American countries, but this is mostly because the United States, Great Britain, and Canada have very large pension funds. Once these three countries are dropped from the sample, the size (expressed as a share of GDP) of Latin American pension funds is not too different from (and, if anything, larger than) that of those in the advanced economies (Figure 8.2).

Pension funds located in the advanced economies hold about one-quarter of their assets in government bonds (Figure 8.3). There are, however, substantial differences among countries in this group. In countries with large pension funds like the United Kingdom and United States, funds hold a relatively low proportion of government bonds. Countries with smaller pension funds (such as Austria and Italy) are characterized by much larger holdings of government bonds. Pension funds of emerging market countries located outside Latin America hold more than 50 percent of their assets, on average, in government bonds.[4] The average share of government paper held by Latin American pension funds is 44 percent of total assets, which is larger than the prevailing average share in pension funds in the advanced economies but smaller than the prevailing average share in emerging markets. Again, there are large differences within the region. Government debt is particularly important (close to or greater than 50 percent of total assets) in Mexico, Argentina, Uruguay, and Colombia, but relatively unimportant in Peru, Brazil, and Chile.

Usually, holdings of public sector debt are particularly high when a country's private pension system is initially established. This is in part a result of the design of pension reforms, which often have the objective of helping governments to finance the costs of the transition out of a state-managed social security system, with its remaining liabilities to the retiring population. As high as these requirements may be, pension funds have at times held even higher shares of public debt owing to limited attractive investment opportunities in the private sector and legal limits on foreign asset holdings. Several Latin American countries (including Chile and Mexico) established special guidelines when their private pension systems were initially set up, allowing pension funds to hold a large fraction of their assets in government bonds in order to reduce the financing risks of the transition from a pay-as-you-go system to a fully funded one.[5] The idea was that limits on holdings of government debt would be reduced over time to ensure that pension funds diversified their assets and did not concentrate their exposure in the public sector. In other cases (e.g., Argentina and Uruguay), there were strict limits from the very beginning on the pension system's holdings of govern-

---

[4] Government bonds are particularly important in Central and Eastern Europe, where pension funds are relatively recent. In East Asia, however, there are large cross-country differences: Singapore has a large share of government bonds, Thailand is an intermediate case, and Korea has pension funds with small holdings of government paper.

[5] As noted in Chapter 2, the financing gap associated with these transitions was in most cases almost entirely funded through the placement of government bonds with pension funds.

Figure 8.2
Pension Fund Assets as a Percentage of GDP

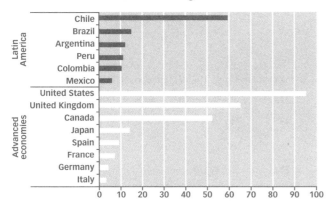

Source: Kiguel (2006).

Figure 8.3
Government Bonds as a Percentage of Pension Fund Assets

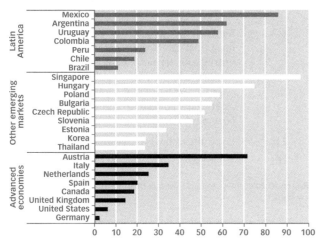

Source: Kiguel (2006).

ment bonds. The existing regulations are diverse, but most countries now impose limits (which are not always enforced) on the holding of government bonds or on overall exposure to the public sector (Table 8.2).

Thus, in Chile, pension fund exposure to the public sector remained at around 50 percent of total assets through most of the 1980s and started to fall gradually only in the 1990s, before dropping sharply in the last six years. One possible reason for this reduction in pension funds' holdings of public debt is that, as Chilean pension funds were confronted with a shortage of public debt (they currently hold roughly 85 percent of the total), they started to find alternative investments in Chile and abroad (aided by a gradual relaxation of the foreign asset share limit).

In Mexico, pension funds' holdings of public debt started at very high levels (97 percent of assets) and remain at very high levels, though they are gradually being reduced. Argentina is clearly an outlier, as the holdings of government bonds significantly increased almost seven years after the inception of the reformed pension system, when the government faced the 2001–2002 debt crisis. This increase in the holdings of government paper was, by and large, not voluntary and was driven by the need to ensure financing prior to the crisis. A similar scenario is observed in Uruguay following the recent debt crisis (Figure 8.4).

The only large Latin American country in which private pension funds hold a small share of total public debt is Brazil. Incidentally, Brazil is also the only large Latin American country that did not implement pension reform in the last few decades and hence has voluntary

Table 8.2 Pension Fund Investments in Government Bonds and Foreign Assets

	Limits on holdings of public sector bonds		Limits on holdings of foreign assets	
	Legal framework	Actual holdings	Legal framework	Actual holdings
Argentina	50% of assets.	62%	Up to 10% of fund's asset value.	9%
Bolivia	None.	77%	10–50% of fund's asset value.	3%
Chile	40–70% of assets, depending on type of fund.	19%	Up to 30% of fund's asset value.	24%
Colombia	50% of assets.	49%	As regards compulsory pensions, up to 10% of fund's total value can be invested in foreign assets (rule effective since September 1, 2001). No qualitative limits have been set for voluntary pensions, although law requires that issuer be awarded "investment grade" status by credit-rating agencies.	7%
Mexico	None.	86%	Although the SIEFORES law determines that total investment in instruments denominated in foreign currencies (U.S. dollars, euros, yen) must not exceed 10% of fund's total asset value, no restrictions have been placed on issuer's origin.	9%
Peru	40% of assets.	24%	Up to 10% of fund's asset value.	10%
Uruguay	50% of assets.	58%	(Information not available.)	0

Sources: Levy Yeyati (2004); Kiguel (2006); Federación Internacional de Administradoras de Fondos de Pensiones (FIAP), available at http://www.fiap.cl.

pension funds.[6] Note that this low level of public debt holdings is due not to the fact that Brazil has small pension funds (in 2004, the assets of Brazilian pension funds were about 16 percent of GDP), but rather to the fact that these funds hold a small amount of government securities. In 2004, only 12 percent of the assets of Brazilian pension funds were invested

---

[6] Brazil's system is voluntary in the sense that there is no Brazilian law that requires all workers to participate in a pension fund. However, the majority of large Brazilian enterprises require their workers to contribute to a pension fund. Therefore, for an employee of, say, Petrobras, participation in a private pension fund is not voluntary.

in government securities (Cowan and Panizza, 2006).[7]

Although their exposure to the public sector is likely to decline in the coming years, pension funds are still likely to be important participants in the public debt market.[8] Moreover, the cited preference for real returns makes them a natural investor base for local currency markets (Levy Yeyati, 2004). While governments should try to take advantage of the needs of pension funds and other institutional investors to fulfill their financial programs, a prudential regulatory framework needs to ensure that the government does not force them to hold more government bonds than these investors consider optimal. In most cases this objective is facilitated by requiring pension funds to mark bonds to market and by limiting their ability to book them as loans or long-term investments that could be considered at technical values until their maturity (for a discussion of this issue, see the last section of this chapter).

One major restriction on the portfolio of pension funds is the limit on the foreign asset share, which aims to ensure that savings are channeled into the domestic economy. The fact that this restriction is binding in most cases (Table 8.2), combined with the dearth of long-run

Figure 8.4
Percentage of Public Debt in Total Assets of Pension Funds

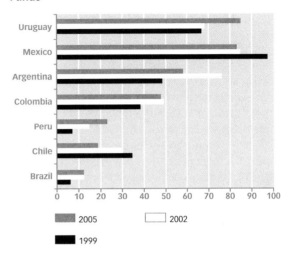

Sources: Kiguel (2006); for Brazil, Associação Brasileira Das Entidades Fechadas de Previdencia Complementar (ABRAPP), available at http://www.abrapp.org.br.

---

[7] This figure may, however, underestimate the real share of Brazilian pension fund assets invested in government securities. Leal and Lustosa (2004) show that in 2004, Brazilian pension funds had 12 percent of their portfolios *directly* invested in treasury securities. However, only 3 percent of their assets were invested in private debt, 5 percent in real estate, and 18 percent in equities. The remainder, 62 percent of the portfolio, was invested in fixed income funds and hedge funds. As these funds invest most of their assets in treasury securities, it is safe to say that the aggregate pension fund holdings of treasury securities is about 12 percent *directly* and more than 50 percent *indirectly*, through other funds. In fact, there seem to be some incentives for pension fund managers in Brazil to hold treasury securities. In the 1990s Brazilian pension funds were subject to rules that specified a minimum amount of their portfolios that should be held in treasury securities. In the late 1990s, new prudential rules were introduced, and instead of minimum holdings, maximum holdings of such securities have been established. Some of the maximum holdings are classified according to their credit risk; as treasury securities are considered to be in the class that has the lowest risk, fund managers have an incentive to hold these assets. In closing, it is important to point out also that Brazilian pension funds cannot hold foreign assets.

[8] One striking feature of pension funds in Latin America is the small amount of stocks that they hold, as these investments represent only 16 percent of total pension system assets in Chile, the most mature system in the region. Peru, whose pension system holds 38 percent of its assets in stocks, is clearly an outlier. One open question is whether pension funds do not hold stocks because there is a lack of supply or whether instead it is a deliberate choice which limits the growth of the equity market in these countries. In several Latin American countries there are limits on the amount of equities that can be held by pension funds, but these limits are rarely binding (Mexico is an exception). In Argentina and Brazil, pension funds are allowed to hold up to 50 percent of their portfolio in stocks, and in Chile, Colombia, and Peru, the ceilings range between 30 and 40 percent (IMF, 2004b).

private investment assets, has certainly contributed to pension funds' marked concentration in government debt. A survey of institutional investors in six Latin American countries suggests that pension funds would like to hold more foreign assets but are prevented from doing so by existing constraints (Cowan and Panizza, 2006). Although there may be a prudential basis for the limit on foreign investment—to avoid a currency mismatch, as pension funds' liabilities are denominated in domestic currency—it is unclear whether this reason justifies the imposed limit or whether the desire to create a captive demand for domestic financial instruments is the driving force of the regulations. Some recent developments may result in a relaxation of these constraints, with several countries opening up their markets to issuers from other countries in the region. For example, a Mexican company (América Móvil) is in the process of issuing long-term bonds in Chile which, under a newly implemented Chilean law, will be registered as domestic bonds and hence become exempt from restrictions based on foreign asset shares. Given the growth potential of the Latin American cross-border market, the IDB's Private Sector Department is considering the possibility of promoting regional integration opportunities by providing guaranties to cross-border issuers.

INSURANCE COMPANIES

Insurance companies are the largest institutional investors in East Asia, but they are much less important players in Latin America (Figure 8.5). However, the increasing importance of pension funds has resulted in positive spillovers into the annuity market and contributed to the growth of the life insurance sector (IMF, 2004b). As a consequence, it is not surprising that Chile is the Latin American country with the largest insurance sector.

One positive aspect of having a large insurance sector is that, in the majority of countries, insurance companies are not required to mark their assets to market on a daily basis,[9] which allows them to face short periods of market volatility without having to book short-term losses. This, together with the fact that the majority of insurers do not benchmark their performance to any specific index, may limit "herding behavior" and is likely to contribute to the overall stability of domestic financial systems.

On a less positive note, in most emerging market economies, insurers are required to match assets and liabilities. As in several Latin American countries a large share of life insurance contracts are specified in foreign currency, and as insurance companies are often not allowed to hold a large share of foreign assets, these companies end up holding a large amount of sovereign dollar-denominated external debt (IMF, 2004b).

MUTUAL FUNDS

Assets of emerging market mutual funds grew rapidly in the second half of the 1990s and then stabilized over the 2000–2003 period. This trend was due to a contraction of assets held by mutual funds in emerging Asia and a continuous expansion in Latin America (Figure 8.6). Within Latin America, the countries that experienced the fastest growth were Brazil, Colombia, and Costa Rica.

---

[9] They are usually required to do so on a quarterly basis (IMF, 2004b).

Figure 8.5
Assets under Management by Insurance Companies
(*percentage of GDP*)

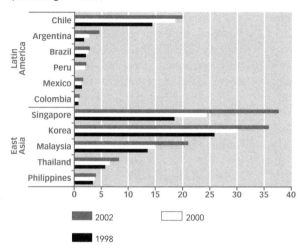

Source: IMF (2004b).

Figure 8.6
Net Mutual Fund Assets
(*percentage of GDP*)

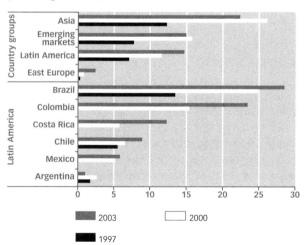

Source: IMF (2004b).
Note: Data for 1997 were not available for Colombia, Costa Rica, and Mexico.

One important difference between the asset composition of mutual funds located in the advanced economies and that of those located in emerging market countries is that in the former, equity funds tend to account for a larger share of the assets than bond funds, while the opposite is true for the latter (this is the case, for instance, in Brazil and Mexico) (IMF, 2004b). This difference is partly due to the fact that in most emerging market countries, stock markets are small, and government bonds are the most liquid instruments in the local capital market. But it is also due to the fact that, in an environment of low short-term interest rates, investors become interested in longer-term bonds and start switching from bank deposits to mutual funds that hold this type of asset. One source of concern with this investment strategy is that retail investors, which are reassured by the low default risk of these instruments, may not understand the market risk associated with their long-term nature, which may amplify market volatility (Box 8.1). In addition, local stock markets are often opaque, with imperfect monitoring and regulation, making them specialists' markets. Finally, unlike those of developed countries, emerging markets' stocks tend to be positively correlated with emerging market bonds, a fact that reduces the hedging benefits of stocks.

Box 8.1 What Happens When Investors Do Not Understand Market Risk

In Colombia, mutual funds were at the center of a "minicrisis" in the treasury bond (TES) market in July-September 2002. Prior to the crisis, many local mutual funds were heavily invested in government bonds with long maturities (10 years), and they had marketed their funds as savings products. Analysts noted, however, that these marketing campaigns stressed the credit ratings of the funds without fully indicating the market risks that were associated with their underlying holdings if interest rates were to rise. When a sharp decline in interest rates occurred between February and June 2002, investors placed money in bond funds because of the attractiveness of the 10-year bond yield and thereby took on significant duration risk. However, an increased perception of regional risk in July 2002 led to a sell-off of Colombia's Yankee bonds and a sharp increase in external debt spreads—in tandem with Brazil spreads. In addition, rising concerns about the country's fiscal situation eventually prompted investors to sell their TES holdings. After this initial sell-off, mutual funds began to experience redemptions by retail investors and were forced to liquidate their positions in a falling market, pushing bond prices down further. In the space of 10 days, the yield on the government bond maturing in 2012 rose from 12 to 20 percent, with a corresponding decrease in the value of the bond, as well as of many mutual funds with significant holdings of the bond. Following this episode, mutual funds shortened the duration of their fixed income portfolios.

Source: IMF (2004b), 140–142.

BANKS IN THE DOMESTIC GOVERNMENT BOND MARKET

Banks are unique players in the government bond market. On the one hand, they invest in government bonds as part of their regular asset management decisions and hold bonds in their portfolios just like other credits. On the other hand, banks are primary dealers and market makers of government bonds, which implies that they participate in regular treasury auctions and provide liquidity for these instruments in secondary markets.[10]

There are least three reasons that lead banks to hold government bonds in their balance sheet:

1. Banks hold government bonds (mainly short-term treasury bills) to manage their liquidity. Government bonds are ideal instruments for this purpose because they generally

---

[10] A key difference between banks and the institutional investors examined in the previous sections is that banks have short-term nominal liabilities. Thus, if there is a fall in the price of government bonds, a bank that holds such bonds takes the loss, while its investors (the depositors) maintain their claims. In addition, banks undertake a liquidity risk, as most of their liabilities (namely, sight deposits) can be claimed on demand, while their assets have longer maturities. As a result, it is riskier for banks to invest in long-term assets, especially if they do not have an adequate level of liquidity.

have a liquid secondary market and can be used for repos with the central bank or with other commercial banks.

2. Banks hold bonds as part of their portfolio decisions. For this purpose they generally buy longer-term treasury bonds that they book in their investment account and hold to maturity. From an accounting point of view these bonds are considered a long-term investment and are included in the "banking" book at their purchase price.

3. Banks hold government bonds for trading and to be market makers in the secondary market for these bonds. These holdings are generally small and valued at market prices.

In the United States banks hold a stock of government bonds equivalent to 14 percent of domestic credit, while in the Euro Area, the average holding of government bonds is 20 percent of domestic credit (Figure 8.7). Banks in Latin America have an average exposure to government bonds of around 25 percent of domestic credit. Banks in Argentina had the largest exposure to the public sector in Latin America in 2003, at close to 50 percent of domestic credit, followed by Mexico, where banks' holdings of government paper represent 42 percent of domestic credit. In contrast, Chilean banks had the smallest exposure to the public sector in the region, well below 10 percent of domestic credit.

There are a number of explanations for the large holdings of government bonds among Latin American banks. In some cases banks in the region hold these bonds as part of their reserve requirements or to comply with regulations—which explains, for instance, roughly one-quarter of banks' holdings of government bonds in Brazil. In the cases of Argentina and Mexico, banks' decision to hold these bonds was not part of a portfolio allocation model, but rather the outcome of the resolution of the banking crises that affected the two countries. In particular, banks exchanged defaulted loans for specially issued government bonds in order to keep operating with an adequate level of capital when the bonds were booked at their technical values. In Argentina banks were also "persuaded" to increase their holdings of government paper in 2001 in order to avoid a government default. So, in a situation in which private credit was shrinking, banks substantially increased their holdings of government assets (Figure 8.8). In other cases, banks might decide voluntarily to hold government bonds because they provide a high yield, are perceived to be less risky (and

Figure 8.7
Banks' Exposure to Public Sector, 2003–2005
(*percentage of total domestic credit*)

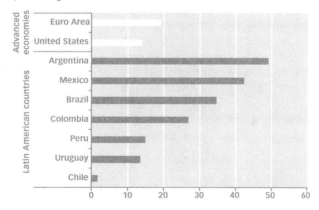

Source: International Monetary Fund, *International Financial Statistics*, lines 32 and 22a.

Figure 8.8
Composition of Bank Lending in Argentina
(*percentage of GDP*)

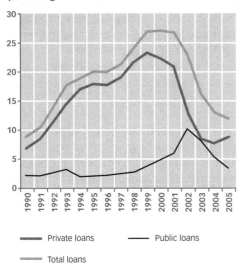

Private loans

Public loans

Total loans

Source: Central Bank of Argentina, available at
http://www.bcra.gov.ar.

implicitly guaranteed by the government) (Box 8.2), and face lower capital requirements than private assets.

In general, it is difficult to know whether banks that hold government bonds are doing so voluntarily or whether they have instead been induced to hold them through regulation or moral suasion. For example, in some cases central banks allow part of a bank's reserve requirements to be held in government instruments, which is one possible incentive to hold public debt.[11] In other cases, regulations can stimulate demand for government bonds by allowing bonds to be on a bank's books at technical values or at the price at which they were originally purchased instead of at market values.

It would thus be useful to separate the portion of banks' exposure to the public sector that is induced through regulation from the portion that arises from their portfolio decisions. One practical way of making this distinction is to force banks to mark to market their exposure to the public sector (Box 8.3).[12]

HOW TO MAKE GOVERNMENT BONDS ATTRACTIVE TO INSTITUTIONAL INVESTORS

Countries with a large base of investors have a greater capacity to deal with reductions in external demand for domestic financial assets. Thus, the relatively small size and number of long-term institutional investors in Latin America may be one of the factors that contribute to the region's vulnerability to external financial shocks.

But there is a two-way interaction between the importance of institutional investors and the functioning of domestic bond markets. While the growth of institutional investors is good for public debt management, a coherent debt management strategy and the development of a sound market microstructure in a country can also foster the growth of institutional investors (Vittas, 1998; Catalan, Impavido, and Musalem, 2000). It is therefore interesting

---

[11] In Argentina, banks have been reducing their exposure to treasury bonds (mainly long-term instruments) consistently since 2002, but they have been increasing their holdings of central bank bills (Lebacs). As a result, banks' overall exposure to the consolidated public sector remains high. Nevertheless, while the initial increase in public sector exposure was essentially compulsory, the most recent was voluntary. So can the resulting high levels of exposure to the public sector be considered totally involuntary?

[12] This might imply an asymmetry with loans to the private sector or mortgages (which typically appear in the balance sheet at book value), but at least it would reduce the chances of induced holding of public debt.

Box 8.2 The Risks of Holding Government Bonds

Is it safe for banks to hold long-term government bonds given the characteristics of their liabilities? There are three risks associated with holding government bonds in general and long-term government bonds in particular: credit risk, market risk, and liquidity risk.

Credit risk. Rating agencies generally have a policy of establishing a sovereign rating credit ceiling, which means that a country's government bonds receive the best credit rating in that country (see Chapter 5). Most countries consider domestic government bonds issued in the domestic currency to be "safe" or risk-free assets, and for that reason they do not impose any capital requirements on holders of these bonds for the credit risk that the bonds might entail.[a] In this respect, there is a difference relative to private debt instruments, especially loans, for which an 8 percent capital requirement is imposed on the holder to cover the credit risk (see Box 8.4 for the implications of the second Basel Accord).

Market risk. Government bonds are subject to market risk, as their prices fluctuate with changes in interest rates (see Box 8.1). The first and second Basel Accords establish capital requirements to cover the market risk of government bonds in case their prices fall as a result of increases in interest. In countries where there is low volatility

of interest rates, these requirements tend to be relatively small. Furthermore, banks can completely avoid these requirements by recording these bonds in their investment account. This is because bonds included in investment accounts are not subject to market risk, as they appear on the books at face (or purchase) value, thus receiving a treatment similar to that for a loan (which is not subjected to mark-to-market regulations, which require an adjustment in valuation to reflect the current market price). Banks are allowed to include government bonds in their investment account (sometimes referred to as the banking book) when they plan to hold the bonds to maturity.

Liquidity risk. This is a minor source of risk because government bonds are often liquid financial instruments, and hence banks can use them to obtain funds either by selling them in the secondary market or by using them as collateral for short-term loans or repos.

---

[a] It has been argued that the Argentine experience indicates that many private creditors were in the end better "credits" and implied less credit risk than the public sector. However, this may be because these private creditors benefited from the fact that their dollar loans were converted into pesos. It is difficult to determine whether the payment record on these loans would have been similar if the debtors had not benefited from the "pesification" of their loans.

to review how a country's public debt management policies may affect the development of institutional investors.

The first set of policies has to do with the *choice of financing instruments*. With respect to the type of bonds to be issued, the government can choose between bullet or amortization bonds; bonds with floating interest rates or fixed interest rates or indexed bonds; bonds

Box 8.3 How Should Banks Value Government Bonds?

It is sometimes difficult to agree on the "correct" valuation of long-term government bonds on a bank's balance sheet, especially whether they should be valued using mark-to-market criteria (i.e., according to their current market value, irrespective of their price at the time they were purchased) or whether banks should instead be allowed to include them at their purchase value. The main argument for this second approach is that this type of valuation is a mechanism for ensuring symmetry with loans, which are always priced at face value. While regulators and many international banks are moving in the direction of using mark-to-market criteria for the valuation of government bonds, several countries allow banks to value at purchase price any long-term bonds that they hold in an investment account.

One could argue that the same reasons that lead analysts and regulators to claim that bonds need to be marked to market are also applicable to loans. What happens if a bank wants to sell a loan prior to its maturity? What price would it get, and is that price, rather than the loan's face value, the one that should be considered on the bank's balance sheet?

issued in domestic or foreign currency; bonds issued under domestic or foreign legislation; and bonds with short or long maturity. It is not clear which type of bonds is preferred by domestic institutional investors, but in practice most Latin American countries are moving towards issuing standardized bonds, which are bullet instruments (i.e., the whole principal is paid at maturity), with semiannual interest payments, and in domestic currency.

The second set of policies is related to the *development of a yield curve*. Investors and other issuers can benefit from a fully developed yield curve for government bonds that sets the "benchmark" interest rates for different maturities (usually ranging from 3 months to 5 or 10 years).

The third set of policies has to do with increasing the *liquidity of government bonds*. A government can increase the liquidity of its bonds by making large benchmark issues (the minimum size of these benchmarks varies across countries). Governments can also improve the liquidity of their bond markets by facilitating the development of the repo market (which allows borrowing against bonds) and by taking measures to reduce transaction costs.

The fourth set of policies has to do with *coordination between the central government and other public sector issuers*. In Latin America the main issuers of domestic debt are the treasury and the central bank, and in many Latin American countries there are explicit agreements between the central bank and the treasury regarding the division of the market. In Uruguay, for instance, the central bank issues mainly in pesos, while the treasury issues in foreign currency. In Argentina, the central bank taps the short end of the market, while the treasury issues at longer maturities.

The fifth set of policies has to do with *providing information about the government's financing strategy*. When institutional investors know the amount of financing that the government needs and the type and timing of instruments to be issued, they can plan their purchases of bonds and ensure that they have the necessary funds to participate in the primary issuance of government bonds. Regular auctions of government bonds are thus desirable. In several countries there are weekly auctions for short-term treasury bills and monthly or quarterly auctions for longer-term treasury bonds.

Finally, governments can improve the attractiveness of their bonds by improving the market microstructure, especially *settlement, clearing system, and custody.* The operational and legal infrastructure that supports the issuance and trading of domestic government debt affects the depth and liquidity of the government bond market. Without the right settlement infrastructure there is a risk of failure to deliver either the cash or the securities in a large transaction, and this could have significant ripple effects on other settlements. Likewise, it is critical to ensure a high-quality custodian for the bonds, with high credit ratings and solid operational procedures. In some countries, the custodian is a public institution, such as the central bank, but in many others there are private custodians. Finally, to minimize credit risk in transactions, most countries have instituted delivery versus payment mechanisms for settling the transactions.

PROTECTING INSTITUTIONAL INVESTORS FROM VORACIOUS GOVERNMENTS

While institutional investors are critical players in domestic government bond markets, they could become victims of their own strength, as financially constrained governments might attempt to capture investors' resources through regulation and persuasion. Therefore, it is essential to have in place good institutional and regulatory frameworks aimed at reducing the risk that a government will pressure institutional investors to buy government bonds when it faces financial strains. Such a system would require an independent regulatory agency able to enforce limits on institutional investors' holdings of government bonds and induce institutional investors to appropriately evaluate the risk-return ratio associated with buying and holding government bonds.

Governments have found creative ways to induce institutional investors to increase their holdings of public debt by offering terms that are more favorable than those prevailing in the markets. For instance, central banks can impose high reserve requirements and then allow banks to fulfill them with government bonds issued at below-market interest rates. This has been the case in Brazil, for instance, where around 25 percent of banks' holdings of government bonds are induced by regulation.

Another way to induce institutional investors to increase their holdings of government bonds is to provide advantages in the way some instruments are valued in the investors' balance sheets. In other cases, authorities create new instruments that allow banks and pension funds to exceed the limits imposed by regulations.

Many of these "innovations" were certainly at work during the recent Argentine financial crisis. Initially, in 2001, the Argentine government attempted to avoid default and "induced" banks and pension funds to increase their holdings of public sector debt. As a result, banks increased their exposure to the public sector from 16.2 percent of assets in 1999 to 26.3 percent in 2001, and pension funds from 48.3 percent to 67.2 percent of total assets. These institutional investors were willing to accept (perhaps reluctantly) an increase in their hold-

Box 8.4 The Second Basel Accord and Bank Holdings of Government Bonds

The 1988 Basel Accord ("Basel I") estab-lished a set of guidelines for capital require-ments governing banks. While banks were required, under the accord, to hold capital equal to 8 percent of risky assets, public sector assets were not considered explicitly, and government bonds were generally con-sidered to be exempt from this requirement; most countries therefore did not enforce any capital requirement on banks for their hold-ings of government bonds. Moreover, many countries relied on historical valuations of these assets rather than current market prices, with the result that when the price of the bonds decreased, banks had inflated asset levels. Basel I is now considered to be outdated and is being replaced by a revised set of guidelines included in the *Interna-tional Convergence of Capital Measurement and Capital Standards—A Revised Frame-work*, also known as "Basel II" or the "Re-vised Framework." The Basel II deliberations

began in early 2001, and the final version of the regulations was issued in November 2005. Implementation of the accord in some G7 countries is expected by 2008.

The Basel II framework allows banks to evaluate the credit risk on their assets using either a standardized approach or an internal rating system. For banks that decide to apply the standardized approach, the risk weight applicable to sovereign debt ranges from 0 percent for sovereigns rated above AA– to 150 percent for sovereigns rated below B–, with unrated sovereigns receiving a risk weight of 100 percent. One problem with this system is that it is not clear whether regulators should apply inter-national ratings or domestic ratings (which tend to be higher than international ratings) in determining risk weights. Furthermore, the Basel II framework allows national super-visors to apply a zero capital requirement on sovereign claims that are denominated and

ings because the new instruments had regulatory advantages over the existing ones, as they could be assessed on balance sheets at "technical" values that were much higher than market values.

In addition, institutional investors may have an incentive to collaborate with the govern-ment once they accumulate a large exposure to the public sector, as a sovereign default or a restructuring of the public debt would then have a significant impact on their balance sheets. Governments can use this "coincidence" of interests to obtain the assistance of such inves-tors. This vested interest in avoiding a debt restructuring could explain the collaboration of banks and pension funds with the Argentine government.

While there is no easy way to insulate institutional investors from governments in des-perate need of financing, there are at least some measures that can mitigate the chances of excessive pressure. The obligation to mark to market all government instruments would be a deterrent to excessive exposure to the public sector, even for pension funds and life insur-ance companies that invest with a long-term horizon. In addition, it would help to require institutions to report their consolidated exposure to the public sector, including indirect funded in domestic currency. If a sovereign claim is in foreign currency, then this special treatment is not permitted, and it is generally understood that foreign currency ratings will apply, along with the provision that if the claim involves a traded security, it must be valued at market prices and capital requirements applied according to the scale discussed above.

For banks that decide to adopt an internal rating system, there are no special guidelines for evaluating sovereign claims, which, in principle, should be evaluated in the same way as any other claim (IDB, 2004). Nevertheless, it is likely that if a domestic bank supervisor allows some banks that are using the standardized approach to take advantage of the special treatment provision and apply a zero capital charge for public sector claims, then it will also allow banks using the more advanced approaches to employ the same treatment.

It is unlikely, therefore, that Basel II will solve the underlying problem. This is probably a reflection of the fact that Basel II was written primarily with G10 countries in mind, and in these countries risky government debt is not a relevant concern. A standard for emerging economies might have included stricter rules with a minimum capital requirement (no special treatment) and perhaps even quantitative limits. This would have provided useful leverage for domestic supervisors attempting to resist political pressure from finance ministries and governments to specify rules that favor holdings of government bonds. It is also worth noting that many countries do indeed have a positive capital charge for holdings of government assets (IDB, 2004).

holdings of government paper through mutual funds and investment companies in which the institutions invest.

In the case of banks, in addition to the obligation to mark to market all government financial instruments, supervisors could include quantitative limits (as part of credit diversification requirements) and introduce capital requirements for holding government bonds. Unfortunately, the new international framework (commonly referred to as Basel II) seems to have missed the opportunity for introducing these kinds of safeguards (Box 8.4).

While implementation of these recommendations would provide useful safeguards, large domestic capital markets are definitely an important first line of defense against financial crises. In the end, however, strong fiscal and debt management policies are the only policy measures that can truly protect a country from a possible default and indirectly support the soundness of institutional investors.

CHAPTER 9 | The Political Economy of Debt

THE STANDARD ECONOMIC MODEL of government debt posits a benevolent government that uses debt to finance capital accumulation or smooth the impact of natural and financial disasters or economic fluctuations. But in fact, decisions on debt and fiscal policy are made by politicians who may have in mind other issues, such as the result of the next election and the interests of their constituencies. If these considerations are important factors in decision making, one needs to formulate a different model of why governments go into debt and what determines debt levels and the evolution of debt over time.

A look at debt levels across countries reveals a wide dispersion that is not easily trace-able to the need to smooth the impact of economic shocks. Figure 9.1 plots the distribution of debt over GDP during the 1995–2005 period and shows that most countries have debt-to-GDP ratios of around 50 percent, but the range goes from 0 to 200 percent. In the advanced economies, average public debt during the 1995–2005 period ranged between 3 and 140 percent of GDP and was characterized by a twin-peaked distribution of public debt (the light green line in Figure 9.1). This group includes three countries (Australia, Luxembourg, and Norway) with public debt below 25 percent of GDP and four countries (Belgium, Greece, Italy, and Japan) with public debt above 100 percent of GDP. In the group of developing and emerg-ing market economies, average public debt over the 1995–2005 period was about 60 percent of GDP. But here also the dispersion was very large, with levels of public debt going from 0 to 200 percent of GDP. In fact, this group includes 16 countries with public debt lower than 25 percent of GDP and 13 countries with debt-to-GDP ratios higher than 100 percent.

The relationship between the level of development (proxied by GDP

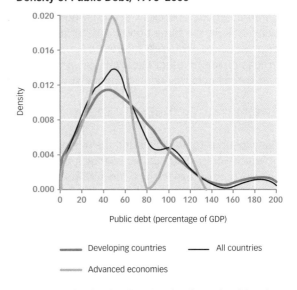

Figure 9.1
Density of Public Debt, 1995–2005

Source: Kernel estimations based on data from Jaimovich and Panizza (2006b).

Figure 9.2
Public Debt and GDP per Capita, 1995–2005

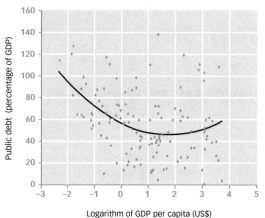

Logarithm of GDP per capita (US$)

Source: Authors' calculations based on data from Jaimovich and Panizza (2006b) and World Bank, *World Development Indicators*.

per capita) and debt ratios appears to be U-shaped rather than linear. At first, debt decreases with the level of GDP per capita, reaching a minimum at an income per capita of approximately $6,000, and then starts increasing again (Figure 9.2). The fit of the line to the data, however, is rather poor. Latin American and Caribbean middle-income countries have levels of per capita income that range between $3,000 and $7,000. Hence, they should be characterized by low levels of debt. However, the region includes countries with low levels of debt (like Chile, Colombia, and Mexico) and countries with high levels of debt (like Jamaica, Argentina, and Uruguay).

As it is difficult to reconcile the enormous dispersion in debt-to-GDP ratios with standard economic theories of public debt, economists have looked for explanations in the political arena (Alesina and Perotti, 1994). It is possible to organize the literature in this area into three groups of theories: (1) theories based on the opportunistic behavior of policymakers whose fiscal choices are intended to maximize voters' support; (2) theories that emphasize the conflict among different politicians, or distributional conflicts between different groups in society; and (3) theories that highlight the importance of budget institutions. Clearly, the three potential determinants of fiscal choices emphasized by these three strands in the literature interact with each other. In fact, distributive conflicts between groups of voters affect fiscal choices partly because officials face opportunistic incentives and are not constrained by budget institutions that work well.

THE FISCAL CHOICES OF OPPORTUNISTIC POLICYMAKERS

Early theories that emphasized the role of opportunistic policymakers relied on a mechanism in which voters value public spending but consistently underestimate its costs in terms of the tax burden, especially if those costs are postponed.[1] Thus, voters support policymakers who provide high levels of deficit-financed expenditures and oust incumbents who are fiscally conservative (Buchanan and Wagner, 1977). This literature has been criticized because of the assumption that voters make systematic mistakes (i.e., they are fooled over and over again by politicians). Opportunistic politicians, however, could be consistent with rational voters if the latter have imperfect information about the competence level of each politician and extract information about the competence of an incumbent running for re-election from

---

[1] This section and the next two draw heavily from Eslava (2006).

his past fiscal choices. According to this class of models, an incumbent who has provided more government programs is inferred to be more competent, and this creates incentives for politicians to run deficits to finance larger expenditures (Rogoff and Sibert, 1988).

This literature has three empirical implications. First, voters should prefer high levels of public expenditure. Second, debt accumulation should be negatively correlated with the transparency of the budget. Third, in countries where fiscal outcomes cannot be observed by voters, electoral periods should be characterized by fiscal expansions. The empirical evidence, however, does not fully support the idea that voters like high levels of public expenditure. Alesina et al. (1998) find that governments that follow tight policies on expenditure are no more likely to be replaced than others. If anything, the opposite seems to be true. Voters' attitude towards expenditure, however, is not independent of the type of government spending. Using data on local elections in Colombia, Eslava (2006) and Drazen and Eslava (2005) show that the share of votes received by an incumbent increases with capital expenditures.

There is, in contrast, clear evidence of a relationship between budget transparency and fiscal outcomes (Alt and Lassen, 2006) and of an interaction between lack of transparency and the possibility of opportunistic use of deficits during election times. Eslava (2006) uses a sample of developing and developed countries and shows a strong negative correlation between accountability and budget deficits. The relationship between accountability and deficit is consistent with the fact that in developing countries there are substantial pre-election increases in public expenditures (Schuknecht, 1994) and that the association between elections and deficits is due to the behavior of "new democracies" (Brender and Drazen, 2005). This indicates that political deficit cycles emerge only in contexts in which voters and the media have not yet developed the ability to efficiently monitor fiscal policy. However, the relationship between deficit and accountability is not purely driven by differences between developing and developed countries; it is also present when the sample is restricted to Latin American and Caribbean countries (Figure 9.3).

DISTRIBUTIONAL CONFLICTS, ELECTORAL SYSTEMS, AND FISCAL POLICY

In a system with two parties with preferences for different publicly provided goods, an incumbent will find that there are at least two advantages to running a deficit. First, she will be able to devote resources to the types of public goods she prefers. Second, she will "tie the hands" of her successor because, if she is replaced, the cost of the deficit will

Figure 9.3
Government Deficit and Government Accountability

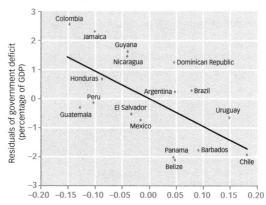

Residuals of Index of Government Accountability

Source: Authors' calculations based on data from Eslava (2006).
Note: The vertical (horizontal) axis measures the residuals of a regression of the variable *Residuals of government deficit* (*Residuals of Index of Government Accountability*) on a set of other exogenous variables.

fall disproportionately on the goods she values less (Tabellini and Alesina, 1990). A related argument arises in the case in which politicians differ in their preferences regarding the optimal size of the government. If faced with a high probability of being replaced, high-spending incumbents may run surpluses to force their successors into high expenditure levels, while low-spending incumbents may do the opposite (Persson and Svensson, 1989).[2]

Excessive fiscal deficits can also result from the presence of heterogeneous interests across groups of voters. If legislators making budget decisions represent geographic units interested in different government-funded projects and government revenues are centralized, each district internalizes the full benefit of specific projects, but only part of the cost. As a result, there is demand for overprovision of government projects (Weingast, Shepsle, and Johnsen, 1981). Similar common-pool problems have been studied by those who emphasize voracity effects (see Chapter 3).

A testable implication of these models is that deficits and debt accumulation should be positively related to the number of groups or districts that are effectively represented in the process of choosing the budget. Empirical research seems to confirm that electoral systems that result in more political cohesion and stability generate more fiscal discipline. Stein, Talvi, and Grisanti (1998) examine the relationship between different electoral systems and fiscal performance in a sample of Latin American countries, finding that electoral systems with more proportionality and a larger number of parties are associated with larger deficits. Figure 9.4 focuses on 17 Latin American and Caribbean countries and shows a negative correlation between a country's deficit and the fragmentation of its legislature.[3]

If the distortionary costs of taxation increase in the level of debt, debt accumulates up to the point at which each group perceives that a new deficit will imply higher costs than benefits. Hence, high levels of debt can be a solution to the common-pool problem (Velasco, 1999). An implication of this model is that higher levels of debt should be associated with a higher probability of a country's undergoing a fiscal adjustment. However, the evidence on the relationship between debt and fiscal adjustments is mixed. Stein, Talvi, and Grisanti (1998) find that debt accumulation in a given period is actually increasing in the initial level of debt. Alesina et al. (1998) and Gupta et al. (2004) find that, conditional on a fiscal stabilization's being under way, the probability that the adjustment is successful is increasing in the initial level of debt. The results of the studies cited above also seem to suggest that no other political or institutional variable has a significant effect on the probability of a country's undergoing an adjustment.

---

[2] While cross-country studies have not found consistent evidence in favor of either model of strategic use of deficits (Lambertini, 2003; Grilli, Masciandaro, and Tabellini, 1991), one study that focuses on the behavior of Swedish local governments supports the Persson and Svensson (1989) theory of strategic debts. In particular, Pettersson-Lidbom (2001) finds that the amount of debt accumulated by a right-wing government increases with its probability of electoral defeat, while the opposite is true for left-wing governments. Using experimental data, Sutter (2003) finds that, as predicted by Tabellini and Alesina (1990), spending is positively correlated with the degree of polarization and negatively correlated with the probability of re-election.

[3] The Fragmentation of the Legislature Index is measured as the negative of the Herfindahl index for the fraction of seats held by different parties. The Herfindahl index takes a value of negative one if all seats are held by the same party and a value of zero if there are as many seats as parties represented in parliament.

BUDGET INSTITUTIONS

The way in which the factors discussed above end up shaping deficit and debt accumulation will depend on the constraints policymakers face when deciding on the budget. Some of those constraints are given by the political environment, as discussed above, while others relate to the set of rules, procedures, and practices according to which budgets are crafted. There are three types of rules that can be used to constrain politicians: numerical targets, procedural rules, and transparency rules. Filc and Scartascini (2006) study the evolution of budget reforms in Latin America and show that procedural rules continuously improved (according to scores on an index constructed by these authors) over the 1992–2004 period and that the budget process became more transparent from 1997 on (Figure 9.5).

Numerical targets may take the form of simple or cyclically adjusted balanced budget constraints. The advantage of a balanced budget constraint is its transparency, and the disadvantage is that it limits a country's ability to conduct countercyclical policies. It is also possible to establish numerical rules that limit the government's ability to borrow (see below). However, the government can often circumvent such rules by borrowing through state-run agencies not included in the main government's budget (Poterba, 1994). While numerical targets are frequently imposed on subnational governments (for instance, most U.S. states have balanced budget rules), they are less common for national governments.[4]

Figure 9.4
Government Deficit and Fragmentation

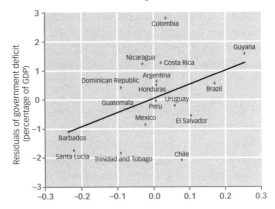

Source: Authors' calculations based on data from Eslava (2006).
Note: The vertical (horizontal) axis measures the residuals of a regression of the variable *Residuals of government deficit (Residuals of Fragmentation of the Legislature Index)* on a set of other exogenous variables.

Figure 9.5
Path of Reforms

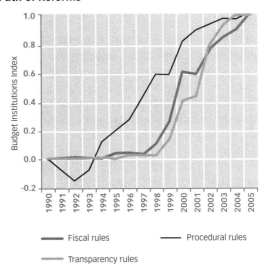

Source: Filc and Scartascini (2006).

---

[4] However, Chile does have a rule aimed at maintaining a structural surplus. See Box 9.3.

Procedural rules are used to establish the functions and rights of the policymakers that participate in the budget negotiations. Existing procedural restrictions can be divided into those that prevent the legislative branch from increasing the total amount of expenditure and those that prevent changes in the levels of deficit. An important distinction is that between "hierarchical" and "collegial" rules. Hierarchical rules often concentrate budgetary power in the finance ministry inside the cabinet, and in the executive vis-à-vis the legislature. Collegial rules, in contrast, are those that allow greater representation of different interests in the budgetary process but risk generating overspending problems. Institutions can be more or less hierarchical at different stages of the budget process. In the drafting of a budget, hierarchical institutions limit the power of spending ministers and centralize drafting power in the minister of finance. At the voting stage, hierarchical institutions limit the legislature's ability to modify the size of the budget proposed by the executive.[5] At the implementation stage, hierarchical institutions impose limits on the congress's ability to propose ex post amendments aimed at modifying the size of the budget.

While more hierarchical procedural rules are likely to increase fiscal discipline, rules can be circumvented through creative accounting, and they will be effective only in the presence of a high degree of transparency. Transparency rules increase information flows and thus enhance other rules. For instance, transparency can increase the effectiveness of numerical and/or procedural rules by limiting the scope for creative accounting. Transparency laws often focus on making publicly available the maximum amount of data covering details on contingent liabilities, a clear explanation of the methodology used to construct projections for fiscal figures, and information on the level and composition of the stock of public debt at all levels of government.

Alesina et al. (1999) study the importance of budget institutions for 20 countries in Latin America and the Caribbean in the 1980s and early 1990s and find that countries with more stringent numerical targets, more hierarchical institutions, and more transparency exhibit lower deficits. Stein, Talvi, and Grisanti (1998) corroborate this finding, after controlling for the fragmentation of the electoral system. Their results indicate that both electoral systems and budget institutions have significant effects on fiscal performance. Recent work by Filc and Scartascini (2006) corroborates this result by showing a strong positive correlation between a country's fiscal balance and (1) the presence of hierarchical rules (Figure 9.6) and (2) an overall indicator that measures the quality of the country's budget institutions (Figure 9.7).

THE ROLE OF THE COURTS

A country's judiciary is a key player in the fiscal policy arena because it can rule some elements of the country's budget unconstitutional and hence effectively modify the government's fiscal policy. Although this institutional feature has received limited attention in the formal literature on the political economy of fiscal policy, it has become a key issue in many countries (IDB, 2005b). In Colombia, for instance, there is an intense debate on the fiscal role of the constitutional court's rulings (Box 9.1).

---

[5] However, these regulations do not always prevent lawmakers from altering budgets, and in some cases, policymakers identify false sources of revenue to cover expenditure increases (Filc and Scartascini, 2006).

Figure 9.8 depicts judicial activism in eight Latin American countries and shows that Costa Rica, Colombia, Guatemala, and Brazil are the countries with the highest degree of judicial activism, Argentina is in an intermediate position, and Mexico, Chile, and Paraguay have the lowest degree of judicial activism. Eslava (2006) examines how judicial activism affects fiscal policymaking in Latin America, and her results strongly support the hypothesis that judicial activism is correlated with larger deficits. Not only are the results statistically significant, but they are also quantitatively important. Eslava's point estimates suggest that, other things being equal, if Costa Rica and Colombia had the same levels of judicial activism as Mexico and Chile, they would observe an improvement in their fiscal balance of close to 3 percent of GDP. While these are exploratory results based on a small sample of countries, they suggest that a country's courts do play a key role in its implementation of fiscal policy.

THE INTERACTION BETWEEN POLITICAL FAILURES AND FINANCIAL MARKET IMPERFECTIONS

While the literature surveyed above focuses on political failures, another strand of the literature on the behavior of emerging market debt has focused on the role of market failures.[6] Rochet (2006) discusses a simple but illuminating theoretical model that unifies these two strands of the literature and shows how financial market and political failures complement one another.

Figure 9.6
Fiscal Outcomes and Hierarchical Rules

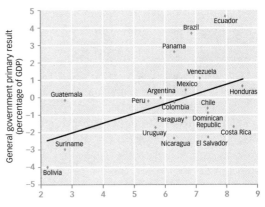

Index of Hierarchical Rules (0–10 scale)

Source: Filc and Scartascini (2006).
Note: The primary result is the average for 2000–2002, and the Index of Hierarchical Rules is for 2000.

Figure 9.7
Fiscal Outcomes and Budgetary Institutions

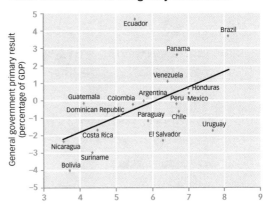

Index of Budgetary Institutions (0–10 scale)

Source: Filc and Scartascini (2006).
Note: The primary result is the average for 2000–2002, and the Index of Budgetary Institutions is for 2000.

---

[6] This section draws heavily from Rochet (2006).

Box 9.1 The Role of Courts in Colombia

Successful fiscal adjustments usually require spending flexibility, especially on items such as transfers, social security contributions, and public sector wages. However, this is not always feasible. In Colombia, for example, the constitutional court has often ruled that certain expenditure cuts violate Article 53 of the country's constitution, which guarantees the right to a "minimum and vital" remuneration. On these grounds, the court has declared the unconstitutionality of various laws aimed at reducing the fiscal deficit. For instance, it deemed too low the increases in public sector wages included in the budget laws of 1999, 2000, and 2002 and forced the government to grant larger raises. The current rule prevents reduction in *real* (as opposed to nominal) salaries of public sector employees over a four-year period that corresponds to each administration's term. On similar grounds, it also ruled unconstitutional a 2002 law aimed at reducing pensions and another 2002 law imposing a 2 percent value-added tax on items that were previously exempt.

Figure 9.8
Index of Judicial Activism in Latin America

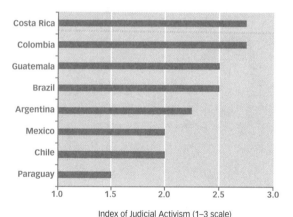

Index of Judicial Activism (1–3 scale)

Source: Cárdenas, Lora, and Mercer-Blackman (2005).

Rochet models an economy in which shortsighted politicians try to borrow as much as they can, while international financiers agree to lend a large amount because they anticipate that other lenders will lend again in the future (making repayment of the original loans more likely). Thus debt accumulates until the country cannot repay, at which point investors refuse to lend any more. There are thus three sources of imperfections: (1) governments are unable to commit to their future borrowing policies (government imperfection), (2) governments care only about the short-term consequences of their decisions (short-termism), and (3) financial markets are unable to provide complete contingent contracts (market incompleteness). Rochet begins by showing that the borrowing policy that would be implemented in the absence of these imperfections is characterized by constant government expenditure, higher levels of borrowing (or smaller debt repayments) during periods of low growth, and lower levels of borrowing (or larger debt repayments)

Box 9.2 Time Inconsistency

Economists describe as "time inconsistent" a situation in which individuals have an incentive to abandon an optimal long-term plan by constantly reoptimizing their policies. It is important to note that these reoptimizations are optimal at each point in time (hence the name) but are not optimal from the point of view of the original long-term plan and thus lead to inferior outcomes. So a fully rational attempt at maximizing an individual's welfare may actually end up leaving the individual worse off.

The story of Ulysses and the Sirens provides a clear illustration of the time inconsistency problem and a possible solution to the problem.[a] According to the ancient Greek poet Homer, the Sirens were creatures whose beautiful singing lured sailors to crash on the rocks close to where they sang. Since the Sirens' singing was so beautiful, the sailors' optimal plan would involve sailing next to them, listening to their singing, but staying far from the rocks. However, a sailor who knows that when he hears the Sirens sing, he will be unable to resist their call and end up crashing his boat will real-

ize that the optimal ex ante policy is "time inconsistent," that is, is no longer optimal at the time when he hears the Sirens singing. As a consequence, he will stay away from the Sirens, save his boat, but miss the show. This is a solution that is superior to listening to the Sirens and crashing the boat but inferior to listening to the Sirens and not crashing the boat. Being the smartest man in Greece, Ulysses knew that he could obtain the first-best solution only by committing ex ante. He asked his crew to plug their ears with wax and tie him to the mast of his ship and ordered them not to listen to his orders when they sailed close to the Sirens. When the Sirens called out to Ulysses, he asked the crew to untie him and change course, but following Ulysses' original orders, they stayed on their course and escaped the danger. Ulysses had understood that only by tying his own hands could he precommit to the first-best solution of listening to the Sirens without crashing his ship.

---

[a] For a less literary version of time inconsistency and an application to economics, see Calvo (1978) and Kydland and Prescott (1977).

during periods of high growth.[7] In other words, the optimal level of debt displays behavior consistent with a countercyclical fiscal policy. Next, Rochet shows that the joint presence of the three imperfections listed above leads to suboptimal procyclical debt policies in which governments borrow in good times and repay in bad times. Interestingly, he shows that the presence of politicians with short-term objectives is not a necessary condition for the suboptimal behavior described in the paper. This is because the optimal policy is not time consistent and, in the absence of a commitment mechanism, even politicians with long-term objectives will have an incentive to reoptimize in each period, borrow more in good times and less in bad times, and hence deviate from the ex ante first-best policy (Box 9.2 discusses the concept of time inconsistency). One possible solution would be to find a commitment

---

[7] This is similar to Barro's (1979) seminal result.

Box 9.3 The Chilean Fiscal Rule

The Chilean budget for the year 2001 introduced a fiscal rule aimed at maintaining a structural fiscal surplus of 1 percent of GDP (there is, however, no law that forces the Chilean authorities to reach this target).[a] Unlike a rule based on the actual fiscal balance, the Chilean rule makes it possible for the government to implement countercyclical policies because it permits the government to run deficits during recessions and requires surpluses during expansions. Formally, the Chilean rule can be described with the following equation:

$$SB_t = B_t + T_t \times \left(\left(\frac{Y_t^*}{Y_t} \right)^\varepsilon - 1 \right) - IC_t + ICE_t = 0.01 \times Y_t^*$$

where SB_t is the structural budget balance, B_t is the actual balance, T_t are net tax revenues, Y_t is actual GDP, Y^* is potential GDP, ε is the output elasticity of tax revenues, IC_t are the gross revenues of the state-owned company that controls copper production (CODELCO), and ICE_t are the revenues of

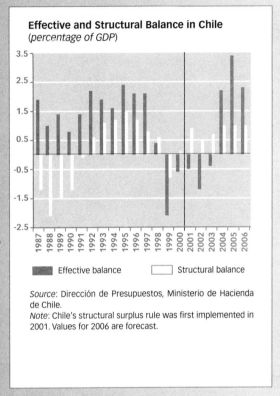

Effective and Structural Balance in Chile
(*percentage of GDP*)

Effective balance ☐ Structural balance

Source: Dirección de Presupuestos, Ministerio de Hacienda de Chile.
Note: Chile's structural surplus rule was first implemented in 2001. Values for 2006 are forecast.

mechanism (like the fiscal rule and fiscal responsibility laws described in Boxes 9.3 and 9.4). Another solution would be to write a state-contingent debt contract. For instance, Rochet (2006) shows that a GDP-indexed bond that makes higher payments in good times and lower payments in bad times can replicate the optimal policy even in the absence of a commitment device. In this sense, removing a financial imperfection (i.e., allowing for state-contingent debt contracts) can solve the problems that arise from a political imperfection. Summing up, Rochet's (2006) results are that (1) if the government could commit to its future borrowing policy, it could implement the first-best policy through perfectly countercyclical borrowing and standard debt contracts, and conversely, (2) if contingent debt contracts were available, even a government without commitment power could implement the first-best policy.

Next, Rochet (2006) studies a case of extreme political instability, in which governments last for only one period and maximize the current level of public consumption without any consideration of future outcomes. He shows that under this extreme assumption, govern-

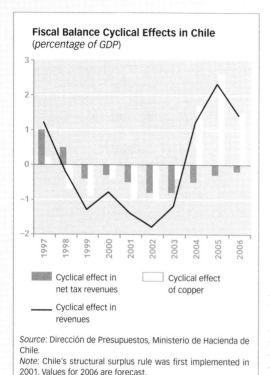

Fiscal Balance Cyclical Effects in Chile
(percentage of GDP)

Cyclical effect in net tax revenues

Cyclical effect of copper

Cyclical effect in revenues

Source: Dirección de Presupuestos, Ministerio de Hacienda de Chile.
Note: Chile's structural surplus rule was first implemented in 2001. Values for 2006 are forecast.

CODELCO that would prevail if the price of copper were at its medium-term level.

So far, the Chilean fiscal rule has worked well. While structural balances mimicked the actual balance before the adoption of the rule, since 2001 the average structural balance has been more or less constant at 0.9 percent of GDP, which has allowed the Chilean government to run effective deficits during periods of low growth and high surpluses during the more recent years characterized by sustained GDP growth and high copper prices, as shown in the figures to the left and on the facing page.

---

[a] The design of the Chilean rule requires a structural surplus because the authorities have the objective of reducing the structural deficit of some public enterprises and the Central Bank of Chile and accumulating funds to face possible contingent liabilities associated with the public pension system.
Source: Based on Valenzuela (2006).

ments always borrow as much as they can, and hence indebtedness is completely determined by the market's willingness to lend. This willingness to lend in turn depends on the market expectations of the government's future income, but also on markets' willingness to lend again in the future. Rochet shows that these simple assumptions lead to a situation in which debt grows continuously until the country becomes unable to pay and defaults. However, as ability to pay is partly determined by investors' willingness to lend, the maximum amount of sustainable debt is determined not only by a country's level of income, but also by the characteristics of the country in terms of growth and volatility. Hence, the model does *not* generate a situation in which the maximum amount of debt is just a fraction, constant for all countries, of the country's GDP. This heterogeneity is an important component of the model and is consistent with the real-world observations that countries tend to have debt crises at very different debt levels (and with the fact that there is a very poor correlation between debt ratios and sovereign ratings, as shown in Figure 1.1). Using a simulation,

Box 9.4 The Brazilian Fiscal Responsibility Law

In May 2000, Brazil enacted a Fiscal Responsibility Law (LRF) that strengthened fiscal institutions and established a broad framework of fiscal planning, execution, and transparency at the federal, state, and municipal levels. Among other provisions, the LRF requires the presentation of fiscal administration reports at four-month intervals, with a detailed account of budget execution and compliance with the LRF provisions. In terms of expenditure, the LRF sets ceilings on personnel spending—inclusive of pensions and payments to subcontractors—at 50 percent of federal government spending and 60 percent of state and local government spending. If these limits are breached in any given four-month period, the lapse must be redressed within the following eight months. There are strict penalties, including prison terms, for public officials who violate the provisions of the LRF or engage in other proscribed fiscal actions, as legislated in the Fiscal Crimes Law.

In terms of public debt, the LRF and complementary legislation set a ceiling of 120 percent of current revenue at the national and state levels. If this ceiling is breached, the debt has to be brought back within the ceiling over the following 12 months, and no form of borrowing is permitted until that happens. There is also a "golden rule" provision, stating that net borrowing cannot exceed the volume of capital spending. Loans between the national, state, and municipal governments are outlawed.

The LRF contains two escape clauses which suspend the application of the debt ceiling. The first escape clause applies in the case of a congress-declared state of national calamity or state of siege. The second one applies in case of economic recession, defined as a growth rate of less than 1 percent of GDP over a period of one year. In the latter case, the period for redressing a breach in the debt ceiling is doubled to two years. The escape clauses also apply to the limits on personnel spending.

Sources: Nascimento and Debus (2002) and de Mello (2006).

Rochet (2006) shows that there are two key determinants of the probability of default and the maximum level of sustainable debt. The first is long-run GDP growth, and the second is the volatility of GDP growth. The effect of GDP growth is straightforward, as countries with higher levels of long-run growth can sustain higher levels of debt. The effect of volatility is less obvious. Contrary to the classic result of Eaton and Gersovitz (1981), in which higher volatility is associated with a higher level of sustainable debt (because volatility increases the insurance value of debt), Rochet finds a U-shaped relationship between volatility and the maximum amount of sustainable debt, a finding that seems to be in line with the empirical evidence presented by Catão and Kapur (2004).

One other interesting result of Rochet's (2006) relatively simple setup is that political and financial imperfections may lead to a situation in which a country's ability to borrow may reduce welfare because it increases (instead of decreasing) the volatility of public expenditure and generates a constant probability of debt crisis.[8] One reason that it is not clear whether preventing a country from borrowing may increase welfare is that in Rochet's model, there are two justifications for sovereign debt: income smoothing and "front loading," or benefiting in advance from future growth of government income. Political and financial failures prevent government from achieving the first objective (and generate a situation in which the ability to borrow increases volatility), but the second objective is partially attained.[9] He suggests that, even if one were to find that the first effect dominates the second, welfare could be improved through less extreme forms of policy intervention than preventing the government from borrowing. One such intervention is a constitutional reform that prevents the government from borrowing more than a certain fraction of current income. As welfare is presumably increased by the reform, at least up to the point at which the front-loading motive becomes dominant, such a reform would require an evaluation of the "optimal" level of debt.[10]

Rochet (2006) argues that a country could reach an even higher level of welfare through a second type of intervention: by combining a cap on borrowing and an insurance policy from the international financial institutions. With such a setup, a country that agrees to put a cap of this type into its constitution would then benefit from contingent credit lines (or equivalently, credit risk insurance) financed ex ante by actuarial premiums. The country could then borrow at a constant rate, face a lower probability of crisis, and pay lower spreads on its debt.[11]

---

[8] This pattern of sovereign debt comes from the multiplicity of lenders and their collective inability to commit not to lend again in the future. This is related to the "common-agency problem" identified by Tirole (2002).

[9] Rochet and von Thadden (2006) provide a complete welfare analysis and find examples in which preventing a government from borrowing increases welfare.

[10] The reader should keep in mind, however, the discussion in the previous sections that highlights the idea that, without the necessary level of transparency, such a policy has serious implementation problems.

[11] A similar proposal is put forward by Cohen and Portes (2006), who argue in favor of the IMF's behaving as a lender of first resort, in exchange for a commitment by the country to refuse borrowing at interest rates above a certain cap. This is also in line with the role of the IMF as seen by Tirole (2002, 114–115), who states that "[t]he IMF's role is to substitute for the missing contracts between the sovereign and individual foreign investors and thereby to help the host country benefit from its capital account liberalization."

CHAPTER 10 | Debt and Development

A SUBSTANTIAL PART OF THIS REPORT focuses on the relationship between public debt and economic crises. This is not surprising, given the fact that Latin America's history has been punctuated by devastating debt and financial crises. However, it should not be forgotten that one of the reasons that countries issue debt is to finance investment in both human and physical capital, which enhances long-run growth. So, in theory, the net effect of higher levels of debt on economic development depends on whether the positive effect of the investment that it finances is stronger than the effects of potential crises. In fact, countries may face a trade-off in which higher levels of external debt could potentially increase growth in the long run but also increase short-run volatility.

A better understanding of the relationship between debt and economic outcomes is also key to forming an opinion on the desirability of debt relief for poor countries. In fact, there are two standard arguments for debt relief. The first has to do with the composition of public expenditure, especially the need to free up resources to increase social spending on health and education and to address infrastructure bottlenecks. The second has to do with the growth-reducing effects of high debt. The first argument is straightforward. For a given path of government revenues, debt relief permits an expansion in public spending by easing a government's budget constraint. In fact, in the enhanced Heavily Indebted Poor Countries (HIPC) initiative, countries receiving debt relief are required to use the resources saved as a result of debt relief to finance increased public spending in areas like health and education. The second argument is based on the idea that large debts have negative effects on private investment and hence depress growth.

With this question in mind, this chapter examines the interaction between debt and economic development, discusses how debt affects the composition and level of public expenditure, and reviews the economic literature on the desirability of debt relief. As the following discussion will show, the literature does not provide clear support for either of these two views. In fact, while there is no clear evidence that debt relief promotes growth and social outcomes across the board, there is some evidence that debt relief has had a positive effect in a restricted group of countries.

THE COMPLEX INTERACTION BETWEEN DEBT AND ECONOMIC GROWTH

The reason that foreign borrowing by developing countries should have a positive effect on growth is straightforward. Almost by definition, developing countries tend to be capital scarce and hence have numerous unsatisfied investment needs with a potential return that

Box 10.1 Debt Overhang

The term "debt overhang" originated in the corporate finance literature and indicates a situation in which a firm's debt is so large that any earnings generated by new investment projects are entirely appropriated by existing debt holders, and hence even projects with a positive net present value cannot reduce the firm's stock of debt or increase the value of the firm (Myers, 1977). The concept of debt overhang migrated to the international finance literature in the mid-1980s, when the debt crisis motivated a series of influential papers by Krugman (1988, 1989) and Sachs (1989). These authors argued that, as sovereign governments service their debt by taxing firms and households, high levels of debt imply an increase in the private sector's expected future tax burden. Debt overhang characterizes a situation in which this future debt burden is perceived to be so high that it acts as a disincentive to current investment, as investors think that the proceeds of any new project will be taxed away to service the pre-existing debt.[a] A weaker version requires only uncertainty by investors as to whether the

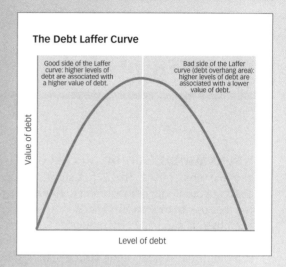

The Debt Laffer Curve

Good side of the Laffer curve: higher levels of debt are associated with a higher value of debt.

Bad side of the Laffer curve (debt overhang area): higher levels of debt are associated with a lower value of debt.

Value of debt

Level of debt

government will expropriate the return on their investment, or even uncertainty on the part of lenders to investors who may not be sure whether their claims will take precedence over—or be superseded by—the government's taxing power.[b] Lower levels of current investment, in turn, lead to lower growth and, for a given tax rate, lower government revenues, lower ability to pay, and

is higher than the international interest rate.[1] In a perfect world, the funds borrowed by developing countries would be used to finance these investments with high returns, and this would not only make the country better off, but also generate the resources necessary to repay the debt. As a consequence, foreigners would profit handsomely from lending to developing countries and would thus have an incentive to provide these countries with all the capital needed to equalize returns to investment across countries.

Unfortunately, the real world is not perfect. Politicians may forgo high-return projects and overborrow to finance "white elephant" projects to satisfy their own egos or a particular constituency.[2] They may also try to maximize their probability of re-election by financing

---

[1] This statement abstracts from the possibility that lack of human capital may lead to low returns to investment even in these capital-scarce countries (see Lucas, 1990).

[2] Alternatively, poor institutions or lack of government capacity may not allow a government to identify the most productive investment projects. Pritchett (1999) provides several examples showing that public investment may not necessarily translate into capital accumulation.

lower expected value of the debt. Countries that suffer from debt overhang will have no net resource flows because, by definition, any new loan that might be issued would be worth less than its nominal value, and no new creditor will be willing to lend when a loss is certain.

Countries that suffer from debt overhang may be located on the wrong side of the "Debt Laffer curve" described in the figure on the facing page and are characterized by a situation in which partial debt cancellation that reduces the expected tax burden can make both lenders and borrowers better off by increasing investment and growth and thus tax revenues and the value of debt. Even if creditors could be better off by canceling debt, debt cancellation requires a coordination mechanism that forces all creditors to accept some nominal losses. In the absence of such a coordination mechanism, each individual creditor will prefer to hold out while other creditors cancel part of their claims.

The key question is, at what level does debt become a debt overhang? It is easy to find this level in a theoretical model with the help of convenient assumptions (Borensztein, 1990). But it is harder to find debt overhang in the data. There is also an important distinction between emerging markets (which economists had in mind in the 1980s when the issue was first debated) and developing countries, where there is little borrowing from private sources and repayment obligations on official debt tend to be soft, as debt is often rolled over continually.

---

[a] According to Krugman's (1988) definition, a country suffers from debt overhang when the expected present value of future country transfers is less than the current face value of its debt.
[b] Corden (1989) extended the concept of debt overhang to explain a lack of motivation on the part of governments to implement economic stabilization and policy reforms, in the expectation that any revenues generated by an improvement in the domestic economy will go entirely to servicing debt.

---

consumption booms (Chapter 9 includes a discussion of various political economy theories of debt and deficit). In the worst of cases, corrupt politicians may steal from the public purse.[3] This leads to a situation in which foreign lenders, who cannot perfectly monitor the uses of the financial resources they are supplying, may be subject to panic episodes and suddenly decide to stop lending. Thus, even countries that are indeed using foreign borrowing to finance high-return projects may be subject to destructive sudden stop episodes (Calvo, 2005c).

Furthermore, debt could have a negative impact on growth even if politicians do not misuse or steal money. Debt overhang theories show that high levels of debt may lead to lower levels of investment and, possibly, worse policies (Box 10.1). In addition, high levels of debt may reduce growth because they make countries vulnerable to herding phenomena

---

[3] This emphasis on public borrowing led to the Lawson doctrine suggesting that only external public borrowing generates vulnerabilities. Several waves of debt crises discredited the Lawson doctrine (Edwards, 2001).

Table 10.1 External Debt and Growth: Results from the Recent Literature

Reference	Effect of external debt over GDP
Chowdury (2001)	Linear negative effect.
Hansen (2001)	No significant effect.
Pattillo, Poirson, and Ricci (2002)	Nonlinear effect. The marginal effect of debt becomes negative for debt-to-GDP ratios that range between 10 and 20 percent. The total impact of debt becomes negative when the debt-to-GDP ratio reaches 35–40 percent.
Clements, Bhattacharya, and Quoc Nguyen (2003)[a]	Nonlinear effect. The marginal effect of debt becomes negative for a debt-to-GDP ratio of about 50 percent. The total impact of debt becomes negative when the debt-to-GDP ratio exceeds 20 percent.
Cordella, Ricci, and Ruiz-Arranz (2005)	Identifies a debt overhang and a debt irrelevance threshold. The marginal effect of the debt-to-GDP ratio becomes negative at about 20 percent (this is the debt overhang threshold) and irrelevant at about 80 percent. Countries with good policies have higher debt overhang and irrelevance thresholds, and countries with bad policies have lower thresholds.
Imbs and Rancière (2005)	The marginal effect of debt becomes negative when the face value of debt reaches 55–60 percent of GDP, but thresholds are higher for countries with good institutions. The negative effect of debt on growth disappears at high levels of debt. Debt overhang is less likely to occur in countries with good institutions. Investment collapses and policies deteriorate in overhang countries.

[a] The sample includes only low-income countries.

and self-fulfilling crises regardless of domestic policies (Calvo, 2005c). In fact, one issue that has not been addressed by the literature on the link between debt and growth is the volatility channel. Interesting questions include the following: (1) Does debt increase output volatility? (2) Does debt favor long-run growth if a crisis is avoided? (3) Does debt favor long-run growth even after the higher propensity for crisis associated with debt is factored in? (4) If so, does the extra growth pay for the loss in welfare due to added volatility?

So much for the theory; what do the data say? Dijkstra and Hermes (2001) survey the early empirical literature on the relationship between debt and growth and find that there is no conclusive evidence in support of the debt overhang hypothesis. One problem with this early empirical literature is that it assumed a linear relationship between debt and growth and hence did not allow for the possibility that moderate levels of foreign borrowing can be associated with higher levels of growth (because they permit the financing of high-return investment projects) and that high levels of debt can be detrimental to growth through debt overhang effects. Recent work (summarized in Table 10.1) explicitly recognizes the possibility of a nonlinear relationship between debt and growth. Pattillo, Poirson, and Ricci (2002) and Clements, Bhattacharya, and Quoc Nguyen (2003) find that low levels of debt have a positive effect on growth, but that growth reaches a maximum at intermediate levels of debt (point A in Figure 10.1 is the debt overhang threshold) and becomes negative when debt reaches another threshold (point B in Figure 10.1). The key difference between these two studies is in the estimated threshold. While the former authors find that the growth-maximizing debt level is 10–20 percent of GDP, the latter authors (who use the same methodology but focus on a sample of low-income countries) find that growth reaches a maximum when debt is about 50 percent of GDP. This difference in turning points is extremely important for the debt relief debate. In fact, the results of Clements, Bhattacharya, and Quoc Nguyen indicate that the amount of debt reduction considered by the HIPC initiative will bring the

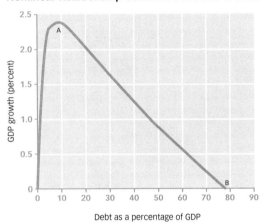

Figure 10.1
Nonlinear Relationship between Debt and Growth

beneficiary countries close to the debt levels that maximize growth, but the results of Pattillo, Poirson, and Ricci suggest that the debt relief offered by the HIPC initiative will not be enough to maximize growth in the beneficiary countries.

More recent studies suggest that the nonlinear estimations adopted by Pattillo, Poirson, and Ricci may be too simple to capture the complex relationship between external debt and growth. Cordella, Ricci, and Ruiz-Arranz (2005) show that there is both a "debt irrelevance threshold" and a debt overhang threshold. Focusing on the full sample of countries for which they have data, these authors show that the debt level that maximizes growth is about 20 percent of GDP (point A in Figure 10.2); at this point debt overhang kicks in and higher debt becomes associated with lower growth until a second threshold (the debt irrelevance threshold, point B in Figure 10.2) is reached; beyond this second threshold, there is no significant correlation between debt and growth. The debt overhang and debt irrelevance thresholds tend to be higher for countries with good policies and lower for countries with bad policies. In fact, it is not even clear whether debt is relevant to growth at all for countries with bad policies. Again, these results have important implications for the debt relief debate because they suggest that, for countries (like most HIPCs) that are situated in the debt irrelevance region, a moderate amount of debt relief (for instance, enough for them to move from point

Figure 10.2
Debt Overhang and Debt Irrelevance

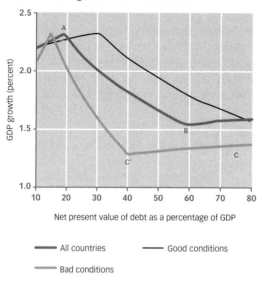

Net present value of debt as a percentage of GDP

— All countries   — Good conditions

····· Bad conditions

Source: Cordella, Ricci, and Ruiz-Arranz (2005).

C to point *C'* in Figure 10.2) would be completely useless. The implications of this study are thus that only a large amount of debt relief—enough to move a country away from the debt irrelevance area—can have a positive effect on the country's growth rate.

Along similar lines, Imbs and Rancière (2005) find that there is no statistically significant relationship between debt and growth regardless of whether debt is low or high, indicating that there might be two debt irrelevance areas. These authors also provide direct tests for the channels through which debt may reduce growth and find that debt overhang episodes are indeed associated with lower levels of investment and worse policies.[4]

All the studies surveyed above focus on the relationship between external debt and GDP growth rather than on the relationship between total public debt and GDP growth. These are different concepts, because total external debt includes both public and private external debt but does not include domestic public debt. At the same time, total public debt does not include private external debt. Tanzi and Chalk (2000) are among the few authors who explicitly focus on total public debt.[5] They argue that there are several channels through which public debt may affect growth. The first is the standard crowding-out channel, through which debt leads to higher interest rates, which are in turn detrimental to private investment. Tanzi and Chalk test the crowding-out hypothesis using a sample of European countries and find that, contrary to what is predicted by Ricardian equivalence (see Chapter 1 for a discussion of this concept), higher levels of public debt do seem to be associated with higher interest rates and lower private investment. Similarly, back-of-the-envelope estimates for the U.S. economy show that, through crowding out, each dollar of debt reduces net output by approximately six cents every year (Elmendorf and Mankiw, 1999). This suggests that in the case of the U.S. economy, only projects that have a social return higher than 6 percent are worth being financed through the issuance of public debt.[6]

---

[4] Pattillo, Poirson, and Ricci (2004) also test for the channels through which debt affects growth and find that the effect acts through both factor accumulation (such as investment in human and physical capital) and productivity.

[5] However, they focus on advanced economies. Replication of the statistical analyses of Pattillo, Poirson, and Ricci (2002) and Cordella, Ricci, and Ruiz-Arranz (2005) by using total public debt is complicated by the fact that few developing countries have long series for domestic public debt (see Chapter 2). However, an analysis based on the data set assembled by Jaimovich and Panizza (2006b) suggests that the relationship between debt and growth is dominated by the external component of debt.

[6] This is a loose statement that implicitly assumes that all other alternative forms of financing are more distortionary than issuing public debt.

The second channel has to do with the fact that governments that face high levels of debt are often forced to reduce public expenditure drastically and often end up doing so by cutting the most productive but least politically costly component of expenditure, that is, public investment and operation and maintenance expenditure. Data for European countries show that higher levels of debt are associated with lower levels of public investment (Tanzi and Chalk, 2000), a result that does not seem to hold for Latin America (Lora, 2006). Financial repression is another channel though which public debt may affect growth. There are several examples in which countries with high levels of debt adopted tax structures that favored public debt and forced institutional investors to hold a large amount of public debt (Tanzi and Chalk, 2000).[7] Finally, countries with a large amount of public debt denominated in domestic currency are likely to be tempted to resort to higher inflation to reduce the burden of debt service. Whether or not such an inflationary policy is implemented, the fact that high levels of public debt generate inflationary expectations may lead to a climate of uncertainty that makes agents reluctant to engage in long-term contracts and translates into lower growth.

DEBT AND PUBLIC SECTOR INVESTMENT IN PHYSICAL AND SOCIAL CAPITAL

The previous discussion highlighted the idea that debt may affect growth through both productivity and factor accumulation and suggested that higher levels of public debt can have a negative effect on the most productive components of public expenditure.[8] Unless it is totally wasteful, public investment in infrastructure is likely to be associated with the accumulation of physical capital, and social expenditure is likely to be associated with the accumulation of human capital.[9] Hence, it is relevant to consider whether there is a relationship between public debt and these components of public expenditure.

Public Debt and Investment in Infrastructure

While in fast-growing East Asian developing countries, investment in infrastructure ranges between 4 and 6 percent of GDP (Fay and Morrison, 2005), during the late 1990s, Latin America's investment in infrastructure was hovering around 2.25 percent of GDP, about two-thirds of which was private and one-third public (Figure 10.3). It is interesting to ask whether these relatively low levels of public investment in infrastructure (PII) were driven by the high debt levels and recurrent debt crises that affected the region in the previous decade.

---

[7] Chapter 8 includes a discussion of these issues.

[8] This section draws heavily from Lora and Olivera (2006) and Lora (2006).

[9] Canning and Bennathan (1999) show that investment in infrastructure can have a high social return in countries characterized by infrastructure bottlenecks. Reinikka and Svensson (1999) also show that underprovision of public investment can have a large negative effect on private investment. However, Pritchett (1999) warns that public investment does not necessarily translate into capital accumulation. With respect to human capital accumulation, Pritchett (2001) finds no correlation between an increase in education and growth of GDP per worker.

Figure 10.3
Investment in Infrastructure in Latin America
(*percentage of GDP, weighted by constant GDP in 2000 US$*)

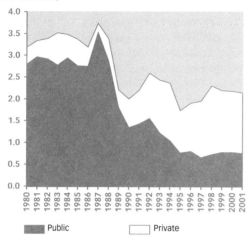

Public Private

Source: Calculations based on Calderón and Servén (2004).
Note: Based on data that include Argentina, Bolivia, Brazil, Chile, Colombia, Ecuador, Mexico, Peru, and Venezuela.

Although there are several studies that focus on the relationship between the composition of public expenditure and fiscal retrenchments,[10] work on the relationship between public capital expenditure and debt levels is more limited and tends to yield inconclusive results. While Mahdavi (2004) finds that external debt has an adverse effect on capital expenditure in a sample of 47 developing countries (the effect is not significant for the Latin American subsample), Clements, Bhattacharya, and Quoc Nguyen (2003) find that the stock of external debt has no significant effect on public investment. Instead, they find that higher levels of debt service (as opposed to the stock of external debt) crowd out public investment. All of these studies focus on capital expenditure, but none of them examines the behavior of PII. These are different concepts, because capital expenditures reported by standard cross-country data sets such as the International Monetary Fund's *Government Finance Statistics* are an incomplete measure of actual PII, which in many countries is mostly carried out by state-owned enterprises or local governments, whose operations are not well captured by this source.

Lora (2006) looks at the experience of the seven largest Latin American economies and is the only study that explicitly focuses on PII. The most striking finding is that PII seems to be positively correlated with the stock of public debt. In particular, a 10 percentage point increase in the debt-to-GDP ratio is associated with an increase of PII of approximately 0.13 percent of GDP. While this effect may seem small in absolute terms, it is very large in relative terms, as it corresponds to approximately 10 percent of average PII in Latin America. Furthermore, the long-run effect is almost twice as large. There is also a strong negative association between fiscal balance and PII, implying that PII tends to decline during periods of fiscal adjustment, a result which is consistent with the findings of previous studies. PII also responds directly to changes in total primary expenditures, confirming that PII is susceptible to expenditure cuts (though not to changes in fiscal revenues).

---

[10] Hicks and Kubisch (1984) and Hicks (1989) find that capital expenditure is the type of expenditure most exposed to cuts during periods of fiscal retrenchment. Diamond and Heller (1990) focus on a sample of developing countries over the 1975–1986 period and conclude that the shifts in the composition of government expenditures tend to be the most pronounced against fixed assets and capital transfers. Consistent with these studies, Calderón, Easterly and Servén (2003) calculate that in Latin America, infrastructure investment cuts contributed to half or more of the total fiscal adjustment during the 1980s and 1990s.

A topic of intense debate is whether lending by international financial institutions has an impact on the level and the composition of public expenditure. In theory, if governments have access to international capital markets, multilateral lending does not necessarily increase public expenditure or alter its broad composition, though such lending may affect the quality and economic and social impact of public expenditure. However, when access to private external finance is limited, two opposing effects may operate. On the one hand, multilateral loans may finance projects that could not take place otherwise. On the other hand, the international financial institutions may make their support conditional on tighter fiscal policy and hence reduced overall expenditure. Lora (2006) finds that official lending as a whole has a minor and negative, though not statistically significant, effect on PII. However, when official lending is broken down by type of lender, it becomes clear that lending by the International Monetary Fund is associated with lower PII. There are two possible reasons for this finding. The first (supported by the critics of the IMF) is that this institution's conditionality results in lower investment in infrastructure. The second (and more likely) reason is that the IMF tends to step up lending at times of crisis, which are also times when fiscal adjustments are required.

Lora (2006) further tests how public debt affects the composition of public expenditure and finds that an increase in the stock of public debt equivalent to 1 percent of GDP leads to a short-run *increase* of 0.15–0.18 percentage points in the share of PII in primary expenditures (or an increase of 0.22–0.30 in the long run).[11] These results point towards a symbiotic relationship between PII and public debt that may operate in the following way. Like other primary expenditures, PII increases when fiscal resources grow. However, when public debt is on the rise, PII is at an advantage vis-à-vis other primary expenditures, possibly because infrastructure is considered a more productive type of expenditure than, say, social expenditure, especially in the short to medium run, and possibly because there are legal and institutional constraints that tie debt to physical investment projects. In periods of fiscal consolidation, PII is adversely affected through a decline in expenditures and a reduced use of (or access to) credit.

On a note of caution, it is important to mention that while the above results suggest that higher levels of public debt are good for public investment, they also convey the more standard message that fiscal retrenchment is associated with lower PII. Hence, the fact that debt accumulation may eventually lead to fiscal retrenchment is likely to mitigate, or even reverse, the result described above. In fact, calculating the total effect of debt accumulation on PII would require a statistical model that jointly estimated how debt accumulation affects both PII and the probability of a future fiscal consolidation—a difficult task indeed.

Public Debt and Social Expenditure

Human capital accumulation is another channel through which public debt can affect economic growth, and if well used, social expenditure can promote human capital accumulation. The conflict between honoring public debt commitments and alleviating the lot of the poor

---

[11] The lower coefficient comes from the statistical model that includes the fiscal balance, suggesting that part of the increase in PII comes from the relaxation of fiscal discipline associated with periods of debt expansion.

is a recurrent topic among social policy activists and politicians in the developing world. For instance, at the World Social Forum held in Porto Alegre, Brazil, in 2002, participants claimed that external debt payments absorb a substantial amount of resources and that poor developing countries should stop repaying their debt. Funds previously earmarked for debt repayment should be redirected, the participants asserted, to finance socially just and ecologically sustainable development (Toussaint and Zacharie, 2002). Debt relief, either granted by lenders or obtained unilaterally through outright default, is often seen as an expeditious way to increase social public expenditure and improve the welfare of the poor. As argued by the World Bank and the IMF in support of the HIPC initiative, "debt relief can also be used to free up resources for higher social spending aimed at poverty reduction to the extent that cash debt-service payments are reduced" (IMF and World Bank, 1999). Economist Jeffrey Sachs (quoted in Fritschel, 2004) has gone even further: "No civilized country should try to collect the debts of people that are dying of hunger and disease and poverty." These arguments resonate strongly in Latin America, where interest payments on debt absorb on average 2.8 percent of GDP, which would be enough to increase total social expenditures by 25 percent (Lora and Olivera, 2006).

Considering the attention that this issue attracts in public debate, it is striking how little empirical research has been devoted to assessing whether countries burdened with heavier debt commitments do indeed spend less in social sectors. While there are a few studies that look at the impact of fiscal adjustment measures on social expenditure,[12] these studies do not shed any light on the impact that debt and debt service payments may have on levels of social expenditure or their share in total expenditures. Lora and Olivera (2006) is the only study that aims at assessing the effects of total public debt (external and domestic) on social expenditure worldwide and in Latin America. Lora and Olivera find that higher debt ratios do reduce social expenditures, as popular opinion holds, but that the effect is rather small. Quantitatively, they find that an increase of 10 percentage points in the debt-to-GDP ratio is associated with a decline of approximately 0.15 percentage points in the ratio of social expenditure to GDP.[13] As the average social expenditure in Lora and Olivera's sample is 6 percent of GDP, these estimates suggest that a 10 percentage point increase in the public debt ratio will reduce social expenditures by approximately 2.5 percent. Lora and Olivera also find that fiscal adjustments have a negative impact on social expenditure and that a one-dollar reduction in the overall or the primary fiscal deficit is associated with an *average* decline in social expenditures of around 3 cents in the current year (or nearly 5.5 cents in the long run). It is important to note that this is an average effect which varies widely depending on how fiscal adjustment is achieved. If primary expenditures are cut by one dollar, the decline in social expenditures may be as high as 13 cents, while if the same adjustment is achieved by raising more revenues, social expenditures may increase by 4 cents.

Lora and Olivera (2006) also show that higher levels of debt have a negative effect on the share of social expenditures in total primary expenditure. A 10 percentage point increase in the debt-to-GDP ratio leads to a decrease in the share of social expenditure in total government expenditure of approximately 0.5 percentage points (with long-run effects about twice

---

[12] Hicks and Kubisch (1984) and Hicks (1989) find that social expenditures are well-protected during periods of fiscal retrenchment, a finding that is confirmed by Baqir (2002), who uses a much larger sample of countries.

[13] Interestingly, this estimate is of similar magnitude (but with the opposite sign) to that obtained when estimating the impact of debt on PII. This suggests that there are offsetting effects between the two types of expenditure.

as large). Social and other public expenditures behave in different ways. When total primary expenditures *decline* by 1 percent of GDP, the share of social expenditures in primary expenditures *increases* by nearly 0.4 percentage points (a finding consistent with previous literature showing that social expenditures are resilient in the face of fiscal adjustments). Ironically, this amplifies the negative effect of debt on social expenditure. In fact, an increase of one dollar in the stock of debt is associated with an increase of 4.9 cents in the primary balance and 1.3 cents in interest payments on debt in the following year. Hence, the net effect on the overall fiscal balance is an increase of 2 cents in the short run (or 3 cents in the long run). The typical response that produces the improvement in the primary balance is a mix of higher revenues (2.6 cents in the following year or 3 cents in the long run) and lower expenditures (2.5 cents in the following year or 4.4 cents in the long run).

Thus, following an increase in the stock of debt, governments typically react by reducing total expenditures and increasing total revenues by an amount beyond the increase in interest payments resulting from the increase in the debt stock, thus in general tightening the overall fiscal balance. In the process, social expenditures are hit twice, as they are sensitive not only to changes in total expenditures (and somewhat less to changes in revenues), but also to the direct impact of the stock of debt. A surprising finding is that increases in debt service payments (which may be the result of higher debt ratios) have only a minor effect on social expenditures. This suggests that debt displaces social expenditure not so much because it raises a country's debt burden, but because it reduces the country's space (or appetite) for further indebtedness.

Another interesting question is whether borrowing from international financial institutions makes a difference in regard to social expenditures. Loans from official sources in general, and from multilateral organizations in particular, do not seem to ameliorate the adverse consequences of debt for social expenditures. However, while increases in total official debt have no additional effect on social expenditures, different types of official lending have different effects on social expenditure. In particular, borrowing through bilateral lending and from the IMF attenuates the negative effect of debt on social expenditure, and borrowing from the other multilaterals amplifies this negative effect (Lora and Olivera 2006).[14] When social expenditure is measured as a share of total expenditure (rather than as a share of GDP), the effect of all types of official lending on social expenditures becomes insignificant, suggesting that the differential influence that each type of official lending has on social expenditures is due basically to how it influences total expenditures and not social expenditures directly.

As Latin America is often associated with macroeconomic instability and debt crises and has levels of social expenditures which are well below both the world average and the average for other developing regions, it is interesting to examine whether the previous results also hold for a subsample of Latin American countries.[15] Increases in debt stocks and

---

[14] These results should be interpreted with caution, because official lending (especially IMF lending) tends to increase during times of crisis. However, this simultaneity problem should bias the results against the findings of Lora and Olivera (2006).

[15] When expressed as a share of GDP, social expenditures in Latin America are 1.7 percentage points below the developing country average. The bulk of this gap is in the education sector, where the gap is 1.2 percent of GDP. However, when measured as a share of total primary expenditures, social expenditures in Latin America turn out to be *higher* than in the rest of the developing world. Therefore, if the region spends too little in social sectors, it is because of the low levels of total public expenditure that characterize the region.

Figure 10.4
Effect of Fiscal Tightening on Social Expenditures:
Initial Fall Followed by Substained Recovery

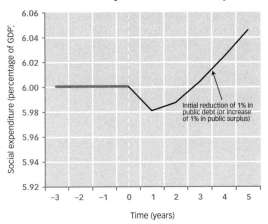

Time (years)

Source: Authors' calculations based on Lora and Olivera (2006).
Note: Fiscal tightening occurs at year 0.

in interest debt payments have much larger effects on social expenditures in Latin America than in the rest of the developing world. When debt stocks in Latin America increase by one dollar, social expenditures decline by 3 cents more than in other regions (where the decline is about 1 cent). For each additional dollar of debt payments in Latin America, social expenditures decline by around 23 cents (while in the rest of the world they *increase* by about 8 cents) (Lora and Olivera, 2006).[16]

Summing up, Lora and Olivera's findings give credence to many of the widely held views about the deleterious effects of high levels of indebtedness. Higher debt ratios do reduce social expenditures, and not just because of the extra cost in interest payments (an effect that is especially important in Latin America), but because these higher debt ratios are associated with cuts in total expenditures that affect the social sectors.

These findings suggest that orthodoxy in debt management may be the best way to protect social expenditures. In fact, an improvement equivalent to 1 percent of GDP in the primary balance should initially cause a decline in social expenditures of 0.034 percent of GDP, but this initial reduction should be partly offset by an increase in social expenditures of 0.014 percent of GDP the following year because the stock of debt has fallen. In the third year, the initial reduction should be fully offset, and beginning with the following year, social expenditures should rise above the initial level (Figure 10.4). Furthermore, it should be possible to have social expenditures rising from the outset if the fiscal adjustment is based on an increase in revenues rather than on a reduction of expenditures, which is the reason why social expenditures fall in periods of fiscal retrenchment.

WHAT CAN BE LEARNED FROM THE DEBT RELIEF EXPERIENCE?

Supporters of debt relief argue that canceling the debt of the poorest countries has several potential advantages. First of all, it is an exercise in transparency, as several institutions are de facto granting debt relief by continuously evergreening past loans and refusing to recognize that some of their loans cannot be collected. Second, debt relief may create

---

[16] The higher sensitivity of social expenditures to interest payment shocks in Latin America is even more apparent when the share of social expenditures in total expenditures is considered.

space for much-needed expenditure on poverty-reducing activities. Third, debt relief can kick-start growth in countries that suffer from debt overhang. Those who oppose debt relief argue, instead, that recipient governments use the resources freed up as a result of debt relief for wasteful activities and that debt relief makes it possible to perpetuate bad policies. Furthermore, providing debt relief to highly indebted countries may just end up promoting bad behavior and distributing resources to countries with a history of poor macroeconomic policies.

So far, this chapter has concentrated on the relationship between debt and economic outcomes, but it has not focused specifically on attempts to test directly the economic impact of debt relief (Boxes 10.2 and 10.3 provide a description of the main debt relief initiatives). A set of interesting questions on the impact of debt relief includes the following:

1. Has debt relief been successful in permanently reducing debt levels?
2. Has debt relief been successful in increasing GDP growth and social expenditure?
3. Is debt relief preferable to aid?
4. Does debt relief bring additional resources?

Has Debt Relief Been Successful in Permanently Reducing Debt Levels?

Past experience suggests that the answer to the question "Has debt relief been successful in permanently reducing debt levels?" is nuanced. Easterly (2002) studies the behavior of a set of countries that received substantial debt relief and finds that the net present value of debt service for these countries increased throughout the period during which these debt relief initiatives were implemented. How can increasing debt be reconciled with a sizable debt relief effort? A possible explanation is bad luck. However, Easterly finds no evidence that HIPCs suffered worse shocks than other developing countries. Easterly's favored explanation is that high levels of debt are due to the presence of policymakers with a high discount rate (economic jargon to describe individuals who prefer to consume as much as they can today without worrying too much about what will happen tomorrow) who always borrow as much as they can. If higher levels of debt are due to the government's high discount rate and if debt relief does not affect the government's discount rate, then debt relief will be ineffective in the long run and lead to a merely temporary consumption boom.[17] Easterly argues that the data support the above interpretation. In particular, he studies the outcome of debt relief in 41 HIPCs and finds that, while debt relief over the 1989–1997 period amounted to US$33 billion, new borrowing by the countries receiving this debt relief was US$41 billion, consistent with the idea that debt relief leads to new borrowing.

However, a formal test leads to less striking conclusions. A regression of new borrowing on debt relief finds that for each 1 percent of GDP in debt relief, there is new net borrowing of 0.34 percent of GDP, suggesting that one dollar of debt relief leads to about 65 cents of effective debt reduction. Furthermore, the effect is not constant across periods. By splitting the sample into three periods, Easterly (2002) shows that debt relief was accompanied by increasing debt over the 1979–1987 period, constant debt over the 1988–1994 period,

---

[17] Even worse, debt relief may have perverse incentive effects, as countries may borrow and delay reforms in the expectation of becoming part of a debt forgiveness program.

Box 10.2 Pre-HIPC Debt Relief

Debt relief is not a new idea.[a] In 1967, UNC-TAD declared that "debt-service payments have risen to the point at which a number of countries face a critical situation" (quoted in Easterly, 2002, p. 1678). A series of UNC-TAD meetings held in 1977–1979 led official creditors to write off US$6 billion of debt to 45 countries. The 1981, 1984, 1986, and 1991 World Bank Africa Reports contained repeated calls for debt relief, and the 1988, 1990, and 1991 G7 summits agreed on the need for additional debt relief, which led to more relief and concessional lending. In 1996, the Heavily Indebted Poor Countries (HIPC) program was launched. Besides explicit debt relief initiatives, there has also been implicit debt relief in the form of substitution of concessional debt for non-concessional debt (Easterly, 2002).

The Brady Plan, which is probably the largest private sector debt relief effort ever implemented, was triggered by the global debt crisis which followed the Mexican announcement on August 12, 1982, that it was unable to meet debt obligations. The Mexican default gave way to a series of other defaults and failed debt-restructuring attempts which, in February 1987, culminated in Brazil's declaration of a debt moratorium. In the following months, several international banks announced large increases in their loan loss reserves and hence explicitly recognized that an important share of their portfolio of loans to developing countries was nonperforming (Arslanalp and Henry, 2005). In early 1989, Nicholas Brady, who was then Secretary of the U.S. Treasury,

put forward a debt relief plan which had the aim of lengthening maturity, forgiving principal, and reducing interest payments for developing country governments. With the Brady Plan, banks were offered a US$25 billion credit enhancement package and four different methods for restructuring their defaulted loans: (1) discount bonds, (2) par bonds, (3) new money, and (4) cash buybacks.[b] Between August 1989 and October 1995, 16 countries participated in Brady swaps and restructured more than US$200 billion in bank loans, with debt relief amounting to US$65 billion.[c] Most of the existing Brady bonds have now been retired (see Chapter 5), another indication of the success of this initiative.

---

[a] This box borrows heavily from Easterly (2002) and Arslanalp and Henry (2005).

[b] Discount bonds were 30-year collateralized bonds (the collateral consisted of U.S. Treasury bonds) with lower face value (about 30 to 35 percent less than the original claim), an interest rate of LIBOR plus 13/16, and a single (bullet) payment at maturity. Par bonds were similar to discounts but were issued at face value and had a fixed interest rate of 6 percent. With new money, banks retained the full value of their claims but committed to issuing new loans amounting to at least 25 percent of the original claim. Cash buybacks involved repurchases of the debt at a pre-established price.

[c] These countries (and their years of first participation) were Argentina (1992), Bolivia (1993), Brazil (1992), Bulgaria (1993), Costa Rica (1989), Dominican Republic (1993), Ecuador (1994), Jordan (1993), Mexico (1989), Nigeria (1991), Panama (1995), Peru (1995), Philippines (1989), Poland (1994), Uruguay (1990), and Venezuela (1990).

and decreasing debt over the 1995–1997 period. The latter result provides some evidence that the latest debt relief initiative may have been more successful than the previous ones, probably because HIPC debt relief is conditional on the implementation of macroeconomic policies that should lead to debt sustainability. It should be noted, however, that according to IMF reports, up to half of the countries that received debt relief under the enhanced HIPC initiative will soon return to an unsustainable debt situation (Birdsall and Deese, 2004).[18]

While Easterly (2002) favors the high discount rate interpretation, an alternative, and to some extents observationally equivalent, interpretation of these facts is that borrowing by poor countries remains high not because of the behavior of spendthrift politicians who waste resources, but because these countries have many unsatisfied basic needs. According to this interpretation, as soon as a debt relief program relaxes their budget constraint, politicians spend as much as they can trying to satisfy these unmet basic needs. Hence, money is not wasted but used trying to escape from a poverty trap; the problem is that there is too little money coming in, and hence poor countries cannot escape from their poverty traps. A policy consistent with this interpretation is to cancel debt and also provide more aid. In fact, Sachs's (2005) proposal for ending poverty and the United Nations (2005) report on how to achieve the Millennium Development Goals make this point explicitly. Poor countries need to increase their expenditure on poverty reduction activities, and this can be achieved only through cancellation of their debt and increases in aid flows to them. A debt cancellation without an increase in aid flows would just result in an immediate buildup of debt—an interpretation consistent with Easterly's empirical finding, but not necessarily an indication that debt relief is useless.[19]

Has Debt Relief Been Successful in Increasing GDP Growth and Social Expenditure?

In regard to whether debt relief has been successful in increasing GDP growth and social expenditure, the answer again is not so clear. Arslanalp and Henry (2005, 2006b) provide convincing evidence that debt relief is beneficial for countries that suffer from debt overhang. In particular, they show that the debt reduction brought about by the Brady Plan provided substantial benefits for both lenders and borrowers. However, they argue that, while debt relief may be beneficial for middle-income countries, HIPCs do not suffer from debt overhang, because in these countries the main obstacle to investment is not excessive debt but the lack of basic market institutions. Bird and Milne (2003) also argue that debt overhang should not matter for low-income countries, because this group of countries receives a positive net resource transfer. Furthermore, while high levels of debt can affect growth by increasing the probability of a financial crisis in the presence of volatile capital flows, this is an unlikely scenario for low-income countries, which have most of their debt with official creditors (Rajan, 2005a).

---

[18] This may not be the result of excessive spending but of negative external shocks that were not taken into consideration in the calculations of the HIPC initiative. However, a World Bank (2006) evaluation of the HIPC initiative also suggests that several participating countries are moving back toward high debt levels.

[19] Easterly (2006) provides a critique of the Sachs and UN plans. Sen (2006) provides a critique of Easterly's view.

Box 10.3 The New Debt Relief Initiatives: HIPC and MDRI

The Heavily Indebted Poor Countries (HIPC) initiative was launched by the IMF and the World Bank in 1996. The objective of the HIPC initiative was threefold: (1) removing the debt overhang for countries that pursue economic and social reforms targeted at measurable poverty reduction, (2) reducing multilateral debt, and (3) helping countries exit from endless debt restructuring to lasting debt relief.[a] The HIPC initiative constituted a radical departure from previous initiatives because it included cancellation of debt owed to multilateral institutions (such as the IMF, World Bank, and IDB), a first in the history of debt relief. At the G7 meeting held in Cologne, Germany, in the fall of 1999, donors and multilaterals agreed that debt relief was moving slowly and decided on a major expansion of the HIPC initiative. The enhanced HIPC initiative more than doubled the amount of debt relief provided under the original HIPC, reduced the debt ratios that qualified a country's debt as unsustainable, and adopted procedures for faster and easier debt relief.

In order to receive debt relief under HIPC, a country has to meet three conditions; it must (1) face an unsustainable burden of debt, beyond traditionally available debt relief mechanisms such as the Paris Club; (2) establish a track record of reforms and sound policies through programs supported by the World Bank and IMF; and (3) prepare a Poverty Reduction Strategy Paper (PRSP). These eligibility criteria are operationalized by a three-step process which involves an eligibility point, a decision point, and a completion point. The *first step* consists of a debt sustainability analysis aimed at assessing whether a low-income country faces an unsustainable level of external debt and hence should be considered for participation in the HIPC initiative. In the *second step*, the country needs to demonstrate some progress towards adjustment and reform programs and submit a first draft of its PRSP. After successful evaluation of the country's efforts in this second step, there is a *decision point* at which multilateral institutions that are granting debt relief formally decide on the country's eligibility, compute a sustainability threshold, and commit to reducing the debt to this threshold. After the decision point, the country starts receiving interim debt relief. In the *third step*, the country needs to establish a further track record of good performance. The length of the period for this may vary, but it must include the satisfactory implementation of the policies agreed upon at the decision point, the maintenance of macroeconomic stability, and the adoption and implementation of the PRSP for at least one year. After all these conditions are met, the country reaches the *completion point* and receives the full debt relief committed to at the decision point.[b]

Depetris Chauvin and Kraay (2005) and Hepp (2005) provide empirical evidence on the effects of debt relief on growth and the composition of public expenditure. Depetris Chauvin and Kraay use a sample of 62 low-income countries during the 1989–2001 period. They find that (1) there is a positive but not statistically significant correlation between debt relief and GDP growth; (2) there is a positive and statistically significant correlation between debt relief and government spending in health and education, but this positive correlation is mostly

The enhanced initiative includes 40 countries (of which 33 are in Africa, 5 in Latin America and the Caribbean, and 2 in Asia), of which 19 have reached the completion point (including Bolivia, Guyana, Honduras, and Nicaragua), 10 have reached the decision point, and 11 (including Haiti) are completing the steps prior to the decision point. The IDB is part of the enhanced HIPC initiative and has already committed $1.9 billion ($1.1 billion in net present value) to debt relief for Bolivia, Guyana, Honduras, and Nicaragua.[c]

At the July 2005 summit held in Gleneagles, Scotland, G8 leaders agreed to cancel all the debt owed to the IMF, the International Development Association (IDA), the concessional branch of the World Bank), and the African Development Fund (AfDF) by all countries that reached or will reach the completion point of the HIPC initiative. This proposal came to be known as the Multilateral Debt Relief Initiative (MDRI), which aims to help HIPCs make progress towards the United Nations Millennium Development Goals, which have the objective of halving poverty by 2015.

Donors agreed to compensate the IDA and AfDF for the debt relief, while part of the relief provided by the IMF will be financed with internal resources.[d] Unlike the HIPC initiative, the MDRI does not propose any contemporaneous debt relief by other creditors beyond the IMF, IDA, and AfDF. This is a thorny issue, because some HIPCs (including all those located in Latin America and the Caribbean) have large debts with multilateral institutions which are not included in the initiative.

---

[a] http://www.worldbank.org/hipc/progress-to-date/May99v3/may99v3.htm.

[b] The HIPC initiative contains a sunset clause designed to prevent the initiative from becoming a permanent facility. Originally, the clause established late 2004 as the ultimate deadline for initial consideration, but the deadline has successively been moved to the end of 2006.

[c] It is important to note that all debt relief initiatives focus on external debt. However, for some countries the main problem is domestic debt. In the case of Nicaragua, for instance, domestic debt dwarfs external debt, and it is likely that most of the resources freed up from debt relief will simply be used to service the domestic debt.

Haiti has not as yet become eligible for the initiative, but it is among the countries that can be included in the HIPC process.

[d] The IMF decided to finance with its own resources (mostly though sales of IMF gold) debt relief to all member countries (whether HIPCs or not) with annual per capita incomes below US$380. Debt relief to HIPCs with incomes above that threshold (which include Bolivia, Guyana, Honduras, and Nicaragua) will instead be administered by the IMF but financed by bilateral contributions.

driven by two outliers (Mozambique and Yemen); (3) there is a positive but not very robust correlation between debt relief and changes in policies; and (4) there is no significant correlation between debt relief and investment. Depetris Chauvin and Kraay interpret these findings as indicating that past debt relief efforts, which amounted to US$100 billion, were ultimately wasted, as they did not yield any concrete result. A more positive view would suggest that debt relief did not hurt any country and was beneficial in some countries.

Hepp (2005) shows that debt relief has a differential effect in HIPCs and non-HIPCs and provides support for Arslanalp and Henry's (2005, 2006a) claim that HIPCs do not suffer from debt overhang. In particular, Hepp finds that, within the sample of HIPCs, neither debt service nor debt stock relief have any significant effect on growth. When he focuses on the sample of non-HIPCs, however, he finds that debt relief that leads to a one percentage point drop in debt service generates a 0.2 percent increase in GDP growth.[20]

One possible assertion is that the current debt relief wave (under the HIPC initiative and the Multilateral Debt Relief Initiative) is better designed and will have a bigger impact on growth than previous initiatives. World Bank (2006) evaluates the HIPC initiative and also finds modest progress in policy performance, growth, and poverty reduction but argues that lack of data makes it extremely hard to provide an evaluation of this initiative.

Is Debt Relief Preferable to Aid?

The question of whether debt relief is preferable to aid has not been systematically addressed by the empirical literature. Arslanalp and Henry (2006a) argue that the answer to this question depends on the type of country. In particular, they claim that debt relief is preferable in middle-income countries that suffer from debt overhang. However, they argue that in low-income countries that are part of the HIPC initiative, low growth is driven not by debt overhang, but by the lack of appropriate market institutions and economic infrastructure.[21] To support this claim, they show that HIPCs always have positive net transfers (a fact inconsistent with debt overhang) and that only a negligible part of capital flows to HIPCs goes to the private sector, indicating that international investors never considered these countries as having vibrant private sectors with viable investment projects. While some authors claim that (at least in the short run) countries care only about net resource flows,[22] Arslanalp and Henry (2006a) stress that debt relief and aid are different concepts and argue that aid is more efficient than debt relief in building market institutions. As aid might be crowded out by debt relief, they conclude that HIPCs should be the target of aid and not debt relief. Along similar lines, Rajan (2005a) points out that if the main obstacle to growth in a particular country is an impossible business climate, reducing the level of debt without providing additional resources or improving policies is unlikely to have any positive effect on growth in that country.

Birdsall and Deese (2004) agree that debt relief and aid are different concepts, but they present a completely different view. According to these authors, debt relief is one of the most effective forms of aid for at least five reasons. The first is the standard debt overhang reason. The second is that debt relief cannot be tied ("tied" refers to a situation in which aid donors force recipient countries to purchase goods or services from the donor country), and they point out that tying aid reduces the value of that aid by as much as 30 percent. The third

---

[20] Hepp's (2005) results should be taken with caution because when he uses an alternative (admittedly less precise) measure of debt relief, he obtains the opposite result.

[21] Cordella, Ricci, and Ruiz-Arranz's (2005) finding that debt may not affect growth in countries with bad policies is in line with this interpretation.

[22] See, for instance, Rajan (2005a). Net resource flow is defined as total capital inflows (aid plus new lending) minus outflows (mostly debt service).

reason is that debt relief stops defensive lending—lending that is not dictated by a country's needs or the quality of its policies but by the level of its debt stock.[23] The fourth reason is that debt relief reduces the transaction costs of conventional aid programs because it liberates recipient countries' government officials from satisfying the different needs and approaches to development of the various donor agencies (which implies that the marginal value added in the requests of these agencies is lower than the efforts that the recipient countries need to make in order to satisfy these requests).[24] The fifth reason is that debt relief provides flexible budget support and increases government accountability because it allows governments of recipient countries to set their own priorities instead of focusing on the pet projects of the various donors.

It should be clear from the above discussion that different views on debt relief versus aid depend partly on differing opinions regarding the value added that can be provided by donor agencies. Those who think that such agencies can increase the development impact of public expenditure by directing external resources towards the development of better institutions and infrastructure will tend to favor aid. Those who think that these agencies will only generate a useless bureaucratic apparatus and result in waste of resources will tend to favor debt relief.

Does Debt Relief Bring Additional Resources?

Systematic research on whether debt relief brings new money is limited. Birdsall, Claessens, and Diwan (2002) look at debt relief to African countries over the 1990s and conclude that because of poor data quality, it is hard to find solid evidence in either direction. However, their results provide some evidence suggesting that the debt reduction of the 1990s crowded out other forms of aid and hence did not provide any additional resources. Ndikumana (2002) finds that beneficiaries of debt relief received more aid than similar countries that did not benefit from debt relief. While this result points towards additionality of debt relief, Ndikumana also finds an overall decline in aid disbursements since the early 1990s, generating a situation in which beneficiaries of debt relief receive more net transfers than nonbeneficiaries, but not necessarily more than what they were receiving before becoming beneficiaries. Powell (2003) finds that debt relief neither crowds out nor generates additional resources. This, when considered along with the fact that economic aid to poorer nations has been decreasing overall, is consistent with the previous results that suggest no increase in net resource transfers to HIPCs. This point is also made by Arslanalp and Henry (2006a), who show that over the 2000–2003 period, net resource transfers to HIPCs were lower than those prevailing over 1980–1995 in terms of both recipient and donor countries' GDP (Figure 10.5).

A World Bank (2006) evaluation of the HIPC initiative which uses more recent data provides a more positive view of the potential additionality of the initiative and shows that since

---

[23] Defensive lending is a situation in which creditors provide new financing to avoid explicitly recognizing that a debtor country is in default. Marchesi and Missale (2004) present strong evidence of defensive lending and defensive granting.

[24] Of course, debt relief is also conditional on some activities and policies, but the conditions are likely to be less burdensome in number than those attached to traditional loans.

2000 there has been a substantial increase in net resource transfers to HIPCs. In particular, this evaluation finds that net annual transfers to the 28 decision point HIPCs increased from US$7.3 billion in 2000 to US$15.8 billion in 2004 and that more than half of this increase was due to debt relief. The same study also conducts a counterfactual exercise in an attempt to explore what would have happened without debt relief and finds that the HIPC initiative did bring additional resources in at least 17 of the 28 HIPCs considered.

THE RESEARCH AND POLICY AGENDA IS STILL OPEN

Well-used public debt can be a powerful tool for economic development. However, political distortions may lead to overborrowing, and volatile capital markets may lead to economic instability even with moderate debt levels. The main message of this chapter is that it is not easy to identify the relationship between debt and economic development, but there is some evidence that moderate levels of debt can promote growth, while higher levels of debt are likely to have a negative effect on growth. The problems with operationalizing these results is that, depending on countries' economic and debt structures, "moderate" may mean very different things. In fact, one of the main themes of this report is that debt levels are only one—and probably not the most important—factor that determines debt vulnerabilities.

The chapter also explores the relationship between debt levels and the composition of public expenditure and does provide evidence suggesting that, while Latin American countries do borrow to finance investment in infrastructure,[25] higher levels of debt have a negative effect on social expenditure.

Finally, the chapter points out that there is still much that is not known on how debt relief affects economic growth and poverty reduction. The two key unanswered questions are whether debt relief is associated with more and better poverty reduction policies and higher growth and whether debt relief initiatives bring additional resources or only crowd out aid and concessional lending.

Figure 10.5
Net Resource Transfers to Heavily Indebted Poor Countries

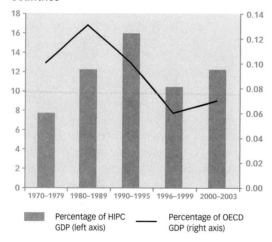

Percentage of HIPC GDP (left axis)

Percentage of OECD GDP (right axis)

Source: Authors' calculations using data from Arslanalp and Henry (2006a), Table 8.

---

[25] In particular, the chapter shows that in Latin America, public debt is positively associated with public investment in infrastructure. The chapter does not tackle the more complex issue of whether this public investment in infrastructure adds to the productive capital stock.

While lack of good data has been one of the main obstacles to detailed evaluations of past debt relief initiatives, one positive aspect of the HIPC initiative is that the coordinating role of the multilateral financial institutions and the need for these institutions to conduct internal evaluations of the initiative has greatly improved the information available to the research community. Furthermore, the high visibility of the initiative is providing incentives to conduct in-depth evaluations of debt relief not only among the multilateral financial institutions, but also in the academic and nonprofit communities. The recent World Bank (2006) update evaluation of the HIPC initiative is a welcome step in this direction and, although some of the results of this evaluation are inconclusive, it is important to note that this was also the case for the early evaluations of the Brady exchange (Husain and Diwan, 1989; Fernández-Arias, 1993), which is now considered a very successful debt relief program.

Fiscal Sustainability in Latin America: Old and New Approaches

CHAPTER 11

THE CONCEPT OF FISCAL SUSTAINABILITY asks whether current debt levels in a country can be serviced given the government's current fiscal position. Thus, it makes no judgment as to whether the country's debt should be different from its current level based on some optimization criterion (see Chapter 10 for a discussion of these issues).

Several of the now-standard approaches to fiscal sustainability were initially devised with developed countries in mind, stressing mostly long-run solvency matters, but ignoring the characteristics of debt and the macroeconomic environment that are typical of developing countries and key for assessing the sustainability of their debt. For example, issues of currency composition of public debt and exposure to large external shocks are fundamental elements that need to be considered in the case of developing countries.

This chapter introduces different fiscal sustainability tools, taking standard sustainability analysis as a starting point, and then moving on to issues that are specific to developing countries. Those issues include fiscal sustainability in the face of uncertainty from various sources, and in particular, the real exchange rate and public revenue fluctuations. As sovereign credit ratings are important benchmarks for investors, the correlation of the fiscal indicators examined here with credit ratings provides a useful measure of the extent to which credit risk analysts focus on these emerging market issues. In other words, what do rating agencies have in mind, directly or indirectly, when assessing solvency risk?

THE STANDARD APPROACH

The meaning of fiscal sustainability is often blurred. A first point to clarify is the difference between solvency and sustainability. Insolvency refers to a situation in which the future paths of spending and revenue do not generate sufficient net financial resources to service the existing government debt. A policy stance is sustainable if "a borrower is expected to be able to continue servicing its debt without an unrealistically large future correction to the balance of income and expenditure" (IMF, 2002a, 4). Thus, solvency is only a necessary condition for sustainability, because solvency can be achieved with very large and costly future adjustments. In other words, sustainability requires achieving solvency without major policy changes.

The starting point for virtually all standard methods of calculating debt sustainability is a government's current period budget constraint, which states that the portion of debt payments falling due (inclusive of interest) that cannot be covered by the primary surplus is financed with new debt.[1] This assumes away any direct financing of the deficit through money printing by the central bank. In the long run, for debt to be sustainable, the government must be able to meet the following condition:

$$s = (r - g)d, \tag{11.1}$$

where d is the level of debt as a share of GDP, r is the real interest rate, g is the growth rate of the economy, and s is the government's primary surplus as a share of GDP. This condition has an intuitive interpretation: the level of the sustainable debt-to-GDP ratio is such that the primary surplus is enough to cover the "effective" interest cost of servicing it. The effective interest rate is the real interest rate net of the growth rate of GDP. As all the variables are assumed to be constant over time (or to reflect an appropriately computed average), this equation states that the stream of future long-run primary surpluses—appropriately discounted—has to fully cover existing debt levels.[2]

While sustainable debt thus measured is a useful benchmark, debt sustainability does not necessarily require a government to constantly satisfy a debt target calculated in this way. For example, a government could be faced with a temporary shock and might want to use debt markets to smooth it out. To account for situations in which there are short-run deviations from the long-run debt level but debt will eventually return to sustainability, some studies focus on a more dynamic interpretation.[3] For example, some methods evaluate whether a country's primary surplus tends to increase when public debt increases.[4] Another, more recent approach makes a short-run evaluation of a country's current fiscal stance by assessing its current debt stock, its current primary surplus, and ongoing interest and growth rates to determine whether they are consistent with convergence to a targeted long-run debt-to GDP ratio (see Croce and Juan-Ramón, 2003). The advantage of this approach is that it allows for departures from long-run values in the current debt stock and the primary balance. It analyzes whether deviations of the primary surplus from its steady state value, and/or deviations of current debt levels from target debt levels, are sufficiently large to put convergence in peril, thus rendering a policy stance unsustainable.

SUSTAINABILITY IN LATIN AMERICA USING THE STANDARD APPROACH

Despite some episodes of fiscal stress in some Latin American countries in the late 1990s and early 2000s, the region has become more fiscally sound than in the 1980s. The sharp decline in inflation rates is an indirect indicator of fiscal improvement, showing that governments

---

[1] For comprehensive discussions see Buiter (1985) and Blanchard (1990). The former focuses on sustainability based on stabilizing government net worth, whereas the latter considers sustainability based on stabilizing the debt-to-GDP ratio. Given the empirical difficulties in measuring net worth, the second approach has been more widely used. See also Chalk and Hemming (2000) and Izquierdo and Panizza (2006) for detailed surveys.

[2] For all calculations in this chapter, the discrete-time version of this formula was used, namely,

$$s = (\frac{1+r}{1+g} - 1)d.$$

[3] In essence, these tests attempt to rule out explosive paths on public debt. See, for example, Hamilton and Flavin (1986) and Chalk and Hemming (2000).

[4] See Bohn (1998). See Abiad and Ostry (2005) for applications to developing countries.

have not needed to resort to monetary financing of their deficits. Another commonly used indicator of ability-to-pay performance through noninflationary sources is the debt-to-fiscal revenue ratio, which had declined by 2004 relative to the early 1990s. Although on average Latin American countries have improved their ability to pay as measured by this indicator (which fell from about 460 percent in 1991 to 320 percent in 2004), the indicator is still much higher than in developed countries, where the average debt-to-revenue ratio for the general government was slightly over 130 percent by the end of 2004.[5] Looking within the region, this improved performance as measured by lower debt-to-revenue ratios is confirmed for most countries when informa-tion for 1991 is compared to that for 2004 (Figure 11.1).

These measures hint at improvements in com-parison with the 1990s, but how has the region performed in terms of the standard sustainability ap-proach? To answer this question, a more compre-hensive indicator based on the standard sustainability approach was constructed based on equation (11.1). This is the real interest rate that would have been required to make prevail-ing debt levels sustainable given prevailing primary surpluses, current debt stocks, and average GDP growth rates. It is equiva-lent to a "slackness" inter-est rate to the extent that it represents the maximum interest rate consistent with fiscal sustainability. This indicator is convenient, because accurate data on average real interest rates are very hard to come by. Although there are some available measures of effective real interest rates—obtained by computing interest payments as a share of beginning-of-period debt levels, net of infla-tion—these are subject to substantial measurement problems (and/or lack of information

Figure 11.1
Public Debt as a Percentage of Total Revenues in Latin America and the Caribbean, 1991 versus 2004

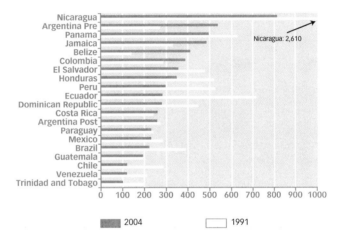

Sources: Cowan et al. (2006) database; Martner and Tromben (2004b); IMF, World Economic Outlook; central banks.
Note: "Argentina Pre" represents figures for Argentina before the debt-re-structuring process. "Argentina Post" represents figures for Argentina after the restructuring process.

---

[5] Countries included in the "Latin America and the Caribbean" group are Argentina, Bolivia, Brazil, Chile, Colombia, the Dominican Republic, Ecuador, Guatemala, Honduras, Jamaica, Nicaragua, Mexico, Panama, Paraguay, Suriname, Trinidad and Tobago, and Venezuela. Developed countries in the sample are Australia, Austria, Belgium, Canada, Den-mark, Finland, France, Germany, Greece, Iceland, Ireland, Italy, Japan, Luxembourg, Netherlands, Norway, Portugal, Spain, Switzerland, the United Kingdom, and the United States.

Figure 11.2
"Slackness" Interest Rate for Sustainability, 1991 versus 2004
(*percent*)

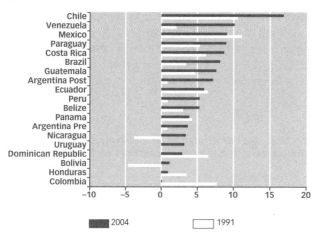

| | 2004 | | 1991 |

Sources: Cowan et al. (2006) database; Martner and Tromben (2004b); IMF, *World Economic Outlook*; central banks.
Note: The slackness interest rate is calculated as $r = ((s/b) * (1 + g)) + g$, where r is the slackness interest rate; s is the primary surplus-to-GDP ratio; b is the total debt-to-GDP ratio; and g is the GDP growth rate. "Argentina Pre" represents figures for Argentina before the debt-restructuring process. "Argentina Post" represents figures for Argentina after the restructuring process. Data for 1991 for Uruguay are unavailable.

for the early 1990s).[6] Figure 11.2 shows values of this variable for each country in the region in 1991 vis-à-vis 2004. The lower interest rates that would have been required, on average, in the early 1990s to make debt sustainable—particularly in a context of higher international interest rates than in 2004—suggest that the countries' fiscal position was more precarious at that time relative to 2004.

Focusing on more recent periods for which data on effective real interest rates are available, a standard debt sustainability exercise is to compute the "required" vis-à-vis the observed levels of the primary surplus. The required primary surplus is defined as the one that would make current debt sustainable, as indicated by equation (11.1). As a first approximation, required primary surpluses were calculated on the basis of effective real interest rates paid in 2004, average growth for the 10-year interval covering the period 1994–2004, and current debt-to-GDP levels.[7] Results are shown in panel (a) of Figure 11.3, and at first glance they suggest a very favorable scenario, as most countries' observed primary surpluses are higher than their required levels.[8]

A more conservative estimate of required primary surplus would be based on a longer-term average of interest rates. Effective real interest rates for 2004 are probably far from being long-run real interest rates for several reasons. International real interest rates in recent times have been quite low and may not remain at current levels in the future. Ad-

---

[6] For example, measurement problems may arise when expected inflation incorporated in interest rates differs substantially from effective short-run inflation. These measurement problems will become apparent in the section linking standard sustainability measures using effective real interest rates to credit ratings.

[7] Effective real interest rates were obtained primarily from IMF country documents. Ideally, if the debt service profile of government debt is known and a long-run real interest rate benchmark is used, the net present value of that debt can be computed and sustainability evaluated at that net present value debt level, given assumptions for the long-run real interest rate and long-run growth rate. However, this is beyond the scope of this report, given lack of information.

[8] This analysis was performed at the central government level, and for some particular cases (such as Colombia), in which balances from the remainder of the nonfinancial public sector are important, this measure may not accurately represent the consolidated nonfinancial public sector position.

ditionally, countries that have recently restructured their debt may also be making lower-than-usual interest payments. For these reasons, and in order to stress-test fiscal performance with respect to interest rate fluctuations, an alternative exercise was performed, this time assuming that countries would eventually roll over their debt stocks at the median real interest rate that prevailed for the period 1992–2004, based on behavior of the aggregate Latin Eurobond Index yield.[9] Recomputed required primary surpluses are contrasted with observed surpluses in panel (b) of Figure 11.3. This time, the results are significantly different, with several more countries now facing required primary surpluses above actual levels, highlighting the fact that current fiscal positions may look much more comfortable than they would if interest rates returned to the higher levels that prevailed in the past. The large fluctuations in real interest rates that Latin American countries have faced in the past—and their profound impact on fiscal standing—suggest that, although fiscal positions have improved, vulnerability to real interest rate increases still remains. It is also worth noting that, at least in the experience of the 1990s, much of the increase in interest rates was due to increases in spreads rather than increases in the risk-free interest rate. Thus, several countries could be as exposed as they were in the 1990s to shocks resulting from increases in real interest rates, even if risk-free interest rates were to remain low.

Figure 11.3
Observed and Required Primary Surplus, 2004

a. Effective real interest rates, 2004

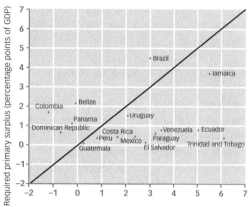

Observed primary surplus (percentage points of GDP)

b. Median real interest rate (Latin Eurobond Index yield)

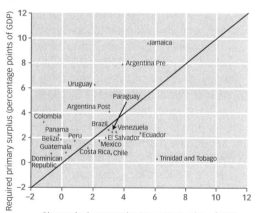

Observed primary surplus (percentage points of GDP)

Sources: Bloomberg; IMF country reports (various years); IMF, *World Economic Outlook* database; central banks; and authors' calculations.
Note: "Argentina Pre" represents figures for Argentina before the debt-restructuring process. "Argentina Post" represents figures for Argentina after the restructuring process. Heavily Indebted Poor Countries (Bolivia, Honduras, and Nicaragua) (both panels) and Chile and Argentina (panel a only) are not included, given that the effective real interest rate in these countries is lower than the average GDP growth rate.

---

[9] The real interest rate used in this case was 7.5 percent.

Furthermore, the current high primary surpluses reflect in part the current favorable conditions for export demand and high commodity prices that increase government revenue. Again, this favorable phase may pass. It is worth noting, however, that under similar favorable conditions in the early 1990s, primary surpluses were lower on average, which indicates that the region has expended significant policy effort toward achieving stronger fiscal positions.

INCORPORATING VOLATILITY

Developing countries differ in many respects from developed countries. To begin with, developing countries face substantially greater volatility in real exchange rates, real interest rates, and terms of trade. Developing countries also frequently have to cope with sudden loss of access to international credit markets, which in many cases is completely unexpected. Additionally, the magnitude of shocks faced by developing countries can be so large and these shocks so persistent that, especially in the presence of relatively low credibility in fiscal policy and budget institutions, countercyclical policies may not be an option at all.

This higher volatility and persistence in shocks introduces various additional sources of vulnerability that must be considered when debt sustainability is analyzed, suggesting that until developing countries are able to reduce volatility, it may be relevant to consider debt levels to be "safe" when they can both be sustained in the long run and withstand the pressure of large shocks. In particular, to the extent that shocks are large and persistent, as, for example, was the case of the capital flow standstill experienced by Latin America in the late 1990s, solvency issues may quickly come into play. Thus, the concept of sustainability should be expanded to ensure solvency not only against realistic adjustment scenarios, but also against realistic external volatility.

These issues can be considered from three different perspectives. The first focuses on financial frictions that have played a major role in recent emerging market crises and their effect on fiscal sustainability. The second addresses the issue that emerging market governments are typically confronted with considerable sources of aggregate uncertainty as they try to assess the pattern of government revenue and expenditure, as well as the level of debt they can afford.[10] A third perspective extends the uncertainty analysis to the evaluation of net worth performance, focusing on novel techniques that account for the valuation of assets.

Currency Mismatches, Sudden Stops, and Valuation Effects

Liability dollarization is a major source of vulnerability to sudden stops in capital flows, and the combination of the two can have devastating effects on fiscal sustainability.[11] For instance, loss of access to credit markets need not be the result of overindebtedness in the context of a good equilibrium, but can instead be the result of an economy's having fallen into a bad equilibrium triggered by a sudden stop in capital flows (see Calvo, Izquierdo, and

---

[10] See Mendoza and Oviedo (2002) for a very useful discussion on these issues.

[11] Following Calvo (1998), a sudden stop is defined as a large and unexpected stop in capital flowing to a particular country. See Calvo, Izquierdo, and Mejía (2004) for empirical definitions of a sudden stop.

Mejía, 2004). This *inverse fiscal view*—in the sense that there is little that is fiscal in the origin of the crisis—finds support in the fact that sudden stop episodes tend to occur around the same time, and for countries exhibiting a variety of fiscal situations before the shock.

Sudden stops in capital flows force abrupt adjustments in the current account deficit that may require sizable currency depreciation in real terms when the capital flow standstill is highly persistent—otherwise, real exchange rate fluctuations would be short lived, and solvency would not necessarily be at stake.[12] This adjustment may have large valuation effects that multiply the cost of servicing foreign currency debt because of excessive liability dollarization, thus pushing a country's debt out of the sustainable range.

The best example of the effect of external conditions on fiscal sustainability can be found in the Russian debt default of August 1998 and the spread of this shock to global capital markets, an event that would lead to generalized capital flow reversals in emerging markets. In many ways, the Russian crisis worked as a liquidity shock to international investors, who spread it across different countries as they sold assets in their portfolios to restore liquidity and cover margin calls resulting from collapsing Russian bond prices (Calvo, 2005b). This shock turned into a full-fledged crisis in countries that had two key domestic vulnerabilities: a small supply of internationally tradable goods (such as exports) and domestic liability dollarization (Calvo, Izquierdo, and Mejía, 2004). These vulnerabilities can be summarized in the following "mismatch" ratio (see Calvo, Izquierdo, and Talvi, 2005):

$$m = \frac{B \, / \, eB^*}{Y \, / \, eY^*} \, , \qquad (11.2)$$

where e is the real exchange rate, B is domestic currency debt, B^* is foreign currency debt, Y is output of nontradables, and Y^* is output of tradables. Mismatches between debt and output composition can lead to substantial differences in valuation of the debt-to-GDP ratio following depreciation. For example, consider a limit case in which all valuation effects take place on debt only, because debt is fully denominated in foreign currency, and output is fully nontradable (that is, when $m = 0$). This is the worst-case scenario, in which real exchange rate depreciation hits fully on sustainability. Another case that is particularly relevant is that in which the composition of debt (in terms of tradables vis-à-vis nontradables) matches that of output (that is, when $m = 1$). When this condition holds, real exchange rate depreciation has no effect on the debt-to-GDP ratio and thus on fiscal sustainability. The effect can be compounded by the fact that contingent liabilities, such as those emanating from banking sector bailouts, can materialize simultaneously. When firms in nontradable sectors are heavily indebted in foreign currency to the banking system, substantial depreciation brings along bankruptcies and an urge for the government to bail out the banking system in an effort to preserve the payments system. Thus, public sector debt can skyrocket once the direct and indirect effects of depreciation add up.

---

[12] See the model presented in Calvo, Izquierdo, and Talvi (2005), which assumes that the sudden stop in capital flows is permanent, and thus that real exchange rate depreciation is permanent as well (and may lead to unsustainable fiscal positions at the new real exchange rate level).

Figure 11.4 shows how Latin American countries ranked in terms of the mismatch ratio defined in equation (11.2) in 1998 (at the time of the Russian crisis) and in 2004.[13] As the figure shows, from a liability perspective, Latin American countries were more exposed to exchange rate fluctuations in 1998 than in 2004. Following the sudden stop episode that plagued the region after the Russian crisis, many countries reacted by reducing mismatches and expanding issuance of debt in domestic currency, in many cases indexed to the CPI.

In terms of ranking within the region, in the healthier range of the spectrum are countries like Chile, with a high level of domestic debt issuance and a large supply of tradable goods. Countries with past inflationary experiences and a tradition of liability dollarization are typically more mismatched (Argentina, Peru, Uruguay).[14] For example, Argentina before debt restructuring had a much lower matching ratio, which has substantially improved since debt restructuring (from 0.15 at the end of 2004 to 0.40 right after debt restructuring in June 2005). Although this index cap-

Figure 11.4
Currency Matching Ratio

a. 1998

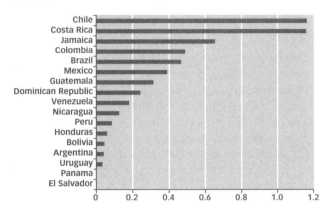

b. 2004

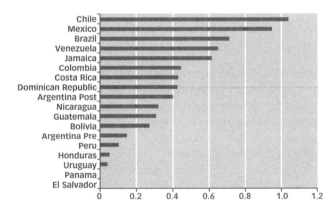

Sources: Cowan et al. (2006); central banks; World Bank, *World Development Indicators* online database; authors' calculations.
Note: "Argentina Pre" represents figures for Argentina before the debt-restructuring process. "Argentina Post" represents figures for Argentina after the restructuring process. The currency matching ratio is calculated as $(B/eB^*)/(Y/eY^*)$, where B is debt in domestic currency; B^* is debt in foreign currency; Y is output in nontradables; Y^* is output in tradables; and e is the real exchange rate.

---

[13] Tradable output is proxied by the share of the sum of agriculture and industry in total GDP at constant prices.

[14] Special consideration should be given to the case of fully dollarized countries such as Panama, Ecuador, and El Salvador. In some cases, as in Panama, the development of a major stable financial center following dollarization may have reduced the likelihood of disruption in capital markets, in which case mismatches are not such a relevant issue. However, to the extent that full dollarization does not diminish the likelihood of a sudden stop, such countries may be heavily exposed.

Figure 11.5
Exposure of Nonfinancial Public Sector to Real Currency Depreciation

a. 1998

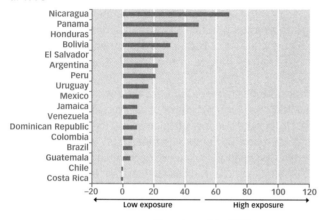

Low exposure ← → High exposure

Percentage points of GDP

b. 2004

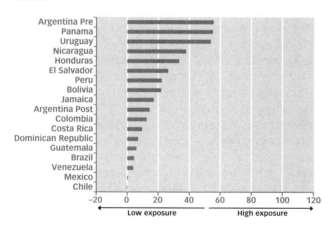

Low exposure ← → High exposure

Percentage points of GDP

Sources: Cowan et al. (2006); central banks; World Bank, *World Development Indicators*; and authors' calculations.
Note: "Argentina Pre" represents figures for Argentina before the debt-restructuring process. "Argentina Post" represents figures for Argentina after the restructuring process.

tures the main determinants of exposure to sudden stops, it does not comprise all sources of vulnerability to events of this type. Where domestic currency debt is short term, expectations of currency depreciation can make interest rates soar and have a significant impact on public finances to the extent that devaluation is resisted (see Chapter 13).

The mismatch ratio can be expanded to reflect the interaction of mismatches and debt levels. For example, a highly mismatched country with very low debt levels would not be seriously affected by the aggregate effects of debt valuation following real currency depreciation. For this reason, a second measure was calculated, this one evaluating the debt increase in terms of GDP that would take place were a country subject to real depreciation of 100 percent (see Figure 11.5).[15] Although in general, the ordering is similar to that obtained using equation (11.2), some heavily indebted countries, like Nicaragua, jump up in the vulnerability rankings, while other less-indebted countries, like Guatemala, are on safer ground.

---

[15] In terms of the notation introduced previously, it is equivalent to computing $d(d)/(d(e)/e)*100$.

THE UNCERTAINTY APPROACH

Standard sustainability analysis was originally conceived for developed countries, in which volatility issues are generally less important. For emerging markets, it becomes essential to incorporate key sources of uncertainty into fiscal analysis and redefine what should be considered "safe" debt levels, taking into account possible changes in economic conditions. The key question that emerging market governments face is whether their debt levels will still be sustainable given the range of possible changes in the international and domestic economic environments.

Most of the debt sustainability literature has explored the use of stochastic methods to obtain representations of the process that drives the dynamics of public debt or net worth.[16] For example, Barnhill and Kopits (2003) adapt the concept of value at risk used in the finance industry to the analysis of government net worth by computing measures of dispersion relative to present values of a government's assets and liabilities to determine the value at risk or exposure to negative net worth. In an application to the case of Ecuador, they find that net worth valuation could not resist large shocks without turning negative. Xu and Ghezzi (2003) instead follow a liquidity approach, in which a government may be exposed to depletion of treasury reserves. Through estimation of the processes followed by variables that influence treasury reserves (such as exchange rates, interest rates, and the primary fiscal balance), the probability of default, that is, a depletion of treasury reserves, can be estimated at any point in time.[17] Garcia and Rigobón (2004) estimate the joint behavior of key variables affecting the evolution of government debt and perform simulations of the joint paths of these variables (the real interest rate, GDP growth, the primary deficit, the real exchange rate, inflation, and shocks to debt or "skeletons"), which amount to repeated simulations of the path of government debt. Based on this information, the probability that debt will reach a level considered unsustainable can be computed.

Celasun, Debrun, and Ostry (2006) emphasize that the high-frequency data used in Garcia and Rigobón (2004) for the primary balance may not be a good indicator of a government's policy stance, because in many cases high-frequency data are quite noisy, as they reflect cash management operations which may differ substantially from true fiscal policy response to changes in the environment. For this reason, Celasun, Debrun, and Ostry separately estimate, using annual data, how the fisc reacts to a key set of variables—a fiscal reaction function—and they combine this with an estimation, based on quarterly data, of the joint behavior of nonfiscal determinants of public debt dynamics (real foreign and domestic interest rates, GDP growth, and the real exchange rate), very much in the vein of Garcia and Rigobón (2004). Using these two pieces of information, they produce "fan charts" indicating the associated potential paths of the debt-to-GDP ratio, which allow for evaluation of the probability that debt as a share of GDP will lie below a particular threshold at any point in time.

Mendoza and Oviedo (2004, 2006) provide a framework that rationalizes why governments may want to impose a debt threshold on themselves. In this framework, a govern-

---

[16] These representations do not address the factors underlying this process but instead focus on reduced-form links between debt and other variables.

[17] This approach is different from most of the material discussed in this chapter, as it is closer to the concept of liquidity than to that of solvency.

ment may want to provide insurance to society by keeping government outlays as smooth as possible (except for inevitable adjustments in times of crises), given uncertainty in regard to public revenue and an environment in which such insurance cannot be bought from financial markets. The framework determines sustainable debt ratios based on the ability of a government to credibly commit to debt repayment, that is, the ability to repay debt even after fiscal revenue hits very low levels for a prolonged period of time. Under these conditions, the government will determine the maximum liability position that it can sustain—or "debt limit"—and will set a contingent plan for adjusting expenditures so as to smooth outlays as much as possible while abiding by the debt limit.

This concept of debt limit is similar to that introduced in equation (11.1) for the standard sustainability approach, except that it considers the primary balance that can be achieved in a fiscal crisis (when revenue is at its minimum and expenditures are adjusted as much as possible in times of crisis). Thus, the debt limit is not the same as the sustainable debt, except in times of crisis.

A key determinant of the debt limit is the volatility of government revenue.[18] As Mendoza and Oviedo show, in general, higher revenue volatility will imply lower debt limits. Figure 11.6 plots revenue volatility for Latin American and Caribbean countries by computing the volatility of the cyclical component of the revenue-to-GDP ratio for the period 1990–2004.[19] The mean volatility for the sample of developed countries used here is 3.3 percent. A one standard deviation interval around that mean yields volatility coefficients ranging roughly between 2 and 4 percent. Only 6 out of 24 countries in the Latin American and Caribbean sample fall within that range or lower, providing an indication of the significance of the volatility problem facing the region.

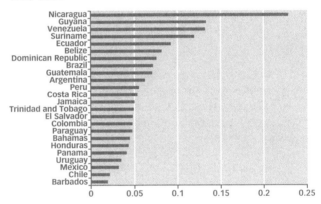

Figure 11.6
Volatility of Cyclical Component of Revenue-to-GDP Ratio, 1990–2004

Source: Authors' calculations based on the IMF's *World Economic Outlook* database.

The relevance of revenue volatility highlighted by the Mendoza-Oviedo framework becomes apparent in the computation of the minimum tolerable level of government expenditure in a time of crisis that would make current debt levels sustainable (and barely below

---

[18] However, it must be noted that revenue volatility implicitly captures volatility in other exogenous variables (such as the terms of trade), and thus revenues should not be considered in and of themselves the source of volatility.

[19] Using a Hodrick-Prescott filter to detrend the series.

Figure 11.7

Minimum Expenditure in Times of Crisis Using Current Debt Levels as Debt Limit

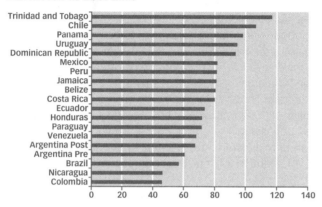

Minimum expenditure (percentage of 2004 expenditure)

Source: Authors' calculations.

Note: "Argentina Pre" represents figures for Argentina before the debt-restructuring process. "Argentina Post" represents figures for Argentina after the restructuring process.

the debt limit) given historical revenue volatility.[20] This exercise provides an idea of the level of insurance that a government would be able to provide given its current fiscal position (as it represents the level of expenditure that could be sustained during a crisis assuming that current debt levels are barely below the debt limit). Results for the Latin American and Caribbean sample are shown in Figure 11.7, in which the minimum level of primary expenditure during a fiscal crisis is expressed as a share of prevailing primary expenditure levels in 2004. As is clear from an examination of the figure, very few countries in the sample could sustain current expenditure levels in a time of fiscal crisis. On average, current expenditure levels would need to be adjusted by 22.3 percent in times of crisis in order to make current debt levels sustainable at the debt limit. This points to relatively low insurance levels for expenditure in times of crisis, even when current debt levels are used as threshold levels.[21]

Changes in revenue volatility have a strong impact on debt limits. To illustrate this point, Latin American and Caribbean countries were ranked according to Moody's credit rating and split into two categories: lower-risk and higher-risk countries.[22] Figure 11.8 shows that the average higher-risk country could benefit substantially from reducing its revenue volatility to avoid a fiscal crisis: if it could bring down revenue volatility from 9.5 percent to that of the average lower-risk country (6 percent), it could increase its debt limit from 42 to 108 percent of GDP.[23] Thus, its chances of hitting a fiscal crisis could be greatly reduced.

---

[20] In the Mendoza-Oviedo framework, the debt limit (b^*) is set by $b^* \equiv (t^{min} - e^{min}) \frac{1+g}{r-g}$, where t^{min} is the lowest possible realization of revenue (as a share of GDP), e^{min} is the crisis expenditure level (as a share of GDP), r is the interest rate, and g is the economy's growth rate. This identity is used to obtain the crisis expenditure level that would make the current debt level the same as the debt limit, when the lowest realization of revenue is set at two standard deviations below the revenue mean. Since under this framework debt (including the debt limit) can always be repaid, and there is no strategic default, interest rate r is in principle a risk-free rate.

[21] However, it must be noted that insurance in this case is against the very unfavorable scenario of a long sequence of the worst possible realization in revenues. An issue that this type of approach must still address is whether it is optimal to purchase this level of insurance.

[22] Countries belonging to Moody's credit-rating categories Ba3 or better are classified in the first group.

[23] Assuming that expenditure can be adjusted by 20 percent in times of crisis.

THE NET WORTH APPROACH REVISITED

While most of the approaches presented in this chapter have focused on vulnerability to shocks to government liabilities, government assets are equally affected by economic shocks. For example, the results of exercises considering the effect of real exchange rate depreciation could change substantially once assets such as oil or copper reserves are added to the equation. A typical representation of the government balance sheet is displayed in Table 11.1. A key component of the balance sheet is the net present value of the stream of future revenues, which can be highly susceptible to changes in the macroeconomic environment and is a key determinant of sustainability.

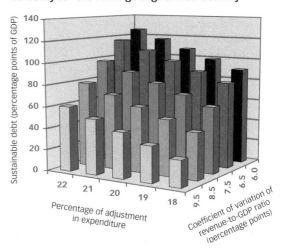

Figure 11.8
Debt Limit Sensitivity to Changes in Revenue Volatility for the Average Higher-Risk Country

Source: Authors' calculations.

Building upon the framework established by Barnhill and Kopits (2003), Levy Yeyati and Sturzenegger (2006) explicitly estimate the behavior of different types of revenue (income tax, value-added tax, etc.) as a function of GDP growth and the real exchange rate (they also do this for different types of government expenditures).

In this framework, the joint behavior of GDP growth, the real exchange rate, and international interest rates is estimated to produce simulations of future joint paths for these three variables that are replicated several times. Results from each simulation are fed into the estimated equations of revenues and expenditures in order to come up with a stream of revenues and expenditures whose net present value can be calculated and included in net worth estimations. Thus, for each replication of GDP growth, real exchange rate, and interest rate paths, a net worth position can be obtained. After a sufficient number of replications, a distribution for net worth can be constructed. This distribution is quite useful, as it allows for the estimation of the probability that net worth may fall into negative territory, that is, the probability that the government may become insolvent. In contrast to the approach pursued in other studies that model the primary surplus as a function of the three key variables previously mentioned, this approach has as an additional benefit that, through the estimation of separate revenue and expenditure elasticities, simulations can be estimated relative to the *actual* value of taxes and expenditures, which is tantamount to estimating the elasticity of the primary surplus for the *current* fiscal policy mix.

With a focus on the particular cases of Argentina and Chile, several interesting results emerge from the net worth approach. An examination of Argentina's balance sheet shows that bonded debt (i.e., explicit liabilities) adds up to just 8 percent of total liabilities, a result that stresses the relevance of including all elements of the balance sheet when assessing

Table 11.1 The Government's Balance Sheet

Assets	Liabilities
Liquid assets	Explicit liabilities
Physical assets	Contingent liabilities
Net present value of taxes	(Net present value of social security)
Net worth of state-owned enterprises	(Net present value of health insurance)
	(Net present value of other expenditures)
	Net worth

Source: Levy Yeyati and Sturzenegger (2006).

Table 11.2 Effect of Real Exchange Rate Shock on Net Worth

(percentage points of GDP)

	Argentina		Chile	
	Basic simulation	With exchange rate shock	Basic simulation	With exchange rate shock
Mean	1.79	0.63	2.34	2.79
Median	1.63	0.52	2.24	2.66
Maximum	12.99	7.76	6.00	7.10
Minimum	−0.32	−2.63	0.95	1.11
Standard deviation	1.04	0.72	0.61	0.75

Source: Levy Yeyati and Sturzenegger (2006).

solvency. More interesting are the findings regarding the effects of real exchange rate depreciation. As expected, in the case of Argentina—a relatively dollarized country—net worth falls following depreciation (see Table 11.2). But an appealing claim that Levy Yeyati and Sturzenegger make is that most of this effect comes from the fact that, with real depreciation, the tax base shrinks as a share of GDP, thus highlighting the relevance of income effects on fiscal accounts (however, this statement should be weighed against the fact that dollar liabilities themselves could be responsible for the obtained income effect).

This result differs from that for Chile (see Table 11.2). With a high share of its income base linked to the tradables sector (due in part to resources provided by copper production), Chile would experience an improvement in its net worth position following depreciation (despite a countervailing increase in expenditure).

DEBT SUSTAINABILITY AND CREDIT RATINGS IN LATIN AMERICA

Are these different perspectives on debt sustainability reflected in any way in how solvency risk is perceived by rating agencies? Do agencies focus on measures associated with standard sustainability analysis only, or are recent concerns brought up by the sustainability literature also considered when default risk is assessed?

A first pass at the data in regard to these questions suggests that standard sustainability measures may have an impact on credit ratings. Panels (a) and (b) in Figure 11.9 show the relationship between indicators associated with standard sustainability analysis and credit ratings assigned by Moody's. Panel (a) shows that the difference between required and observed primary surpluses, using prevailing real effective interest rates in 2004, has a low correlation with credit ratings. However, as mentioned previously, real effective interest rates are subject to several sources of measurement error. Given this shortcoming, credit ratings are contrasted next against "slackness" real interest rates, or the maximum level of real interest rates that would make a country's current fiscal position sustainable. The results are displayed in panel (b), indicating a much tighter relationship (the correlation coefficient in this case is 0.49).

Figure 11.9
Credit Ratings versus Different Sustainability Measures

a. Required minus observed primary surplus

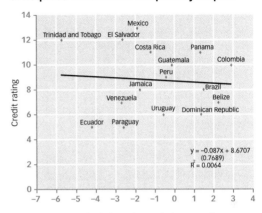

Required minus observed primary surplus
(percentage points of GDP)

b. "Slackness" interest rates for sustainability

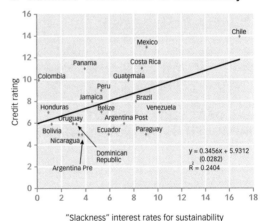

"Slackness" interest rates for sustainability
(percentage points)

How about measures associated with currency mismatches? Panels (c) and (d) in the figure provide a preliminary answer. Panel (c) plots the mismatch measure of equation (11.2) against credit ratings, while panel (d) does the same using the augmented mismatch measure that also takes into account debt size. Interestingly, both measures indicate a relatively strong association with credit ratings (the correlations are 0.38 and −0.40, respectively).

Finally, panels (e) and (f) in Figure 11.9 show associations with measures of revenue volatility and minimum expenditures derived from the Mendoza-Oviedo framework. This time there is indication of negative cor-relation between credit ratings and the volatility of the cyclical component of the revenue-to-GDP ratio, and of posi-tive correlation between credit ratings and minimum levels of expenditures that can be "guaranteed" in times of crisis (correlations are −0.49 and 0.51, respec-tively). These results open up interesting venues for future research exploring further links between revenue volatility and credit ratings.

Many of these partial, cross-sec-tion regression plots may in one way or another be capturing a common el-ement taken into account by credit-rating agencies. However—and despite the limitations of the sample—there is some evidence that, directly or indi-rectly, these new measures may provide pieces of information which could be relevant in and of themselves, as indi-cated by a simple regression of credit ratings on the matching measure that takes debt size into account and the measure of revenue volatility previously described.[24]

HAS DEBT SUSTAINABILITY IMPROVED IN LATIN AMERICA?

Latin America made some strides in terms of debt sustainability coming out of the 1980s, which has been aptly termed the "debt crisis" decade. How-ever, several indicators suggest that, on

Figure 11.9 (continued)

c. Currency matching ratio

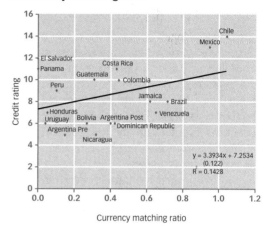

d. Financial exposure

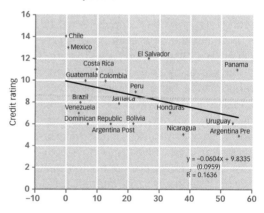

average, the region is far from being safe. To begin with, the region remains vulnerable to interest rate fluctuations. Although some progress has been made in reducing liability dol-larization, fiscal sustainability in many countries remains susceptible to large shocks in the real exchange rate, given lingering currency mismatches and relatively high debt levels.

---

[24] Despite the limitations of the sample (16 observations in one particular region), mismatch and volatility variables are significant at the 6 and 3 percent level.

e. Volatility of cyclical component of revenue-to-GDP ratio

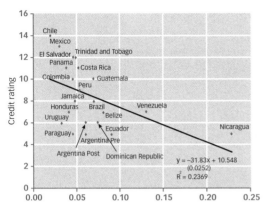

Volatility of cyclical component of revenue-to-GDP ratio

f. Minimum expenditure in times of crisis

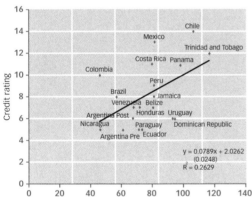

Minimum expenditure (percentage points)

Sources: Moody's; Cowan et al. (2006); IMF, *World Economic Outlook* database; World Bank, *World Development Indicators*; central banks; and authors' calculations.
Note: Data are for 2004. "Argentina Pre" represents figures for Argentina before the debt-restructuring process. "Argentina Post" represents figures for Argentina after the restructuring process. Values in parentheses are *p*-values for the independent variable.

Furthermore, volatility is far from over in Latin America. Periods of systemic capital market turmoil could well return to haunt the region. Although many countries in the region have improved their current account balances, partly as a result of the current bonanza in export prices, they are still exposed to potential interruptions in capital flows that could trigger substantial changes in the real exchange rate and in debt sustainability. In such situations, countries would need to resort to large expenditure adjustments. In this regard, several exercises suggest that reducing revenue volatility could be beneficial in terms of the ability to sustain higher debt levels.

Fiscal sustainability analysis is undergoing a quantum leap with the incorporation of the effects of economic and financial volatility into analysis frameworks. Exposure to volatility in government revenues and real exchange rate fluctuations are particularly important in the Latin American context, as underscored by the fact that credit ratings seem to reflect these vulnerabilities as well. Although progress made in modifying the debt structure in Latin American countries has reduced the exposure to exchange rate fluctuations, debt sustainability could be further enhanced by fiscal and institutional reforms that limit the impact of volatility in government revenues.

CHAPTER 12 | The Costs of Default

EVALUATING DEBT SUSTAINABILITY requires determining what level of debt is high enough to trigger a default by a sovereign country.[1] This is relatively straightforward in the case of a private firm. The "default point" of a private company is the point at which its debt liabilities are equal to the total market value of its assets, that is, the point at which the equity value of the firm becomes zero (Merton, 1974). Finding the default point of sovereign debt is much more complicated, because a government's assets, which include, for example, the ability to tax its citizens, do not have an observable market value.[2] Moreover, governments typically do not stop paying pensions or disband the military to make room for debt service payments—and are not expected to do so.

Rules of thumb are not likely to provide very useful approximations of the level of debt that triggers default. For example, the debt-to-GDP ratio, at the time of the events of default, of countries that have defaulted since the 1980s has had a wide range of values, from around 0.4 to more than 1.5. Figure 12.1 displays defaulting countries' level of debt at the end of the year preceding the default, but a similar picture emerges if debt levels in the default year are used. Needless to say, many countries have had debt levels within the same range and have not fallen into default. This suggests that finding the default point of sovereign debt requires a more elaborate analysis.

Furthermore, creditor rights are less effectively enforceable for sovereign debt than private debts. If a private firm becomes insolvent, legal authorities have the means to enforce creditors' claims on the company's assets, even if those assets may be insufficient to cover the totality of the debt. By contrast, in the case of sovereign debt, despite the fact that the claim and the relevant legal authority are typically well-defined, the enforcement capacity is limited to assets in the same legal jurisdiction, which limits the efficacy of the legal recourse.[3]

---

[1] Note that in this report, default is not taken to mean a repudiation of debts or a unilateral suspension of payments, but instead an event when either scheduled debt service is not paid on the due date or the sovereign makes a restructuring offer which contains terms less favorable than the original debt. This is in line with the technical definition applied by credit-rating agencies, for example.

[2] Gapen et al. (2005) attempt to apply this approach to valuation of sovereign debt.

[3] Because of this, recent litigation against defaulting sovereigns, rather than focusing on direct enforcement of the claim, have hinged on the threat of seizing sovereign assets abroad, such as international reserves or, most notably, payments on external debt on which the sovereign is current, so as to force an out-of-court settlement. See Sturzenegger and Zettelmeyer (2006).

Figure 12.1
Debt Levels at Default

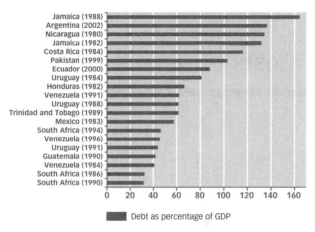

Sources: Cowan et al. (2006); Borensztein and Panizza (2006a); Jaimovich and Panizza (2006b).

This has led economists to posit that sovereign defaults are a reflection of a government's "willingness to pay" rather than its "ability to pay." The theoretical economic literature has traditionally seen the sovereign as calculating the cost implied by a debt default and comparing it to the burden of servicing its debt to decide whether to continue meeting its debt obligations. Defaults are then the result of a strategic decision to obtain a financial gain, rather than the result of a legitimate situation of bankruptcy. In fact, the existence of significant costs of default is considered the mechanism that makes sovereign debt possible in the first place. Otherwise, why would sovereigns repay their debts? If sovereigns did not suffer some type of cost in the event of default, no investor would be willing to lend any money to them (see, for example, Dooley, 2000).

Yet this type of strategic behavior is not in line with what has been observed in sovereign debt crises. Sovereign defaults have taken place after a country's economy has gone through a serious downturn and other measures have failed. The precise timing seems to respond to economic considerations which are far removed from the strategic factors hypothesized by the sovereign debt literature. In fact, there is evidence that, rather than engaging in strategic considerations and trying to avoid repayments, in moments of crisis, countries go to great lengths to adopt policies aimed at preventing default.

WHAT IS A DEFAULT?

Identifying sovereign default episodes and measuring their duration is not a straightforward exercise. There are multiple definitions of what constitutes a default episode and different ways of determining the precise time at which a default event occurs. Moreover, the nature of a default event is clearly distinct depending on whether the underlying debt is with private creditors or an official lender, and within the latter group, a bilateral or a multilateral creditor. This issue is of consequence from the point of view of empirical research on the effects of default, as the correct identification of the default episode and its precise timing may be critical for dealing with causality and simultaneity issues that arise in econometric work.

The most commonly used catalogs of default events are defaults with official bilateral creditors that are members of the Paris Club (available in the Paris Club database); defaults on private bank loans and bond instruments, as classified by rating agencies like Standard &

Poor's (S&P); and defaults on commercial and official debt under Detragiache and Spilimbergo's (2001) methodology, which is largely based on the database of the World Bank's *Global Development Finance*.

While there is substantial coincidence among the three databases, the correspondence is far from perfect. Some mismatches can be traced to differences in the methodology used to measure the length of a default episode. For instance, the methodology used by Detragiache and Spilimbergo is based on the existence of arrears and rescheduling negotiations and considers as defaults several episodes that are not classified as such by S&P.[4] Conversely, S&P classifies as defaults Argentina's 2001 and Uruguay's 2003 exchanges on the basis of their less than voluntary nature, although no arrears were incurred at the time. Not even the well-documented Paris Club defaults are free from methodological ambiguity. In the case of the Paris Club database, only two dates are provided: the date of signature of the restructuring agreement and the cutoff date that determines the debt under renegotiation (where debt incurred after that date is excluded). While the former date has often been used as the starting point of the default episode, a case can be made that it signals the completion of negotiations and therefore the end of the default and that the starting point is likely to be more appropriately proxied by the cutoff date that separates pre- and postdefault debt. This is the criterion used in this report.

Figure 12.2 shows the number of defaults per decade between 1970 and 2004 and before 1970. Episodes tend to lump together at several points, most notably during the debt crisis of the early 1980s, suggesting a dependence on common external factors. However, the incidence of default episodes is by no means restricted to particular periods. On the contrary, there has hardly been a year in the recent period without a default event.

The duration of default episodes—the amount of time that passes between the default event and when the debt is restructured in one way or another—has tended to vary over time, particularly in recent years, declining from an average of about eight years in the period 1970–1990 to roughly four years since 1991. This reflects in part the fact that, for a growing group of emerging market countries, bonds have substituted for banks as the primary borrowing form and that, contrary to what was once thought, bonded debt restructuring through unilateral exchange offers has proven to be much faster to complete than bilateral bank debt restructurings. Additionally, there seems to have been a relative decline in the incidence of default with official lenders, possibly reflecting the diminishing importance of bilateral lending (see Chapter 6).

COSTS OF DEFAULT

The theoretical literature on sovereign debt has traditionally focused on two channels through which costs of default may materialize: reputation (that is, higher borrowing costs that, in the limit, could result in absolute exclusion from financial markets in the future) and direct sanctions (such as legal attachments of property and international trade sanctions imposed by creditors' countries of residence).

---

[4] Examples include Nigeria, Zambia, and Sierra Leone in the 1970s, Egypt and El Salvador in the 1980s, and Sri Lanka, Thailand, Korea, and Tunisia in the 1990s.

Figure 12.2
Defaults over Time

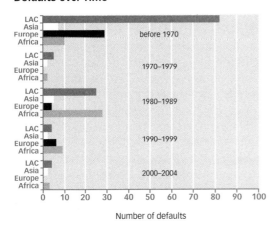

Number of defaults

Source: Authors' calculations based on Standard & Poor's.
Note: LAC = Latin America and the Caribbean.

The reputation argument assumes that sovereign debt is used primarily to insure against income shocks by increasing disposable income in bad states of the world, at the expense of a smaller income (resulting from repayment) in good states. In their seminal paper, Eaton and Gersovitz (1981) showed that such a debt contract can be sustained solely on the basis of a country's credit record (reputation), inasmuch as the loss involved in being deprived of the insurance benefits provided by sovereign debt exceeds the maximum payment under the contract.[5] In a well-known critique, Bulow and Rogoff (1989) showed that a country can always use a fraction of the payment due under the original (defaulted) debt contract to pay in advance for an insurance policy that offers the same benefits, concluding that reputational concerns alone are not sufficient to ensure that sovereign debt can be sustained and that direct sanctions are needed to counteract default risk.[6] However, this critique hinges on three nontrivial assumptions: (1) that the new lender (the insurer) can commit to paying the sovereign as stipulated by the insurance policy (there is no lender commitment problem); (2) that the sovereign can find a new lender while in default (lenders do not collude); and (3) that the sovereign does not spend its debt payment money in the current period (investing in insurance is time consistent for the government). These assumptions have been recently questioned by Kletzer and Wright (2000), Wright (2002), and Amador (2002). Thus, the theoretical debate appears to have gone full circle back to the insurance view.

One problem with the insurance view is that it implies that, in the absence of financial imperfections, net transfers should be negatively correlated with deviation from expected long-run income. Hence, defaults should occur only in good times, when a debtor that has the funds to repay chooses to keep the payment entirely for itself. In other words, default should be, almost by definition, *strategic*: a deliberate opportunistic decision to repudiate previous obligations.[7] However, both the assumption and the implication appear to be starkly at odds with reality. Private cross-border debt flows are not countercyclical and, as a result, defaults tend to occur in the context of economic contractions, casting doubt on the rel-

---

[5] In an interesting spin-off, Grossman and Van Huyck (1988) apply the same argument to motivate the existence of nominally denominated sovereign debt in a context in which the sovereign can inflate away the debt burden.

[6] Sachs, Bulow, and Rogoff (1988), Kletzer (1988), and Lindert (1989) also support the sanctions view.

[7] In this context, it is easy to see the distinction between willingness and ability to pay, since defaults are, by assumption, *positively* correlated with the former. The more frequent case of a default during a recession, however, calls for a more nuanced definition of those terms.

evance of the insurance benefits of international debt flows—and the reputational costs of losing access to those benefits (Levy Yeyati, 2006b).

While there is no evidence of the imposition of direct trade or economic sanctions following the latest sovereign default episodes, the literature has highlighted alternative channels through which a country may face immediate real economic cost as a result of default. One such channel is the presence of externalities on sovereign contracts that cannot be readily insured (Cole and Kehoe, 1996) or in the domestic private sector in the form of reduced access to financing (Sandleris, 2006).

More recently, recognizing that holders of government debt are often primarily resident investors, more attention has been paid to a third channel, namely, the immediate consequences of default for the domestic economy (in particular, the impact of default on the solvency of the banking sector and its income effect on domestic demand). This channel has been particularly relevant in recent defaults in emerging economies in which banks held significant amounts of government liabilities and the anticipation of default may have fueled, at least in part, a run on bank deposits.[8]

A natural corollary of this last channel is that a default may involve sizable political cost for the government. A declining economy and a banking system in crisis typically combine in this case with the effect of the default on domestic debt holders to undermine the image of incumbent policymakers, a channel that has been noted in the context of currency devaluations but has been overlooked in the case of debt defaults.

In light of this extensive theoretical literature on sovereign debt, there is surprisingly little empirical work to substantiate these alternative views of the reasons why a sovereign is expected to repay its obligations. Only recently a number of papers have attempted to assess the different channels suggested by the analytical models. These papers do not find much support for the traditional "willingness to repay" explanations of default. Sovereign defaults occur after a country's economy has gone through a serious downturn and other measures have failed, and the precise timing responds to both economic and political considerations that are far removed from the strategic factors highlighted above.

Access to International Capital Markets

Studies that provide empirical evidence in support of the "market exclusion" view implicitly assume that access to international markets is valuable for a country. Starting from this premise, Tomz (2004) uses the case study method to argue that Argentina repaid its debt with the United Kingdom in 1930 in order to strengthen its reputation as a good debtor, rather than to avoid a trade embargo from the United Kingdom, as had been previously interpreted by, for example, Díaz-Alejandro (1983). In turn, English (1996) studies the evidence on U.S. states that defaulted between 1841 and 1843. While states that were in default were mostly excluded from the capital market, they were able to regain access after renegotiating debt payments, even when the latter involved partial write-offs of debt.

This is in line with the conventional view that a *temporary* default does not lead to *permanent* exclusion from the international capital market: a country is likely to lose access to

---

[8] Chapter 8 discusses the importance of institutional investors' holding of government bonds.

this market while in default, but once the restructuring process is behind it and the country becomes current on its debt once again, the market does not discriminate, in terms of access, between defaulters and nondefaulters; nor does an absence of default in a country's record guarantee it access to the market. Examples that lend support to this account can be found in the period that goes from the 1930s to the 1960s, in which all Latin American countries were largely excluded from the world capital market regardless of whether they had defaulted in the 1930s, and in the lending boom of the 1990s, which did not exclude countries that had defaulted in the 1980s. More recently, countries that defaulted in the late 1990s regained access to the international capital market almost immediately after their debt renegotiations were concluded.[9]

However, access cannot be analyzed solely as a binary variable according to whether a country is or is not excluded from borrowing. It may well be the case that countries regain access to markets after default, but at a higher financial cost or to a lesser degree.

In this regard, the studies that estimate the impact of past defaults on current sovereign spreads or credit ratings (which tend to correlate closely with spreads) find weak or short-lived effects. While defaults after 1970 are associated with a two-notch drop in a country's credit rating (Cantor and Packer, 1996), the effect exhibits low persistence: only defaults in the previous five years are found to display any significant correlation with current ratings (Borensztein and Panizza, 2006a). Along the same lines, a number of studies have looked at the direct impact of default on borrowing costs and found generally small or extremely short-lived effects.[10]

By contrast, there appears to be some evidence that in recent years the volume of capital flows to a country has been correlated with its reputation as a debtor. Figure 12.3 illustrates this pattern. In the left panel, the figure compares net private capital flows (as a share of GDP) to two groups of sovereign borrowers over the 2000–2004 period: those that had been in default at some point since 1970, and those that had a completely clean record over the same period. The figure shows substantially higher net flows to the nondefaulting sovereigns. The same can be said about total private cross-border debt flows to these countries, comprising both sovereign and private borrowers. In the right panel of the figure, the same data are displayed after the effect of several variables, including the state of the business cycle and country- and time-specific factors, have been controlled for using econometric methods (see Levy Yeyati, 2006b).

This evidence, however, should be taken with caution, since the reduced inflows may well be reflecting a country's policy decision to cut indebtedness that has proved excessive in the past, rather than a lessening of the country's ability to borrow in international finan-

---

[9] Gelos, Sahay, and Sandleris (2004) find that countries that defaulted in the 1980s were able to regain access to credit in about four years.

[10] Lindert and Morton (1989) and Chowdhry (1991) find that defaults in the nineteenth century and the 1930s did not imply higher borrowing cost in the 1970s, Ozler (1993) reports a small premium on sovereign bank loans extended over the 1968–1981 period for countries that defaulted in the 1930s, and Flandreau (2004) finds that defaults in the 1880–1914 period were associated with a 90 basis point increase in spreads in the year following the end of the default episode. For the current emerging bond markets period, Ades et al. (2000) show that default history had no significant effect on sovereign spreads in the late 1990s except for a small "Brady bond premium," while Dell'Ariccia, Schnabel, and Zettelmeyer (2002) report a small "Brady country premium" that widened only somewhat at the time of the Russian default of 1998.

Figure 12.3
Defaults and Debt Flows, Average, 2000–2004
(*percentage of current GDP*)

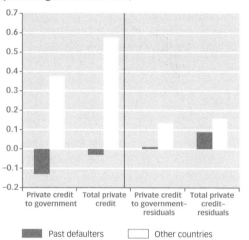

Past defaulters   Other countries

Source: Levy Yeyati (2006b).

cial markets. Indeed, it has been shown in historical studies—such as English (1996) on U.S. states—that defaulting states that regained access to international markets have nonetheless been net payers in the postdefault years.

Trade Sanctions and Trade Credit

While the idea that defaults may lead to trade retaliation has been around for a long time in the economic literature (see, for instance, Díaz-Alejandro, 1983), there have been a limited number of empirical studies on the link between default and international trade. An influential recent study (Rose, 2005) focuses on Paris Club debt renegotiations. Using "gravity" models of bilateral trade (models that estimate natural levels of trade based on variables such as geographic proximity and historical affinity), the study finds that defaults on bilateral official loans appear to be associated with a persistent decline in bilateral trade that lasts for 15 years.[11] There is also some evidence that sovereign defaults with the private sector involve significantly more economic costs for export-oriented industries than for other manufacturing sectors, although in this case the effects have been found not to be persistent once the default is resolved (Borensztein and Panizza, 2006b).

This evidence does not shed light on the specific channels through which defaults may affect trade or, more specifically, exports. The sovereign debt literature has often assumed that reduction in trade following a default comes from restrictive measures imposed by the country of residence of the defaulted investors. However, there is not much evidence of countries' imposing quotas or embargoes on—let alone initiating direct military actions against—defaulting countries in modern times. Moreover, bondholders do not appear to be an effective political lobby today, as perhaps was the case in the historical period of the nineteenth-century bond market.

A more realistic candidate for explaining the effect of default on a country's trade is the deterioration in the credit quality of exporting firms in the defaulting country after the default—resulting from confiscation or convertibility risk—which could restrict access to trade credit. There is anecdotal evidence that international trade credit tends to be affected when markets become concerned with the creditworthiness of a government. In 2002, Brazil arranged financing from the IDB and the World Bank to offset the cutting off of international

---

[11] The result is somewhat weakened, but not eliminated, by the inclusion of time effects (Martínez and Sandleris, 2004).

credit lines to Brazilian exporters in the context of country risk concerns (Financial Times, 2002). This support from the international community, together with intervention by Brazil's central bank and banking system, was successful in protecting the country's export sector from a credit crunch. At the aggregate level, OECD data on trade credit flows from private and official sources show that defaults have a negative effect on trade credit, but this decline seems to be small in magnitude (Borensztein and Panizza, 2006a; Love and Zaidi, 2004; World Bank, 2004b).[12]

Financial Sector

Possibly the most important collateral effects of government debt crises have been those that have occurred in the domestic financial sector. When banks are heavily exposed to government debt (as is often the case in Latin America; see Chapter 8), government defaults may cause a banking crisis or at least a period of weakening in banking credit to the private sector. This may happen for several reasons. First of all, default episodes may cause a collapse in confidence in the domestic financial system and may lead to bank runs, resulting in banking crises or at least a credit crunch. Second, even in the absence of a bank run, default episodes will have a negative effect on banks' balance sheets, especially if the banks' holdings of the defaulted paper are large, and lead banks to adopt more conservative lending strategies. Finally, default episodes are often accompanied by a weakening of creditor rights or at least more uncertainty about them, which may also have a negative effect on bank lending. This result will be a magnification of the economic recession associated with the default. A detailed analysis of four recent sovereign defaults—those of Ecuador (1999), Pakistan (1999), Russia (1998), and Ukraine (1998)—has highlighted this association between debt crisis and banking distress (IMF, 2002c).

There is a fairly close association between sovereign defaults and domestic banking crises. Based on data between 1975 and 2000, it has been estimated that the probability that a banking crisis will occur within one to two years of a default is as high as 14 percent. By contrast, banking crises do not precede defaults very often, despite the fact that defaults tend to be anticipated by the public and deposit runs are likely in such an event (Borensztein and Panizza, 2006a).[13]

Economic Growth

Whatever the specific channel through which a sovereign default affects the domestic economy, if defaults exert a significant influence on economic growth, this must be observed in a direct link between default events and GDP growth. Indeed, there is a strong association between defaults and recessions when annual GDP data are considered (Sturzenegger, 2004; Borensztein and Panizza, 2006a).

---

[12] Note that other forms of international lending are also cut off at times of turbulence, but export activities are more dependent on external finance, and thus they are hurt disproportionately more by a credit crunch.

[13] However, in most cases, debt and banking crises tend to occur simultaneously, and the lead pattern may simply reflect the fact that defaults are often delayed until both crises are well underway. See Beim and Calomiris (2000a, 2000b, 2000c), Levy Yeyati, Martínez Pería, and Schmukler (2004), and Sturzenegger and Zettelmeyer (2006).

Figure 12.4
Default and Output

a. Argentina

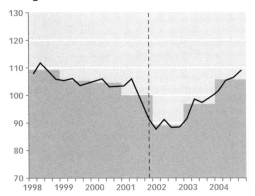

b. Ecuador

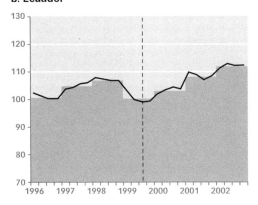

c. Uruguay

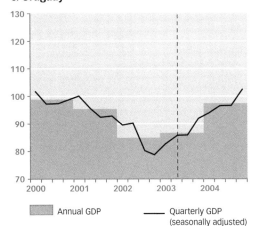

▨ Annual GDP   ▬ Quarterly GDP (seasonally adjusted)

Source: Levy Yeyati and Panizza (2006).

Looking at annual data, however, may not bring out the full picture of the relationship between debt crises and growth (Levy Yeyati and Panizza, 2006). Consider, for instance, two recent default episodes: those in Ecuador (1999) and Argentina (2001). Judging from annual data, Ecuador's GDP contracted by 6 percent in 1999 (the default year), and Argentina's output declined by 12 percent in 2002 (the official date of the Argentine default was December 2001). The quarterly evolution of GDP in these two countries suggests that the collapse in output occurred just before the default event. This is illustrated in Figure 12.4, which also portrays the case of Uruguay in 2003. Annual data may mask the timing of events, because the start of a recession may spill over from one year into the following year in the data, as annual GDP is an average of what happened during the year. Thus, for example, the sharp GDP contraction in Argentina in late 2001 is largely registered as an output decline in 2002, despite the fact that the economy started to recover in that year. Even more striking is the case of Uruguay, in which a recovery was already incipient when the government launched its debt exchange.

Figure 12.5 takes a somewhat longer view of the evolution of GDP around default episodes. The figure shows, for a sample of emerging economies that have experienced default, quarterly GDP levels in a six-year window centered on the default period.[14] Time 0 in the figure indicates the year of the default episode, time −4 indicates one year (four quarters) before the event, and time 4 indicates one year after the event. As the figure

---

[14] GDP levels are seasonally adjusted (excluding the default period) and normalized by the mean over the window.

Figure 12.5
Output around Default

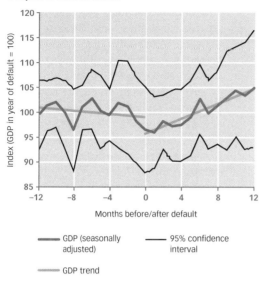

Months before/after default

GDP (seasonally adjusted) — 95% confidence interval

GDP trend

Source: Levy Yeyati and Panizza (2006).

shows, GDP drops in the period preceding default and, while it still falls slightly in the quarter after the event, it reverses its trend in the following quarter. Recovery is quick, and long-term growth does not appear to suffer in the period after default.[15] Naturally, as in the case of the drop in output at the time of default, the growth improvement may be related to recovery from deep currency and financial crises. However, this does not appear to be the case here, as the same pattern emerges when the immediate postdefault recovery period is excluded.[16]

These findings do not imply that policies that lead to default have no cost; on the contrary, the large GDP decline that typically precedes a default may reflect in part the anticipation of the default decision, and the postdefault recovery observed in the data may not be independent of the cost paid in the preceding periods.[17] Moreover, to some degree, the fact that output contractions precede an event of default may be a consequence of the fact that the default is already widely anticipated, and residents may start to hoard financial assets abroad and postpone investment projects in view of the uncertain prospects. Likewise, the official timing of the default may in some cases be somewhat later than the time when the debt crisis that generates the default actually started. Bond payments, for example, typically have a grace period before the bonds are technically considered in default.

But the evidence on defaults, recessions, and recoveries flies in the face of stories of "strategic" sovereign default. A sovereign choosing to default on the assumption that it could obtain a financial gain by doing so, even if it faced exclusion from financial markets, would always default in a situation of economic strength, namely, when it did not need to resort to borrowing in the near future. Recessions are periods when incomes are low and financing needs are high, and far from being the result of punishments or sanctions imposed by creditors as retaliation for the default, as posited by the traditional theoretical models of sovereign debt, they often precede (and may cause) the default decision. Defaults coming after, or in the midst of, a period of economic weakness are an indication of a situation of financial insolvency on the part of the sovereign, not a sign of a calculated, strategic action.

---

[15] Long-run output is obtained using the Hodrick-Prescott filter. A similar result is obtained using the log-linear trend instead.

[16] Alternatively, faster growth may reflect some learning from the crisis: an improvement in policies and the instauration of a new and more credible economic and political team that may signal a "new start."

[17] In addition, there is some preliminary evidence that countries that do manage to resist default tend to do better than countries that give up and actually default (Borensztein and Panizza, 2006a).

Politics

Postponing a default that has been widely anticipated by the market may be costly for at least three reasons: (1) it requires adjustment policies that may be perceived to be excessively costly (at least in the short run) and hence not fully credible; (2) default risk, as long as it is not realized, translates into high interest rates and overall business uncertainty that hamper investment and deepen banking fragility through greater nonperformance ratios; and (3) the liquidity crunch typically associated with debt crises leads to fire sales of assets and to the validation of unreasonably high rollover costs, compromising the solvency of both public and private debtors.

And yet, politicians and technocrats in ministries of finance and central banks seem to go to great lengths to avoid default. In the case of Argentina in 2001, for instance, it has been reported that, prior to the default, even Wall Street bankers tried to persuade Argentine policymakers to face reality and initiate a debt-restructuring operation (Blustein, 2005).

Why the reluctance? A possible hypothesis is that defaults can be politically costly for the careers of finance ministers and top executive politicians. In fact, the evidence on the political impact of recent events of default reveals that in 18 out of the 19 cases studied, the ruling coalitions lost votes after the default. In addition, ruling governments in defaulting countries faced, on average, a 16 percent decline in electoral support and, in 50 percent of the cases, a change in the chief executive in the year of the default or the following year—more than twice the probability in normal economic times (Borensztein and Panizza, 2006a).[18]

This political cost may relate to the fact that electors may interpret a default as an explicit sign that the policies in place prior to the default were not working. However, this would explain reluctance to default only among politicians and technocrats who have been in charge for a long period of time and hence can be blamed for past policies. But new politicians and technocrats who are appointed with the explicit or implicit objective of saving a country from default may also try to delay default, because default would be a clear signal that they had not been able to accomplish their mission.[19] These politicians may have an incentive for "gambling for resurrection," namely, taking extreme measures that have a low chance of success but, if they do succeed, will bring clear political gains to the ruling administration. A more benign interpretation is that politicians know that the market will severely punish a strategic default, and in delaying default, they go to great lengths to make sure that everybody agrees that a default is indeed inevitable and hence not strategic. According to this interpretation, politicians who delay default are actually maximizing social welfare and not just their own.

---

[18] These arguments on the political cost of default relate to the familiar literature on the political cost of sharp devaluations (Cooper, 1971; Frankel, 2005).

[19] Accepting default would instead be easier for politicians and technocrats who are appointed after almost everybody agrees that default is unavoidable.

ABILITY TO PAY OR WILLINGNESS TO PAY?

There is a disconnect between the theoretical literature on sovereign debt and the empirical evidence on sovereign defaults and renegotiations. The theoretical literature presents a paradigm of sovereign debt as a contract in which the costs of default only slightly exceed the benefits of pocketing the money otherwise needed for repayment. Hence, according to this literature, default events occur in good times, when countries enjoy a strong financial position and do not anticipate the need of market financing in the near future. These are strategic defaults rather than bankruptcies such as those that occur in the business world. There is little evidence, however, of strategic sovereign defaults ever occurring, and time after time default events occur in situations in which a country has reached a condition that can be described as sovereign bankruptcy.[20]

A central finding of this chapter is that while defaults may have costs in terms of higher spreads, lower international trade, and more limited access to finance, these costs tend to be short lived. More interestingly, the chapter provides preliminary evidence that economic crises take place before defaults and that recoveries start soon after the event. This suggests that sovereigns may sometimes delay debt-restructuring decisions too long. Clearly, more work needs to be done in this area, but if further analysis confirms this conjecture, the next challenge will be to find out why this is the case and what the policy implications of this finding are.

The chapter provides two conjectures as to why a political administration may postpone the moment of reckoning. The first focuses on self-interested politicians who are worried about the effect on their careers, as there is clear evidence of accelerated political turnover following a debt default. The second interpretation assumes that, while strategic defaults would be very costly in terms of reputation—and that is why they are never observed in practice—"unavoidable" defaults carry limited reputation loss in the markets (Grossman and Van Huyck, 1988). Hence, policymakers may postpone default actions to ensure that there is broad consensus, prior to the actual occurrence of default, that the decision is unavoidable and not strategic. The idea is that politicians choose the lesser of the two evils and are willing to pay the additional cost brought about by the delayed default rather than subject the country to punishment by the market. This would be consistent with widely anticipated defaults that happen in situations when the economy is very weak.

These two interpretations have widely different policy implications. If the problem is self-interested politicians who do not maximize social welfare, then reforms should focus on the policymaking process (see IDB, 2005b). If the problem is that politicians delay default in order to guarantee that markets will perceive the default, when it does occur, as necessary, then part of the solution may be a better, faster understanding of the economic situation of countries that are headed for default, an area in which the international financial institutions could make a valuable contribution.

---

[20] Such a situation is often driven by a combination of negative external shocks and misguided policies.

The Risks of Sovereign Finance

CHAPTER 13

SOVEREIGN BORROWING CAN GENERATE RISKS for essentially two reasons. The first relates to the link between sovereign debt and the probability of financial and debt crises. The second relates to the constraints that sovereign debt places on the ordinary conduct of monetary and fiscal policies.[1] Chapter 11 made the point that, among the determinants of country risk, the structure of debt may be more important than the level of debt. The same is true for the risks of sovereign finance, for which the *quality* of debt matters more than the *quantity* of debt. In this context, debt quality refers to the degree of risk associated with any given level of debt. Debt quality depends critically on two dimensions: denomination and maturity. The premise here is that the currency and maturity *composition* of the debt stock largely determines the debt burden relative to the country's repayment capacity at each point in time. In particular, currency and maturity composition determine the probability of a debt default and, as a result, the sovereign's borrowing costs and their sensitivity to both domestic and external factors—as well as to self-fulfilling runs.

Hence, any analysis that aims at offering diagnostic and policy advice on how to limit the risk of sovereign finance should focus on policies with the objective of improving debt structure, so that sovereign borrowing becomes an instrument of growth rather than an impediment to it. Devising such policies (the subject of the next chapter) requires a thorough understanding of the sources of risk.

Before looking into its underlying sources, it is necessary to define risk in an operational way that makes it possible to assess quantitatively the policy responses to particular sources of risk. Unfortunately, this is easier said than done. In the context of efficient financial markets, the most natural measure of sovereign risk (understood as the probability that the issuer does not comply with the terms of the debt contract) is provided by the yield paid by sovereign debt instruments in a continuously trading secondary market. This measure, however, has conceptual and practical drawbacks. The conceptual problem is that it refers to a narrow definition of risk that overlaps only partially with the risk of sovereign finance. More precisely, it measures the risk from the bondholder's perspective, which is narrower than the risk for the sovereign issuer as defined above. The practical problem is data availability: secondary market prices are limited to the subsample of developing countries that

---

[1] These constraints include limited ability to have a countercyclical monetary policy and to have a truly floating exchange rate (fear of floating), inflation bias, and low credibility. Constraints on fiscal policy may result in procyclical and excessively restrictive policies.

have issued a large stock of liquid global bonds (the emerging economies).[2] An alternative measure of the same concept is provided by the sovereign ratings assigned by credit agencies. While still subject to the first criticism, ratings have the advantage of being available for a larger set of countries. The caveat here is that ratings are highly influenced by outcomes and therefore may overstate risk in the upswing and understate it when the situation deteriorates (see Chapter 5).

Conceptually, the most accurate way of assessing the risk to the sovereign entails an evaluation of the influence of debt size and composition on economic performance (output growth and volatility). This chapter presents some evidence in this direction, but the reader should keep in mind that the causal relationship between debt and economic outcomes is bound to run in both directions, and a quantitative identification of these mutual influences is extremely difficult.

CURRENCY AND MATURITY RISK

There is a large literature showing that *currency denomination* can substantially increase the risk of sovereign finance. This literature has shown that, in the presence of foreign currency debt, net debtor countries have an aggregate currency mismatch, and a depreciation in the real exchange rate will increase the stock of net liabilities in terms of the national product, whereas a real appreciation will reduce it, creating a potentially perilous exposure to currency fluctuations.

Debtor countries can adopt policies aimed at eliminating the mismatch or preventing it from arising in the first place, but often at considerable expense. For example, they can try to change the denomination of their debt from foreign to domestic currency; however, in the short run, such a policy may sometimes turn out to be exceedingly expensive or unfeasible. Alternatively, countries can eliminate the mismatch by deciding to borrow only to the extent allowed by the supply provided by domestic currency markets, which would in most cases entail a significant reduction in net borrowing. Such self-restraint does not eliminate the problem, however, as countries still need to manage their outstanding stock of debt. Furthermore, countries that decide to become financially autarchic will not be able to benefit from the opportunities for risk diversification and access to resources offered by foreign borrowing. As an intermediate strategy, countries may decide to eliminate the mismatch implicit in short-run flows by accumulating foreign reserves. In this way, they ensure that they will not face a foreign currency liquidity shortage in the near future, at the cost of financing low-return reserves with high-cost sovereign debt.

The currency denomination problem is particularly important in Latin America and the Caribbean, a region characterized by narrow domestic markets and a dependence on external funds. Because the economies of the region are also relatively closed in terms of international trade, balance sheet effects arising from adjustments of the real exchange rate become magnified (Calvo, Izquierdo, and Talvi, 2005). There is evidence that a large share of

---

[2] In principle, one could derive comparable information from the lending rates charged by private international banks on public or publicly guaranteed loans. However—even ignoring the fact that bank rates tend, because of loan evergreening, to underreact to changes in perceived risk—systematic data on interest rates are very difficult to compile.

foreign-currency-denominated external debt is associated with lower credit ratings, higher volatility of both GDP growth and capital flows, and limited ability to conduct an independent monetary policy (Eichengreen, Hausmann, and Panizza, 2005b). Additionally, foreign currency external debt increases the sensitivity of spreads to real exchange rate fluctuations (Berganza and García-Herrero, 2004) and leads to contractionary devaluations (Bebczuk, Galindo, and Panizza, 2006).

Furthermore, although there is incomplete cross-country data on the structure of domestic public debt, there seems to be a close correlation between the dollarization of government debt and bank loans (Cowan et al., 2006), and dollarization of the domestic bank sector also presents macroeconomic risks. Dollarization of bank loans increases a country's propensity to suffer disruptive sudden stop episodes (Calvo, Izquierdo, and Mejía, 2004) and leads to high relative price volatility and thus macroeconomic instability (Calvo, Izquierdo, and Loo-Kung, 2005). Along similar lines, the dollarization of bank deposits increases financial fragility and leads to higher output volatility and lower economic growth (Levy Yeyati, 2006a).

Another major factor that affects the risk of sovereign borrowing is the *maturity structure* of debt. Short-term debt, by bunching debt payments together (specifically, by increasing the size of the obligations maturing at each point in time) deepens rollover risk and paves the way to possible debt crisis. This is especially true when debt is denominated in foreign currency, but even if all debt is denominated in domestic currency and the government is running a primary budget surplus, the bunching of payments induced by short-term debt creates a financing gap that opens the door to self-fulfilling liquidity runs (Obstfeld, 1994).

Most of the literature on debt crises has focused on the combination of these two risks and shows that short-term external (hence, mostly foreign-currency-denominated) debt is a strong predictor of debt crises. In particular, studies have found that the higher the ratio of a country's short-term dollar debt to international reserves, the higher the probability of a crisis in that country (Manasse, Roubini, and Schimmelpfennig, 2003). This provided a rationale for what became known as the Guidotti-Greenspan rule of reserve adequacy, which states that countries should always hold enough reserves to cover at least their external liabilities falling due within one year.[3]

Not surprisingly, there is much less evidence of a link between debt crises and short-term domestic debt denominated in domestic currency. This is because, in the event that the sovereign's capacity to pay is severely affected, domestic currency debt offers an alternative to outright default: the government can keep servicing debt by "printing money" at a seemingly negligible immediate cost. The result, of course, is inflation and also higher interest rates in anticipation of the expected inflation over the life of the bond. If inflation wins the race against nominal interest rates—which is always possible but may require accelerating inflation until levels of hyperinflation are reached—the real value of the debt is effectively diluted, and the government regains solvency. In fact, in most cases, governments faced by

---

[3] While there are no formal studies on the dangers of domestically issued short-term foreign currency debt, the Mexican Tequila crisis of December 1994 (sparked by problems rolling over the short-term dollar-indexed Tesobonos) should be sufficient to convince most readers that the dangers implied by this fragile currency-maturity combination are not exclusive to international placements.

a large amount of domestic currency debt have preferred to recur to inflation (sometimes to hyperinflation) rather than defaulting (the Russian default on ruble-denominated GKOs is a notable exception).[4]

Does this mean that short-term domestic debt denominated in domestic currency is less risky than foreign currency debt? Not necessarily. First of all, high inflation is costly economically and socially. It creates uncertainty and reduces growth, and stabilizing from high inflation has been a long and costly process in Latin America. Moreover, inflation hits especially hard the poorest segments of the population, who have more limited ways of protecting their savings from sudden increases in prices and for whom basic necessities can become suddenly unaffordable with a price increase. Second, there have been cases in which the presence of a substantial amount of short-term domestic currency debt was one of the fundamental causes of a financial crisis even though, by the time the crisis came, most of this debt had been swapped into foreign currency.

The 1994 Mexican crisis provides an example of this situation. At the beginning of 1994, Mexico had basically no domestic debt in foreign currency, but it had about 60 percent of its domestic debt denominated in short-term peso notes (called CETES, for Certificados de la Tesoreria de la Federación). During the year, pre-electoral political turmoil, amplified by the assassination of presidential candidate Luis Donaldo Colosio and an insurgency in the state of Chiapas, led to expectations of a currency devaluation and a surge in the interest rate on CETES (which, given their short maturity, needed to be rolled over during the year). In fact, in the month of the Colosio assassination, the rate on CETES jumped from 10 to 16 percent. Deeming a devaluation unlikely to become necessary, Mexican authorities decided to substitute dollar-denominated Tesobonos for some of its CETES holdings. The result was a significant leveraging of risks: if the exchange regime survived the attack on the Mexican currency, the cost of defending the country's exchange rate peg would have been much lower, but if a currency devaluation became unavoidable (as happened), the government's losses would be much higher. With the benefits of hindsight, the swap of CETES for Tesobonos was probably a bad decision, but the alternatives (either pay a high real interest rate or accommodate the inflationary expectations by abandoning the peg) were extremely costly from both a political and an economic perspective. These alternatives were determined to no small degree by the presence of short-term domestic debt denominated in domestic currency and by the fact that the Mexican authorities knew well that the arithmetic of diluting short-term debt with inflation can be unforgiving, as the path to high inflation can be gradual, unplanned, and hard to reverse.[5]

---

[4] The default came after the GKO had reached an interest rate of 100 percent.

[5] An example may be helpful in illustrating the difficulty of diluting short-term debt. Assume that a country has an excessive debt that needs to be reduced by, say, 30 percent. Assume as well that investors have adaptive expectations and that debt can be diluted only if inflation in the current period is higher than inflation in the previous period. Consider now a country where all public debt has a remaining maturity of three years. If it starts with zero inflation, such a country can simply generate 10 percent inflation (actually it needs a little bit less than that) and dilute the debt over a three-year period. Inflation will permanently move from 0 to 10 percent, and the new debt issued after three years (i.e., when the old debt matures) will have a higher nominal interest rate but the same real interest rate as the old debt. Consider now a country with the same problem, but where all public debt has a remaining maturity of one month. If the country wants to dilute the debt before rollover time, it will need to generate *monthly* inflation of 30 percent; this corresponds to annual inflation of 2,300 percent! Of course, the country could decide to move

IS THERE A CURRENCY-MATURITY TRADE-OFF?

Inflation and currency depreciation risks have been pervasive elements in the structure of government debt in Latin America. Seeking protection against those risks, investors have gravitated towards foreign-currency-denominated debt. Two notable exceptions to the prevailing dollarization cases are Chile, where financial instruments are widely indexed to inflation, and Brazil, where a large fraction of domestic currency debt is indexed to the overnight interest rate. These cases suggest, at an anecdotal level at least, that there is a trade-off between currency and maturity, namely, that countries can avoid foreign currency debt, but only by going heavily to the short end of the maturity spectrum.

At a more systematic level, the evidence on a trade-off between maturity and denomination is more mixed. Firm-level data on liabilities show that in highly dollarized countries (Uruguay, Argentina, Costa Rica, and Peru) there is a strong positive relationship between the degree of dollarization and maturity of debt, suggesting that firms that issue dollar debt are able to extend the maturity of their obligations. Interestingly, this pattern is not present in economies characterized by low levels of dollarization (such as Brazil and Chile), probably because these countries can extend maturity by using other forms of indexation (to prices or interest rates rather than foreign currency). But the sign of the relationship between dollarization and long-termism reverses when a cross-section of countries is examined. Countries that have on average higher degrees of firm liability dollarization have on average a lower share of long-term liabilities in total debt (Kamil, 2004).[6] One possible interpretation of the above results is that country-specific factors like policies and the credibility of policymakers affect in the same direction both dollarization and short-termism, leading to the positive cross-country relationship between these two variables. There is some debate, however, on the extent to which economic policies affect the structure of countries' debt. Some studies have failed to find a strong correlation between policies and the structure of external debt (see Eichengreen, Hausmann, and Panizza, 2005a). However, Hausmann and Panizza (2003), Jeanne and Guscina (2006), and Mehl and Reynaud (2005) find that policies may matter for the structure of domestic debt.

Cross-country government debt data show less evidence of a trade-off between currency and maturity. Although data for 19 emerging market countries suggest that a movement towards lower levels of dollarization is associated with an increase in the share of short-term debt, the effect is completely driven by the behavior of Russia (Figure 13.1).[7] If Russia is excluded from the sample, there is little evidence of a correlation between changes in dollarization and changes in maturity structure. Furthermore, there seems to be no short-

---

gradually and deflate the debt a little bit at a time. But also in this case, the adaptive nature of expectations will lead to ever-increasing inflation. (For instance, the country could decide to dilute the debt by 1 percent a month. In this case, it will start with 1 percent monthly inflation and then increase it gradually, so that it will take 30 months to dilute the debt by 30 percent. By the 30th month, monthly inflation will be 30 percent, and annual inflation about 2,300 percent.) Clearly these are extreme examples that resort to unrealistic assumptions, but they should make it clear that, in the presence of short-term debt, pursuing the option of diluting the debt may mean hyperinflation.

[6] Again, in the currency mismatch literature there is no clear distinction between dollarization of the financial sector and dollarization of public debt. But as argued before, these two types of dollarization tend to be correlated, at least in Latin America.

[7] The figure reports the results of a fixed effects regression that measures the effect of changes in maturities on changes in dollarization.

Figure 13.1
The Currency-Maturity Trade-Off

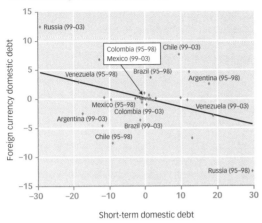

Source: Authors' estimations based on data from Jeanne and Guscina (2006).
Note: Graph plots the results of a regression that includes country fixed effects.

ening of debt maturities associated with recent dedollarization in Latin America and the Caribbean (Cowan et al., 2006).

From a more conceptual point of view, it can be argued that the currency-maturity trade-off should be analyzed in terms of cost. Namely, governments can always issue long-term, domestic currency debt that pays the currency premium that the market demands. Of course, this premium may be too high, and hence the sovereign will decide not to pursue this option. But what does "too high" mean? If the difference between the interest rate paid on long-term domestic currency debt and that paid on foreign currency debt correctly reflects inflation or devaluation expectations (that is, if uncovered interest parity holds), then the costs of all instruments will be equal ex ante. Why, then, would a sovereign choose to borrow in foreign currency or in short-term domestic instruments?

One reason has to do with the fact that the sovereign cares about the level of inflation, which carries heavy economic and political costs. If the structure of debt affects expected inflation, the government can use dollar debt or short-term debt to provide a signal that it is committed to maintaining low inflation. In this way, it will end up paying the same interest rate as with long-term debt denominated in the domestic currency, but the economy will have a lower inflation rate.

Another reason has to do with the fact that long-term domestic currency debt may indeed be more costly in term of the ex post real cost. This can happen if the maturity or currency premium overstates inflation or devaluation expectations, possibly as a result of information asymmetry between the government and investors. Suppose, for instance, that there are two types of governments: a good one (which desires to avoid inflation and currency depreciation) and a bad one (which has a tendency to use inflation and currency depreciation). Also suppose that the current government is of the good type, but investors do not know this for sure and hence assign a 50 percent probability that the government will inflate and/or devalue the currency. As a consequence, investors will ask a currency/maturity premium that the good-type government knows to be excessive, and hence the government will decide to issue either short-term or foreign currency debt.[8]

A similar situation arises from the absence of a mechanism to commit a government to maintaining low inflation. If the government cannot make a credible commitment to this

---

[8] If the government were of the bad type, investors could correctly infer the type and hence ask to be fully compensated for expected inflation. Arida, Bacha, and Lara-Resende (2005) argue that the high real interest rates that characterize the Brazilian market are a consequence of the decision to avoid dollar-denominated contracts.

objective in the eyes of investors, they will demand a premium on local currency debt, and then the best option for the government will be to reduce its borrowing costs by resorting to inflation (Calvo, 1988). This will lead to a situation characterized by two equilibria: in the good equilibrium, credible governments will be able to borrow cheaply long term in local currency and will fulfill lenders' expectations by maintaining low inflation; in the bad equilibrium, however, noncredible governments will be required to pay a premium and will end up fulfilling lenders' high inflation expectations. Faced with such a situation, a government characterized by low credibility can do better by borrowing either short term or in an indexed unit, be it inflation indexed or in foreign currency, because it will end up paying the same interest rate but without needing to resort to inflation. In other words, a risky form of debt (such as foreign currency or short-term debt) is a commitment mechanism that can solve the time inconsistency problem faced by governments with low credibility.[9] Tirole (2003) focuses on the currency denomination of private debt and also highlights that risky debt may serve as a commitment device. Similarly, Alfaro and Kanczuk (2006) conduct a welfare analysis that suggests that, under certain conditions, risky debt is welfare improving, and nominal debt may not be sustainable in volatile emerging economies. An additional reason why foreign currency debt may be relatively cheap is that foreign currency debt instruments may be perceived as implicitly senior to local currency debt instruments, as defaults usually are associated with a highly depreciated real exchange rate, which increases the value of dollar claims relative to local currency claims (Chamon, 2001).

Summing up, when a government has low credibility in regard to inflation, short-term domestic currency debt often turns out to be a more feasible option than long-term domestic currency debt. From the point of view of investors, it is reasonable to assume that the risk of an inflation outbreak is increasing over time, simply as a result of increasing uncertainty. There is in fact a tendency for countries with lingering inflation fears to shorten the maturities on their debt instruments or to employ frequently adjustable interest rates. From the point of view of the government, there is also a tendency to prefer short tenors if the authorities expect inflation to stay low and credibility to increase gradually. In this type of situation, governments would not want to lock in high interest rates that incorporate high-inflation fears in long-term instruments and would prefer instead to issue short-term debt until credibility improves and maturity can be lengthened at lower interest rates.

It is critical to note, however, that even if local currency borrowing at long maturities is indeed excessively costly for some of the reasons noted above, there are cases in which foreign currency borrowing still might not be a better alternative. The higher expected cost of long-term local currency debt may be worth paying in exchange for the insurance benefits it provides. The final decision will hinge, more generally, on the price that a sovereign is willing to pay to increase debt quality and limit the risks of sovereign finance.

This suggests a less benign view of why a government may choose not to issue long-term debt in the local currency. Even in the absence of distortions, a fair currency premium would typically incorporate the incidence of a possible sharp devaluation in the future—much in the same way as an insurance fee against sudden real exchange rate adjustments.[10] Finding

---

[9] For a discussion of time inconsistency, see Box 9.2.

[10] This was particularly so in the past, when Latin America and the Caribbean was characterized by limited exchange rate flexibility.

that the premium exactly compensates for currency risk, a forward-looking policymaker may opt for the safer local currency debt factor because of its insurance benefits. By contrast, a myopic policymaker who cares only about the present will disregard negative events that may materialize when he is no longer in office. If, as usual, the probability of a currency adjustment increases with the time horizon, such a policymaker will find the premium expensive relative to short-term risk and will opt for either foreign currency debt or short-term debt, which will command a lower premium but leave the next government exposed to the risk of sovereign finance.

In addition, one should factor in the positive externalities of issuing domestic currency debt—an aspect ignored in the static cost-benefit framework discussed above—in terms of the development of a new market and the creation of an investor base for domestic currency instruments, which may flourish once credibility is finally built. In the presence of start-up costs, a sovereign may then decide to issue part of its debt in the domestic currency even if costs are excessive, simply to keep open the option of resorting to domestic currency borrowing in the future.

INFLATION INDEXATION

The above discussion has addressed the conventional view that governments with credibility problems face a trade-off between short-term domestic currency debt and long-term foreign currency debt. But neither time inconsistency nor asymmetric information necessarily implies that the only viable option is foreign-currency-denominated government debt. More precisely, the government may have another method for committing to low inflation: by issuing local currency long-term bonds indexed to inflation. Indexed debt is not as safe as nominal debt, because a crisis that causes inflation to accelerate can undermine fiscal solvency, potentially with self-fulfilling implications. But inflation is a slowly moving variable, and from the sovereign's point of view, inflation-indexed bonds are clearly safer than short-term local currency bonds or long-term foreign currency bonds because they reduce rollover risk and do not generate negative balance sheet effects in the presence of devaluation of the real exchange rate. It is therefore puzzling that Latin American countries (with the exception of Chile) have made such a limited use of price indexation in recent years.[11]

There are three possible answers to this puzzle. The first has to do with negative past experience with indexation. In some countries, past indexation of financial contracts spilled over to the whole economy, generating a situation in which everything was indexed (including wages, pensions, and subsidies). Such a pervasive indexation system amplified inflationary cycles, as increases in prices led to rapid increases in wages, which would then immediately feed back to prices (Bernanke, 2005). As a consequence, the widespread conventional wisdom was that it was best to steer clear of any form of indexation, although that view seems to have been reconsidered more recently.[12]

---

[11] For a detailed discussion of Chile's successful experience with CPI indexation, see Herrera and Valdés (2005).

[12] This may explain why some countries made attempts to limit the use of CPI indexation and replace it with floating rate debt indexed to the short-term interest rate, which because of its lower duration increases the sensitivity of debt service to the monetary policy stance and, in particular, to episodes of financial distress much in the same way as short-term debt.

A second aspect that explains the unpopularity of price indexation has to do with the fact that, while more difficult to dilute than nominal long-term bonds, inflation-indexed bonds are easier to dilute than dollar-indexed bonds. To the extent that the price index is measured with a lag—or averaged over a longer period—it will not fully protect investors from an acceleration of the inflation rate, and hence it will not protect investors from hyperinflation. Whereas this could have been a problem in the early 1990s, when most Latin American countries were emerging from a period with recurrent hyperinflation episodes, it should be less of a problem in the current context, when most central banks in the region have made important gains in monetary credibility.

A third, more practical reason has to do with the fact that inflation-indexed bonds may simply be too expensive given inflation expectations, an anomaly that may be related to a number of distortions. The premium may reflect the incipient nature of the markets for such bonds—associated with the lack of both trading volume and specialized traders—the mistrust of government-produced inflation statistics, or simply lack of familiarity with this new instrument. It should be clear that none of these reasons constitutes a fundamental objection to the use of inflation-indexed bonds; rather, they are transient obstacles to the use of such bonds that should be taken into account in the design of policies to promote them. The small-market problem is certainly transitory and can be mitigated with the help of international financial institutions, which can fund themselves using CPI-indexed bonds on the borrowing members' currencies. Investors' mistrust can also be attenuated by international financial institutions, which can serve as auditors to increase the credibility of official statistics. In turn, the contractionary devaluations at the core of the implicit seniority problem should be gradually eliminated by dedollarization. It is thus not surprising that several Latin American countries have started to rely more on domestic debt indexed to prices as a mechanism for lengthening maturities while avoiding currency risk.[13]

OTHER SOURCES OF RISK

So far, the discussion in this chapter has focused on rollover and exchange rate risks. However, developing and Latin American and Caribbean countries are also subject to several other sources of risk. The most important ones are terms-of-trade shocks; catastrophic events (such as earthquakes and hurricanes), which can have a very high cost in poorly diversified small countries; and, more generally, high output volatility.

A simple exercise can illustrate how different debt structures can affect the evolution of public debt in an economy that faces these different types of risk (details are provided in Box 13.1). Consider the public finances of a government that faces uncertainty in regard to the key economic variables that determine its financial position, including interest rates, the exchange rate, and economic growth (which determines tax revenue and, indirectly, the fiscal surplus before interest payments). To be sure, the volatilities of each of these variables are not independent of one another, but this exercise ignores that complication. The government has choices in terms of the structure of its liabilities. For simplicity, these choices are limited

---

[13] Ize and Powell (2005) discuss the advantages of inflation indexation over dollarization in the case of the banking system.

Box 13.1 How Debt Management Can Reduce Vulnerability: An Example

This exercise shows the distribution of probable outcomes for the debt-to-GDP ratio under different assumptions about the debt structure. The government in this exercise starts from a fairly sound position: a debt-to-GDP ratio of 45 percent (in the year 2005, which is the start of the simulation period) and a projected fiscal balance over the next five years. This means that the primary surplus of the budget (f_t) is projected to be equal to the expected interest cost. The simulation considers that the government can use three different debt instruments: foreign currency debt (with a share of s^f and paying interest rate r^f), domestic currency debt (s^d and r^d), and GDP-linked debt (s^{gdp} and r^{gdp}).

The evolution of the debt-to-GDP ratio follows the standard equation:

Assumptions

	Δy_t	r_t^d	r_t^f	Δq_t
Mean	0.050	0.140	0.130	0.037
Standard deviation	0.080	0.075	0.075	0.070

probability of occurrence. In other words, after the 20 percent of the simulations that yield the most extreme values for the debt-to-GDP ratio are excluded, the remaining values span the fan in the figure.[a]

The results are striking. When all the debt is denominated in foreign currency, debt can, with an 80 percent probability, reach values anywhere between 25 and 66 percent of GDP in five years. With a debt composition which is 50 percent in foreign currency and 50 percent in domestic cur-

$$d_t = \left(\frac{(1+r_t^d)s_t^d + (1+\Delta q_t)(1+r_t^f)s_t^f + (1+\Delta q_t)(1+\Delta y_t)(1+r^{gdp})s_t^{gdp}}{1+\Delta y_t} \right) d_{t-1} - f_t,$$

where d_t is the debt-to-GDP ratio, Δq_t is the rate of depreciation of the exchange rate, and Δy_t is the rate of growth of GDP. For simplicity, the exercise assumes zero inflation.

In the baseline case, the government issues only foreign-currency-denominated debt. By means of the simulation of 1,000 stochastic series of Δy_t, r_t^d, r_t^f, and Δq_t, with means and standard deviations shown in the table at the top of the next column, Figure 13.2 illustrates the range of likely debt-to-GDP ratios for the period between 2005 and 2010. The "fan" in the figure represents the range of values that have an 80 percent

rency, the range of the fan tightens significantly. With a debt composition that is equal parts of each of the three instruments, the fan closes even further, and now the 80 percent confidence interval ranges only from 41 to 52 percent of GDP. This simulation illustrates the potential gains from using instruments that provide implicit insurance against the volatility of the exchange rate and economic growth.

---

[a] This exercise is very similar in spirit to Celasun, Debrun, and Ostry (2006) and Ferrucci and Penalver (2003).

to three instruments: a foreign-currency-denominated bond, a domestic-currency-denominated bond, and a bond whose payments are linked to the evolution of GDP.

Figure 13.2 plots the probable evolution of a country's debt-to-GDP ratio over time, after the government makes a choice regarding debt structure and the level of spending. The line in the center of the figure is the country's projected debt-to-GDP ratio if there are no shocks to the economy. In this case, the debt-to-GDP ratio is projected to remain constant (at 0.45). But when economic uncertainty is considered, a "fan" of possible values for the debt-to-GDP ratio opens up. The fan reflects the fact that in the face of uncertainty, the variance is larger at points more distant in the future. The figure shows the range of values of the debt-to-GDP ratio that may be obtained with an 80 percent probability under various mixes of currency and indexation. When all of a country's debt is denominated in foreign currency, the fan is the widest. When the country's debt structure is composed of foreign currency and domestic currency instruments in equal parts, the fan is less wide, and when its debt structure comprises equal parts of foreign-currency, domestic-currency, and GDP-linked instruments, the fan is even narrower. This illustrates how a government can reduce the variance of its debt ratio or, equivalently, how it can reduce the fiscal adjustment that would be necessary to preserve debt sustainability if a negative shock were to occur.

This example assumes that the government can issue three different types of instruments at a cost that roughly reflects the expected return to investors.

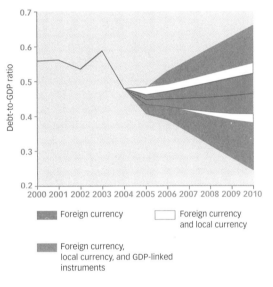

Figure 13.2
Debt-to-GDP Ratio Distribution

Source: Authors' calculations.

This is not always the case, because numerous factors—like the liquidity of the instrument and concerns that investors may have about possible capital controls, the manipulation of the exchange rate or economic statistics that determine the value of the asset—may affect the cost of instruments other than foreign-currency-denominated bonds issued in global markets. Further, in the case of innovative instruments, there is a "novelty" premium to be paid, as investors may prefer to stay away from less familiar assets unless the expected payoff is sufficiently rewarding. Debt management must balance these costs of more favorable instruments against the gains of a more resilient debt structure and protect the country against the need for costly fiscal adjustment in times of economic malaise.

DOES IT MATTER WHERE TO ISSUE?

Another possible source of risk is the jurisdiction where bonds are issued. There are two ways in which the jurisdiction in which sovereign debt is issued could influence the risk of sovereign finance. The first relates to the fact that, for emerging markets, most financial assets are denominated in the currency of the market in which they are issued, with only a few exceptions. If there are deep-seated reasons for this feature of global financial markets, such as perhaps the absence of deep markets for many emerging economies' currencies in the major global markets, any dedollarization effort must involve primarily the development of domestic markets, as has been mostly the case recently in Latin America.[14]

A second aspect relates to the differential legal treatment that a sovereign may receive from local and international courts in the event of a debt restructuring. Domestically issued sovereign debt may be thought of as a way of reducing overlending, under the assumption that, unlike in courts abroad, international lenders cannot enforce any of their rights in domestic courts and will therefore be more reluctant to volunteer funds (Bulow, 2002). Furthermore, if domestic courts are more amenable to a debt restructuring that is believed to improve the country's welfare, they may take into account the social costs of debt service and legitimize a renegotiation under more favorable con-

---

[14] This is due to the combination of investors' home bias (the fact that residents tend to invest more—or relatively more—in domestic assets) with what could be labeled the "home currency bias," namely, the fact that the preference for local currency assets is higher among residents than among nonresidents.

Figure 13.3
Pricing of International and Domestic Bonds
a. Argentina
(foreign currency)

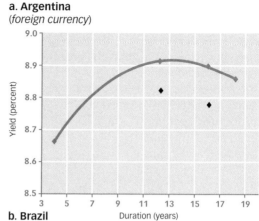

b. Brazil
(domestic currency)

c. Colombia
(domestic currency)

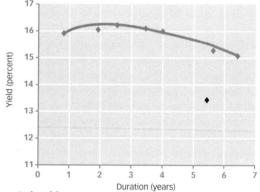

Source: Authors' calculations based on Bloomberg data.

ditions than a judge in New York or London.[15] While this may make domestic debt less risky than external debt from the perspective of the sovereign issuer, it will also make it more expensive. Figure 13.3 is consistent with the idea that issuing in international markets is marginally cheaper than issuing in domestic markets, but the difference is small and could be due to a variety of factors (like tax treatment, regulatory issues, and market segmentations) other than a difference in risk.[16]

CAN RISKS BE REDUCED?

Most discussion on the risks of sovereign finance has focused on the problems related to currency and maturity risks and on a possible trade-off between these two forms of risk. Countries can try to avoid having to make such a trade-off using forms of debt, such as inflation-indexed long-term bonds or bonds indexed to real variables (like the GDP), that expand the efficiency frontier, but there are several reasons why countries still make only limited use of these (apparently superior) forms of financing. The next chapter will focus more specifically on policies aimed at removing the perceived obstacles to countries' use of these forms of financing.

---

[15] Perhaps the main example comes from a developed country: the decision of the U.S. Supreme Court to uphold the government's decision to nullify gold indexation clauses after the country abandoned the gold standard in 1933. One interpretation of this decision is that it offered a way of improving overall social welfare at the expense of a few sovereign debt holders (Kroszner, 2003).

[16] Another difference is that domestically issued foreign currency debt is usually indexed to the foreign currency but payable in domestic currency, while foreign-issued debt is usually payable in foreign currency. This may be an important issue in the presence of capital controls or multiple exchange rates.

Lowering the Risks of Sovereign Finance

A banker is a fellow who lends you his umbrella when the sun is shining and wants it back the minute it begins to rain.

—Mark Twain (1835-1910)

NOWHERE HAS THE HISTORY of sovereign debt been more dramatic than in Latin America and the Caribbean, where dependence on often unpredictable international capital flows poses risks that have often resulted in financial and economic grief. The nineteenth century, starting from the immediate aftermath of the independence of the Latin American republics, was characterized by ambitious schemes of government borrowing for infrastructure development and other public projects. All too often these waves of borrowing culminated in market panics, debt crises, and sovereign defaults, notably in the 1830s, 1850s, 1870s, and 1890s (and in the twentieth century as well, in the 1930s and the 1980s). These crises left Latin American and Caribbean countries shut out of international financial markets and often were highly disruptive to their economic development. From the very start, then, sovereign debt has been a mixed blessing for Latin America and the Caribbean.

The current phase of Latin American sovereign debt history started in the early 1990s, when the Brady exchanges converted external bank debt into bonds, established emerging market bonds as an asset class, and opened the door for the re-emergence of bond markets as a source of external finance. This marked a return to the first era of globalization of 1880–1914, when Latin American sovereign bonds were a major component of a thriving global market for financial instruments issued by emerging economies. The current phase is evolving: Brady bonds have been almost entirely retired well ahead of their maturity dates, and domestic debt markets have started to emerge as the venue of choice for sovereign finance. This shift in the composition of public debt has led some observers to conclude that Latin American countries are gradually reducing their vulnerabilities, on the grounds that foreign-currency-denominated external debt held by international investors is more sensitive to global factors than domestically issued debt held by resident investors.

More generally, current trends point to a steady enlargement of the menu of financing sources and instruments. With the acceptance by increasingly sophisticated investors of contingent provisions in bond covenants—of clauses indexing returns to a country's rate of growth or the occurrence of a natural disaster, for example—it will become easier for prudent governments to manage higher levels of debt. That these higher levels apply to *prudent* governments should be emphasized, because the proliferation of instruments (derivative securities, for example) also increases the scope for things to go wrong. That said, the development of new instruments opens opportunities for debt managers to achieve superior combinations of expected cost and risk for any given level of public debt, relative to what was available before.

At the same time, the development and deepening of financial markets is also enhancing access to international financing by private borrowers from emerging economies, including those of Latin America. Traditionally, foreign borrowing was done by governments. During the early 1980s, more than two-thirds of the stock of all debt owed by Latin American and Caribbean countries to private international lenders was debt incurred by the public sector. By 1990, that share had risen to nearly 90 percent. (See Figure 14.1, which shows analogous figures for East Asia for purposes of comparison.) But in recent years, private firms and banks have been drawing finance from international markets in record amounts. While domestic bond markets are still overwhelmingly dominated by public issuers, private sector issuers are beginning to gain access (see Chapter 7). There are visible signs, in other words, of the development of economically significant corporate bond markets, although the small size of many Latin American firms still limits their access to bond finance.

Policy analyses of public debt management in Latin America and the Caribbean should be placed in this context. The fact that a growing range of private sector entities are now able to access debt finance, both at home and abroad, implies a diminished need for public borrowing. The fact that others can borrow on domestic and foreign markets weakens the argument that the government must borrow for them, whether to finance investment in infrastructure and productive capacity or for the purpose of smoothing consumption spending across good and bad times.[1]

This suggests that globalization and financial market development create two forces that influence the role of public debt, one expanding it, and the other reducing it. The availability of a wider range of instruments and a broader investor base increases the scope of the sovereign to borrow safely and finance its operations. Conversely, the private sector's growing access to financial markets diminishes the traditional role of the state as intermediary for such financing. These two opposing tendencies operate with different degrees of intensity in different countries. Imagining the role of public debt in the twenty-first century therefore requires analyzing these dynamic forces and developments in individual countries in more detail.

WHY DO SOVEREIGNS BORROW?

The history of debt crises in Latin America underscores the risks involved in sovereign borrowing. Is government debt a threat to a country's financial stability? Should governments therefore give up borrowing altogether, or limit their debt to such small amounts that any risk of financial instability is ruled out? A judicious answer to these questions should ac-

---

[1] This statement is valid only if sudden stops have the same effect on private and sovereign borrowers. If sovereign borrowers have better access to finance in bad times (perhaps through lending by multilaterals), then there is still a role for sovereign borrowing in this regard.

Figure 14.1
International Debt by Type of Borrower
a. Latin America and the Caribbean
(*US$ billion*)

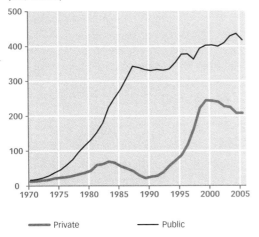

b. East Asia and the Pacific
(*US$ billion*)

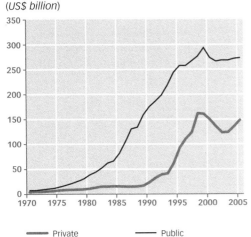

Source: World Bank, *Global Development Finance* database.

knowledge that the risks of sovereign borrowing should be balanced against the benefits, that is, the functions that governments fulfill and whose execution requires resorting to debt. Chapter 1 discussed three primary economic justifications for government borrowing: (1) to redistribute income from wealthier future generations to those currently alive, (2) to fund development projects, and (3) to fund policies aimed at smoothing the effect of business cycles and other shocks.

The first rationale for public borrowing, borrowing for redistributive purposes, should be assessed within the framework of the political motivations for government borrowing, discussed in Chapter 9. The existence of shortsighted politicians, together with the fact that future generations are not represented in the current decision-making process, creates a tendency toward excessive current consumption and hence overborrowing. A case in point is social security systems, which often run deficits, taxing future generations to cover the shortfall created by the level of benefits provided to current recipients under the retirement system. Moreover, the progressive development of private insurance and annuity markets will eventually weaken the case for a government role in retirement benefits, or at least create the opportunity for alternative systems that do not involve the buildup of future public liabilities. At a minimum, the presence of such markets should help in evaluating the actuarial fairness of retirement systems and the extent of redistribution from future to current generations that such systems involve.

The second rationale, namely, development borrowing, seems self-evident. There can be little doubt that developing countries would benefit from an increase in investment in human and physical capital of such a magnitude that it cannot be financed entirely from current taxes. Indeed, there is evidence that infrastructure bottlenecks are particularly serious in Latin America and the Caribbean (see Chapter 10). But does this justify public borrowing and spending? Although many infrastructure projects have a clear public-good content, the private sector can now provide more of the investment needed to finance them.[2] Indeed, the data indicate that private infrastructure projects have increased substantially over the last 20 years, although their growth has not fully offset the observed decline in public investment. This shortfall provides an immediate explanation for the persistence of infra-structure bottlenecks.[3] Another area in which the government should retain an important role is human capital investment. Here, there are problems that private capital markets are unlikely to solve. In practice, it simply is not possible, for example, for poor households, lacking negotiable collateral, to finance an education by borrowing against their offspring's future earnings.[4]

While the development of private capital markets has also weakened the argument for government spending to smooth the impact of business cycles and other shocks, the case remains strong. In downturns, households and firms experience reductions in the value of their tangible collateral, limiting their ability to borrow to smooth consumption and invest-ment. Moreover, when contemplating whether to borrow, they have no reason to take into account the aggregate (macroeconomic) effects, which accrue to the country as a whole in the form of an externality. Large shocks, such as those associated with natural disasters and financial rescue operations, also require abrupt increases in government spending. Such increases cannot be financed out of current revenues; it is desirable to smooth over long periods the impact of such events on tax rates, which implies a prolonged period of public indebtedness. The problem here is that the credit risk premium on borrowed funds often rises sharply in bad times, precisely when the country is most in need of financing. The in-crease may be sharpest on global markets, which is where it makes the most sense to seek financing during a domestic recession. Thus, instead of borrowing more during periods of weakness, emerging economies often must cope with a more limited and more costly sup-ply of finance.[5]

---

[2] Additionally, the proper discount rate for the public sector has long been the subject of debate, with some econo-mists arguing that the government's discount rate should be different from the market interest rate faced by private investors (Spackman, 2004, provides a recent survey of this literature). If the government's discount rate is lower than the private rate, then the government should be willing to finance investment projects that the private sector is not willing to finance. However, this difference in discount rates does not necessarily require that the government borrow to finance investment projects that are not pursued by the private sector, as the government could achieve its desired investment plans by giving the private sector a subsidy which is equal to the difference between the two discount rates.

[3] There is in fact some evidence that public and private investment in infrastructure may be complements rather than substitutes: that there is a continuing role for the public sector in infrastructure investment that enhances the efficiency of and incentives for private sector infrastructure investment. Of course, this assumes that the govern-ment is willing and able to invest in activities with high levels of social return. As discussed in Chapters 9 and 10, this is often not the case.

[4] Of course, this does not say anything about whether the government should promote investment in human capital through subsidies or education loans or by directly financing public schools. For a discussion of these issues, see Shleifer (1998).

[5] In contrast, advanced economies are only marginally affected by credit quality deterioration during cyclical down-turns.

SOVEREIGN DEBT IN THE TWENTY-FIRST CENTURY

The conclusion that emerges is that there are still legitimate reasons for governments to borrow, although imperfections in political systems and financial markets pose the risk that the recourse to sovereign debt may be used poorly or unduly restricted. To limit the vulnerabilities that result from sovereign debt and maximize its economic value, policy should be directed at three targets:

- *Setting essential controls on the flow of debt.* This implies creating a fiscal policy framework that ensures that debt stays within sustainable levels.
- *Appropriately managing the inherited stock of debt.* This involves using a combination of debt instruments to minimize vulnerability to a debt crisis and to lessen the constraints imposed by debt on monetary and fiscal policies while keeping the cost of debt service at acceptable levels.
- *Improving the international financial environment in which these decisions occur.* This entails reforms to the global financial environment to make sovereign borrowing safer.

CONTROLLING THE FLOW OF DEBT

What can countries do to better manage the ongoing process of debt accumulation? Domestic reform should start with measures to ensure that governments borrow for the right reasons (i.e., for tax smoothing, high-return infrastructure investment, or socially desirable intergenerational redistribution, as described above). In contrast, borrowing on an ongoing basis to, inter alia, pay the salaries of redundant civil servants is not sound practice.

Political motivations and electoral considerations can distort borrowing decisions, however, as discussed in Chapter 9. Political and procedural reforms and greater fiscal transparency can help to limit problems associated with such distortions. A large empirical literature now shows that more centralized fiscal procedures that leave less autonomy to spending ministries are conducive to better fiscal outcomes. Federal fiscal systems that limit vertical fiscal transfers from the central government to subnational governments similarly limit the scope for the latter to spend now and demand additional transfers from the center later. Finally, political systems that produce majority governments or stable coalitions not prone to excessive turnover encourage politicians to adopt reasonably long horizons when making fiscal decisions.

A mechanism for ensuring that debt policies are not distorted by political influences is to rely on *fiscal rules* that impose limits on unwarranted use of fiscal expansions. The most common fiscal rules are automatic stabilizers and fiscal targets. Automatic stabilizers are taxes and transfers that adjust over the business cycle. Progressive income taxes are a good example: income tax revenues are higher when incomes are higher. Automatic stabilizers have a number of advantages over discretionary tax changes. For one, symmetrical automatic stabilizers do not give rise to a deficit bias. Symmetry implies that the increase in revenues relative to expenditures during expansions is more or less equal to the reduction in revenues relative to expenditures during contractions. In contrast, the temptation to raise spending during bad times may not be matched by the desire or ability to cut it in good times when countercyclical stabilization is undertaken on a discretionary basis. Of course automatic stabilizers can be used only by countries that can access resources during bad times. In order to do this, countries need either to have continuous access to the international capital markets or to accumulate resources in a stabilization fund.

Fiscal targets, including legally mandated balanced budgets and deficit caps, are included in some of the fiscal responsibility laws that have been adopted in many Latin American countries over the past decade, and they figure prominently in Europe's Stability and Growth Pact. These fiscal policy rules differ in the measure of fiscal performance that they involve, in whether they involve a strict ceiling or simply a target, and in their provisions in case targets are missed or special circumstances arise. The range of performance indicators includes the budget deficit, debt levels, and public spending at various levels of government. Some of the rules allow for margins around the target or for time averaging to provide an opportunity to make up for shortfalls, and many allow for departures in case of international crisis or natural disasters. At the same time, the laws provide for stiff financial or judicial sanctions for noncompliance (see Kopits, 2001).

To be sure, there are also costs associated with such measures. Rules are rigid; such is their nature. Under extreme circumstances, such as an unusually severe recession, a financial crisis or a natural disaster, it may be desirable for stabilization purposes to cut taxes or increase public debt by more than would be appropriate in a typical downturn. Some rules do include "escape clauses" to provide for such contingencies. But this may raise problems of its own. Politicians inclined to use public spending to advance their re-election prospects will be tempted to cite an unanticipated contingency justifying a discretionary increase in spending whenever an election approaches. This problem can be ameliorated by assigning responsibility for declaring the existence of a relevant contingency to an independent, extrapolitical body but, in practice, it is difficult to do this. Nevertheless, rules can be designed to be more responsive to current economic conditions. In this regard, the Chilean rule, described in detail in Box 9.3, is a step forward because it targets a structural measure which adjusts the actual budget balance for the state of the economy and the price of copper, a mineral export that contributes substantially to the country's fiscal position. Similarly, the Brazilian fiscal responsibility law sets limits on debt accumulation and contingent liabilities with some well-defined escape clauses related to the state of the economy (see Box 9.4).

A further problem is that a major component of debt accumulation is the result of contingent liabilities (or "skeletons") and balance sheet effects that are not recorded in the traditional measure of the fiscal deficit that is the subject of the pertinent fiscal policy rule (see Chapter 3). One way around this problem may be to set a ceiling on public debt rather than on the government's deficit. However, contingent liabilities can derive from unfunded obligations of the sovereign (such as unfunded pension obligations), implicit obligations for servicing the debts of subnational governments, and implicit responsibility for the liabilities of public enterprises, banks, etc. This means that it may be difficult for a government to ignore these liabilities even if there is no room to accommodate them if the debt rule is respected. And it may be equally hard to impose a rule on the volume of contingent liabilities. The magnitude of these contingent liabilities tends to be difficult to estimate—this is their nature, since they are contingent, after all. In this regard, enhancing the transparency of fiscal policy and making the budget as comprehensive as possible, which is desirable under all circumstances, can be especially valuable. Special interests pushing for bailouts with narrow benefits but widely dispersed social costs will find it more difficult to do so when fiscal poli- cies are formulated in the light of day and additional expenditures cannot be easily hidden as off-budget activities. Transparency will generally strengthen the operation of market forces, whereby interest rates and credit ratings will more accurately provide an assessment of fis- cal sustainability. More intense market discipline will in turn put pressure on authorities to refrain from creating too many skeletons.

Rules-based institutions can also help countries manage volatile revenue flows result- ing from commodity exports, either through taxation or by direct ownership of the natural resource. Commodity stabilization funds have in fact been widely used for some time in Latin America and the Caribbean (Engel and Meller, 1993). The idea is to save resources in good times and use them in bad times, which is a sound principle. However, actual experience with stabilization funds has not been entirely happy. Many stabilization funds have been ex- propriated (in other words, their rules were changed and their assets spent prematurely, and they ended up stabilizing very little). Moreover, even when a stabilization fund is working as envisaged, the government can go on a spending binge involving the central budget during a commodity price bonanza, in effect offsetting the savings accumulated by the stabilization fund. This is a problem not with the concept of stabilization funds per se, but with the design of many stabilization funds that have been implemented in the past, and with the broader fiscal institutional framework within which they operate (see Box 14.1).

MANAGING THE STOCK OF DEBT

Even when countries have good policies in place to control deficits, management of inherited stocks of debt poses several challenges. High economic volatility and low policy credibility are often more serious issues in Latin American and Caribbean economies than in other emerging markets, let alone advanced economies (see IDB, 1995). The volatility of funda- mentals (GDP, terms of trade, exchange rates, tax revenues) in the region has been linked to factors ranging from limited diversification of the economy to a narrow tax base. Partly as a result, political processes in Latin America and the Caribbean tend to be less effective and transparent, detracting from the credibility of economic policies and the confidence of resident and international investors.[6] Latin American and Caribbean countries are often es- pecially dependent on foreign borrowing, but volatility and a tendency toward investor panic makes access to foreign markets unreliable. The implication is that maintaining reasonably low public deficits is not enough to eliminate the possibility of a debt crisis.[7] Creating a debt structure that makes public finances less vulnerable to shocks is also essential in the Latin American and Caribbean context.

Gaining credibility requires creating and enhancing the perception that public debt is not a liability to be serviced in good times and restructured in bad times, but rather an obligation that will be serviced under all reasonable circumstances. Budgetary reform that raises the likelihood that a country's debt will be limited to prudent levels can enhance this percep-

---

[6] The effectiveness of the policymaking processes was analyzed in depth by IDB (2005a).

[7] After all, Chapter 3 shows that recorded deficits explain only 5 percent of the variance in debt growth in Latin America and the Caribbean.

Box 14.1 Making Stabilization Funds Work

The first problem with the design of past stabilization funds is that they were implemented as saving rules and not spending rules. From the theoretical point of view, a saving rule is exactly the same as an expenditure rule. However, in practice they are not the same, because with saving rules politicians will have a greater temptation to spend the resources saved in stabilization funds (this is the appropriability problem). If a country has a large proportion of its GDP saved in an account for stabilization, the temptation to spend those funds is extremely large, and if the law prevents politicians from using the money accumulated in the fund, it can be offered as collateral for new borrowing. Alternatively, the law can be reinterpreted to allow withdrawal of the resources, or the executive can declare a state of emergency, allowing it to reassign the funds. In the end, if there is too much saved, some of it will be withdrawn.

Substituting expenditure rules for saving rules can address part of the appropriability problem. Consider the following example: assume that there is a target for fiscal revenue of $10 billion, and the actual income is $11 billion. The saving rule would require

$1 billion to be placed in the stabilization fund. The government could follow the law and put $1 billion in the fund, then put it up as collateral to borrow an extra billion dollars and use that to increase expenditure to $11 billion. The letter of the law is respected (because the law does not say anything about the government's ability to borrow), but its spirit is not respected, because there has been no net saving. On the other hand, an expenditure rule would have said that the government could spend only $10 billion. If congress then decides to increase expenditures, it will have to explain why it is violating a law. This is why it is much harder to appropriate under expenditure rules than under saving rules. Expenditure rules attack the source of misbehavior directly. Indeed, stabilization funds based on expenditure rules can be consistent with fiscal responsibility laws, while saving rules have to be changed yearly in order to achieve this. Of course, both saving and expenditure rules can be violated, but stabilization funds defined as saving rules are easier to breach.[a]

The next problem that stabilization funds have to deal with is the issue of governability. Most of the time, if a country has several

---

tion. So too can the creation of a domestic investor class that holds the government's debt and is likely to be less prone to herding than international investors. Such an investor group could also become a strong political constituency in favor of responsible fiscal policies and dependable debt service.

Using Contingent Contracts

Even with the strongest willingness to honor debts, the probability that an extreme adverse shock will tip the balance toward renegotiation would still be greater in an emerging economy. This is where well-designed debt management policies can improve the trade-off sources of fiscal risk, it tends to adopt one stabilization fund for each source of risk (the funds are created sequentially, and each new law does not change the existing ones). From a practical point of view, having several funds to achieve the same objective is inefficient, and the funds become unmanageable.

A third problem with the design of stabilization funds is the way in which fund resources are invested. The financial instrument that provides the best stabilization is one in which the returns to the asset are negatively correlated with the fiscal shocks faced by the country, but almost all stabilization funds invest their resources in short-term treasury bonds issued by the United States or other advanced economies. The objective of this investment strategy is to maximize the liquidity of the stabilization fund. The problem is that these financial instruments have a very limited correlation with the risk against which the country needs to be insured. Consider, for instance, an oil importer that wants to insure itself against a sudden increase in the price of oil. Wouldn't a fund invested in stocks of oil-producing companies be better than a fund invested in U.S. treasuries? The latter have no correlation (or a limited correlation) with the price of oil; the former tend to do poorly when oil prices are low (i.e., when the country does not need the money) and do well when the price of oil is high (i.e., when the country needs the money). Consider instead an oil producer that wants to insure itself against a sudden drop in the price of oil. An ideal investment strategy would be to invest in securities traded on the Japanese stock market, which tends to move in the opposite direction with respect to the price of oil, delivering high returns when the price of oil is low (i.e., when the oil-producing country needs resources) and low returns when the price of oil is high (i.e., when the oil-producing country does not need extra resources). Clearly, these are just rough examples; the point is that countries can do better than holding their stabilization funds in short-term government paper issued by advanced economies.

_____

[a] Of course, the rule could also be broken in less transparent ways, such as through the assumption of contingent liabilities, like credit guarantees, through the stabilization fund.

Source: Based on Rigobón (2006).

between the risk of debt crises and the cost of sovereign finance. As highlighted in Chapter 13, the structure of public debt contributes to the burden the debt imposes as importantly as the level of debt itself. In Latin America, in particular, that structure is often biased towards foreign-currency-denominated instruments. In this case, a real exchange rate adjustment has a powerful impact on the most widely used indicator of sustainability, the debt-to-GDP ratio, and in most cases on actual measures of how burdensome debt service is. But a number of other factors, such as commodity prices and other real shocks, or exogenous contagion and panics, can also turn debt sustainability indicators around very quickly (see Chapter 12).

This creates an argument for introducing into debt contracts contingencies with equity-like features that allow for more efficient sharing of this volatility.[8] These would be instruments that offer lower payoffs during bad times and higher payoffs during good times, which should make them safer for investors and would afford governments the opportunity to manage their fiscal policy stance better over the business cycle. Interest payments can be indexed to commodity prices, the terms of trade, or the rate of growth of GDP. While indexing to the price of a commodity has been the traditional recommendation—and still makes the most sense in some cases—emerging economies are diversifying, and a debt contract indexed to the country's growth rate is likely to be applicable to a broader set of countries nowadays (see Anderson, Gilbert, and Powell, 1989; Borensztein and Mauro, 2004; Caballero and Panageas, 2006; Hausmann and Rigobón, 2003; and Eichengreen and Hausmann, 2005, for discussion of different forms of indexed debt). Under such a contract, when commodity prices drop or growth rates slow, the burden of debt servicing on the government will decline, as investors will share part of that debt-servicing burden with the government.[9] Chapter 13 illustrated how making use of such provisions can reduce the volatility of a country's debt-to-GDP ratio and effectively reduce the probability of a debt crisis. The opportunities for sovereigns to make use of a broader set of debt instruments have increased significantly in recent years, as noted above.

Another option is to obtain contingent coverage directly from international financial markets, through the use of derivative contracts. An example would be the case of a commodity producer subject to fiscal shocks due to fluctuating commodity prices. Such a country can reduce uncertainty by using futures, forwards, and options markets for the commodity. In practice, however, there are problems with this approach. First, many futures and options markets lack depth and liquidity and therefore offer only limited scope for insurance. The lack of markets is more acute in respect to events such as fluctuations in tourism revenue, hurricanes, and other natural disasters. Fortunately, financial market innovation is increasing the scope for using this type of market coverage as insurance, as in the case of the recent operation by Mexico securing earthquake insurance for three at-risk geographical areas (see Box 14.2). Second, contracts aimed at isolating countries from external shocks are likely to be very large and complicated and may present significant demands in terms of management, and it may be difficult to allow traders sufficient leeway to operate in the markets while ensuring that their trades and risk taking are aligned with the objectives of the government.

Finally, obtaining some form of market insurance, either through derivative contracts or through indexed debt, must also surmount a more fundamental obstacle. By its very nature, any such device implies a cost that must be paid during good times. This is analogous to paying an insurance premium and takes the form of losses in a futures or option contract or high coupon payments on debt. As these contracts are relatively complex, such losses can be easily misunderstood and become politically costly. This creates little incentive for politicians to enter into large-scale contracts of this type, especially for myopic politicians, considering that the cost is likely to be paid up front but the payoff from the insurance may accrue only years later.

---

[8] For a general treatment on the benefits of contingent contracts, see Shiller (2003).

[9] In the limit, indexation of the principal to GDP or terms of trade can automatically stabilize the debt-to-GDP or the debt-to-export ratio.

Box 14.2 Mexico's Catastrophe Bond

In May 2006, Mexico placed a new financial instrument that provides the country with compensation in the case of an earthquake in three at-risk areas of the country's Pacific coast and around Mexico City. This is the first "catastrophe bond" placed by a Latin American country and is expected to be the first step in the Mexican government's plan to secure insurance against natural disasters, including hurricanes.

The operation comprises two instruments: a straight "parametric" insurance, under which Mexico will receive payments if an earthquake of a certain magnitude hits the prescribed regions over the next three years, and two catastrophe bonds whose principal will be written off if such a disaster occurs. The total face value of the two bonds is $160 million which, when added to the monetary compensation provided by the insurance contracts, totals $450 million in compensation ($150 million contingent on occurrence of an earthquake in each region). The cost to Mexico also has two parts: an annual spread of 230 basis points on the catastrophe bonds, and the direct insurance premium of about $14 million.

An operation of this type illustrates the economic advantages of using market insurance to obtain protection from potential shocks—in this case, natural disasters. Market insurance is more cost effective than the alternative of "self-insurance." It is also an instrument less subject to manipulation or distortions by the political system. The importance of these issues should not be underestimated. Even this fairly modest initiative is reported to have taken almost three years to structure, largely because of the intricacy of the budgetary approval process. It is noteworthy that obtaining the insurance as part of a bond offering may be simpler because the public debt management offices generally have broad authority to issue debt instruments, and interest payments do not require specific budgetary allowances.

Currency-Maturity Trade-Offs

Another trade-off that often arises in the context of dedollarization of sovereign debt (that is, the shift from foreign- to local-currency-denominated instruments) is between currency and rollover risk. Debt denominated in local currency is often placed at short tenors, largely because of steep currency premiums—the result of lingering fears of inflation, which has long been a concern in Latin America—that make long-term local currency borrowing excessively costly (see Chapter 13). Furthermore, when credibility can be regained only gradually, governments should avoid locking in high risk premiums in long-term bonds. If the menu is limited to long-term, fixed rate foreign currency debt and short-term domestic currency debt, it makes sense for the issuer to maintain a diversified portfolio. Fixed rate foreign currency debt insulates the issuer from sharp fluctuations in interest rates on local currency instruments, while short-term domestic liabilities protect the issuer against a sharp increase in the debt burden when the domestic currency depreciates. Inflation-indexed instruments provide an alternative that can help improve the terms of this trade-off. It may be possible to issue long-term inflation-indexed instruments at moderate cost, as investors are protected from the risk of unexpected inflation. But governments may have been wearied by past experiences in which financial indexation spearheaded widespread indexation of wages, pensions, subsidies, and so on and created a situation of stubborn inflation and inflexibility of relative prices. Still, some countries have been successful in using indexed financial instruments widely without perceptibly worsening inflation persistence.

Since recent experience has pointed to currency fluctuations as an important source of vulnerability, Latin American governments have reacted by favoring local currency debt over dollar debt.[10] But trading one risk for another (in this case, currency risk for rollover risk) is not a panacea. If the next shock to the region's economy is a rise in local currency funding costs rather than a fall in exchange rates, concentrating exposure on the maturity side may prove not to have been a prudent bet. A large investor base for debt that is denominated in the domestic currency at fixed nominal rates and reasonably long maturities does not yet exist. Interestingly, it would appear that foreign investors are more interested in these types of instruments, as such investors are less troubled by a history of inflation (see Chapter 7). But at the same time, these investors may be highly sensitive to changes in credit quality or less favorable prospects in short-term returns, which means that market access may be unreliable for Latin American sovereigns.

This suggests that eliminating (or decreasing) the existing trade-off between currency and maturity will also require the development of liquid, well-functioning bond markets for domestic currency instruments that are underpinned by a stable investor base. Domestic institutional investors, such as pension funds, are increasingly forming the core of such an investor base in many countries. By the nature of their liabilities to beneficiaries—and also as a result of direct regulation—pension funds are naturally stable, dedicated investors in domestic bond markets. As policies and institutions in the countries of the region gain credibility and inflation fears continue to recede, the core investor base will grow broader. A better debt structure will, in fact, make the policy framework in these countries sounder and itself contribute to gains in credibility on price and exchange rate stability. Thus, the strategy for gaining access to long-term, fixed rate, high-credit-quality, domestic-currency-denominated debt should be based on these two elements: improving credibility through sound policies and developing local bond markets.

Managing Rollover Risk

Even when countries are in a sound position in terms of debt sustainability, they may face liquidity problems. Countries need to roll over maturing debt and cover their annual financing needs, and this can become virtually impossible in the event of a sudden stop in global financial markets. Moreover, a liquidity crisis can trigger more fundamental insolvency problems by causing a large exchange rate depreciation, a recession, and/or bank failures. When debt is denominated in foreign currency, only the accumulation of a large stock of international reserves can protect a country from potential liquidity crises. In recent years, emerging economies, especially those in Asia, have accumulated vast international reserves

---

[10] Yet foreign currency debt still represents about half of sovereign obligations in the region (see Chapter 2).

(Figure 14.2). The accumulation of reserves in Latin America has been one of the least extensive in all of the regions, but still significant. While in some cases, notably Middle Eastern oil exporters, the level of reserves goes well beyond what may seem necessary from a financial stability standpoint, for many emerging economies the main purpose of accumulating international reserves is crisis prevention.

But the accumulation of international reserves is expensive. Reserves are held in safe liquid assets so that they can be mobilized when there is a need to intervene in the foreign exchange market, either to avoid wide fluctuations in the exchange rate under disorderly market conditions or simply to smooth out the effect of temporary shocks. But safe and liquid assets such as U.S. Treasury bonds carry low interest rates. For emerging markets, the spread of their own debt over the yield on U.S. treasury bonds can be significant. Self-insurance thus entails a "cost of carry" that the government has to pay in excess of the return on liquid foreign assets to finance the purchase of excess reserves, namely, the sovereign risk premium, which for most Latin American countries—as opposed to Asian countries—tends to be large.[11]

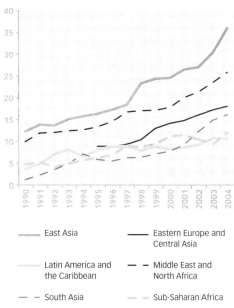

Figure 14.2
International Reserves
(percentage of GDP)

East Asia

Eastern Europe and Central Asia

Latin America and the Caribbean

Middle East and North Africa

South Asia

Sub-Saharan Africa

Source: IMF, *International Financial Statistics* database.

Self-insurance is, by its own nature, an inefficient strategy. Any car driver would recognize the efficiency of buying a car insurance policy instead of saving and stashing away millions of dollars for possible liability claims before owning a car. Essentially along these lines, some authors have proposed ways of improving on this self-insurance strategy, for example, by investing reserves in assets that are negatively correlated with country risk (as opposed to high-grade foreign currency assets) or, in the case of commodity exporters, through the use of derivatives (Caballero and Panageas, 2005, 2006; Rigobón, 2006). This is a sound strategy assuming that there exist assets or commodity derivatives with a reliable correlation with country risk and a sufficiently liquid market. A number of obstacles may have to be overcome to implement such a strategy, however, including the already noted political cost of paying the insurance fee (in this case, the derivative losses when the economy is in a good state). But the case for this strategy is easier to make in countries where the volume

---

[11] Note that in some cases, notably China, reserve accumulation has been financed largely by issuing domestic currency (a non-interest-bearing debt). This massive increase in money has not had any inflationary consequences thanks to the high growth rates of the economy and the increasing monetization resulting from the transformation of the economy into a modern, market-based system. In this case, the cost of reserve accumulation is not obviously high.

of reserves amply exceeds what may be needed purely for the purpose of ensuring stability in the foreign exchange market.[12]

Self-insurance through the accumulation of reserves has a further drawback. Any readily available pool of public resources is subject to political capture. In other words, reserves could be spent before the "rainy day." This has been highlighted in the literature on stabilization funds but applies more generally to any type of public savings.

An alternative strategy would be to obtain liquidity insurance from the private financial markets, for example, in the form of credit lines that can be activated if there is an incipient sudden stop, as measured by an increase in spreads or some other variable. In fact, such credit lines were implemented for a handful of countries, including Mexico and Argentina (see IMF, 1998). Private liquidity insurance, however, faces some serious challenges. In particular, private lenders want to reduce their exposure when conditions deteriorate and can effectively undo in other markets the loans that are activated through the liquidity insurance agreement.

REFORMING THE INTERNATIONAL FINANCIAL ARCHITECTURE

The financial crises of the 1990s resulted, at least in part, from market imperfections that led to "herd" behavior by investors, contagion, and panics resulting in self-fulfilling liquidity runs (Calvo, 2005b). This suggests a role for the international community, and the international financial institutions (IFIs) in particular, in implementing initiatives to limit the consequences of instability in international financial markets. Efforts in this direction gained momentum after the Asian and Russian crises of 1997–1998 and continue to evolve as the global financial system continues to pose challenges.

The traditional role of the IFIs has been to provide financial and policy support when a country facing a currency or financial crisis requests it. But it is clear that the best way of minimizing the costs of crises is to avoid them in the first place. While this depends on prudent fiscal policies on the part of the countries themselves, the IFIs' role is to help minimize the risks that arise from global financial markets, mainly rollover and contagion risks. In addition, the IFIs have been working to eliminate major obstacles that emerge in connection with the resolution of debt crisis events.

Rollover Risk

To strengthen crisis prevention, the international community needs to implement plans to prevent or mitigate sudden hard currency liquidity shortages. Credit facilities to prevent liquidity runs that can turn into debt crises are referred to as *country insurance facilities*.[13] A country insurance facility would consist of a liquidity window that lends in the short term to eligible countries at predetermined interest rates—in much the same way as the central

---

[12] Summers (2006) suggests that reserves exceeding the requirements of the Guidotti-Greenspan rule (stating that reserves should be enough to cover one year of capital account liabilities) should be invested in stocks rather than advanced economies' treasury bills.

[13] A precedent in this regard is the Contingent Credit Line (CCL) facility that the IMF implemented in 1999. Design problems made this facility unattractive to potential users, and it was finally deactivated in 2003 without ever having been requested by a member country. On this, see IMF (2003b).

bank, acting as lender of last resort, lends to domestic financial institutions. Since rollover risk (that is, uncertainty about access to sources of finance) is the main aspect driving liquidity runs, the availability of liquidity with certainty is a strong deterrent to the start of a self-fulfilling run.

Although facilities of this type have been recognized to be the best response to liquidity and contagion risks,[14] there are also some implementation difficulties that must be worked out. A commonly voiced concern is the potential for moral hazard. This concern relates to the possibility that a government could adopt risky policies with high short-term political rewards once it has secured a country insurance line. Indeed, moral hazard is an issue that comes up in relation to any insurance contract. As with private insurance, there are also mechanisms for dealing with moral hazard issues in the case of countries. The facility can avoid moral hazard by applying appropriate eligibility conditions, based on triggers that are exogenous to the assisted country (such as international interest rates or natural disasters), or a policy prequalification condition. The latter condition could determine the volume of resources to which a country has access based on consistent and transparent indicators of the soundness of the country's policies. An alternative mechanism would be the requirement of a commitment by countries not to borrow in international markets at above a predetermined spread, which would put an early stop to risky "borrow and spend" runs (Cohen and Portes, 2006). Eligibility rules may also face problems related to the governance of institutions managing the credit facility (Powell and Arozamena, 2003). For example, a declaration by the institution which is providing insurance that a country has become ineligible (perhaps because of a deterioration of fundamentals) may lead to a market run and precipitate a crisis.

As a partial response to the liquidity risk, some emerging economies have started to develop *regional country insurance* schemes. These typically take the form of regional swap agreements under which participating countries can borrow from other members on short notice for limited periods of time. These agreements include the North American Swap Agreement (NAWA), the Chiang Mai Initiative (CMI), and the Latin American Reserve Fund (FLAR, after its Spanish name, Fondo Latinoamericano de Reservas). NAWA, set up in April 1994 among Canada, Mexico, and the United States, provides 90-day renewable collateralized loans. CMI, launched in May 2000 by the 10 members of the Association of Southeast Asian Nations (ASEAN) plus China, Japan, and Korea, involves bilateral currency swap arrangements.[15] FLAR originated in 1978 as the Andean Reserve Fund (FAR) and was expanded to include all interested Latin American countries (with the name changing to FLAR) in 1988. Currently, FLAR includes six countries (Bolivia, Colombia, Costa Rica, Ecuador, Peru, and Venezuela) and has a size (as measured by the capital subscribed by its members) of $2.1 billion.

While these arrangements are close in spirit to a multilateral country insurance facility, in that they offer immediate access to short-term liquidity while avoiding the hedging problems that may arise with private insurers, their effectiveness is hampered by their limited (albeit growing) size and, in the Latin American case, by the absence of a large country with

---

[14] See, among others, Fischer (1999), Jeanne and Zettelmeyer (2001), Ostry and Zettelmeyer (2005), Cordella and Levy Yeyati (2006a), and Rajan (2006). A new proposal along these lines has been recently endorsed by the IMF (2006a).
[15] While currency swaps among ASEAN countries date back to 1977, they have rarely been used due to their small volumes.

reliable access to dollar liquidity in the arrangement—a factor that severely reduces the scope to leverage central bank resources without raising borrowing costs and, as a result, the size of available credit lines.

These problems notwithstanding, there seems to be scope for regional insurance in Latin America, potentially leveraging the liquidity support that could be provided by a country insurance facility. FLAR has been able to leverage its capital to some extent by funding itself in international markets at interest rates below those of the participating countries (Figure 14.3). This implies that this regional arrangement entails a lower insurance cost relative to what member countries would have to pay individually. A similar effect is observed in the rates paid by the Andean Financial Corporation (CAF, for Corporación Andina de Fomento), a regional development bank, which suggests that there may be efficiency gains associated with this type of arrangement, stemming from risk pooling or from the perception that these facilities enjoy a preferred creditor status.[16]

Absent large creditor countries, the IFIs could have a potentially important supporting role in such arrangements by guaranteeing, under certain conditions, the debt placed by the multilateral insurance fund or even contributing resources to the pool (Cordella and Levy Yeyati, 2006b).[17] This could significantly leverage the size of the fund at a reasonably low cost, while keeping the intended countercyclical pattern of IFI lending. In other words, the IFIs would shift from making loans to offering guarantees in good times when alternative sources of finance are abundant, and back to making loans in recessions when funds become scarce (given that the insurance fund has already been built up). Alternatively, the IFIs could go further to provide a global arrangement along the lines of the existing multilateral insurance schemes, which would be superior to a group of regional ones, because liquidity shocks tend to be regionally correlated, because neighboring economies are subject to similar risks, because neighboring economies trade with one another, and because contagion tends to have strong regional links.

Risk of Contagion

Contagion has escalated individual emerging market crises to regional or even global events in several past episodes (Chapter 5). While a well-implemented and fully credible country insurance mechanism could eliminate contagion episodes, regulators and supervisors could also play a role by putting in place mechanisms to limit the damage caused by disorderly markets. In many domestic exchanges, rules such as circuit breakers that suspend trading temporarily when price fluctuations become too large have been implemented to help prevent market failures from developing into full-fledged crises. There is no equivalent mechanism in the global market for sovereign debt.

---

[16] It has to be noted, however, that CAF also benefits from high capitalization and a broader membership that includes investment grade countries like Mexico and Chile, as well as an advanced economy, Spain.

[17] Large creditor countries like Japan and China in the CMI, or the United States and Canada in NAWA, enhance the coverage provided by those arrangements in two ways: (1) contributing to diversification of liquidity shocks (which tend to display a low correlation between developing and developed countries) and (2) lending their creditworthiness to the developing members, strengthening the capacity to borrow countercyclically from outside the region in the case of a regional shock (thus reducing the need to keep a liquid reserve pool) or, alternatively, lowering the cost of holding reserves ex ante. The IFIs could play essentially this second role.

Although it may not be feasible for an international institution to act as a global regulator, there are proposals that could provide circuit-breaker-type benefits to limit contagion effects. For example, Calvo (2005b) proposes the creation of an Emerging Market Fund (EMF) aimed at stabilizing an emerging market index, such as the JPMorgan Emerging Markets Bond Index Plus (EMBI+). The fund would be endowed with G3 debt instruments and, in the event of a disturbance, could limit contagion by making a credible commitment to buy bonds from the emerging markets that are not at the center of the crisis. The EMF could thus slow down or even stop a generalized collapse in the asset class, preventing fire sales from sending the wrong signal to investors. According to Calvo, the fund would not try to fight trends but only intervene in special circumstances. Action could be triggered only by a financial meltdown, defined as a drop in the index of more

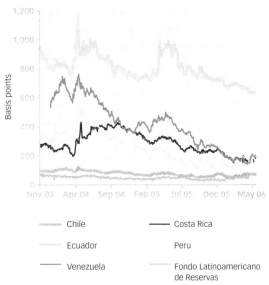

Figure 14.3

Multilateral Insurance: Fondo Latinoamericano de Reservas and Latin American Spreads

— Chile
— Costa Rica
— Ecuador
  Peru
— Venezuela
  Fondo Latinoamericano de Reservas

Source: Cordella and Levy Yeyati (2006b).

than a certain percentage relative to a moving average. If the initial drop reflected a change in fundamentals and prices did not recover from the initial drop, the moving average would decline over time, and the EMF would sell its emerging market bonds and revert to holding only G3 bonds. The same thing would happen if the intervention was successful and prices recovered to the precrisis level. In both cases, the EMF would have negligible holdings of emerging market bonds in tranquil times. Calvo shows that creating such a fund would require less than 1 percent of the public debt of G3 countries and could even be profitable, as long as the majority of the crises were indeed due to contagion and not deterioration of fundamentals.[18]

Crisis Resolution

Even in the best-planned system, train wrecks sometimes happen. When sovereign debt crises occur, there are no well-established procedures for restructuring debts and restoring

---

[18] One criticism of this proposed EMF is that while it could limit moral hazard from the borrower's point of view (by focusing on the asset class rather than an individual country), it might create moral hazard for investors, insofar as it slows down the adjustment of bond prices. In recent crises, contagion has been less important than in the previous ones, and by its own design, the EMF could deal only with contagion; hence it would not help with crises that affected just one country. In the absence of contagion, however, the EMF would be useless but also harmless.

financial normalcy.[19] Restructuring typically occurs through a bond exchange offer in which new bonds are exchanged for the existing debt. Because exchanges are voluntary, there is always a fraction of bondholders that do not accept the offer. The value of the claims of these holdout investors creates legal uncertainty and litigation. Consequently there has been considerable debate over proposals to establish a statutory mechanism to adjudicate defaulted claims, such as the Sovereign Debt Restructuring Mechanism (SDRM) proposed by the IMF.

While there has been disagreement in the international community regarding the desirability of an SDRM, there is consensus on the desirability of a more modest initiative to include collective action clauses (CACs) in bond covenants (see Eichengreen and Portes, 1995). CACs provide for changes in the payment terms of a bond if a supermajority of bondholders—usually 75 percent—accept the changes. This automatically solves holdout problems by binding in dissidents. CACs have become commonplace in emerging markets' global bond issues since Mexico pioneered them in 2003. Recent CACs have also included "aggregation" clauses that permit a supermajority of bondholders—typically 85 percent—to restructure all outstanding bonds and binding the minority to accept the write-down. This solves the problem that the simple version of a CAC applies only bond by bond, and many sovereigns have issued tens, or even hundreds, of bonds.

While CACs have become standard in new bond contracts, older bonds still in circulation do not include them. In most cases, it will take many years for the stock of outstanding bonds to mature and be replaced by new instruments containing CACs and aggregation clauses. This means that holdout uncertainty will not disappear quickly. The lack of collective action created by holdouts has not been a major impediment to recent sovereign restructuring operations, although a large mass of holdout claims remain unresolved, and the outcome of ongoing litigation and possible new legal strategies by holdouts may change the situation again (see Sturzenegger and Zettelmeyer, 2005b).

New Financial Instruments

The international community can help to improve debt management by supporting the development of new markets and new instruments to allow countries to minimize the risks of sovereign borrowing, keep the costs of borrowing at moderate levels, and improve the cyclical timing of fiscal policy.

Developing Local Currency Bond Markets

There is broad consensus that it is desirable for the universe of debt instruments issued by a government to include a significant share of domestic currency debt. As noted above, Latin American countries have started to change the structure of their debt in response to this recognition.

The IFIs could accelerate this process by helping to increase the scope of available local currency instruments at home and abroad. One option is for them to enlist their own mar-

---

[19] As crisis resolution is not the main topic of this report, this section is necessarily short; for a more comprehensive treatment, see Roubini and Setser (2004) and Ghosal and Miller (2003a, 2003b).

ket liabilities. Already the multilaterals have begun issuing bonds denominated in emerging economies' currencies, although often the objective has been mainly to minimize their own borrowing costs. (Box 14.3 comments on the experience of the IDB in this regard.)

By borrowing in local currencies, the IFIs could also support the development of markets for such instruments. One of the main factors limiting a country's ability to issue external debt in its own currency is the small size of the market. While the largest Latin American economies, Brazil and Mexico, for example, may not be seriously affected, the currencies of many emerging markets are considered "exotic" and carry substantial liquidity premiums (Eichengreen, Hausmann, and Panizza, 2005a). An ambitious proposal along these lines is to create a synthetic unit of account that pools currency risk from a large and diversified group of emerging economies, and to have the international financial community take steps to develop liquidity in this unit (see Eichengreen and Hausmann, 2005).[20]

Some observers have noted the influence of sovereign (credit) risk in the underdevelopment of local currency markets and have pointed to the IFIs' bonds in exotic currencies as a way to decouple sovereign risk from currency risk. This is implicit in the previous proposal, where the IFIs are seen as the first issuers of bonds in a basket of currencies. But it is even more critical for resident (particularly institutional) investors, who are more naturally inclined to invest in their home currencies but may shy away from domestic assets for fear of default. Absent an international market in their domestic currencies, the offshoring that characterizes many non-investment-grade Latin American countries may lead to the dollarization of domestic savings for reasons unrelated to currency risk. It follows that IFI bonds in domestic currencies may find their main investor base among residents.

Contingent Bonds

Debt sustainability and risk sharing can be enhanced by instruments with equity-like features, which provide for lower payments in the event of adverse shocks like natural disasters, recessions, and commodity price busts, but these markets are grossly underdeveloped. To be sure, creating a market in such securities poses a number of challenges. New, original instruments may have shallow markets initially and command an illiquidity premium. Designing a new type of instrument is costly, creating a first-mover problem.

Markets in such instruments do not spring up spontaneously. Someone has to sink the costs of designing the new instrument, and someone has to be the first to issue in a nonexistent or illiquid market. In the past, official intervention has been instrumental in the development of pathbreaking financial instruments, such as the market for mortgage-backed securities in the United States. In the case of contingent bonds, the international community can provide technical assistance on instrument design and expected pricing. In the case of GDP-linked debt, for example, the international community could strengthen the quality and reliability of statistics by various means, enhancing their credibility for investors. As in the

---

[20] The plan has four steps: (1) development of a basket of inflation-indexed currencies of emerging markets (the "EM index"); (2) issuance by multilateral development banks of debt denominated in the EM index, to fund lending in the same exotic currencies; (3) having G10 sovereigns do the same, issuing a portion of their debt in this index and then swapping a portion of their currency exposure with the countries whose currencies are represented in the EM index; and (4) encouraging institutional investors and mutual funds to create products that add credit risk to the index.

Box 14.3 Latin American Currency Bonds by the IDB

Over the last few years, the IDB has contributed to the expansion of domestic currency bond markets by issuing its own debt in the currencies of the member countries. In April 2004, the IDB became the first institutional issuer to launch a global bond denominated in Mexican pesos, offering a new asset class for domestic and international investors. This was the first international bond issue made available in the domestic capital market under the new financial regulatory framework adopted by Mexico in 2003 and the first AAA bond issued in the Mexican capital market. Since this first issue, the IDB has issued 18 other bonds in the currencies of Latin American countries, raising a total of approximately 1.3 billion. While most of the issues tapped the Mexican peso market (for a total of more than US$900 million), the bank has also issued bonds denominated in Brazilian *reais*, Chilean pesos, and Colombian pesos.

The IDB's issues in domestic currencies may serve two purposes. First, they may provide funding that can be used for local currency loans to its member countries, which is a sensible option for many projects whose revenues are not at all related to the exchange rate. Second, given its prime borrower rating, the IDB expands the range of available credit risks in local currencies, in both domestic and international markets. This can help attract more investors to local currency instruments and develop a benchmark yield curve, which is valuable for pricing and giving liquidity to instruments issued by a range of borrowers.

Of particular interest is the potential use of local currency bonds to finance local currency lending. As the IDB cannot take on currency risk, it cannot "create" local currency lending but must simply act as a financial intermediary. It has two options for doing so: borrowing from savers in local currency and on-lending the proceeds, or borrowing in a foreign currency, lending in local currency, and hedging the exchange rate risk.

The effects of local currency financing on the aggregate level of available credit and distribution of currency mismatches throughout an economy are complex and will depend on

1. how IDB intermediation in the local currency markets (for debt and derivatives) affects the currency composition of the domestic supply of credit in the country;
2. how IDB intermediation in the local currency markets affects the allocation of local currency debt across firms and government;
3. how substituting intermediation in local currency markets for intermediation in foreign currency markets affects the total (domestic and foreign) supply of credit available to the country.

In the best case, the IDB could fund itself in a way that increases the willingness of savers to lend more in local currency or take on local currency risk and contributes to assigning available local currency credit where it is most needed in a way that reduces balance sheet currency mismatches, all without reducing the total supply of credit available to the country. In the worst case, the IDB would tap into the existing supply of local currency debt, favoring its clients but crowding out other borrowers. If these other borrowers, in turn, are more currency mismatched than the IDB clients, this might render the entire operation counterproductive, as aggregate vulnerability to exchange rate shocks will increase.

IDB (2005a) suggests that the positive effects of its participation in local currency markets are likely to dominate the negative ones. In particular, the IDB suggests that as its assets are default risk free, they will lead to increased saving by domestic residents. Since domestic residents hold a portion of their savings in local currency, this will translate into an expansion of local currency savings, supporting local currency debt. This effect will be largest in countries with the highest default risk. Furthermore, domestic residents may replace foreign assets in their portfolios with IDB local currency bonds, generating a capital inflow that reverses previous capital flight. In particular, pension funds may choose to shift from foreign-currency-denominated AAA assets to local currency AAA assets. This shift in the currency composition of domestic savings will have a positive effect on the aggregate supply of local currency credit. The reduction in the risk associated with local currency assets may also increase the demand for these assets by foreigners

(who may have previously been reluctant to lend in domestic currencies because they were bundled with default risk). IDB local currency instruments may also play an indirect role in increasing the supply of local currency financing by fostering the development of domestic financial markets. Furthermore, in those countries with low monetary credibility, issues indexed to inflation linked to a consumer price index certified by a credible institution could benefit the local bond market.

On the negative side, an expansion in the supply of local currency credit in a particular country may result in a contraction in the supply of dollar credit to the extent that the traditional funding sources of the IDB (foreign international investors) are not tapped and remain inaccessible to that country. Countries with easy access to foreign savings will not experience measurable negative effects on dollar credit supply and in fact may actually benefit from tapping increased domestic onshore dollar savings. Countries with difficult access to foreign savings, however, may lose the allocation ensured by the traditional IDB intermediation through dollar lending and end up with less total credit available.

Sources: IDB Finance Department, and IDB (2005a).

case of collective action clauses, the international community could help in the drafting of a model contract and resolve legal uncertainties (for example, questions about the legal standing of a GDP warrant relative to other sovereign instruments). It could provide guidance on the drafting of GDP link clauses to ensure the reliability and integrity of their application.[21]

A more ambitious idea would be for some of the international financial institutions to become the first issuers of an instrument of this type and sow the seeds of a market that countries themselves could tap later. The risk could be unloaded by swapping this instrument with the beneficiary country, although it can be argued that the international financial institutions already carry an equity-type risk in regard to their member countries, because the institutions will need to help these countries if the countries suffer an adverse shock. Alternatively, an international financial institution could issue a bond on an index of real variables of several countries, in a form analogous to the currency basket referred to above. In the same vein, the IFIs could guarantee contingent instruments, or at least the part of the instruments that is contingent. This might be seen as a subsidy to spur innovation in the market by compensating for novelty premiums, setup costs, and concerns about manipulation of certain indices (see Anderson, Gilbert, and Powell, 1989).

FINAL REMARKS

While it is trivially true that pushing the region's debt to zero would eliminate Latin America's vulnerability to debt crisis, this is neither feasible in the short run nor economically desirable. The central conclusion of this report is that, more than the level, it is the structure, namely the quality, of the debt issued by Latin American and Caribbean countries, and the inherent volatility of their economies, that makes the region prone to crises. While the specific design and parameters of a debt management strategy for the region's countries would differ from case to case, some general principles are valid. Latin American and Caribbean countries should continue to shift their debt structures away from foreign-currency-denominated debt and into debt denominated in domestic currency. However, there are trade-offs that need to be considered carefully as they advance in this process. In particular, to avoid locking in excessive interest costs, countries sometimes need to issue instruments with very short maturities. Otherwise, vulnerability to a debt crisis—or to an inflationary outburst—will not disappear but only change its nature. The development of sound domestic bond markets, based on a core set of institutional investors and the use of inflation-linked instruments, can help improve the terms of this critical trade-off. Foreign currency debt will maintain a share in each country's liabilities both because of the need to tap foreign investors and because the structure of revenues in the country may be partly related to foreign currency and thus make it advisable from a risk management perspective. Countries should explore more aggressively the use of contingent debt as a mechanism for obtaining insurance from foreign investors against adverse shocks such as recessions, commodity price collapses, and natural disasters.

---

[21] The United Nations Department of Economic and Social Affairs (UNDESA) and the United Nations Development Programme (UNDP) are sponsoring a working group that is making progress in this direction. See http://www.un.org/esa/ffd/GDP-indexed%20Bonds.

Debt management is crucial in the volatile Latin American environment, but limiting the risks of sovereign finance also demands gaining the markets' (and their citizens') trust in the institutional and policymaking framework. In particular, the flow of new debt, namely, budget deficits, must be controlled to ensure both that the ability to borrow is not abused by the political leadership and that fiscal policy does not worsen economic fluctuations. Although design problems have impaired some experiences, fiscal rules and stabilization funds continue to be ideal mechanisms for underpinning a sound approach to fiscal deficit controls.

The current relatively benign global environment is partly due to better policies and safer debt management, but it heightens the risk that the international community will become complacent and needed initiatives will be postponed. Tranquil times are the best for discussing and introducing new initiatives aimed at reducing the vulnerabilities that still lurk in the global financial system.

In recent years, the international community has focused on the process of resolution of debt defaults, and progress is being made in this area, with the widespread introduction of collective action clauses in debt contracts. But progress has not been made in the area of crisis prevention, and available instruments were designed in a pre-financial-globalization era. In this area, the IFIs could contribute a great deal by designing workable credit facilities to prevent liquidity runs and self-fulfilling market panics and by supporting in various ways reserve-pooling arrangements by emerging market economies. The IFIs also have an important new role to play as facilitators of reforms aimed at limiting the risk of sovereign finance. The IFIs can promote the development of markets for local currency instruments and new contingent debt instruments in various ways. They can provide assistance with the design of those instruments, and they can help to overcome the externalities and start-up costs of new markets and attract new investors. Finally, the IFIs can change the nature of their own loans to member countries by offering a wide menu of domestic currency loans and contingent facilities and thus contribute to the dedollarization process.

Public Debt in Latin America and the Caribbean: Country Profiles

THIS APPENDIX PRESENTS debt profiles for 26 Latin American and Caribbean countries. The methodology used to collect the data is summarized in Box 2.2 and described in greater detail in Cowan et al. (2006). It is important to note that, during 2004–2006, several countries in the region experienced real appreciation and robust GDP growth, and this allowed them to reduce their debt ratios to implement policies aimed at improving their debt profiles. These recent changes are not reflected in this appendix, which uses data up to 2004. The analysis stops at that point for two reasons. First, while it is possible to find more recent data, these more recent data could not be made comparable using the methodology described in Box 2.2. Second, while historical debt statistics are extremely hard to collect, more recent data can easily be found in publications of the multilaterals (such as IMF Article IV agreements) and of major investment banks or commercial providers of economic data (such as the Economist Intelligence Unit). The data used in this appendix are available at www.iadb.org/res/pub_desc.cfm?pub_id=DBA-007.

ARGENTINA

In the mid-1980s Argentina accumulated substantial external debt, mostly in the form of international bank loans, but with a large official (both bilateral and multilateral) component (Figure A.1). In 1989 there was a sharp increase in the external debt-to-GDP ratio (from 32 percent of GDP in 1988 to 53 percent in 1989) which was due not to an increase in the dollar value of debt, but to a deep economic crisis and real devaluation, which reduced the dollar value of GDP by 35 percent.[1] Subsequently, the Brady swap led to a reduction in debt held by foreign banks and a switch toward sovereign bond issuances (foreign bonds went from 1 percent of GDP in 1992 to 13 percent of GDP in 1993, and foreign bank loans dropped from 9 percent of GDP to less than 1 percent of GDP). From the mid-1990s, the country's external debt increased gradually until the economic crisis and devaluation of 2001, which reduced the dollar value of GDP by 62 percent and led to a sudden jump in the external debt-to-GDP ratio from 30 to 82 percent of GDP.

The early 1990s witnessed a gradual decline in the total debt-to-GDP ratio in Argentina. As external debt was either constant or increasing during this period, this decline was

---

[1] In 1988 Argentina defaulted on foreign bank loans and hence was not making payments on these loans (it exited from default in 1993).

Figure A.1 Argentina
External Government Debt by Creditor Type
(US$ million)

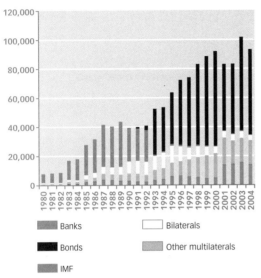

Legend:
- Banks
- Bonds
- IMF
- Bilaterals
- Other multilaterals

Source: Authors' calculations based on Cowan et al. (2006).

Figure A.2 Argentina
Structure of Government Debt
(percentage of GDP)

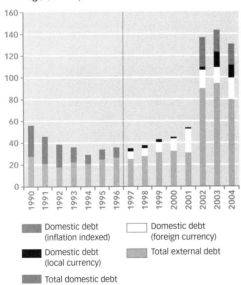

Legend:
- Domestic debt (inflation indexed)
- Domestic debt (local currency)
- Total domestic debt
- Domestic debt (foreign currency)
- Total external debt

Source: Authors' calculations based on Cowan et al. (2006).
Note: Data for currency composition of domestic debt available from 1997 on.

entirely the result of lower domestic debt. At the beginning of the 1990s, the country's debt was evenly distributed between domestic and foreign holders, but by 1994, 72 percent of Argentina's public debt was external. During the 1994–2001 period the increase in Argentina's debt was gradual and mostly financed by foreign-currency-denominated domestic debt.[2] The crisis of 2001 led to a sudden jump in the debt-to-GDP ratio (which went from 54 percent in 2001 to 135 percent in 2002). This increase in the debt-to-GDP ratio was partly due to the large real devaluation resulting from the crisis, but it was also due to the costs of rescuing the country's financial system and to bonds issued to retire some of the debt issued by provincial governments. The bank rescue operations and the "pesification" of foreign currency debt held by domestic institutions and individuals led to a reduction in the share of foreign currency debt to 70 percent of total debt (30 percent of domestic debt) from a peak of 90 percent in 1997 (68 percent of domestic debt) (Figure A.2). In January 2006, Argentina was able to repay all of its debt to the IMF for the first time since 1982.

In Argentina, local governments issue a substantial amount of debt. Subnational debt (issued mostly by the provinces but also by the City of Buenos Aires) grew from 4 to 6 percent of GDP over the 1996–2000 period and then jumped to 10 percent of GDP over the 2000–2002 period; most

---

[2] Data on currency composition for domestic debt are available from 1997.

of this debt was denominated in foreign currency.[3] Over the 2002–2004 period the central government assumed a large amount of subnational debt by issuing "Bonos Garantizados" (Bogar) for an amount close to 6 percent of GDP. This led to a substantial reduction in subnational debt, which by 2004 had fallen back to 6 percent of GDP.

Methodological issues. The main source of data for Argentina is the ministry of the economy, which does not, however, separate domestic from foreign bank debt. As a consequence, domestic bank debt was obtained by subtracting the foreign bank debt reported by the World Bank's *Global Development Finance* (GDF) from total bank debt reported by the ministry of the economy. As the ministry of the economy classifies data on marketable debt by the holder's place of residence, it was necessary to reclassify this information in order to match the methodology described in Cowan et al. (2006).

THE BAHAMAS

The Bahamas has moderate levels of public debt even though public debt grew at a fast pace over 2000–2003 (Figure A.3) and total public debt is much higher than central government debt (the debt of public enterprises is above 10 percent of GDP, leading to a level of debt in the general government of close to 50 percent of GDP). Traditionally, The Bahamas has had a debt structure similar to that of industrial countries, with almost all debt issued domestically and denominated in domestic currency. However, over 2002–2003 external central government debt more than doubled (this was partly compensated for by a reduction in the external debt of state-owned enterprises).

Figure A.3 The Bahamas
Domestic Government Debt, External Debt, External Government Debt by Creditor Type, and Total Government Debt

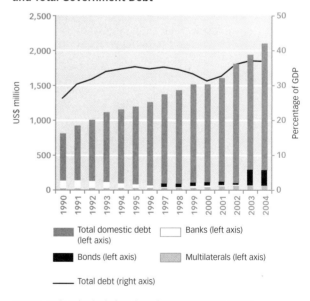

Source: Authors' calculations based on Cowan et al. (2006).

BARBADOS

Barbados has levels of debt which are above the Latin America and Caribbean averages. Public debt grew very rapidly over the 1980–1994 period, then decreased somewhat in the second half of the 1990s, but started growing

---

[3] These figures do not include debt owed to the central government (mostly through the Fondo Fiduciario para el Desarrollo Provincial, FFDF), which in 2002 reached a peak of 11 percent of GDP and in 2004 still stood at 9.5 percent of GDP.

Figure A.4 Barbados
Domestic Government Debt, External Debt, External Government Debt by Creditor Type, and Total Government Debt

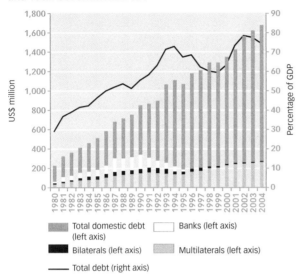

Total domestic debt (left axis)

Banks (left axis)

Bilaterals (left axis)

Multilaterals (left axis)

Total debt (right axis)

Source: Authors' calculations based on Cowan et al. (2006).

Figure A.5 Belize
Domestic Government Debt, External Government Debt by Creditor Type, and Total Government Debt

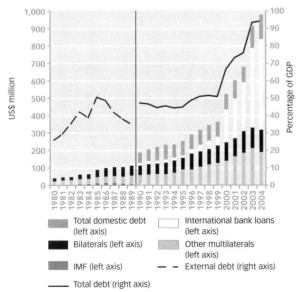

Total domestic debt (left axis)

International bank loans (left axis)

Bilaterals (left axis)

Other multilaterals (left axis)

IMF (left axis)

External debt (right axis)

Total debt (right axis)

Source: Authors' calculations based on Cowan et al. (2006).
Note: Data for domestic debt available from 1990 on.

again in 1999 (Figure A.4). On the positive side, about three-quarters of the country's total public debt is domestic and denominated in domestic currency, and this makes Barbados much less vulnerable to a possible debt crisis than countries with similar levels of debt but a larger share of external debt and debt denominated in foreign currency.

BELIZE

Belize's external debt increased steadily in the first half of the 1980s (from 25 percent of GDP in 1980 to 50 percent in 1985) and then decreased over the 1985–1993 period from 50 percent of GDP to 30 percent of GDP (Figure A.5). Until the late 1990s most of Belize's external debt was held by official creditors (with a large share of bilateral debt), but starting in 2000, international bank loans became increasingly important, and they now account for more than 50 percent of the country's external debt (they represented only 7 percent of its external debt in 1995). This increase in foreign bank debt coincided with an explosion in Belize's debt-to-GDP ratio, which went from around 60 percent in 2000 to more than 95 percent in 2004. Data for domestic debt are available from 1994 (there are no data on the currency composition of domestic debt). Domestic debt did not change much during the period for which data are available (ranging from 10 to 13 percent of GDP), and its share in total debt dropped substantially over the 1994–2004 period. Following the methodology discussed in Cowan et al. (2006), the data in Figure A.5 do not include debt issued by the Development Finance Corporation, a state-owned development bank which issues a large amount of debt and is considered by the IMF to be a drain on the country's public finances (IMF, 2004a).[4]

BOLIVIA

Bolivia has had a high debt-to-GDP ratio and has benefited from debt relief initiatives. The country's external debt grew through most of the 1980s, from 53 percent of GDP to a peak of 107 percent in 1987. This increase was mostly financed through bilateral official lending, which rose from 19 percent of GDP in 1980 to 56 percent in 1987. Multilateral official lending has also become increasingly important for Bolivia, and its share increased from 18 percent of GDP in 1985 to 46 percent of GDP in 2004 (Figure A.6). Bilateral debt gradually declined beginning in 1999, with relief provided under the Heavily Indebted Poor Countries (HIPC) Initiative. This decline, however, was offset by the increase observed in both multilateral external debt and domestic debt. The latter experienced a particularly sharp rise, from 1 percent of GDP in 1994 to 23.3 percent in 2004, mostly coinciding with the marked deterioration in public finances in the period 1999–2003. More recently, Bolivia's total public debt decreased substantially, from 76.4 percent of GDP in 2004 to an estimated 50.8 percent of GDP in 2006, principally as a result of major debt relief initiatives (HIPC, Enhanced HIPC, and the Multilateral Debt Relief Initiative [MDRI]). As in several other countries with a large share of concessional debt, reported public debt overstates

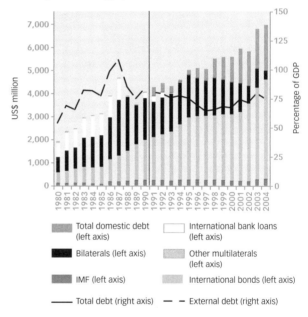

Figure A.6 Bolivia
Domestic Government Debt, External Government Debt by Creditor Type, and Total Government Debt

Total domestic debt (left axis)   International bank loans (left axis)

Bilaterals (left axis)   Other multilaterals (left axis)

IMF (left axis)   International bonds (left axis)

—— Total debt (right axis)   – – External debt (right axis)

Source: Authors' calculations based on Cowan et al. (2006).
Note: Data for domestic debt available from 1991 on.

the level of indebtedness when measured in net present value (NPV). In NPV terms, Bolivia's total public debt declined from 57.7 percent of GDP in 2004 to an estimated 32.3 percent in 2006. Most of the country's domestic debt is denominated in foreign currency, although in

---

[4] Belize is making a substantial effort to decrease its debt level. Fiscal tightening measures were adopted in 2005. One of the central pieces in Belize's debt reduction strategy is the winding down and closure of the Development Finance Corporation.

recent years local-currency-indexed debt (tied to the Unidad de Fomento de Vivienda inflation index) has been issued. Bolivia's central bank reserve position has been increasing (net
international reserves as of the end of July 2006 were approximately US$2.6 billion, or 136
percent higher than in 2004). If Bolivia's total public debt net of international reserves were
used in the calculation, it would lower the nominal debt-to-GDP ratio to an estimated 27
percent at the end of 2006.

Methodological issues. The data for multilateral and bilateral debt were obtained from
GDF and the Central Bank of Bolivia. The data for foreign bank and marketable debt were
obtained from GDF.

BRAZIL

In the early 1980s Brazil's external debt averaged 25 percent of GDP, but in 1982 it jumped to
41 percent of GDP, and it reached 49 percent of GDP in 1984. Starting in 1984, the country's
external debt-to-GDP-ratio decreased steadily until 1997 (due to a growing GDP and a constant dollar value of external debt), when total external debt reached 15 percent of GDP
(Brazil was in default between 1983 and 1994), and then started increasing again, reaching
a peak of 32 percent of GDP in 2003
(but decreasing to 25 percent of GDP
in 2004).

Until 1993, most of Brazil's external
debt was owed to international banks
(over the 1980–1993 period foreign
bank loans represented 70 percent of
total external debt). The Brady swap led
to a sudden increase in bond financing,
and bond debt now represents more
than 15 percent of GDP and about 55
percent of external debt (Figure A.7).
IMF financing became increasingly important over the 1990–2004 period and
reached 16 percent of GDP in 2004
(all of Brazil's IMF debt was repaid in
2006).

The reduction in external debt documented above was accompanied by a
net increase in domestic debt (which
went from 22 percent of GDP in 1994 to
55 percent of GDP in 2004). As a consequence, Brazil's total debt increased
substantially over the 1994–2001 pe-
riod (from about 40 percent of GDP to about 80 percent of GDP). The country's domestic
debt is mainly denominated in domestic currency (however, there were significant issuances
indexed to foreign currencies during 1999–2001). In the late 1990s there was an increase
in the proportion of the country's domestic debt indexed to foreign currency or to prices

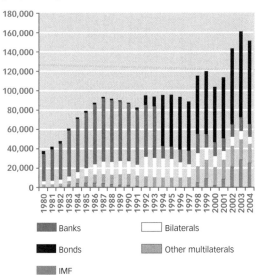

Figure A.7 Brazil
External Government Debt by Creditor Type
(US$ million)

Banks Bilaterals
Bonds Other multilaterals
IMF

Source: Authors' calculations based on Cowan et al. (2006).

(Figure A.8), but then this component of debt showed a net decrease between 2001 and 2004. A large share of Brazil's debt is floating rate debt (this is local currency debt indexed to the overnight interest rate) (Figure A.9). The amount of this debt, however, decreased in late 2005 and early 2006, reducing the vulnerability of the Brazilian debt structure (over the 2000–2006 period the share of fixed rate debt rose from 9.5 to 28 percent of total domestic debt, and the share of debt indexed to inflation increased from 6 to 20.5 percent of total domestic debt).

Methodological issues. The data for Brazil used in this report tend to differ from the data reported by official sources because Brazil focuses on net rather than gross debt. One major source of difference is the treatment of state and local governments. These governments have issued large amounts of bonded debt over the years and were bailed out several times by the central government (in 1989, 1993, and 1997). As a consequence, state and local governments now have a large debt to the federal government. In official statistics, this debt is reported as subnational debt and netted out from the federal government debt. In this report, subnational debt is included in the federal government debt and not reported as debt of the subnationals. In fact, under the definition of subnational debt used in this report, state and local government debt went from 9 percent of GDP in 1992 to 4.5 percent of GDP in 1997 and then remained below 1 percent of GDP for most of the 2000–2004 period. Official figures, in contrast, show higher and increasing (close to 20 percent of GDP in 2003) levels of net subnational debt. When one considers total debt

Figure A.8 Brazil
Structure of Government Debt
(*percentage of GDP*)

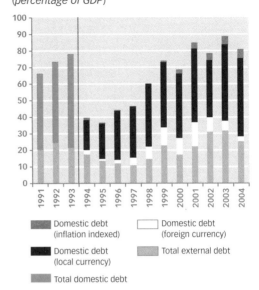

Source: Authors' calculations based on Cowan et al. (2006).
Note: Data for currency composition of domestic debt available from 1994 on.

Figure A.9 Brazil
Federal Bonded Debt Composition
(*constant million* reais)

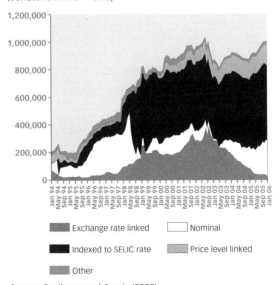

Source: Bevilaqua and Garcia (2002).
Note: SELIC = Sistema Especial de Liquidação e de Custódia (Special System for Settlement and Custody).

Figure A.10 Brazil
Gross and Net Public Debt:
CLYPS Data versus Central Bank Data
(*percentage of GDP*)

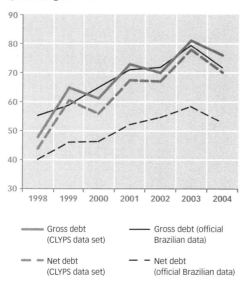

Gross debt
(CLYPS data set)

Gross debt (official
Brazilian data)

Net debt
(CLYPS data set)

Net debt
(official Brazilian data)

Source: Authors' calculations based on Cowan et al. (2006)
and Central Bank of Brazil.
Note: CLYPS = Cowan, Levy Yeyati, Panizza, and Sturzenegger (2006).

(federal plus state and local), however, the debt figures used in this report are similar to official statistics.

As Brazil focuses on net debt, the composition of the debt was available only for net debt, and hence it was necessary to assume that the composition of gross debt was the same as that of net debt.

The netting strategy used in this report differs substantially from the netting strategy used by the Brazilian authorities (for more details see Box 2.3). Figure A.10 compares the data used here with the official figures reported by Brazil's central bank. All data refer to the nonfinancial public sector (i.e., excluding the central bank). In spite of not being identical, the two data sets yield similar figures for gross public debt (in fact, in both cases the average value of the debt-to-GDP ratio over the 1998–2004 period was exactly 67 percent of GDP). However, there are large differences for the net debt figures. In particular, the netting strategy used in this report would yield much higher levels of net debt. Focusing on Net Debt 2 (see Chapter 2 for details), this report finds that the average debt-to-GDP ratio over the 1998–2004 period was 61 percent, while official figures suggest an average debt-to-GDP ratio of approximately 50 percent.

CHILE

Chile's external debt increased steadily during the early 1980s, reaching 44 percent of GDP in 1986. This increase was mainly accounted for by higher debt due to credit from multilateral institutions (which went from 1 percent of GDP in 1980 to 12 percent in 1986) and foreign bank loans (which went from 3 percent of GDP in 1980 to 22 percent in 1986) (Figure A.11).[5] The dollar value of external debt stopped increasing in the late 1980s and, thanks to economic growth, the external debt-to-GDP ratio started decreasing, reaching a minimum of 3 percent of GDP in 1998 (over the 1987–1997 period, debt owed to foreign banks declined from 18 percent of GDP to less than 1 percent of GDP, and official debt decreased from 23 percent of GDP to less than 3 percent of GDP). The dollar value of external debt increased

---

[5] In 1984 approximately 37 percent of Chile's total external debt was owed to official creditors; by 1993 this share had increased to 70 percent. Chile was in default between 1983 and 1990.

over the 2001–2004 period but, thanks to rapid GDP growth, the external debt-to-GDP ratio remained well below 10 percent. In 2004 external debt was 5 percent of GDP, with 3 percent of GDP in bonded debt and 2 percent of GDP owed to official creditors.

In 1989 domestic debt stood at 73 percent of GDP, representing 71 percent of total debt (which was 104 percent of GDP). Starting in 1990, domestic debt decreased gradually, reaching 43 percent of GDP in 2004. (As domestic debt decreased at a slower rate than external debt, however, its share in total debt rose, reaching 90 percent.)

Among countries covered in this appendix, Chile has the largest share of indexed debt; the peak of indexation was reached in 1997, when more than 80 percent of domestic public debt was indexed to prices. By 2004, 60 percent of domestic debt was indexed to prices, 14 percent was denominated in foreign currency, and the remaining 26 percent was in nominal pesos.

Chile's central bank holds a substantial amount of reserves and government paper (in some cases up to 30 percent of GDP); if these assets are netted out from the gross debt, the country's debt-to-GDP ratio drops dramatically. In 2003 gross debt was 58 percent of GDP (48 percent in 2004), but net debt stood at 28 percent of GDP (in 2004 it was 25 percent of GDP). The line in Figure A.12 shows the debt-to-GDP ratio obtained if central bank debt is not included in the total.

Methodological issues. Interpreting the Chilean data is complicated, because the central bank issues a large amount of debt (including bonds related to support of weak banks in the 1980s), but it also holds a large amount of assets (part of these assets are through the Petroleum

Figure A.11 Chile
External Government Debt by Creditor Type
(*US$ million*)

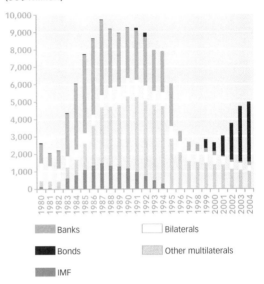

Source: Authors' calculations based on Cowan et al. (2006).

Figure A.12 Chile
Structure of Government Debt
(*percentage of GDP*)

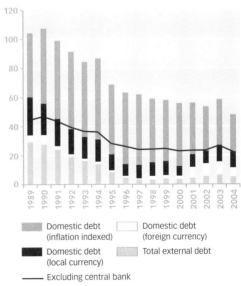

Source: Authors' calculations based on Cowan et al. (2006).

Stabilization Fund and the Copper Compensation Fund). According to the methodology described in Cowan et al. (2006), some of these assets have not been netted out of the total debt, so this methodology yields debt-to-GDP ratios which are much higher than those reported by Chilean authorities. Dropping debt issued by the central bank from the figures reported here yields data which are similar to standard Chilean debt statistics.

COLOMBIA

Colombia's external debt increased substantially during the first half of the 1980s, going from US$4.6 billion (14 percent of GDP) in 1980 to more than US$13 billion (32 percent of GDP) in 1987. The increase was financed by foreign bank loans (which went from 5 percent of GDP in 1980 to 12 percent of GDP in 1985) and lending by multilaterals (which went from less than 10 percent of GDP in 1980 to 15 percent of GDP in 1987). Over the 1990s, foreign bank loans became gradually less important, and by 2004 they represented only 8 percent of external debt, with the decrease being offset by an increase in bonded debt, which rose from less than 1 percent of external debt in 1986 to 50 percent in 2004 (Figure A.13). The swap of foreign loans for bonds was not as dramatic as in other Latin American countries, because Colombia did not default on its loans and therefore did not participate in the Brady exchange. Thanks to economic growth, external debt as a percentage of GDP started decreasing in 1990 (the dollar value remained more or less constant until 1995), reaching a minimum of 15 percent in 1997. The subsequent increase (which brought external debt back to 27 percent of GDP) was financed mostly by issuing foreign bonds (which went from 4 percent of GDP in 1997 to 13 percent of GDP in 2004).

Figure A.13 Colombia
External Government Debt by Creditor Type
(US$ million)

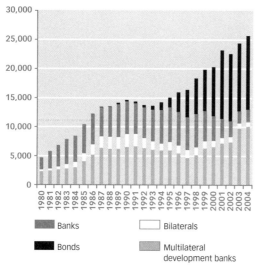

Source: Authors' calculations based on Cowan et al. (2006).

While Colombia's external debt-to-GDP ratio stabilized after 2001, domestic debt kept growing over the 1995–2004 period (going from 11 percent of GDP in 1995 to more than 30 percent of GDP in 2004). Colombia substantially increased the share of its domestic debt issued in foreign currency over the 1995–2002 period, from 14 percent to 29 percent of total domestic debt. This trend has reversed, however, since 2003. Hence, while domestic debt was substituted for foreign debt, the currency denomination of the country's debt did not vary substantially over the period under observation, and the share of foreign currency debt remained more or less constant, hovering at around 60 percent of total debt (Figure A.14).

Colombia's central bank holds substantial reserves; if these reserves are netted out from total debt, the country's debt-to-GDP ratio drops by almost 15 percentage points.[6] Furthermore, regional governments in Colombia also hold a substantial amount of central government debt. Netting out these holdings would further reduce the Colombian debt-to-GDP ratio.

COSTA RICA

Costa Rica's external debt increased dramatically in the early 1980s, going from US$1.5 billion (37 percent of GDP) in 1980 to more than US$2.6 billion (100 percent of GDP) in 1982, with the increase triggered by both an increase in the dollar value of debt (Figure A.15) and an economic crisis and real devaluation which reduced the dollar value of GDP by almost 50 percent. External debt started decreasing in the late 1980s (Costa Rica was in default between 1983 and 1990) and stabilized at about 20 percent of GDP in the late 1990s (Figure A.16). Multilateral and bilateral debt decreased gradually (the former went from 24 percent of GDP in 1983 to 8 percent of GDP in 2004, while the latter decreased from about 20 percent of GDP to 2 percent of GDP), and nonofficial debt decreased drastically at the time of the Brady exchange. The Brady swap led to a decline in foreign bank loans from about 10 percent of GDP in 1990 to less than 1 percent of GDP in 1991 and an increase in foreign bonds from less than 1 percent of GDP to 8 percent of GDP. From 1991, debt issued to bilateral lenders was reduced

---

[6] Some of these reserves are not owned by the central bank but are reserves held to back dollar deposits in the banking system.

Figure A.14 Colombia
Structure of Government Debt
(*percentage of GDP*)

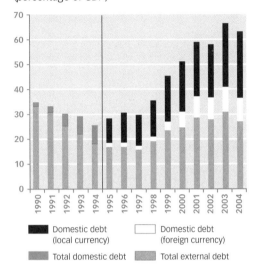

Source: Authors' calculations based on Cowan et al. (2006).
Note: Data for currency composition of domestic debt available from 1995 on.

Figure A.15 Costa Rica
External Government Debt by Creditor Type
(*US$ million*)

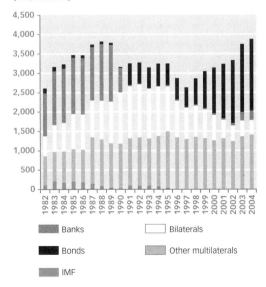

Source: Authors' calculations based on Cowan et al. (2006).

Figure A.16 Costa Rica
Structure of Government Debt
(*percentage of GDP*)

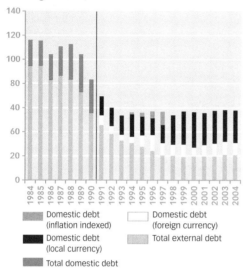

Domestic debt
(inflation indexed)

Domestic debt
(foreign currency)

Domestic debt
(local currency)

Total external debt

Total domestic debt

Source: Authors' calculations based on Cowan et al. (2006).
Note: Data for currency composition of domestic debt available from 1991 on.

Figure A.17 Dominican Republic
Domestic Government Debt, External Government Debt by Creditor Type, and Total Government Debt

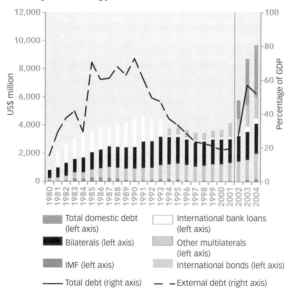

Total domestic debt
(left axis)

International bank loans
(left axis)

Bilaterals (left axis)

Other multilaterals
(left axis)

IMF (left axis)

International bonds (left axis)

——— Total debt (right axis)

— — External debt (right axis)

Source: Authors' calculations based on Cowan et al. (2006).
Note: Data for domestic debt available from 2002 on.

significantly and was offset by a further increase in bonded debt.

The counterpart to the decrease in external debt documented above was a steady increase in domestic debt, which went from 25 percent of GDP in 1984 to 38 percent of GDP in 2004. While domestic debt in Costa Rica has traditionally been denominated in domestic currency, the share of foreign-currency-denominated domestic debt has been increasing since the mid-1990s and in 2004 was close to 30 percent of total domestic debt. Costa Rica's central bank holds large reserves, and if these reserves are netted out, the debt-to-GDP ratio drops by approximately 10 percentage points.

Methodological issues. The data were constructed using information provided by Costa Rica's central bank. Although state-owned institutions hold a significant part of the country's domestic debt, these cross-holdings were not subtracted from gross debt in the computation of net debt.

DOMINICAN REPUBLIC

External debt in the Dominican Republic grew rapidly during the first half of the 1980s, going from 15 percent of GDP in 1980 to 70 percent of GDP in 1985 (Figure A.17).[7] The sudden reduction in the country's external debt in 1984 and the large jump the following year are explained by a large real appreciation (which increased the dollar value of GDP by 50 percent) and a subsequent large

---

[7] Reliable historical series for domestic debt are not available.

real depreciation (which decreased the dollar value of GDP by 60 percent). The country's external debt started decreasing in the early 1990s, reaching a minimum of 18 percent of GDP in 2000 (the Dominican Republic was in default from 1982 to 1994).

After the Brady swap implemented in 1993 (which led to a reduction of foreign bank debt from 13 percent of GDP in 1993 to 1 percent in 1994 and an increase in bonded debt from 0 to 5 percent of GDP for the same period) and until 2001, most of the Dominican Republic's external debt was owed to official creditors (with bilateral creditors being the largest group). A banking crisis in the country in 2003 was soon followed by an explosion of both external and domestic debt.

ECUADOR

At the beginning of the 1990s Ecuador was characterized by extremely high levels of public debt (117 percent of GDP in 1990) (Figure A.18). Over the 1990–1997 period, external debt displayed a decreasing path, reaching a minimum of 59 percent of GDP in 1997 (Ecuador was in default between 1992 and 1995). The country's debt increased slightly in 1998 and, after a large real devaluation, jumped back to 100 percent of GDP in 1999. Thanks to a debt restructuring and favorable macroeconomic conditions, Ecuador's debt decreased substantially over the 1999–2004 period, reaching 49 percent of GDP in 2004.

Ecuador's debt is mainly external (even though domestic debt increased from 3 percent of GDP in 1990 to 11 percent of GDP in 2004), with significant official debt (in 2004 bilateral and multilateral debt represented more than one-third of total debt and almost 50 percent of external debt). In the early 1990s most of Ecuador's nonofficial external debt was with foreign banks, and after the Brady swap, which took place in 1995, this form of financing almost completely disappeared.

Methodological issues. The currency composition of Ecuador's domestic debt is not available. However, anecdotal evidence suggests that this debt has been traditionally denominated in foreign currency. In 2000, Ecuador adopted the U.S. dollar as its official currency and, since then, all of its domestic debt has been denominated in U.S. dollars.

Figure A.18 Ecuador
Domestic Government Debt, External Government Debt by Creditor Type, and Total Government Debt

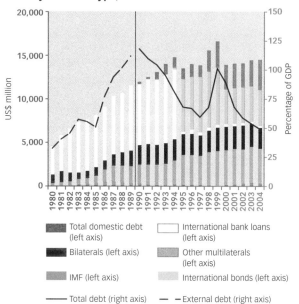

Total domestic debt (left axis)

International bank loans (left axis)

Bilaterals (left axis)

Other multilaterals (left axis)

IMF (left axis)

International bonds (left axis)

—— Total debt (right axis)   – – External debt (right axis)

Source: Authors' calculations based on Cowan et al. (2006).
Note: Data for domestic debt available from 1990 on.

Figure A.19 El Salvador
Domestic Government Debt, External Government
Debt by Creditor Type, and Total Government Debt

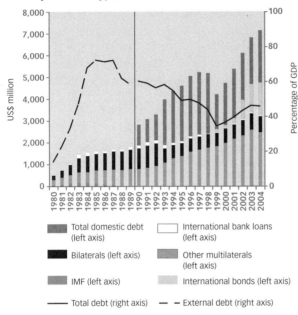

Total domestic debt (left axis)

Bilaterals (left axis)

IMF (left axis)

International bank loans (left axis)

Other multilaterals (left axis)

International bonds (left axis)

—— Total debt (right axis)   — — External debt (right axis)

Source: Authors' calculations based on Cowan et al. (2006).
Note: Data for domestic debt available from 1990 on.

EL SALVADOR

El Salvador's external debt rose sharply during the first half of the 1980s (this was the worst period of the country's civil war, and public debt went from 14 percent of GDP in 1980 to 71 percent of GDP in 1986), with an increase in its multilateral, IMF, and bilateral components (until recently almost all of El Salvador's external debt was with official creditors). In 1987 the country's external debt-to-GDP ratio started decreasing, falling from 72 percent of GDP in that year to 20 percent of GDP in 1998 (over the 1987–1998 period, El Salvador's multilateral debt decreased from 31 percent to 15 percent of GDP, and its bilateral debt decreased from 35 percent to 5 percent of GDP). This decrease was due to GDP growth in the presence of a constant dollar value of external debt (Figure A.19). El Salvador's external debt started increasing again in the late 1990s and reached 21 percent of GDP in 2004 (this increase was mainly financed through the issuance of foreign bonds, which went from 5 percent of external debt in 1999 to 32 percent of external debt in 2004); the main reason for this increase in debt was reconstruction following a major earthquake that hit the country in 2001. Domestic debt was around 20 percent of GDP in 1990, and it escalated to between 23 and 30 percent of GDP over the 1993–1998 period. In fact, during this period, the increase in the country's external debt was partly compensated for by higher levels of domestic debt. As a consequence, El Salvador's total debt decreased at a much slower pace (going from 60 percent of GDP in 1990 to 44 percent of GDP in 1998). Over the 1998–2004 period, the country's domestic debt did not change much, oscillating between 13 and 16 percent of GDP.

El Salvador's central bank holds large international reserves (up to 16 percent of GDP in 1999), and netting these reserves from total debt substantially reduces the country's debt-to-GDP ratio. In 2004, the country's gross debt was 45 percent of GDP, but its net debt was close to 33 percent of GDP.

GUATEMALA

Guatemala's total debt increased substantially over the 1980s, going from 19 percent of GDP in 1980 to 49 percent of GDP in 1987 (Figure A.20). In the first half of the 1980s, the increase in the country's debt was financed by issuing both domestic and external debt, but from 1985 on, debt issued to foreign creditors gradually became more important. Guatemala's debt started declining at the beginning of the 1990s, reaching 17 percent of GDP in 1998. Over the 1990s most of Guatemala's external debt was held by official creditors (both bilateral and multilateral lenders), but since then bonds have become increasingly important, and by 2004 they had become the country's second-largest source of external financing. Domestic debt, which was around 9 percent of GDP in 1980, increased during the first half of the 1980s, to 22 percent of GDP in 1984, but declined subsequently, reaching 6 percent of GDP in 2004 (domestic debt dropped from 50 percent of total debt in the 1980s to about 30 percent in 2004).

Since 1995, Guatemala's central bank has been accumulating large reserves, and the difference between its gross and net debt (which was negligible in the mid-1990s) is now substantial (in 2004, the country's gross debt was 21 percent of GDP, and its net debt was 7 percent of GDP).

Methodological issues. As GDF data differ substantially from the data provided by the Guatemalan

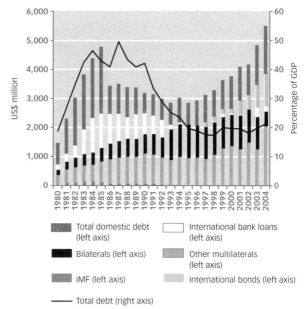

Figure A.20 Guatemala
Domestic Government Debt, External Government Debt by Creditor Type, and Total Government Debt

Total domestic debt (left axis)
International bank loans (left axis)
Bilaterals (left axis)
Other multilaterals (left axis)
IMF (left axis)
International bonds (left axis)
Total debt (right axis)

Source: Authors' calculations based on Cowan et al. (2006).

authorities (with the former source reporting much higher debt levels, the average difference over the 1990–2003 period was 2.5 percent of GDP), the following procedure was used to calculate the debt levels used in this report.[8] Total external debt reported by the central bank was used to compute the total debt of the central bank, the central government, and the rest of the public sector. Next, the debt was broken down into various subgroups using information from IMF reports, Bloomberg (for bonded debt), and GDF (for multilateral and bilateral debt). One source of discrepancy is that some bonds are guaranteed by the World Bank and hence are classified as multilateral debt by GDF. For the classification of this

---

[8] This difference may be due to the fact that the GDF statistics include debt of the Corporación Financiera Nacional (CORFINA), which is not included in official government statistics.

Figure A.21 Guyana
Domestic Government Debt, External Debt,
External Government Debt by Creditor Type, and
Total Government Debt

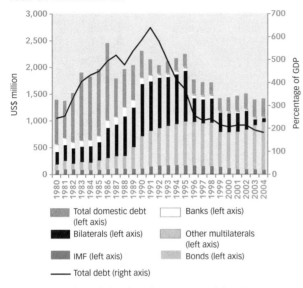

Source: Authors' calculations based on Cowan et al. (2006).

Figure A.22 Haiti
Domestic Government Debt, External Debt, External
Government Debt by Creditor Type, and Total Government
Debt

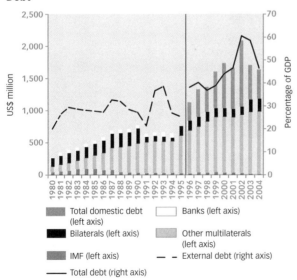

Source: Authors' calculations based on Cowan et al. (2006).
Note: Data for currency composition of domestic debt available from
1996 on.

report, these bonds were subtracted from the multilateral debt.
Data on the amount of foreign
bank loans were obtained as a
residual entity.

GUYANA

Guyana is characterized by high
levels of debt, both domestic and
external, and it is part of the HIPC
initiative. Its total public debt decreased dramatically in the first
half of the 1990s and then decreased again after 1998 thanks
to the debt relief provided by
the initiative. While the data reported here end in 2004, more
recent data would show a further
decline in debt due to additional
debt relief brought about within
the framework of the MDRI. It is
also worth mentioning that, as
a large share of Guyana's debt
is concessional and as the data
in Figure A.21 focus on nominal
figures, they greatly overstate the
net present value of the country's
debt ratio.

HAITI

Haiti has high levels of debt, both
domestic and external, and is part
of the HIPC initiative even though
it has yet to qualify for debt relief. As a large share of Haiti's
debt is extended with concessional terms, the data in Figure
A.22 overstate the actual level of
debt, which is much lower when
measured in net present value.
Haiti has not reached the HIPC
decision point and hence has not
received debt relief as yet. Debt

relief under the HIPC initiative and MDRI is likely to substantially reduce the country's external public debt.

HONDURAS

Honduras is part of the HIPC initiative, and its main source of external financing is official creditors. Over the period under study, the country's official debt averaged more than 90 percent of total debt and, since 1995, official creditors have financed virtually all of Honduras's external debt (Figure A.23). Throughout the 1980s, external debt in Honduras grew steadily (going from US$1 billion in 1980 to US$2.6 billion in 1989) but remained below 60 percent of GDP. In 1990 an increase in the dollar value of debt (which rose to approximately US$3 million), together with a large devaluation which halved the dollar value of GDP, brought external debt to about 100 percent of GDP. The country's external debt-to-GDP ratio continued to increase in the next few years, reaching 120 percent of GDP in 1994. The external debt-to-GDP ratio started decreasing in the mid-1990s and stabilized at about 70 percent of GDP in the 2000–2004 period. The country's debt ratios are expected to decrease further thanks to debt relief provided through the MDRI.

Honduras's total debt has followed a pattern similar to that of external debt (Figure A.24). Its domestic debt increased from 13 percent of GDP in 1980 to 27 percent in 1989. It then decreased over the 1990–1995 period (reaching a minimum of 9 percent of GDP) and subsequently increased again (partly substituting for external debt), reaching 17 percent of GDP in 2004. Most of Honduras's domestic debt is denominated in domestic currency, but there have been some foreign currency issuances in the last few years. In the late 1990s, Honduras's central bank started accumulating larger

Figure A.23 Honduras
External Government Debt by Creditor Type
(*US$ million*)

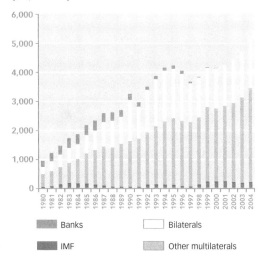

- Banks
- IMF
- Bilaterals
- Other multilaterals

Source: Authors' calculations based on Cowan et al. (2006).

Figure A.24 Honduras
Structure of Government Debt
(*percentage of GDP*)

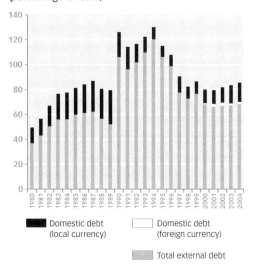

- Domestic debt (local currency)
- Domestic debt (foreign currency)
- Total external debt

Source: Authors' calculations based on Cowan et al. (2006).

Figure A.25 Jamaica
External Government Debt by Creditor Type
(*US$ million*)

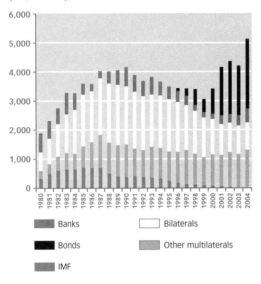

■ Banks	□ Bilaterals
■ Bonds	▦ Other multilaterals
▨ IMF	

Source: Authors' calculations based on Cowan et al. (2006).

Figure A.26 Jamaica
Structure of Government Debt
(*percentage of GDP*)

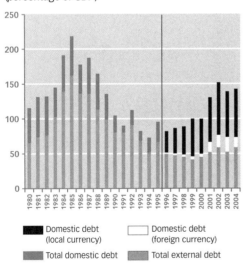

■ Domestic debt (local currency)	□ Domestic debt (foreign currency)
▨ Total domestic debt	▦ Total external debt

Source: Authors' calculations based on Cowan et al. (2006).
Note: Data for currency composition of domestic debt available from 1996 on.

reserves, and by 2004, those reserves had reached 25 percent of GDP. As a consequence, Honduras's net debt (which until recently was almost identical to its gross debt) is substantially smaller than its gross debt (in 2004, they were 60 and 85 percent of GDP, respectively).

JAMAICA

Total external debt in Jamaica increased substantially over the course of the 1980s, going from US$1.8 billion (66 percent of GDP) in 1980 to about US$4 billion (more than 150 percent of GDP) in the late 1980s (Figure A.25). This increase was mostly financed by official lenders, with bilateral creditors playing a major role; over this period, the country's bilateral debt rose from 22 percent of GDP to 80 percent, its multilateral debt increased from 10 percent of GDP to 34 percent, and its IMF debt went from 11 percent of GDP to 31 percent. The dollar value of Jamaica's external debt decreased steadily over the 1990–1999 period and this, together with GDP growth, substantially reduced the country's external debt-to-GDP ratio. However, Jamaica's external debt started increasing again over the 2000–2004 period, with an increasing share of bonded debt (going from 6 percent of GDP in 1999 to 27 percent of GDP in 2004) and a smaller share of official debt (from 33 percent of GDP in 1999 to 26 percent of GDP in 2004).

During the 1980s, Jamaica's debt-to-GDP ratio was above 100 percent, reaching a peak of 218 percent in 1985 (Figure A.26). It then decreased over 1986–1994, reaching a minimum of 72 percent of GDP in 1994, and subsequently increased again over the 1994–2004 period, returning to figures over 100 percent of GDP after 2001 (by 2004, the country's total debt was about 140 percent of GDP).

During the early part of the 1980s, Jamaica's domestic debt remained at about 50 percent of GDP, but then it started decreasing along with external debt, reaching 10 percent of GDP in 1991. Starting in the mid-1990s, Jamaica's domestic debt increased steadily, and by the late 1990s, it had become larger than the country's external debt (in 2004, domestic debt was 84 percent of GDP and 59 percent of total debt).[9] Domestic debt in Jamaica is mainly issued in domestic currency, but the share of foreign currency debt has increased over the last few years (reaching 24 percent of domestic debt in 2003).

Jamaica's central bank holds large international reserves, and once these reserves are netted out, the country's debt-to-GDP ratio drops substantially.

MEXICO

Mexico's total external debt increased substantially after the country's debt and currency crisis in 1982 (Figure A.27). Its dollar value increased by more than 40 percent (from US$58 billion to more than US$80 billion) over the 1982–1987 period and almost doubled in terms of GDP (going from 34 to more than 50 percent of GDP). The dollar value of the country's external debt stabilized in 1987, and the external debt-to-GDP ratio started decreasing and fell below 20 percent of GDP in 1993 (Mexico was in default between 1982 and 1990; it exited default with the Brady swap, which led to a reduction of its bank debt and an increase in its bonded debt). The currency crisis that hit the country at the end of 1994 led to another sudden jump both in the dollar value of debt and in the external debt-to-GDP ratio (this time, the ratio doubled in one year, reaching 41 percent at the end of 1995). The IMF and other multilateral and bilateral lenders provided substantial financing at this point (by 1995, official creditors held more than one-third of Mexico's external debt). The country's external debt then decreased over the 1996–2001 period and subsequently stabilized at around 10 percent of GDP, with a much smaller component owed to official creditors.

Mexico's domestic debt increased in the 1980s, but over the 1990–1994 period, its domestic debt dropped both in absolute terms and as a share of total debt; after 1995, however, the country's domestic debt started increasing in both absolute and relative terms, reaching about 62 percent of total debt in 2004 (Figure A.28). In fact,

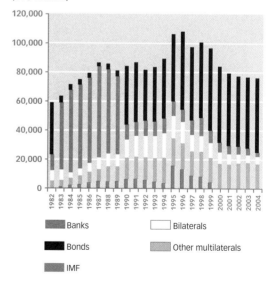

Figure A.27 Mexico
External Government Debt by Creditor Type
(US$ million)

Banks   Bilaterals
Bonds   Other multilaterals
IMF

Source: Authors' calculations based on Cowan et al. (2006).

---

[9] A financial sector crisis was one of the main drivers of this increase in debt.

Figure A.28 Mexico
Structure of Government Debt
(*percentage of GDP*)

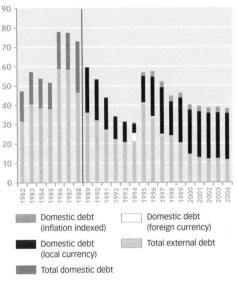

Domestic debt (inflation indexed)

Domestic debt (foreign currency)

Domestic debt (local currency)

Total external debt

Total domestic debt

Source: Authors' calculations based on Cowan et al. (2006).
Note: Data for currency composition of domestic debt available from 1989 on.

Figure A.29 Mexico
Composition of Central Government Bonded Debt
(*percentage*)

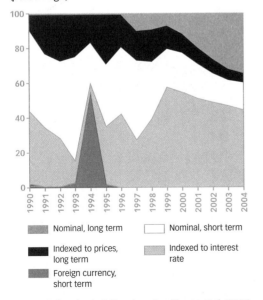

Nominal, long term

Nominal, short term

Indexed to prices, long term

Indexed to interest rate

Foreign currency, short term

Source: Authors' calculations based on Cowan et al. (2006).

the large drop in external debt in the first half of the 1990s was partly compensated for by larger issuances of domestic debt. Traditionally, domestic debt in Mexico has been denominated in domestic currency, with the exception of 1994, when the Mexican government issued a large amount of foreign currency short-term domestic debt (the (in)famous Tesobonos). Although most of the country's debt is denominated in domestic currency, the share of that debt attributable to long-term nominal debt was basically nil until the late 1990s (Figure A.29). In 2004 more than one-third of domestic bonds issued by the central government were indexed to the interest rate, and another third were either short term or indexed to prices.

It is worth noting that the Mexican central bank holds large levels of international reserves, and if these reserves are subtracted from gross debt, the 2004 debt-to-GDP ratio drops from 38 percent to 29 percent of GDP.

Methodological issues. The Mexican authorities track two types of debt: "traditional" debt and "augmented" debt. Traditional debt, according to the authorities' definition, includes only debt issued by the federal government. Augmented debt includes the debt of the agency that rescued the banking system after the Tequila crisis (FOBAPROA), which later became a deposit guarantee agency (IPAB), the debt of a trust fund created to rescue toll roads (FARAC), publicly guaranteed debt issued by private companies that are developing public infrastructure projects (PIDIRIEGAS), and debt issued by national development banks. This report uses an intermediate definition that includes the debt of FOBAPROA/IPAB and FARAC but not of PIDIRIEGAS and national development banks (for details on how these different definitions of debt compare, see Cowan et al., 2006).

NICARAGUA

Nicaragua has a high debt ratio and is part of the HIPC initiative. In 1980 Nicaragua's external debt was about US$2 billion (about 130 percent of GDP). It grew steadily over the 1980s, reaching US$8 billion in 1988 (corresponding to 800 percent of GDP) and more than US$9 billion in 1989 (1,025 percent of GDP) (Figure A.30). External debt remained above 500 percent for the next four years. In 1994, Nicaragua's external debt-to-GDP ratio started decreasing, reaching 120 percent of GDP in 2004.

During the early 1990s Nicaragua had some debt with foreign banks, but since 1995 the totality of Nicaragua's external debt has been issued by official creditors (with bilateral debt playing an extremely important role). Domestic public debt was basically nonexistent in the country until 1991, but thereafter it grew from 5.7 percent of GDP (1 percent of total debt) to 54 percent of GDP (30 percent of total debt) in 2004. All of Nicaragua's domestic debt is in domestic currency. Two important components of the country's domestic debt are the long-term bonds that were issued to compensate for the confiscations and expropriations that took place in the 1980s and central bank instruments issued for monetary purposes. The country's debt is expected to decrease further, thanks to debt relief provided through the MDRI.

Figure A.30 Nicaragua
Domestic Government Debt, External Government Debt by Creditor Type, and Total Government Debt

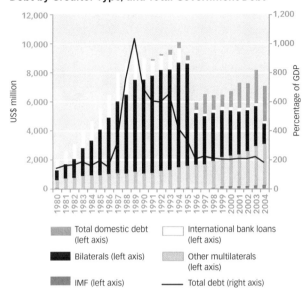

Source: Authors' calculations based on Cowan et al. (2006).

PANAMA

Over the 1990s the dollar value of Panama's external debt remained more or less constant (Figure A.31), and its external debt-to-GDP ratio dropped from 120 percent of GDP (in 1990) to around 70 percent of GDP (in 1995), then remained more or less stable, oscillating between 64 and 72 percent of GDP.[10] Most of the reduction in the external debt-to-GDP ratio was due to GDP growth and a drop in official debt (both its bilateral and multilateral components). The Brady exchange led to a reduction in external debt and a switch from bank loans to bonded debt (which went from 5 percent of GDP in 1995 to 38 percent in 1996). Domestic

---

[10] Panama was in default between 1983 and 1996. Data for Panama start in 1990 because for earlier periods, the figures provided by the ministry of finance differ substantially from the data provided by GDF, and it is impossible to reconcile the two sources.

Figure A.31 Panama
Domestic Government Debt, External Government Debt by Creditor Type, and Total Government Debt

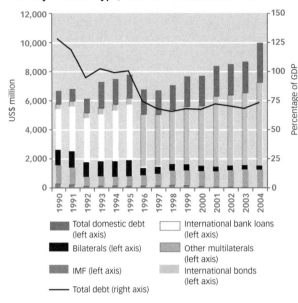

Total domestic debt (left axis)

Bilaterals (left axis)

IMF (left axis)

International bank loans (left axis)

Other multilaterals (left axis)

International bonds (left axis)

Total debt (right axis)

Source: Authors' calculations based on Cowan et al. (2006).

Figure A.32 Paraguay
Domestic Government Debt, External Government Debt by Creditor Type, and Total Government Debt

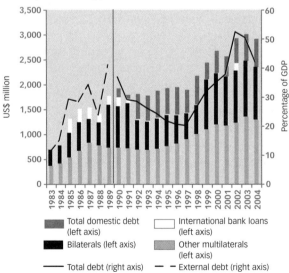

Total domestic debt (left axis)

Bilaterals (left axis)

International bank loans (left axis)

Other multilaterals (left axis)

Total debt (right axis)

External debt (right axis)

Source: Authors' calculations based on Cowan et al. (2006).
Note: Data for domestic debt available from 1990 on.

debt remained constant at about 20 percent of GDP. Hence, its relative importance grew with the decline of external debt. In particular, the share of domestic debt in total debt went from 14 percent in 1990 to 28 percent in 2004.

The National Bank of Panama (Banco Nacional de Panamá) holds a substantial amount of reserves and government bonds; when these assets are netted from total debt, the debt-to-GDP ratio drops by more than 10 percentage points (up to 20 percentage points in certain years).

The official currency of Panama is the U.S. dollar, and hence the differentiation between domestic and foreign currency debt is meaningless.

PARAGUAY

Over the 1980s Paraguay's external debt increased from 15 to 41 percent of GDP (Figure A.32). After 1989, the dollar value of the country's external debt started decreasing, and the external debt-to-GDP ratio reached a low of 14 percent in 1996. In 1997, Paraguay's external debt started increasing again, reaching 34 percent of GDP in 2004 (Paraguay was in default between 1986 and 1992).

Paraguay's external debt is almost completely held by official creditors (there was some borrowing from foreign banks in the late 1980s) and evenly distributed between multilateral and bilateral creditors. Domestic financing became progressively more important starting in the 1990s, increasing from 3 percent of GDP (10 percent of total debt) in 1990 to 8 percent of GDP (20 percent of total debt) in 2004.

Paraguay's central bank holds large international reserves. In 2004 these reserves were about 16 percent of GDP, yielding a net debt of 26 percent of GDP (versus a gross debt of 42 percent of GDP).

PERU

Peru's external debt increased from about US$5 billion (30 percent of GDP) in 1980 to about US$20 billion (more than 70 percent of GDP) in the early 1990s (Figure A.33). The two major creditors were bilateral lenders and foreign banks, followed by multilateral banks and the IMF. Between 1993 and 1996, the dollar value of Peru's external debt was still increasing, but not as fast as the dollar value of GDP, leading to a reduction in the external debt-to-GDP ratio from 66 percent to 47 percent (Figure A.34). This ratio then dropped to 33 percent after the Brady swap (implemented in March 1997). Over the late 1990s, the dollar value of the country's external debt remained more or less constant, but it started increasing again in the 2003–2004 period. However, the external debt-to-GDP ratio did not change much and, starting in 1997, oscillated between 33 and 39 percent without any clear trend.[11] Over the 1997–2004 period the composition of the country's debt did not vary significantly, with official debt financing around 75 percent of external debt and bonds the remaining 25 percent. In 2005 Peru's external debt stock decreased by more than US$2 billion, mainly as a result of the prepayment of debt operations with Paris Club and suppliers. In both cases, the payment operations were financed with issues of domestic and external sovereign bonds, which allowed a change in the country's debt structure, reducing external debt and increasing domestic debt from 21 percent of total public debt in 2004 to 25 percent in 2005.

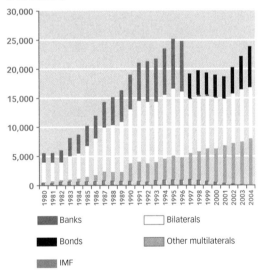

Figure A.33 Peru
External Government Debt by Creditor Type
(*US$ million*)

Banks · Bilaterals
Bonds · Other multilaterals
IMF

Source: Authors' calculations based on Cowan et al. (2006).

---

[11] Over the 1976–1984 period, Peru defaulted several times; it exited from default in 1997.

Figure A.34 Peru
Structure of Government Debt
(*percentage of GDP*)

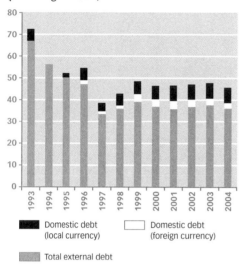

- ■ Domestic debt (local currency)
- □ Domestic debt (foreign currency)
- ▨ Total external debt

Source: Authors' calculations based on Cowan et al. (2006).

Domestic debt was low in the early 1990s but grew in the second half of the decade, stabilizing at about 16 percent of GDP and 25 percent of total debt.[12] About one-quarter of Peru's existing domestic debt was issued in foreign currency, and the remaining 75 percent in domestic currency.

Peru's central bank has accumulated large reserves (up to 20 percent of GDP), yielding a substantial difference between gross and net debt. In 2004, the country's gross debt was 46 percent of GDP and its net debt 28 percent of GDP.

SURINAME

Until the beginning of the 1980s, Suriname's public debt was extremely low, but it grew—reflecting large deficits—from about 30 percent of GDP in 1983 to more than 100 percent of GDP in the early 1990s.[13] Most of this debt was domestic, with the bulk held by the central bank. This high level of central bank financing translates into money creation and high inflation. Suriname's public debt started decreasing in the early 1990s, reaching a minimum of 28 percent of GDP in 1997 (20 percent of GDP owed to external creditors and 8 percent owed to domestic creditors). However, the country's public debt started increasing again in the late 1990s, reaching about 75 percent of GDP in 2000.[14] A fiscal adjustment reversed this trend, and by 2004 Suriname's total public debt stood at about 47 percent of GDP (of which 33 percent of GDP was owed to external creditors).

TRINIDAD AND TOBAGO

In 1980 Trinidad and Tobago was characterized by low levels of debt (about US$100 million), but over the subsequent decade, the country's external debt increased rapidly, reaching US$1.8 billion by 1989 (Figure A.35). In terms of GDP, total public debt increased from 6 percent of GDP in 1980 to almost 60 percent in 1990 and reached a peak of 67 percent in 1993 (Trinidad and Tobago was in default between 1988 and 1989). The main drivers of this increase in debt were a devaluation and an economic crisis which led to a 35 percent reduction in the dollar value of GDP. Starting in 1993, the country's total debt began to decrease

---

[12] There are no official figures for domestic debt in Peru in the early 1990s. All figures have been estimated using old IMF reports and hence are subject to a large margin of error.

[13] As Suriname is not included in the CLYPS data set, this section is based on IMF Article IV reports.

[14] IMF (2002d), Table 2, page 29, and IMF (2003c), Table 1, page 21.

gradually, reaching 25 percent of GDP in 2004.

Trinidad and Tobago's increase in debt over the 1984–1993 period was financed by issuing both domestic and external debt (unlike other countries in the region, Trinidad and Tobago did not make exclusive use of foreign bank loans, as it was already issuing a large amount of international bonds in the 1980s), with official debt growing rapidly over the 1986–1995 period. The decrease in the country's total debt after 1993 was instead due to the behavior of external debt, which decreased from 44 percent of GDP in 1993 to 12 percent of GDP in 2004 (the largest decrease was in official debt, especially bilateral debt, and foreign bank loans). Domestic debt also decreased (going from 20 percent of GDP in 1993 to 13 percent of GDP in 2004), but at a much slower pace.

Figure A.35 Trinidad and Tobago
Domestic Government Debt, External Government Debt by Creditor Type, and Total Government Debt

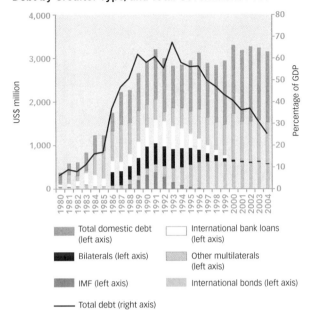

Source: Authors' calculations based on Cowan et al. (2006).

Since the mid-1990s, Trinidad and Tobago's central bank has accumulated substantial reserves which, in 2004, were larger than the country's total gross debt (yielding a negative net debt).

Methodological issues. Assembling data for Trinidad and Tobago was a difficult task, because central bank statistics do not include information on the composition of external debt. Hence, the data were obtained by mixing information from IMF reports, GDF, and the central bank. GDF was the main source of data for the 1980–1993 period. As GDF data did not match well with data from other sources, pre-1993 data should be viewed with caution. Domestic debt data were obtained from central bank statistics, and it is worth noting that these data do not always match the figures presented in IMF reports.

URUGUAY

Uruguay's external debt stood at about US$650 million in 1980 (about 9 percent of GDP) and jumped to more than US$2 billion in 1983 (almost 50 percent of GDP). The increase in the external debt-to-GDP ratio was triggered both by an increase in the dollar value of debt (Figure A.36) and also by an economic crisis and a real devaluation which reduced the dollar value of GDP by more than 50 percent over the 1981–1985 period. During this period, Uruguay's main creditors were international banks, followed by multilateral banks and the IMF. Be-

Figure A.36 Uruguay
External Government Debt by Creditor Type
(*US$ million*)

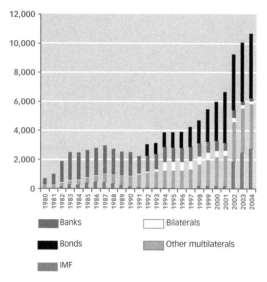

Banks

Bonds

IMF

Bilaterals

Other multilaterals

Source: Authors' calculations based on Cowan et al. (2006).

Figure A.37 Uruguay
Structure of Government Debt
(*percentage of GDP*)

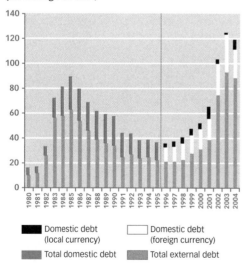

Domestic debt
(local currency)

Total domestic debt

Domestic debt
(foreign currency)

Total external debt

Source: Authors' calculations based on Cowan et al. (2006).
Note: Data for currency composition of domestic debt available from 1996 on.

tween 1985 and 1991, the dollar value of the country's external debt did not change substantially, and economic growth led to a gradual decrease in the external debt-to-GDP ratio, which reached 21 percent of GDP in 1991 (in 1992, Uruguay swapped its bank debt for bonds, whose share of GDP then went from 0 to 6 percent). Over the 1992–2001 period, Uruguay's external debt increased gradually, rising from about US$3 billion to US$6.5 billion.

The Argentine crisis of 2001–2002 had substantial spillovers in Uruguay, which faced both an increase in the dollar value of its external debt (which reached US$9 billion in 2002) and also a large real devaluation, which led to a sudden jump in the external debt-to-GDP ratio (to 71 percent in 2002 and then to 91 percent in 2003) (Figure A.37). The IMF and multilateral banks played an important role in financing this increase in debt (Uruguay's IMF borrowing went from 1 percent of GDP in 2001 to 15 percent of GDP in 2002; debt held by multilateral lenders went from 11 percent of GDP to 22 percent of GDP over the same period). The ratio of bonded debt to GDP also increased substantially (going from 19 percent in 2001 to 31 percent in 2002).[15]

The country's domestic debt increased substantially during the first half of the 1980s, increasing from 6 percent of GDP in 1980 to 27 percent of GDP in 1985, and remained stable throughout the rest of the decade, averaging 24 percent of GDP. It then decreased in the first half of the 1990s

---

[15] The increase in this component of debt was mostly due to a denominator effect and not to new issuances.

(reaching a low of 16 percent of GDP in 1997). After 1997, Uruguay's domestic debt started increasing again, along with the country's total debt. This increase was at first gradual, but then both domestic and external debt soared suddenly beginning in 2002, reaching 30 percent of GDP in 2004 and pushing total debt to well above 100 percent of GDP (the debt-to-GDP ratio was 65 percent in 2001 and was close to 120 percent of GDP in 2004). This increase in the debt-to-GDP ratio was due to both an increase in the dollar value of total debt and a decrease in the dollar value of GDP brought about by a large currency depreciation.

In Uruguay, domestic debt has traditionally been denominated in foreign currency, with the share of domestic-currency-denominated debt oscillating between 5 and 30 percent. The sudden increase in debt documented above was accompanied by central bank accumulation of international reserves and holdings of government paper. By the end of 2004, these assets of Uruguay's central bank were in excess of 30 percent of GDP, yielding a large difference between the country's net and gross debt (in 2004, the latter was 88 percent of GDP).

Methodological issues. As Uruguay's official figures classify external debt as debt held by nonresidents and not as debt issued in foreign jurisdictions, it was necessary to reclassify some of the figures provided by the Uruguayan authorities. This reclassification was conducted using central bank, GDF, and Bloomberg data.

VENEZUELA

Venezuela's external debt increased during the 1980s, from about US$10 billion in 1980 (15 percent of GDP) to almost US$24 billion (59 percent of GDP) in 1989 (with large jumps in 1984 and 1986) (Figure A.38). Until 1989, about 80 percent of Venezuela's external debt was owed to foreign banks (these loans were in default over the 1983–1990 period), but in 1990 the country's bank loans were swapped for bonded debt and official debt (IMF and multilateral debt reached 10 percent of GDP). Over the 1990–1994 period, the dollar value of Venezuela's external debt grew at different rates and, as a consequence, the country's external debt-to-GDP ratio first decreased (dropping to 47 percent of GDP in 1992) and then increased again (to 53 percent of GDP in 1994) (Figure A.39). External debt—both in dollar value and as a share of GDP—decreased substantially over the 1994–2001 period, reaching a minimum of 18 percent of GDP in 2001 (bonded debt decreased from 36 percent of GDP in 1994 to 13 percent of GDP in 2001). External debt

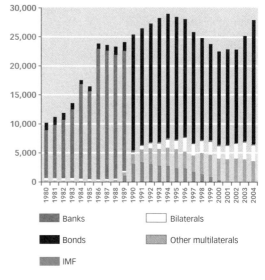

Figure A.38 Venezuela
External Government Debt by Creditor Type
(US$ million)

Legend:
- Banks
- Bonds
- IMF
- Bilaterals
- Other multilaterals

Source: Authors' calculations based on Cowan et al. (2006).

Figure A.39 Venezuela
Structure of Government Debt
(percentage of GDP)

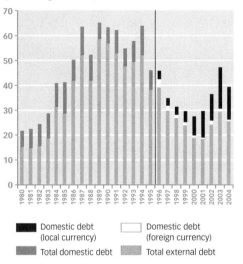

Domestic debt (local currency)

Domestic debt (foreign currency)

Total domestic debt

Total external debt

Source: Authors' calculations based on Cowan et al. (2006).
Note: Data for currency composition of domestic debt available from 1996 on.

increased again in the 2001–2003 period, peaking at 29 percent of GDP in 2003, then decreased slightly, to 25 percent of GDP, in 2004.

Over the 1980–2000 period, domestic debt in Venezuela oscillated between 6 percent and 12 percent of GDP. Between 2001 and 2004, the country's domestic debt remained above 10 percent of GDP, reaching a peak of 18 percent of GDP in 2003. In the mid-1990s, Venezuela's domestic debt was evenly split between domestic currency debt and foreign currency debt, but the share of domestic currency debt has increased over the years, and by 2004, 96 percent of the country's domestic debt was denominated in domestic currency.

Venezuela's central bank holds a large amount of reserves (18 percent of GDP in 2003 and 17 percent of GDP in 2004), yielding substantial differences between the country's gross and net debt figures. In 2003, gross debt was 47 percent of GDP and net debt 28 percent. The corresponding figures for 2004 were 39 percent and 22 percent, respectively.

Methodological issues. The figures included in this report do not include debt issued by the state-owned oil company, Petroleos de Venezuela SA, or the assets of Venezuela's Special Petroleum Fund. In the case of external debt, there were large differences between data reported by GDF and those reported by the IMF and the ministry of finance. The latter sources were used whenever possible.

REFERENCES

Abiad, Abdul, and Jonathan D. Ostry. 2005. *Primary Surpluses and Sustainable Debt Levels in Emerging Market Countries*. IMF Policy Discussion Paper no. 05/6. International Monetary Fund, Washington, DC.

Adams, Charles, Donald J. Mathieson, Garry Schinasi, and Bankim Chadha, eds. 1998. *International Capital Markets: Developments, Prospects and New Issues*. Washington, DC: International Monetary Fund.

Ades, Alberto, Federico Kaune, Paulo Leme, Rumi Masih, and Daniel Tenengauzer. 2000. *Introducing GS-ESS: A New Framework for Assessing Fair Value in Emerging Markets Hard-Currency Debt*. Global Economics Paper no. 45. Goldman Sachs, New York.

Aguilar, Camila, Mauricio Cárdenas, Marcela Meléndez, and Natalia Salazar. 2006. The Development of Latin-American Bond Markets: The Case of Colombia. Paper presented at the Second Workshop on the Development of Latin-American Bond Markets, July 13, Berkeley, CA.

Aizenman, Joshua, and Andrew Powell. 1998. The Political Economy of Public Savings and the Role of Capital Mobility. *Journal of Development Economics* 57(1): 67–95.

Alesina, Alberto F., Silvia Ardagna, Roberto Perotti, and Fabio Schiantarelli. 2002. Fiscal Policy, Profits, and Investment. *American Economic Review* 92(3) June: 571–89.

Alesina, Alberto F., and David Dollar. 2000. Who Gives Foreign Aid to Whom and Why? *Journal of Economic Growth* 5(1) March: 33–63.

Alesina, Alberto F., Ricardo Hausmann, Rudolf Hommes, and Ernesto Stein. 1999. Budget Institutions and Fiscal Performance in Latin America. *Journal of Development Economics* 59(2) August: 253–73.

Alesina, Alberto F., and Roberto Perotti. 1994. *The Political Economy of Budget Deficits*. NBER Working Paper no. 4637. National Bureau of Economic Research, Cambridge, MA.

Alesina, Alberto F., Roberto Perotti, José Tavares, Maurice Obstfeld, and Barry Eichengreen. 1998. The Political Economy of Fiscal Adjustments. In Brookings Institution, ed., *Brookings Papers on Economic Activity* 1998(1). Washington, DC: Brookings Institution Press.

Alesina, Alberto F., and Guido Tabellini. 2005. *Why Is Fiscal Policy Often Procyclical?* NBER Working Paper no. 11600. National Bureau of Economic Research, Cambridge, MA.

Alfaro, Laura, and Fabio Kanczuk. 2006. *Sovereign Debt: Indexation and Maturity*. Research Department Working Paper no. 560. Inter-American Development Bank, Washington, DC.

Alt, James E., and David Dryer Lassen. 2006. Fiscal Transparency, Political Parties, and Debt in OECD Countries. *European Economic Review* 50(6) August: 1403–39.

Amador, Manuel. 2002. A Political Model of Sovereign Debt Repayment. Stanford University, Stanford, CA. Unpublished.

Amato, Jeffery. 2006. The International Debt Securities Market. *BIS Quarterly Review* (March): 31–42.

Anderson, Ronald W., Christopher L. Gilbert, and Andrew Powell. 1989. Securitization and Commodity Contingency in International Lending. *American Journal of Agricultural Economics* 71(2) May: 523–30.

Arida, Persio, Edmar Lisboa Bacha, and André Lara-Resende. 2005. Credit, Interest, and Jurisdictional Uncertainty: Conjectures on the Case of Brazil. In Francesco Giavazzi, Ilan Goldfajn, and Santiago Herrera, eds., *Inflation Targeting, Debt, and the Brazilian Experience, 1999 to 2003*. Cambridge, MA: MIT Press.

Arslanalp, Serkan, and Peter Blair Henry. 2005. Is Debt Relief Efficient? *Journal of Finance* 60(2) April: 1017–51.

———. 2006a. Debt Relief. *Journal of Economic Perspectives* 20(1) Winter: 207–20.

———. 2006b. Helping the Poor to Help Themselves: Debt Relief or Aid? In Chris Jochnick and Fraser A. Preston, eds., *Sovereign Debt at the Crossroads: Challenges and Proposals for Solving the Third World Debt Crisis*. Oxford, UK: Oxford University Press.

Balassone, Fabrizio, Daniele Franco, and Stefania Zotteri. 2004. Public Debt: A Survey of Policy Issues. Paper presented at the Sixth Banca d'Italia Workshop on Public Finance, April 1–3, Perugia, Italy.

Baqir, Reza. 2002. *Social Sector Spending in a Panel of Countries*. IMF Working Paper no. 02/35. International Monetary Fund, Washington, DC.

Barnhill, Theodore, and George Kopits. 2003. *Assessing Fiscal Sustainability under Uncertainty*. IMF Working Paper no. 03/79. International Monetary Fund, Washington, DC.

Barro, Robert J. 1974. Are Government Bonds Net Wealth? *Journal of Political Economy* 82(6) December: 1095–1117.

———. 1979. On the Determination of the Public Debt. *Journal of Political Economy* 87(5) October: 940–71.

Barro, Robert J., and Jong-Wha Lee. 2005. IMF Programs: Who Is Chosen and What Are the Effects? *Journal of Monetary Economics* 52(7): 1245–69.

Bartolini, Leonardo, and Carlo Cottarelli. 1997. Designing Effective Auctions for Treasury Securities. *Current Issues in Economic and Finance* [Federal Reserve Bank of New York] 3(9) July: 1–6.

Bebczuk, Ricardo, Arturo Galindo, and Ugo Panizza. 2006. *An Evaluation of the Contractionary Devaluation Hypothesis*. Research Department Working Paper no. 582. Inter-American Development Bank, Washington, DC.

Beim, David O., and Charles W. Calomiris. 2000a. Building Financial Institutions. In David O. Beim and Charles W. Calomiris, *Emerging Financial Markets*. New York: McGraw Hill/Irwin.

———. 2000b. Information and Control. In David O. Beim and Charles W. Calomiris, *Emerging Financial Markets*. New York: McGraw Hill/Irwin.

———. 2000c. Legal Foundations. In David O. Beim and Charles W. Calomiris, *Emerging Financial Markets*. New York: McGraw Hill/Irwin.

Berganza, Juan Carlos, and Alicia García-Herrero. 2004. *What Makes Balance Sheet Effects Detrimental for the Country Risk Premium?* Documento de Trabajo no. 0423. Banco de España, Madrid.

Bernanke, Ben. 2005. Inflation in Latin America: A New Era? Speech delivered at Stanford Institute for Economic Policy Research Economic Summit, February 11, Stanford, CA. Available at http://www.federalreserve.gov/BOARDDOCS/Speeches/2005/20050211/default.htm.

Bevilaqua, Afonso S., and Márcio G. P. Garcia. 2002. Debt Management in Brazil: Evaluation of the Real Plan and Challenges Ahead. *International Journal of Finance and Economics* 7(1) January: 15–35.

Biais, Bruno, and Richard C. Green. 2005. The Microstructure of the Bond Market in the 20th Century. Tepper School of Business, Carnegie Mellon University, Pittsburgh, PA. Unpublished.

Bird, Graham, and Alistair Milne. 2003. Debt Relief to Low Income Countries. Is It Effective and Efficient? *World Economy* 26(1) January: 43–59.

Birdsall, Nancy, Stijn Claessens, and Ishac Diwan. 2002. *Will HIPC Matter? The Debt Game and Donor Behavior in Africa.* CEPR Discussion Paper no. 3297. Centre for Economic Policy Research, London.

Birdsall, Nancy, and Brian Deese. 2004. *Beyond HIPC: Secure Sustainable Debt Relief for Poor Countries.* Center for Global Development Working Paper no. 46. Center for Global Development, Washington, DC.

Blanchard, Olivier J. 1990. *Suggestions for a New Set of Fiscal Indicators.* OECD Economics Department Working Paper no. 79. Organisation for Economic Co-operation and Development, Paris.

Blustein, Paul. 2005. *And the Money Kept Rolling In (and Out): The World Bank, Wall Street, the IMF, and the Bankrupting of Argentina.* New York: PublicAffairs.

Bobba, Matteo Alessandro. 2004. The Determinants of IMF Loan Programs. *Rivista di Politica Economica* nos. 11–12 (November–December): 21–48.

Bohn, Henning. 1998. The Behavior of U.S. Public Debt and Deficits. *Quarterly Journal of Economics* 113(3) August: 949–63.

Bolton, Patrick, and Xavier Freixas. 2006. Financial Architecture in Emerging Market Economies. Columbia University, New York. Unpublished.

Bordo, Michael D., and Christopher M. Meissner. 2005. *The Role of Foreign Currency Debt in Financial Crises: 1880–1913 vs. 1972–1997.* NBER Working Paper no. 11897. National Bureau of Economic Research, Cambridge, MA.

Bordo, Michael D., Christopher M. Meissner, and Angela Redish. 2005. How Original Sin Was Overcome: The Evolution of External Debt Denominated in Domestic Currencies in the United States and the British Dominions, 1800–2000. In Barry Eichengreen and Ricardo Hausmann, eds., *Other People's Money: Debt Denomination and Financial Instability in Emerging Market Economies.* Chicago: University of Chicago Press.

Bordo, Michael D., and Hugh Rockoff. 1996. The Gold Standard as a "Good Housekeeping Seal of Approval." *Journal of Economic History* 56(2): 389–428.

Borensztein, Eduardo. 1990. Debt Overhang, Credit Rationing and Investment. *Journal of Development Economics* 32(2) April: 315–35.

Borensztein, Eduardo, Marcos Chamon, Olivier Jeanne, Paolo Mauro, and Jeromin Zettelmeyer. 2004. *Sovereign Debt Structure for Crisis Prevention*. IMF Occasional Paper no. 237. International Monetary Fund, Washington, DC.

Borensztein, Eduardo, Kevin Cowan, and Patricio Valenzuela. 2006. The "Sovereign Ceiling Lite" and Bank Credit Ratings in Emerging Markets Economies. Inter-American Development Bank, Washington, DC, and Banco Central de Chile, Santiago. Unpublished.

Borensztein, Eduardo, Barry Eichengreen, and Ugo Panizza. 2006a. Building Bond Markets in Latin America. University of California, Berkeley, and Inter-American Development Bank, Washington, DC.

————. 2006b. *Debt Instruments and Policies in the New Millennium: New Markets and New Opportunities*. Research Department Working Paper no. 558. Inter-American Development Bank, Washington, DC.

————. 2006c. *A Tale of Two Markets: Bond Market Development in East Asia and Latin America*. Occasional Paper no. 3. Hong Kong Institute for Monetary Research, Hong Kong.

Borensztein, Eduardo, and Paolo Mauro. 2004. The Case for GDP-Indexed Bonds. *Economic Policy* 19(38) April: 165–216.

Borensztein, Eduardo, and Ugo Panizza. 2006a. The Cost of Default. Inter-American Development Bank, Washington, DC. Unpublished.

————. 2006b. *Do Sovereign Defaults Hurt Exporters?* Research Department Working Paper no. 553. Inter-American Development Bank, Washington, DC.

Borensztein, Eduardo, and Patricio Valenzuela. 2006. Manias and Panics in the Bond Markets. Inter-American Development Bank, Washington, DC. Unpublished.

Braun, Matías, and Ignacio Briones. 2005. The Development of Bond Markets around the World. Universidad Adolfo Ibáñez, Peñalolén, Chile. Unpublished.

Brender, Adi, and Allan Drazen. 2005. Political Budget Cycles in New versus Established Democracies. *Journal of Monetary Economics* 52(7) October: 1271–95.

Buchanan, James M. 1976. Barro on the Ricardian Equivalence Theorem. *Journal of Political Economy* 84(2) April: 337–42.

Buchanan, James M., and Richard E. Wagner. 1977. *Democracy in Deficit: The Political Legacy of Lord Keynes*. San Diego, CA: Academic Press.

Budina, Nina, and Norbert Fiess. 2004. Public Debt and Its Determinants in Market Access Countries: Results from 15 Country Case Studies. World Bank, Washington, DC. Unpublished.

Buiter, Willem. 1985. A Guide to Public Sector Debt and Deficits. *Economic Policy* 1(1) November: 15–79.

Bulow, Jeremy. 2002. First World Governments and Third World Debt. In William C. Brainard and George L. Perry, eds., *Brookings Papers on Economic Activity* 2002(1). Washington, DC: Brookings Institution Press.

Bulow, Jeremy, and Kenneth Rogoff. 1989. Sovereign Debt: Is to Forgive to Forget? *American Economic Review* 79(1) March: 43–50.

Burger, John D., and Francis E. Warnock. 2004. *Foreign Participation in Local-Currency Bond Markets*. International Finance Discussion Paper no. 794. Board of Governors of the Federal Reserve System, Washington, DC.

Burnside, Craig, and David Dollar. 2000. Aid, Policies, and Growth. *American Economic Review* 90(4): 847–68.

Caballero, Ricardo J., and Stavros Panageas. 2005. *A Quantitative Model of Sudden Stops and External Liquidity Management*. NBER Working Paper no. 11293. National Bureau of Economic Research, Cambridge, MA.

————. 2006. Contingent Reserves Management: An Applied Framework. In Ricardo J. Caballero, César Calderón, and Luis Felipe Céspedes, eds., *External Vulnerability and Preventive Policies*. Santiago: Central Bank of Chile.

Cady, John, and Anthony Pellechio. 2006. *Sovereign Borrowing Cost and the IMF's Data Standards Initiatives*. IMF Working Paper no. 06/78. International Monetary Fund, Washington, DC.

Calderón, César, William Easterly, and Luis Servén. 2003. Latin America's Infrastructure in the Era of Macroeconomic Crises. In William Easterly and Luis Servén, eds., *The Limits of Stabilization: Infrastructure, Public Deficits, and Growth in Latin America*. Stanford, CA: Stanford University Press.

Calderón, César, and Luis Servén. 2004. *Trends in Infrastructure in Latin America, 1980–2001*. Policy Research Working Paper no. 3401. World Bank, Washington, DC.

Calvo, Guillermo A. 1978. On the Time Consistency of Optimal Policy in a Monetary Economy. *Econometrica* 46(6) November: 1411–28.

————. 1988. Servicing the Public Debt: The Role of Expectations. *American Economic Review* 78(4) September: 647–61.

————. 1998. Capital Flows and Capital Market Crises: The Simple Economics of Sudden Stops. *Journal of Applied Economics* 1(1): 35–54.

————. 2005a. Capital Market Contagion and Recession: An Explanation of the Russian Virus. In *Emerging Capital Markets in Turmoil: Bad Luck or Bad Policy?* Cambridge, MA: MIT Press.

————. 2005b. Contagion in Emerging Markets: When *Wall Street* Is a Carrier. In Guillermo A. Calvo, *Emerging Capital Markets in Turmoil: Bad Luck or Bad Policy?* Cambridge, MA: MIT Press.

————. 2005c. *Emerging Markets in Turmoil: Bad Luck or Bad Policy?* Cambridge, MA: MIT Press.

Calvo, Guillermo A., Alejandro Izquierdo, and Rudy Loo-Kung. 2005. *Relative Price Volatility under Sudden Stops: The Relevance of Balance Sheet Effects*. NBER Working Paper no. 11492. National Bureau of Economic Research, Cambridge, MA.

Calvo, Guillermo A., Alejandro Izquierdo, and Luis-Fernando Mejía. 2004. *On the Empirics of Sudden Stops: The Relevance of Balance-Sheet Effects*. NBER Working Paper no. 10520. National Bureau of Economic Research, Cambridge, MA.

Calvo, Guillermo A., Alejandro Izquierdo, and Ernesto Talvi. 2005. Sudden Stops, the Real Exchange Rate, and Fiscal Sustainability: Argentina's Lessons. In Guillermo A. Calvo, *Emerging Capital Markets in Turmoil: Bad Luck or Bad Policy?* Cambridge, MA: MIT Press.

Calvo, Guillermo A., and Enrique G. Mendoza. 2000. Capital-Markets Crises and Economic Collapse in Emerging Markets: An Informational-Frictions Approach. *American Economic Review* 90(2) May: 59–64.

—————. 2005. Petty Crime and Cruel Punishment: Lessons from the Mexican Debacle. In Guillermo A. Calvo, *Emerging Capital Markets in Turmoil: Bad Luck or Bad Policy?* Cambridge, MA: MIT Press.

Calvo, Guillermo A., and Carmen M. Reinhart. 2002. Fear of Floating. *Quarterly Journal of Economics* 117(2) May: 379–408.

Calvo, Guillermo A., and Ernesto Talvi. 2005. *Sudden Stop, Financial Factors and Economic Collapse in Latin America: Learning from Argentina and Chile.* NBER Working Paper no. 11153. National Bureau of Economic Research, Cambridge, MA.

Campos, Camila F. S., Dany Jaimovich, and Ugo Panizza. 2006. The Unexplained Part of Public Debt. *Emerging Markets Review* 7(3) September: 228–243.

Canning, David, and Esra Bennathan. 1999. The Social Rate of Return on Infrastructure Investment. World Bank, Washington, DC. Unpublished.

Cantor, Richard, and Frank Packer. 1996. Determinants and Impact of Sovereign Credit Ratings. *Economic Policy Review* [Federal Reserve Bank of New York] 2(2) October: 37–53.

Caprio, Gerard, and Daniela Klingebiel. 2003. Episodes of Systemic and Borderline Financial Crises. World Bank, Washington, DC. Unpublished.

Cárdenas, Mauricio, Eduardo Lora, and Valerie Mercer-Blackman. 2005. The Policy Making Process of Tax Reform in Latin America. Powerpoint presentation at the Inter-American Development Bank Workshop on State Reform, Public Policies and Policymaking Processes, February 28–March 2, Washington, DC.

Cardoso, Eliana A., and Rudiger Dornbusch. 1989. Brazilian Debt Crises: Past and Present. In Barry J. Eichengreen and Peter H. Lindert, eds., *The International Debt Crisis in Historical Perspective.* Cambridge, MA: MIT Press.

Castellanos, Sara, and Lorenza Martínez. 2006. The Development and Challenges Faced by the Mexican Bond Market. Paper presented at the Second Workshop on the Development of Latin-American Bond Markets, July 14, Berkeley, CA.

Catalan, Mario, Gregorio Impavido, and Alberto R. Musalem. 2000. *Contractual Savings or Stock Market Development—Which Leads?* Policy Research Working Paper no. 2421. World Bank, Washington, DC.

Catão, Luis, and Sandeep Kapur. 2004. *Missing Link: Volatility and the Debt Intolerance Paradox.* IMF Working Paper no. 4/51. International Monetary Fund, Washington, DC.

Celasun, Oya, Xavier DeBrun, and Jonathan D. Ostry. 2006. *Primary Surplus Behavior and Risks to Fiscal Sustainability in Emerging Market Countries: A "Fan-Chart" Approach.* IMF Working Paper no. 06/67. International Monetary Fund, Washington, DC.

Chalk, Nigel, and Richard Hemming. 2000. *Assessing Fiscal Sustainability in Theory and Practice.* IMF Working Paper no. 00/81. International Monetary Fund, Washington, DC.

Chamon, Marcos. 2001. Why Can't Developing Countries Borrow from Abroad in Their Own Currency? Harvard University, Cambridge, MA. Unpublished.

Chowdhry, Bhagwan. 1991. What Is Different about International Lending? *Review of Financial Studies* 4(1) Spring: 121–48.

Chowdury, Abdur. 2001. Foreign Debt and Growth in Developing Countries. Paper presented at World Institute for Development Economics Research (WIDER) Conference on Debt Relief, August 17–18, United Nations University, Helsinki.

Choy, Marylin. 2002. The Development of Debt Markets in Peru. In *The Development of Bond Markets in Emerging Economies* [BIS Papers no. 11]. Basel: Bank for International Settlements.

Cifuentes, Rodrigo, Jorge Desormeaux, and Claudio González. 2002. Capital Markets in Chile: From Financial Repression to Financial Deepening. In *The Development of Bond Markets in Emerging Economies* [BIS Papers no. 11]. Basel: Bank for International Settlements.

Clements, Benedict, Rina Bhattacharya, and Toan Quoc Nguyen. 2003. *External Debt, Public Investment, and Growth in Low-Income Countries*. IMF Working Paper no. 03/249. International Monetary Fund, Washington, DC.

Cline, William R. 1995. *International Debt Reexamined*. Washington, DC: Institute for International Economics.

Cline, William R., and Kevin J. S. Barnes. 1997. *Spreads and Risk in Emerging Market Lending*. Research Paper no. 97-1. Institute of International Finance, Washington, DC.

Cohen, Daniel, and Richard Portes. 2006. *Toward a Lender of First Resort*. IMF Working Paper no. 06/66. International Monetary Fund, Washington, DC.

Cole, Harold L., and Timothy J. Kehoe. 1996. A Self-Fulfilling Model of Mexico's 1994–1995 Debt Crisis. *Journal of International Economics* 41(3–4) November: 309–30.

Cooper, Richard N. 1971. *Currency Devaluation in Developing Countries*. Essays in International Finance no. 86. Princeton University, Princeton, NJ.

Cordella, Tito, and Eduardo Levy Yeyati. 2006a. A (New) Country Insurance Facility. *International Finance* 9(1) Spring: 1–36.

———. 2006b. Multilateral Country Insurance. World Bank, Washington, DC. Unpublished.

Cordella, Tito, Luca A. Ricci, and Marta Ruiz-Arranz. 2005. *Debt Overhang or Debt Irrelevance? Revisiting the Debt-Growth Link*. IMF Working Paper no. 05/223. International Monetary Fund, Washington, DC.

Corden, Max. 1989. Debt Relief and Adjustment Incentives. In Jacob Frenkel, Michael Dooley, and Peter Wickham, eds., *The Analytical Issues in Debt*. Washington, DC: International Monetary Fund.

Corsetti, Giancarlo, Paolo Pesenti, and Nouriel Roubini. 2001. *The Role of Large Players in Currency Crises*. NBER Working Paper no. 8303. National Bureau of Economic Research, Cambridge, MA.

Cowan, Kevin, Eduardo Levy Yeyati, Ugo Panizza, and Federico Sturzenegger. 2006. *Sovereign Debt in the Americas: New Data and Stylized Facts*. Research Department Working Paper no. 577. Inter-American Development Bank, Washington, DC.

Cowan, Kevin, and Ugo Panizza. 2006. Government and Corporate Bonds in Latin America: A Summary of the Country Studies. Inter-American Development Bank, Washington, DC. Unpublished.

Croce, Enzo, and V. Hugo Juan-Ramón. 2003. *Assessing Fiscal Sustainability: A Cross-Country Comparison*. IMF Working Paper no. 03/145. International Monetary Fund, Washington, DC.

Davis, Lance E., and Robert E. Gallman. 2001. *Evolving Financial Markets and International Capital Flows: Britain, the Americas, and Australia, 1865–1914*. Cambridge: Cambridge University Press.

de Brun, Julio, Néstor Gandelman, Herman Kamil, and Arturo C. Porzecanski. 2006. The Fixed-Income Market in Uruguay. Paper presented at the Second Workshop on the Development of Latin-American Bond Markets, July 13, Berkeley, CA.

de la Torre, Augusto, and Sergio L. Schmukler. 2004a. Coping with Risks through Mismatches: Domestic and International Financial Contracts for Emerging Economies. *International Finance* 7(3) December: 349–90.

—————. 2004b. *Whither Latin American Capital Markets?* Washington, DC: World Bank.

de Mello, Luiz. 2006. *Fiscal Responsibility Legislation and Fiscal Adjustment: The Case of Brazilian Local Governments.* Policy Research Working Paper no. 3812. World Bank, Washington, DC.

Dell'Ariccia, Giovanni, Isabel Schnabel, and Jeromin Zettelmeyer. 2002. *Moral Hazard and International Crisis Lending: A Test.* IMF Working Paper no. 02/181. International Monetary Fund, Washington, DC.

della Paolera, Gerardo, and Alan M. Taylor. 2001. *Straining at the Anchor: The Argentine Currency Board and the Search for Macroeconomic Stability, 1880–1935.* Chicago: University of Chicago Press.

—————. 2003. Gaucho Banking Redux. *Economia* 3(2) Spring: 1–42.

—————. 2006. Sovereign Debt in Latin America: History. Research Department, Inter-American Development Bank, Washington, DC. Unpublished.

Demirgüç-Kunt, Asli, and Eduardo Fernández-Arias. 1992. *Burden-Sharing among Official and Private Creditors.* Policy Research Working Paper no. 943. World Bank, Washington, DC.

Depetris Chauvin, Nicolas, and Aart Kraay. 2005. What Has 100 Billion Dollars Worth of Debt Relief Done for Low-Income Countries? Available at http://129.3.20.41/eps/if/papers/0510/0510001.pdf.

Detragiache, Enrica, and Antonio Spilimbergo. 2001. *Crises and Liquidity: Evidence and Interpretation.* IMF Working Paper no. 01/2. International Monetary Fund, Washington, DC.

Diamond, Jack, and Peter Heller. 1990. *International Comparisons of Government Expenditure Revisited: The Developing Countries, 1975–86.* IMF Occasional Paper no. 69. International Monetary Fund, Washington, DC.

Díaz-Alejandro, Carlos F. 1983. Stories of the 1930s for the 1980s. In Pedro Aspe Armella, Rudiger Dornbusch, and Maurice Obstfeld, eds., *Financial Policies and the World Capital Market: The Problem of Latin American Countries.* Chicago: University of Chicago Press.

Didier, Tatiana, Paolo Mauro, and Sergio Schmukler. 2006. *Vanishing Contagion?* IMF Policy Discussion Paper no. 06/1. International Monetary Fund, Washington, DC.

Dijkstra, Geske, and Niels Hermes. 2001. The Uncertainty of Debt Service Payments and Economic Growth of Highly Indebted Poor Countries: Is There a Case for Debt Relief? Paper presented at World Institute for Development Economics Research (WIDER) Conference on Debt Relief, August 17–18, United Nations University, Helsinki.

Dittmar, Robert F., and Kathy Yuan. 2006. Do Sovereign Bonds Benefit Corporate Bonds in Emerging Markets? Stephen M. Ross School of Business, University of Michigan, Ann Arbor. Unpublished.

Dooley, Michael P. 1995. A Retrospective on the Debt Crisis. In Peter B. Kenen, ed., *Understanding Interdependence: The Macroeconomics of the Open Economy*. Princeton, NJ: Princeton University Press.

————. 2000. *International Financial Architecture and Strategic Default: Can Output Losses Following International Financial Crises Be Avoided?* NBER Working Paper no. 7531. National Bureau of Economic Research, Cambridge, MA.

Dornbusch, Rudiger, Federico Sturzenegger, and Holger Wolf. 1991. Extreme Inflation: Dynamics and Stabilization. In William C. Brainard and George L. Perry, eds., *Brookings Papers on Economic Activity: Macroeconomics*. Washington, DC: Brookings Institution Press.

Drazen, Allan, and Marcela Eslava. 2005. *Electoral Manipulation via Expenditure Composition: Theory and Evidence*. NBER Working Paper no. 11085. National Bureau of Economic Research, Cambridge, MA.

Easterly, William. 2002. How Did Heavily Indebted Poor Countries Become Heavily Indebted? Reviewing Two Decades of Debt Relief. *World Development* 30(10) October: 1677–96.

————. 2003. Can Foreign Aid Buy Growth? *Journal of Economic Perspectives* 17(3) Summer: 23–48.

————. 2006. *The White Man's Burden: Why the West's Efforts to Aid the Rest Have Done So Much Ill and So Little Good*. New York: Penguin.

Eaton, Jonathan, and Mark Gersovitz. 1981. Debt with Potential Repudiation: Theoretical and Empirical Analysis. *Review of Economic Studies* 48(2) April: 289–309.

Edwards, Sebastian. 2001. *Does the Current Account Matter?* NBER Working Paper no. 8275. National Bureau of Economic Research, Cambridge, MA.

Eichengreen, Barry. 2000. The Euro One Year On. *Journal of Policy Modeling* 22(3) May: 355–68.

Eichengreen, Barry, and Ricardo Hausmann. 1999. Exchange Rates and Financial Fragility. Paper presented at the symposium New Challenges for Monetary Policy, August 26–28, Jackson Hole, WY.

————. 2005. The Road to Redemption. In Barry Eichengreen and Ricardo Hausmann, eds., *Other People's Money: Debt Denomination and Financial Instability in Emerging Market Economies*. Chicago: University of Chicago Press.

Eichengreen, Barry, Ricardo Hausmann, and Ugo Panizza. 2003. *Currency Mismatches, Debt Intolerance and Original Sin: Why They Are Not the Same and Why It Matters*. NBER Working Paper no. 10036. National Bureau of Economic Research, Cambridge, MA.

————. 2005a. The Mystery of Original Sin. In Barry Eichengreen and Ricardo Hausmann, eds., *Other People's Money: Debt Denomination and Financial Instability in Emerging Market Economies*. Chicago: University of Chicago Press.

————. 2005b. The Pain of Original Sin. In Barry Eichengreen and Ricardo Hausmann, eds., *Other People's Money: Debt Denomination and Financial Instability in Emerging Market Economies*. Chicago: University of Chicago Press.

Eichengreen, Barry, and Pipat Luengnaruemitchai. 2004. *Why Doesn't Asia Have Bigger Bond Markets?* NBER Working Paper no. 10576. National Bureau of Economic Research, Cambridge, MA.

Eichengreen, Barry, and Richard Portes. 1995. *Crisis? What Crisis? Orderly Workouts for Sovereign Debtors*. London: Centre for Economic Policy Research.

Elmendorf, Douglas W., and N. Gregory Mankiw. 1999. Government Debt. In John B. Taylor and Michael Woodford, eds., *Handbook of Macroeconomics*. Volume 1C. Amsterdam: Elsevier Science.

Engel, Eduardo, and Patricio Meller, eds. 1993. *External Shocks and Stabilization Mechanisms*. Washington, DC: Inter-American Development Bank.

English, William B. 1996. Understanding the Costs of Sovereign Default: American State Debts in the 1840s. *American Economic Review* 86(1) March: 259–75.

Eslava, Marcela. 2006. Ciclos políticos de la política fiscal con votantes opuestos al déficit: el caso colombiano. *El trimestre económico* 73(290): 289–336.

Faini, Riccardo, and Enzo Grilli. 2004. *Who Runs the IFIs?* CEPR Discussion Paper no. 4666. Centre for Economic Policy Research, London.

Fay, Marianne, and Mary Morrison. 2005. *Infrastructure in Latin America and the Caribbean: Recent Developments and Key Challenges*. Volume I: Main Report. Washington, DC: World Bank.

Ferguson, Niall, and Moritz Schularick. 2006. The Empire Effect: The Determinants of Country Risk in the First Age of Globalization, 1880–1913. *Journal of Economic History* 66(2) June: 283–312.

Fernández, Roque, Sergio Pernice, Jorge M. Streb, María Alegre, Alejandro Bedoya, and Celeste González. 2006. The Development of Latin-American Bond Markets: The Case of Argentina. Paper presented at the Second Workshop on the Development of Latin-American Bond Markets, July 13, Berkeley, CA.

Fernández-Arias, Eduardo. 1993. *Costs and Benefits of Debt and Debt Service Reduction*. Policy Research Working Paper no. 1169. World Bank, Washington, DC.

Fernández-Arias, Eduardo, and Andrew Powell. 2006. Multilateral and Private Sector Sovereign Lending: What Makes MDB's Different, Are They Catalytic? Inter-American Development Bank, Washington, DC. Unpublished.

Ferri, G., L.-G. Liu, and J. E. Stiglitz. 1999. The Procyclical Role of Rating Agencies: Evidence from the East Asian Crisis. *Economic Notes* 28(3): 335–55.

Ferrucci, Gianluigi, and Adrian Penalver. 2003. Assessing Sovereign Debt under Uncertainty. *Bank of England Financial Stability Review* no. 15 (December): 91–99.

Filc, Gabriel, and Carlos Scartascini. 2006. Budgetary Institutions. In Eduardo Lora, ed., *The State of State Reform*. Stanford, CA: Stanford University Press and Washington, DC: World Bank. Forthcoming.

Financial Times. 2002. Brazil Pledges Loans to Companies. August 13, p. 1.

Fischer, Stanley. 1999. On the Need for an International Lender of Last Resort. *Journal of Economic Perspectives* 13(4) Fall: 85–104.

Fishlow, Albert. 1989. Conditionality and Willingness to Pay: Some Parallels from the 1890s. In Barry J. Eichengreen and Peter H. Lindert, eds., *The International Debt Crisis in Historical Perspective*. Cambridge, MA: MIT Press.

Flandreau, Marc. 2004. *The Glitter of Gold: France, Bimetallism, and the Emergence of the International Gold Standard, 1848–1873*. Oxford, UK: Oxford University Press.

Forbes, Kristin, and Roberto Rigobón. 2000. *Contagion in Latin America: Definitions, Measurement, and Policy Implications.* NBER Working Paper no. 7885. National Bureau of Economic Research, Cambridge, MA.

Frankel, Jeffrey A. 2005. Contractionary Currency Crashes in Developing Countries. *IMF Staff Papers* 52(2) September: 149–92.

Fritschel, Heidi. 2004. Is There a Way out of the Debt Trap? *IFPRI* [International Food Policy Research Institute] *Forum,* December. Available at http://www.ifpri.org/pubs/newsletters/ifpriforum/IF200412.htm.

Gali, Jordi, and Roberto Perotti. 2003. Fiscal Policy and Monetary Integration in Europe. *Economic Policy* 18(37) October: 533–72.

Galiani, Sebastián, and Eduardo Levy Yeyati. 2003. The Fiscal Spending Gap and the Procyclicality of Public Expenditure. Universidad Torcuato Di Tella, Buenos Aires. Unpublished.

Gapen, Michael T., Dale F. Gray, Cheng Hoon Lim, and Yingbin Xiao. 2005. *Measuring and Analyzing Sovereign Risk with Contingent Claims.* IMF Working Paper no. 05/155. International Monetary Fund, Washington, DC.

Garcia, Márcio, and Roberto Rigobón. 2004. *A Risk Management Approach to Emerging Markets' Sovereign Debt Sustainability with an Application to Brazilian Data.* NBER Working Paper no. 10336. National Bureau of Economic Research, Cambridge, MA.

García-Herrero, Alicia, and Álvaro Ortiz. 2005. *The Role of Global Risk Aversion in Explaining Latin American Sovereign Spreads.* Documento de Trabajo no. 0505. Banco de España, Madrid.

Gavin, Michael, and Roberto Perotti. 1997. Fiscal Policy in Latin America. In Ben S. Bernanke and Julio J. Rotemberg, eds., *NBER Macroeconomics Annual 1997.* Cambridge, MA: MIT Press.

Gelos, R. Gaston, Ratna Sahay, and Guido Sandleris. 2004. *Sovereign Borrowing by Developing Countries: What Determines Market Access?* IMF Working Paper no. 04/221. International Monetary Fund, Washington, DC.

Ghosal, Sayantan, and Marcus Miller. 2003a. Managing Financial Crisis in Emerging Markets: New Developments in Review. In Alfredo G. A. Valladão and Pedro da Motta Veiga, eds., *Political Issues in EU-Mercosur Negotiations.* Paris: Chaire Mercosur de Sciences Po.

————. 2003b. Co-ordination Failure, Moral Hazard and Sovereign Bankruptcy Procedures. *Economic Journal* 113(487) April: 276–304.

Glen, Jack. 1994. *An Introduction to the Microstructure of Emerging Markets.* IFC Discussion Paper no. 24. International Finance Corporation, World Bank, Washington, DC.

Goldfajn, Ilan, and Eduardo Refinetti Guardia. 2003. *Fiscal Rules and Debt Sustainability in Brazil.* Banco Central do Brasil Technical Notes no. 39. Banco Central do Brasil, Brasília.

Goldstein, Morris, and Philip Turner. 2004. *Controlling Currency Mismatches in Emerging Markets.* Washington, DC: Institute for International Economics.

González Rozada, Martín, and Eduardo Levy Yeyati. 2006. *Global Factors and Emerging Market Spreads.* Research Department Working Paper no. 552. Inter-American Development Bank, Washington, DC.

Gordon, David B., and Eric M. Leeper. 2005. *Are Countercyclical Fiscal Policies Counterproductive?* NBER Working Paper no. 11869. National Bureau of Economic Research, Cambridge, MA.

Grandes, Martin. 2003. *Convergence and Divergence of Sovereign Bond Spreads: Theory and Facts from Latin America.* Working Paper no. 03. American University of Paris.

Greenspan, Alan. 1999. Do Efficient Financial Markets Mitigate Financial Crises? Remarks before the 1999 Financial Markets Conference of the Federal Reserve Bank of Atlanta, October 19, Sea Island, GA.

Grilli, Vittorio, Donato Masciandaro, and Guido Tabellini. 1991. Political and Monetary Institutions and Public Financial Policies in Industrial Democracies. *Economic Policy* 6(13) October: 341–92.

Grossman, Herschel I., and John B. Van Huyck. 1988. Sovereign Debt as a Contingent Claim: Excusable Default, Repudiation, and Reputation. *American Economic Review* 78(5) December: 1088–97.

Gupta, Sanjeev, Benedict Clements, Emanuele Baldacci, and Carlos Mulas-Granados. 2004. The Persistence of Fiscal Adjustments in Developing Countries. *Applied Economics Letters* 11(4) March: 209–12.

Hamilton, James D., and Marjorie A. Flavin. 1986. On the Limitations of Government Borrowing: A Framework for Empirical Testing. *American Economic Review* 76(4) September: 808–19.

Hansen, Henrik. 2001. The Impact of Aid and External Debt on Growth and Investment: Insights from Cross-Country Regression Analysis. Paper presented at World Institute for Development Economics Research (WIDER) Conference on Debt Relief, August 17–18, United Nations University, Helsinki.

Hausmann, Ricardo, and Ugo Panizza. 2003. On the Determinants of Original Sin: An Empirical Investigation. *Journal of International Money and Finance* 22(7) December: 957–90.

Hausmann, Ricardo, Ugo Panizza, and Ernesto Stein. 2001. Why Do Countries Float the Way They Float? *Journal of Development Economics* 66(2): 387–414.

Hausmann, Ricardo, and Roberto Rigobón. 2003. IDA in UF: On the Benefits of Changing the Currency Denomination of Concessional Lending to Low-Income Countries. Harvard University, Cambridge, MA. Unpublished. Available at http://ksghome.harvard.edu/~rhausma/new/HausmannRigobonWBOS.pdf.

Hawkins, John. 2002. Bond Markets and Banks in Emerging Economies. In *The Development of Bond Markets in Emerging Economies* [BIS Papers no. 11]. Basel, Switzerland: Bank for International Settlements.

Hepp, Ralf. 2005. Can Debt Relief Buy Growth? University of California, Davis. Unpublished.

Hercowitz, Zvi, and Michel Strawczynski. 2004. Cyclical Ratcheting in Government Spending: Evidence from the OECD. *Review of Economics and Statistics* 86(1): 353–61.

Herrera, Luis Oscar, and Rodrigo O. Valdés. 2005. De-dollarization, Indexation and Nominalization: The Chilean Experience. *Journal of Policy Reform* 8(4) December: 281–312.

Herrera, Santiago, and Guillermo Perry. 2002. Determinants of Latin Spreads in the New Economy Era: The Role of U.S. Interest Rates and Other External Variables. World Bank, Washington, DC. Unpublished.

Hicks, Norman. 1989. Expenditure Reductions in High-Debt Countries. *Finance and Development* 26: 35–37.

Hicks, Norman, and Anne Kubisch. 1984. Recent Experience in Cutting Government Expenditures. *Finance and Development* 21: 37–39.

Hopkins, Raúl, Andrew Powell, Amlan Roy, and Christopher L. Gilbert. 1997. The World Bank and Conditionality. *Journal of International Development* 9(4): 507–16.

Huhne, Christopher. 1998. How the Rating Agencies Blew It on Korea. *International Economy* 12 (May/June): 46–63.

Husain, Ishrat, and Ishac Diwan, eds. 1989. *Dealing with the Debt Crisis.* Washington, DC: World Bank.

Imbs, Jean M., and Romain Rancière. 2005. *The Overhang Hangover.* Policy Research Working Paper no. 3673. World Bank, Washington, DC.

Inter-American Development Bank (IDB). 1995. *Overcoming Volatility.* Economic and Social Progress in Latin America: 1995 Report. Washington, DC: IDB.

————. 2004. *Unlocking Credit: The Quest for Deep and Stable Bank Lending.* Economic and Social Progress in Latin America: 2005 Report. Washington, DC: IDB.

————. 2005a. Operational Framework for Lending in Local Currency. Available at http://idbdocs.iadb.org/wsdocs/getdocument.aspx?docnum=706805.

————. 2005b. *The Politics of Policies.* Economic and Social Progress in Latin America: 2006 Report. Washington, DC: IDB.

International Monetary Fund (IMF). 1998. Emerging Markets: The Contraction in External Financing and Its Impact on Financial Systems. In Charles Adams, Donald J. Mathieson, Garry Schinasi, and Bankim Chadha, eds., *International Capital Markets: Developments, Prospects, and Key Policy Issues.* Washington, DC: IMF.

————. 2002a. Assessing Sustainability. Policy paper. Policy Development and Review Department, IMF, Washington, DC.

————. 2002b. Selected Topic: Emerging Local Bond Markets. In IMF, ed., *Global Financial Stability Report: Market Developments and Issues.* September. Washington, DC: IMF.

————. 2002c. Sovereign Debt Restructurings and the Domestic Economy Experience in Four Recent Cases. Policy paper. Policy Development and Review Department, IMF, Washington, DC.

————. 2002d. *Suriname: 2002 Article IV Consultation.* IMF Country Report. IMF, Washington, DC.

————. 2003a. Public Debt in Emerging Markets: Is It Too High? In IMF, ed., *World Economic Outlook: Public Debt in Emerging Markets.* Washington, DC: IMF.

————. 2003b. Review of Contingent Credit Lines. Policy paper. Policy Development and Review Department, IMF, Washington, DC. Available at http://www.imf.org/external/np/pdr/fac/2003/021103.htm.

————. 2003c. *Suriname: 2003 Article IV Consultation.* IMF Country Report no. 03/356. IMF, Washington, DC. Available at http://www.imf.org/external/pubs/ft/scr/2003/cr03356.pdf.

————. 2004a. *Belize: 2003 Article IV Consultation.* IMF Country Report no. 04/102. IMF, Washington, DC. Available at http://www.imf.org/external/pubs/ft/scr/2004/cr04102.pdf.

————. 2004b. *Global Financial Stability Report: Market Developments and Issues.* April. Washington, DC: IMF.

————. 2005a. Development of Corporate Bond Markets in Emerging Market Countries. In IMF, ed., *Global Financial Stability Report: Market Developments and Issues.* September. Washington, DC: IMF.

————. 2005b. *Global Financial Stability Report: Market Developments and Issues.* September. Washington, DC: IMF.

————. 2006a. Consideration of a New Liquidity Instrument for Market Access Countries. Policy paper. Policy Development and Review Department, IMF, Washington, DC. Available at http://www.imf.org/external/np/pp/eng/2006/080306.pdf.

————. 2006b. *Global Financial Stability Report: Market Developments and Issues.* April. Washington, DC: IMF.

————. 2006c. The Influence of Credit Derivative and Structured Credit Markets on Financial Stability. In *Global Financial Stability Report.* April. Washington, DC: IMF.

————. 2006d. Structural Changes in Emerging Sovereign Debt and Implications for Financial Stability. In IMF, ed., *Global Financial Stability Report: Market Developments and Issues.* Washington, DC: IMF.

International Monetary Fund and World Bank. 1999. Modifications to the Heavily Indebted Poor Countries Initiative. Available at http://www.imf.org/external/np/hipc/modify/hipc.htm.

————. 2003. Guidelines for Public Debt Management—Amended. IMF and World Bank, Washington, DC.

Ize, Alain, and Andrew Powell. 2005. Prudential Responses to De Facto Dollarization. *Journal of Policy Reform* 8(4) December: 241–62.

Izquierdo, Alejandro, and Ugo Panizza. 2006. Fiscal Sustainability: Issues for Emerging Market Countries. In Ahmed Galal and Nadeem Ul Haque, eds., *Fiscal Sustainability in Emerging Markets: International Experience and Implications for Egypt.* Cairo: American University in Cairo Press.

Jaimovich, Dany, and Ugo Panizza. 2006a. Procyclicality or Reverse Causality? Inter-American Development Bank, Washington, DC. Unpublished.

————. 2006b. *Public Debt around the World: A New Dataset of Central Government Debt.* Research Department Working Paper no. 561. Inter-American Development Bank, Washington, DC.

Jeanne, Olivier, and Anastasia Guscina. 2006. *Government Debt in Emerging Market Countries: A New Data Set.* IMF Working Paper no. 06/98. International Monetary Fund, Washington, DC.

Jeanne, Olivier, and Jeromin Zettelmeyer. 2001. International Bailouts, Moral Hazard and Conditionality. *Economic Policy* 16(33) October: 407–32.

Jiang, Guorong, Nancy Tang, and Eve Law. 2001. Cost Benefit Analysis of Developing Debt Markets. *Hong Kong Monetary Authority Quarterly Bulletin* (November): 1–18.

JPMorgan. 2002. *Local Markets Guide—Global Edition.* March. New York: JPMorganChase.

————. 2006. *Local Markets Guide—Global Edition.* March. New York: JPMorganChase.

Kamil, Herman. 2004. A New Database on the Currency Composition and Maturity Structure of Firms' Balance Sheets in Latin America: 1990–2002; Definition of Variables, Methodology of Construction and Data Sources. Paper presented at Inter-American Development Bank policy seminar, Currency Mismatches in Emerging Markets, November 2, Washington, DC. Available at http://idbdocs.iadb.org/wsdocs/getdocument.aspx?docnum=770110.

Kaminsky, Graciela L., Carmen M. Reinhart, and Carlos A. Végh. 2005. When It Rains, It Pours: Procyclical Capital Flows and Macroeconomic Policies. In Mark Gertler and Kenneth Rogoff, eds., *NBER Macroeconomics Annual 2004.* Cambridge, MA: MIT Press.

Kiguel, Miguel. 2006. Institutional Investors and Domestic Bond Markets. Centro para la Estabilidad Financiera (CEF), Buenos Aires. Unpublished.

Kletzer, Kenneth M. 1984. Asymmetries of Information and LDC Borrowing with Sovereign Risk. *Economic Journal* 94(374) June: 287–307.

―――. 1988. *Sovereign Debt Renegotiation under Asymmetric Information.* Yale Economic Growth Center Paper no. 555. Yale University, New Haven, CT.

Kletzer, Kenneth M., and Brian D. Wright. 2000. Sovereign Debt as Intertemporal Barter. *American Economic Review* 90(3) June: 621–39.

Kopits, George. 2001. *Fiscal Rules: Useful Policy Framework or Unnecessary Ornament?* IMF Working Paper no. 01/145. International Monetary Fund, Washington, DC.

Kroszner, Randall S. 1997. Global Government Securities Markets: Economics and Politics of Recent Market Microstructure Reforms. In Guillermo Calvo and Mervyn King, eds., *The Debt Burden and Its Consequences for Monetary Policy.* London: Macmillan.

―――. 2003. Is It Better to Forgive Than to Receive? An Empirical Analysis of the Impact of Debt Repudiation. Graduate School of Business, University of Chicago. Unpublished. Available at http://gsbwww.uchicago.edu/fac/randall.kroszner/research/repudiation4.pdf.

Krugman, Paul. 1988. Financing vs. Forgiving a Debt Overhang. *Journal of Development Economics* 29(3) November: 253–68.

―――. 1989. Market Based Debt Reduction Schemes. In Jacob Frenkel, Michael Dooley, and Peter Wickham, eds., *The Analytical Issues in Debt.* Washington, DC: International Monetary Fund.

Kydland, Finn E., and Edward C. Prescott. 1977. Rules Rather Than Discretion: The Inconsistency of Optimal Plans. *Journal of Political Economy* 85(3) June: 473–92.

Lambertini, Luisa. 2003. *Are Budget Deficits Used Strategically?* Working Paper no. 578. Boston College, Boston, MA.

Leal, Ricardo P. C., and Andre L. Carvalhal-da-Silva. 2006. The Development of the Brazilian Bond Market. Paper presented at the Second Workshop on the Development of Latin-American Bond Markets, July 13, Berkeley, CA.

Leal, Ricardo P. C., and Eliane Lustosa. 2004. Institutional Investors and Corporate Governance in Brazil. Coppead Business School, Rio de Janeiro. Unpublished.

Leung, Julia. 2006. Developing Bond Markets in Asia: Experience with ABF2. In *Developing Corporate Bond Markets in Asia* [BIS Papers no. 26]. Basel: Bank for International Settlements.

Levine, Ross, and Sergio L. Schmukler. 2006. Internationalization and Stock Market Liquidity. *Review of Finance* 10(1): 153–87.

Levy Yeyati, Eduardo. 2004. *Dollars, Debt and the IFIs: Dedollarizing Multilateral Lending.* CIF Working Paper no. 11-04. Universidad Torcuato Di Tella, Buenos Aires. (Forthcoming in *World Bank Economic Review.*)

―――. 2006a. Financial Dollarization: Evaluating the Consequences. *Economic Policy* 21(45) January: 61–118.

―――. 2006b. *Optimal Debt? On the Insurance Value of International Debt Flows.* Research Department Working Paper no. 574. Inter-American Development Bank, Washington, DC.

Levy Yeyati, Eduardo, María Soledad Martínez Pería, and Sergio L. Schmukler. 2004. *Market Discipline under Systemic Risk: Evidence from Bank Runs in Emerging Economies.* Working Paper no. 3440. World Bank, Washington, DC.

Levy Yeyati, Eduardo, and Ugo Panizza. 2006. The Elusive Costs of Sovereign Defaults. Inter-American Development Bank, Washington, DC. Available at http://200.32.4.58/~ely/elypan_WP.pdf.

Levy Yeyati, Eduardo, and Federico Sturzenegger. 2006. The Balance-Sheet Approach to Debt Sustainability. Unpublished.

Lindert, Peter H. 1989. Response to the Debt Crisis: What Is Different about the 1980s? In Barry Eichengreen and Peter H. Lindert, eds., *The International Debt Crisis in Historical Perspective.* Cambridge, MA: MIT Press.

Lindert, Peter H., and Peter J. Morton. 1989. How Sovereign Debt Has Worked. In Jeffrey D. Sachs, ed., *Developing Country Debt and Economic Performance, Volume 1: The International Financial System.* Chicago: University of Chicago Press.

Lora, Eduardo. 2006. The Decline of Infrastructure Investment in Latin America: Is Debt the Culprit? Research Department, Inter-American Development Bank, Washington, DC. Unpublished.

Lora, Eduardo, and Mauricio Olivera. 2006. *Public Debt and Social Expenditure: Friends or Foes?* Research Department Working Paper no. 563. Inter-American Development Bank, Washington, DC.

Love, Inessa, and Rida Zaidi. 2004. Trade Credit and Financing Constraints: Evidence from the East Asian Crisis. World Bank, Washington, DC. Unpublished.

Lucas, Robert. 1990. Why Doesn't Capital Flow from Rich to Poor Countries? *American Economic Review* 80(2) May: 92–96.

Luengnaruemitchai, Pipat, and Li Lian Ong. 2005. *An Anatomy of Corporate Bond Markets: Growing Pains and Knowledge Gains.* IMF Working Paper no. 05/152. International Monetary Fund, Washington, DC.

Madhavan, Ananth. 2000. Market Microstructure: A Survey. Finance and Business Development Department, University of Southern California, Los Angeles. Unpublished.

Mahdavi, Saeid. 2004. Shifts in the Composition of Government Spending in Response to External Debt Burden. *World Development* 32(7) July: 1139–57.

Manasse, Paolo, Nouriel Roubini, and Axel Schimmelpfennig. 2003. *Predicting Sovereign Debt Crises.* IMF Working Paper no. 03/221. International Monetary Fund, Washington, DC.

Marchesi, Silvia, and Alessandro Missale. 2004. What Does Motivate Lending and Aid to the HIPCs? University of Siena and University of Milan. Available at http://129.3.20.41/eps/if/papers/0411/0411006.pdf.

Marichal, Carlos. 1989. *A Century of Debt Crises in Latin America: From Independence to the Great Depression, 1820–1930.* Princeton, NJ: Princeton University Press.

Martínez, José Vicente, and Guido Sandleris. 2004. Is It Punishment? Sovereign Defaults and the Declines in Trade. School of Advanced International Studies, Johns Hopkins University, Washington, DC. Unpublished.

Martner, Ricardo, and Varinia Tromben. 2004a. Public Debt Indicators in Latin American Countries: Snowball Effect, Currency Mismatch and the Original Sin. Paper prepared for the Sixth Banca d'Italia Workshop on Public Finance, April 1–3, Perugia, Italy.

————. 2004b. Public Debt Sustainability. *CEPAL Review* no. 84 (December): 97–113.

Mauro, Paolo, Nathan Sussman, and Yishay Yafeh. 2002. Emerging Market Spreads: Then versus Now. *Quarterly Journal of Economics* 117(2): 695–733.

————. 2006. *Emerging Markets and Financial Globalization: Sovereign Bond Spreads in 1870–1913 and Today.* Oxford, UK: Oxford University Press.

McCauley, Robert, and Eli Remolona. 2000. Size and Liquidity of Government Bond Markets. *BIS Quarterly Review* (November): 52–60.

Mehl, Arnaud, and Julien Reynaud. 2005. *The Determinants of "Domestic" Original Sin in Emerging Market Economies.* ECB Working Paper no. 560. European Central Bank, Frankfurt am Main, Germany.

Meltzer, Allan. 2000. Report of the Financial Institution Advisory Commission. Available at http://www.house.gov/jec/imf/meltzer.pdf.

Mendoza, Enrique G., and Pedro Marcelo Oviedo. 2002. Public Debt Sustainability under Uncertainty. University of Maryland, College Park. Unpublished.

————. 2004. *Public Debt, Fiscal Solvency and Macroeconomic Uncertainty in Latin America: The Cases of Brazil, Colombia, Costa Rica and Mexico.* NBER Working Paper no. 10637. National Bureau of Economic Research, Cambridge, MA.

————. 2006. Fiscal Solvency and Macroeconomic Uncertainty in Emerging Markets: The Tale of the Tormented Insurer. Paper presented at 2006 AEA meeting, Iowa State University.

Merton, Robert C. 1974. On the Pricing of Corporate Debt: The Risk Structure of Interest Rates. *Journal of Finance* 29(2) May: 449–70.

Mody, Ashoka, and Diego Saravia. 2003. *Catalyzing Capital Flows: Do IMF-Supported Programs Work as Commitment Devices?* IMF Working Paper no. 03/100. International Monetary Fund, Washington, DC.

Mohanty, Madhusudan. 2002. Improving Liquidity in Government Bond Markets: What Can Be Done? In *The Development of Bond Markets in Emerging Economies* [BIS Papers No. 11]. Basel: Bank for International Settlements.

Moody's. 2003. Moody's Special Comment: Sovereign Bond Defaults, Rating Transitions, and Recoveries (1985–2002). Moody's Investors Service, New York.

Mora, Nada. 2004. Sovereign Credit Ratings: Guilty beyond Reasonable Doubt? Paper presented at the 31st Annual Meeting of the European Finance Association, August 18–21, Maastricht.

Morris, Stephen, and Hyun Shin. 2003. *Catalytic Finance: When Does It Work?* Cowles Foundation Discussion Paper no. 1400. Yale University, New Haven, CT.

Myers, Stewart. 1977. Determinants of Corporate Borrowing. *Journal of Financial Economics* 5(2) November: 147–75.

Nascimento, Edson Ronaldo, and Ilvo Debus. 2002. Entendendo a lei de responsabilidade fiscal. Comments and clarifications on Lei Complementar No. 101/2000. Available at http://federativo.bndes.gov.br/bf_bancos/estudos/e0001737.pdf

Ndikumana, Léonce. 2002. *Additionality of Debt Relief and Debt Forgiveness, and Implications for Future Volumes of Official Assistance.* WIDER Discussion Paper no. 2002/97. World Institute for Development Economics Research, United Nations University, Helsinki.

Nierop, Erwin. 2005. Developing Corporate Bond Markets: A European Legal Perspective. In *Developing Corporate Bond Markets in Asia* [BIS Papers no. 26]. Basel: Bank for International Settlements.

Obstfeld, Maurice. 1994. The Logic of Currency Crises. *Cahiers économiques et monétaires de la Banque de France* 43: 189–213.

Obstfeld, Maurice, and Alan M. Taylor. 2003. Sovereign Risk, Credibility and the Gold Standard: 1870–1913 versus 1925–31. *Economic Journal* 113(487): 241–75.

Organisation for Economic Co-operation and Development (OECD). 2005. *Geographical Distribution of Financial Flows to Aid Recipients, 1999–2003*. Paris: OECD.

Ostry, Jonathan D., and Jeromin Zettelmeyer. 2005. *Strengthening IMF Crisis Prevention*. IMF Working Paper no. 05/206. International Monetary Fund, Washington, DC.

Ozler, Sule. 1993. Have Commercial Banks Ignored History? *American Economic Review* 83(3) June: 608–20.

Pattillo, Catherine, Hélène Koliane Poirson, and Luca A. Ricci. 2002. *External Debt and Growth*. IMF Working Paper no. 02/69. International Monetary Fund, Washington, DC.

————. 2004. *What Are the Channels through Which External Debt Affects Growth?* IMF Working Paper no. 04/15. International Monetary Fund, Washington, DC.

Persson, Torsten, and Lars E. O. Svensson. 1989. Why a Stubborn Conservative Would Run a Deficit: Policy with Time-Inconsistent Preferences. *Quarterly Journal of Economics* 104(2) May: 325–45.

Pettersson-Lidbom, Per. 2001. An Empirical Investigation of the Strategic Use of Debt. *Journal of Political Economy* 109(3) June: 570–83.

Poterba, James M. 1994. State Responses to Fiscal Crises: The Effects of Budgetary Institutions and Politics. *Journal of Political Economy* 102(4) August: 799–821.

Poterba, James M., and Lawrence H. Summers. 1988. Mean Reversion in Stock Prices: Evidence and Implications. *Journal of Financial Economics* 22: 27–59.

Powell, Andrew, and Leandro Arozamena. 2003. Liquidity Protection versus Moral Hazard: The Role of the IMF. *Journal of International Money and Finance* 22(7) December: 1041–63.

Powell, Andrew, and Matteo Bobba. 2006. Multilateral Intermediation of Development Assistance: What Is the Trade-Off for Donor Countries? Inter-American Development Bank, Washington, DC. Unpublished.

Powell, Andrew, Dilip Ratha, and Sanket Mohapatra. 2002. *Capital Inflows and Capital Outflows: Measurement, Determinants, Consequences*. Business School Working Paper no. 25. Universidad Torcuato Di Tella, Buenos Aires.

Powell, Robert. 2003. *Debt Relief, Additionality, and Aid Allocation in Low-Income Countries*. IMF Working Paper no. 03/175. International Monetary Fund, Washington, DC.

Pritchett, Lant. 1999. *The Tyranny of Concepts: CUDIE (Cumulated, Depreciated Investment Effort) Is Not Capital*. Policy Research Working Paper no. 2341. World Bank, Washington, DC.

————. 2001. Where Has All the Education Gone? *World Bank Economic Review* 15(3): 367–91.

Radelet, Steven. 2006. Aid and Growth. Presentation at Multilateral Development Bank Meeting on Debt Issues, June 21, Washington, DC.

Rajan, Raghuram G. 2005a. Debt Relief and Growth. *Finance and Development* 42(2) June [online].

————. 2005b. The Greenspan Era: Lessons for the Future. Speech delivered at the symposium, Financial Markets, Financial Fragility, and Central Banking, August 27, Jackson Hole, WY. Available at http://www.imf.org/external/np/speeches/2005/082705.htm.

————. 2006. The Role of the International Monetary Fund in a Changing World. Lecture delivered at the Kiel Institute, April 10. Available at http://www.imf.org/external/np/speeches/2006/041006.htm#P9_220.

Rajan, Raghuram G., and Arvind Subramanian. 2005. *Aid and Growth: What Does the Cross-Country Evidence Really Show?* NBER Working Paper no. 11513. National Bureau of Economic Research, Cambridge, MA.

Rajan, Raghuram G., and Luigi Zingales. 2003a. *Banks and Markets: The Changing Character of European Finance.* NBER Working Paper no. 9595. National Bureau of Economic Research, Cambridge, MA.

————. 2003b. The Great Reversals: The Politics of Financial Development in the Twentieth Century. *Journal of Financial Economics* 69(1) July: 5–50.

————. 2003c. *Saving Capitalism from the Capitalists: Unleashing the Power of Financial Markets to Create Wealth and Spread Opportunity.* New York: Crown Business.

Ratha, Dilip. 2001. *Complementarity between Multilateral Lending and Private Flows to Developing Countries: Some Empirical Results.* Policy Research Working Paper no. 2746. World Bank, Washington, DC.

Reinhart, Carmen M., Kenneth S. Rogoff, and Miguel A. Savastano. 2003. Debt Intolerance. In William C. Brainard and George L. Perry, eds., *Brookings Papers on Economic Activity* 2003(1). Washington, DC: Brookings Institution Press.

Reinikka, Ritva, and Jakob Svensson. 1999. *How Inadequate Provision of Public Infrastructure and Services Affects Private Investment.* Policy Research Working Paper no. 2262. World Bank, Washington, DC.

Reisen, Helmut, and Julia von Maltzan. 1999. *Boom and Bust and Sovereign Ratings.* OECD Development Centre Working Paper no. 148. Organisation for Economic Co-operation and Development, Paris.

Riascos, Álvaro, and Carlos A. Végh. 2003. Procyclical Fiscal Policy in Developing Countries: The Role of Incomplete Markets. University of California, Los Angeles. Unpublished.

Rigobón, Roberto. 2003. Identification through Heteroskedasticity. *Review of Economics and Statistics* 85(4): 777–92.

————. 2005. Comment. In Mark Gertler and Kenneth Rogoff, eds., *NBER Macroeconomics Annual 2004.* Cambridge, MA: MIT Press.

————. 2006. Fiscal Response to Revenue Uncertainty. Massachusetts Institute of Technology, Cambridge, MA. Unpublished.

Rippy, J. Fred. 1959. *British Investments in Latin America, 1822–1949: A Case Study in the Operations of Private Enterprise in Retarded Regions.* Minneapolis: University of Minnesota Press.

Rochet, Jean-Charles. 2006. *Optimal Sovereign Debt: An Analytical Approach.* Research Department Working Paper no. 573. Inter-American Development Bank, Washington, DC.

Rochet, Jean-Charles, and Ernst-Ludwig von Thadden. 2006. A Theory of Rational Sudden Stops. Université Toulouse I and Universität Mannheim. Unpublished.

Rodrik, Dani. 1995. *Why Is There Multilateral Lending?* NBER Working Paper no. 5160. National Bureau of Economic Research, Cambridge, MA.

Rogoff, Kenneth, and Anne Sibert. 1988. Elections and Macroeconomic Policy Cycles. *Review of Economic Studies* 55(1) January: 1–16.

Rose, Andrew K. 2005. One Reason Countries Pay Their Debts: Renegotiation and International Trade. *Journal of Development Economics* 77(1) June: 189–206.

Roubini, Nouriel, and Brad Setser. 2004. *Bailouts or Bail-Ins? Responding to Financial Crises in Emerging Economies.* Washington, DC: Institute for International Economics.

Sachs, Jeffrey D. 1989. The Debt Overhang of Developing Countries. In Guillermo Calvo, Ronald Findlay, Pentti Kouri, and Jorge Braga de Macedo, eds., *Debt, Stabilization, and Development: Essays in Memory of Carlos Díaz-Alejandro.* Oxford, UK: Basil Blackwell.

—————. 2005. *The End of Poverty: Economic Possibilities for Our Time.* New York: Penguin.

Sachs, Jeffrey D., Jeremy Bulow, and Kenneth Rogoff. 1988. Comprehensive Debt Retirement: The Bolivian Example. *Brookings Papers on Economic Activity* 2: 705–15.

Sandleris, Guido. 2006. Sovereign Defaults: Information, Investment and Credit. School of Advanced International Studies, Johns Hopkins University, Washington, DC. Unpublished.

Schinasi, Garry J., and R. Todd Smith. 1998. *Fixed Income Markets in the United States, Europe and Japan: Some Lessons for Emerging Markets.* IMF Working Paper no. 98-173. International Monetary Fund, Washington, DC.

Schuknecht, Ludger. 1994. *Political Business Cycles and Expenditure Policies in Developing Countries.* IMF Working Paper no. 94/121. International Monetary Fund, Washington, DC.

Scottish Executive News. 2004. Document of the Month January 2005. Scottish Executive News [online], December 30. Available at http://www.scotland.gov.uk/News/News-Extras/doc Jan2005/Q/pno/1.

Sen, Amartya. 2006. The Man without a Plan [Review of William Easterly's *The White Man's Burden*]. *Foreign Affairs* 85(2) March/April [online].

Shiller, Robert J. 2003. *The New Financial Order: Risk in the 21st Century.* Princeton, NJ: Princeton University Press.

Shleifer, Andrei. 1998. State versus Private Ownership. *Journal of Economic Perspectives* 12(4) Fall: 133–50.

Spackman, Michael. 2004. Time Discounting and the Cost of Capital in Government. *Fiscal Studies* 25(4) December: 467–518.

Standard & Poor's. 2006. Sovereign Ratings History since 1975. September 11. Available at http://www2.standardandpoors.com/servlet/ContentServer?pagename=sp/sp_article/ArticleTemplate&c=sp_article&cid=1099333608002&b=10&s=&i=&r=6&l=EN

Stein, Ernesto, Ernesto Talvi, and Alejandro Grisanti. 1998. *Institutional Arrangements and Fiscal Performance: The Latin American Experience.* NBER Working Paper no. 6358. National Bureau of Economic Research, Cambridge, MA.

Stone, Irving. 1977. British Direct and Portfolio Investment in Latin America before 1914. *Journal of Economic History* 37(3): 690–722.

—————. 1999. *The Global Export of Capital from Great Britain, 1865–1914: A Statistical Survey.* New York: St. Martin's.

Sturzenegger, Federico. 2004. Toolkit for the Analysis of Debt Problems. *Journal of Restructuring Finance* 1(1): 201–3.

Sturzenegger, Federico, and Jeromin Zettelmeyer. 2005a. *Haircuts: Estimating Investor Losses in Sovereign Debt Restructurings, 1998–2005*. IMF Working Paper 05/137. International Monetary Fund, Washington, DC.

————. 2005b. Has the Legal Threat to Sovereign Debt Restructuring Become Real? Kennedy School of Government, Harvard University, Cambridge, MA. Unpublished.

————. 2006. *Debt Defaults and Lessons from a Decade of Crises*. Cambridge, MA: MIT Press. Forthcoming.

Summers, Lawrence. 2006. Reflections on Global Account Imbalances and Emerging Markets Reserve Accumulation. L. K. Jha Memorial Lecture, Reserve Bank of India, March 24, Mumbai, India.

Sutter, Matthias. 2003. The Political Economy of Fiscal Policy: An Experimental Study on the Strategic Use of Deficits. *Public Choice* 116(3–4) September: 313–32.

Tabellini, Guido, and Alberto F. Alesina. 1990. Voting on the Budget Deficit. *American Economic Review* 80(1) March: 37–49.

Talvi, Ernesto, and Carlos A. Végh. 2005. Tax Base Variability and Procyclical Fiscal Policy in Developing Countries. *Journal of Development Economics* 78(1): 156–90.

Tanzi, Vito, and Nigel Chalk. 2000. Impact of Large Debt on Growth in the EU: A Discussion of Potential Channels. *European Economy* no. 2: 23–43.

Taylor, Alan M. 1992. External Dependence, Demographic Burdens and Argentine Economic Decline after the Belle Époque. *Journal of Economic History* 52 (December): 907–36.

————. 2003. *Foreign Capital in Latin America in the Nineteenth and Twentieth Centuries*. NBER Working Paper no. 9580. National Bureau of Economic Research, Cambridge, MA.

Taylor, Alan M., and Jeffrey G. Williamson. 1994. Capital Flows to the New World as an Intergenerational Transfer. *Journal of Political Economy* 102(2): 348–71.

Tirole, Jean. 2002. *Financial Crises, Liquidity, and the International Monetary System*. Princeton, NJ: Princeton University Press.

————. 2003. Inefficient Foreign Borrowing: A Dual- and Common-Agency Perspective. *American Economic Review* 93(5) December: 1678–1702.

Tomz, Michael R. 2001. How Do Reputations Form? New and Seasoned Borrowers in International Capital Markets. Paper presented at the 2001 Annual Meeting of the American Political Science Association, August 30–September 2, San Francisco.

————. 2004. Finance and Trade: Issue Linkage and the Enforcement of International Debt Contracts. Paper presented at the annual meeting of the American Political Science Association, August, Chicago.

————. 2006. Sovereign Debt and International Cooperation: Reputational Reasons for Lending and Repayment. Stanford University, Stanford, CA. Unpublished.

Tornell, Aaron, and Philip R. Lane. 1999. The Voracity Effect. *American Economic Review* 89(1): 22–46.

Toussaint, Eric, and Arnaud Zacharie. 2002. Abolish the Debt to Free Development. Speech presented at the World Social Forum, January 31–February 5, Porto Alegre, Brazil.

Tovar, Camilo E. 2005. International Government Debt Denominated in Local Currency: Recent Developments in Latin America. *BIS Quarterly Review* (December): 109–18.

Triner, Gail D. 2001. International Capital and the Brazilian Encilhamento, 1889–1891: An Early Example of Contagion among Emerging Capital Markets? Paper presented at the Economic History Association conference, Finance and Economic Modernization, September 14–16, Philadelphia.

Twomey, Michael J. 2000. *A Century of Foreign Investment in the Third World*. London: Routledge.

Ul Haque, Nadeem, Manmohan S. Kumar, Nelson Mark, and Donald J. Mathieson. 1996. The Economic Content of Indicators of Developing Country Creditworthiness. *IMF Staff Papers* 43(4) December: 688–724.

United Nations. 2005. *Investing in Development: A Practical Plan to Achieve the Millennium Development Goals*. New York: United Nations Millennium Project.

Valenzuela, Patricio. 2006. Presupuesto fiscal estructural del gobierno de Chile: ¿balance o superávit? Inter-American Development Bank, Washington, DC. Unpublished.

Velasco, Andrés. 1999. A Model of Endogenous Fiscal Deficits and Delayed Fiscal Reforms. In James M. Poterba and Jürgen von Hagen, eds., *Fiscal Institutions and Economic Performance*. Chicago: University of Chicago Press.

Vittas, Dimitri. 1998. *Institutional Investors and Securities Markets: Which Comes First?* World Bank Development Research Group Working Paper no. 2032. World Bank, Washington, DC.

Wallack, Jessica S. 2004. Disagreement, Delay, and Deficits. Graduate School of Business, Stanford University, Stanford, CA. Unpublished.

———. 2005. Investing in the Dark: Data Quality and Perceptions of Creditworthiness. University of California, San Diego. Unpublished.

Weingast, Barry R., Kenneth Shepsle, and Christopher Johnsen. 1981. The Political Economy of Benefits and Costs: A Neoclassical Approach to Distributive Politics. *Journal of Political Economy* 89(4) August: 642–64.

World Bank. 2004a. Annex: Commercial Debt Restructuring (Chapter 2). In World Bank, ed., *Global Development Finance 2004: Harnessing Cyclical Gains for Development*. Washington, DC: World Bank.

———. 2004b. Financing Developing Countries' Trade. In *Global Development Finance 2004: Harnessing Cyclical Gains for Development*. Washington, DC: World Bank.

———. 2006. *Debt Relief for the Poorest: An Evaluation Update of the HIPC Initiative*. Independent Evaluation Group, World Bank, Washington, DC.

Wright, Mark. 2002. Reputations and Sovereign Debt. Stanford University, Stanford, CA. Unpublished.

Xu, David, and Piero Ghezzi. 2003. From Fundamentals to Spreads: A Fair Spread Model for High Yield Emerging Markets Sovereigns. Deutsche Bank, Berlin. Unpublished.

Zervos, Sarah. 2004. *The Transactions Costs of Primary Market Issuance: The Case of Brazil, Chile, and Mexico*. Policy Research Working Paper no. 3424. World Bank, Washington, DC.